普通高等学校"十二五"规划教材·应用型本科·高职高专

实用英语语法教程

主 编 赵 萍

国防工业出版社

·北京·

内容简介

《实用英语语法教程》是一部新型的、融合传统语法与现代语言学研究成果,并结合应用型本科(及高职高专)学生特点所编写的英语语法教材。此教材编写过程中,在不影响语法体系的前提下,根据编者多年教学实践的经验,针对在校学生的实际需要,对英语语法的重点和难点作出了详细的阐述并附以大量生动、实用的范例。本书所举范例语言规范、难易适中、生动新颖。此外,针对语法中的难点和重点,本书还附以大量启发性巩固练习,供学生边学边练。本书是一部理论和实践紧密结合,有助于学生英语学习、具有很大实用价值的语法教程。另外,本书对于普通读者也是一本很好的学习参考书。

图书在版编目(CIP)数据

实用英语语法教程/赵萍主编.—北京:国防工业出版社,2011.8(2016.8重印)
普通高等学校"十二五"规划教材.应用型本科·高职高专
ISBN 978-7-118-07634-9

Ⅰ.①实... Ⅱ.①赵... Ⅲ.①英语—语法—高等学校—教材 Ⅳ.①H314

中国版本图书馆 CIP 数据核字(2011)第 166938 号

※

国防工业出版社出版发行
(北京市海淀区紫竹院南路 23 号 邮政编码 100048)
北京京华虎彩印刷有限公司印刷
新华书店经售

*

开本 787×1092 1/16 印张 20½ 字数 509 千字
2016 年 8 月第 1 版第 2 次印刷 印数 4001—5200 册 定价 35.00 元

(本书如有印装错误,我社负责调换)

国防书店:(010)88540777　　发行邮购:(010)88540776
发行传真:(010)88540755　　发行业务:(010)88540717

《实用英语语法教程》编委会

主　编　赵　萍
主　审　王天润
副主编　韩彦枝　黄瑞锋　李　哲
编　者　翟慧敏　何　华　周　卿
　　　　　　郑　帅　边莉娟　王桂林

前　言

　　《实用英语语法教程》是一部新型的、融合传统语法与现代语言学研究成果,并结合应用型本科(及高职高专)学生的特点所编写的英语语法教材。此教材在不影响语法体系的前提下,根据编者多年教学实践经验,针对我国高职高专学生的实际需要,对英语语法的重点及难点作出了详细的阐述,并附以大量生动、实用的范例。本书充分考虑并尊重目前高职高专教育体系的实际,针对学生英语基础差距大、英语课时有限的状况,力求简易和实用。本书所举范例语言规范、难易适中、生动新颖。考虑到学生的兴趣所在及接受倾向,本书精选包括2008年奥运会和四川地震在内的最具时代性的各类内容,让学生在学习语言的同时,随时接受最新信息,了解当前世界的热点、焦点话题,融知识性、实用性和趣味性于一体。此外,针对语法中的难点和重点,本书还附以大量启发性巩固练习,供学生边学边练。本书是一部理论和实践紧密结合,有助于高职高专学生英语学习、具有很大实用价值的语法教程。

　　本书由多位一线教师严格遵循国家教育部对应用型本科(及高职)院校英语教学提出的基本要求,坚持实用型人才培养的目标,注意把握"以应用为目的,实用为主,够用为度"的教材编写原则完成编写的。与以往同类教材相比,本教材具有以下几个特色:

　　(1) 思路清新,框架合理。本教程的设计思路是重点突出,以培养学生应用能力为核心,对英语语法的重点及难点作出了详细的阐述,并提供有针对性的培养和强化学生实践能力的各类练习。

　　(2) 突出实用,注重典型。本教程尽可能多地采用了内容新颖、来源于实际生活的真实材料,多角度地搜集学生可能接触到的范例,突出实用性,注重典型性,力争使学生开阔眼界,培养兴趣。

　　(3) 体例新颖,语言规范。本教程在编写体例上打破普通语法教材的模式,每个章节中,首先让学生从分析实际范例入手,然后理论联系实际,让学生完成一系列有针对性的训练,使学生在掌握了一定理论知识的情况下将其应用到实践中,既体现了理论与实践的结合,又保证了语法知识的连贯性和完整性。

　　(4) 注重实践,形式多样。本教程在巩固练习部分有针对性地设计了大量形式多样的练习,目的就是通过一定数量的练习强化学生的技能,帮助其巩固所学的知识。

　　全书共26章,各章既相对独立,又相互联系、相互渗透,形成一个系统的、完整的体系。每章之后附有形式多样的巩固练习,并附有巩固练习的参考答案。

本书由赵萍主持编写,王天润负责全书的修改定稿。赵萍负责第一章、第四章和第六章的编写;边莉娟负责第七章的编写;韩彦枝负责第三章、第九章、第二十章、第二十一章和第二十二章的编写;黄瑞锋负责第十章、第十一章、第十二章和第十三章的编写;李哲负责第八章、第十四章的编写;翟慧敏负责第五章、第十六章、第十七章和第十八章的编写;何华负责第二章和第十五章的编写;郑帅负责第二十三章、第二十四章的编写;周卿负责第二十五章、第二十六章的编写;王桂林负责第十九章的编写。

本书在编写过程中参考了不少专家、同行的论著及研究成果,在此一并表示真诚的谢意!

由于编者水平有限,加之编写时间仓促,书中难免存在错误和不妥之处,恳请专家和广大读者批评指正。

目　录

第一章　语法概述 …………………… 1
 1.1　词法 ……………………………… 1
 1.2　句法 ……………………………… 3
 巩固练习 ……………………………… 9

第二章　名词 ………………………… 10
 2.1　名词的分类 ……………………… 10
 2.2　名词的数 ………………………… 11
 2.3　名词的性 ………………………… 15
 2.4　名词的格 ………………………… 17
 2.5　名词在句中的作用 ……………… 18
 巩固练习 ……………………………… 18

第三章　冠词 ………………………… 20
 3.1　冠词的定义 ……………………… 20
 3.2　冠词的位置 ……………………… 20
 3.3　冠词的用法 ……………………… 21
 3.4　冠词的省略 ……………………… 23
 巩固练习 ……………………………… 23

第四章　代词 ………………………… 27
 4.1　人称代词 ………………………… 27
 4.2　物主代词 ………………………… 32
 4.3　反身代词 ………………………… 33
 4.4　相互代词 ………………………… 34
 4.5　指示代词 ………………………… 35
 4.6　疑问代词 ………………………… 37
 4.7　关系代词 ………………………… 38
 4.8　不定代词 ………………………… 39
 巩固练习 ……………………………… 50

第五章　数词 ………………………… 53
 5.1　基数词 …………………………… 53
 5.2　序数词 …………………………… 55
 5.3　倍数、分数、小数和百分数的
   表示法 …………………………… 57
 5.4　算式表示法 ……………………… 58
 5.5　编号表示法 ……………………… 59
 5.6　年、月、日表示法 ……………… 59
 5.7　时刻表示法 ……………………… 60
 5.8　币制表示法 ……………………… 60
 巩固练习 ……………………………… 61

第六章　动词 ………………………… 63
 6.1　概述 ……………………………… 63
 6.2　动词的基本形式 ………………… 67
 巩固练习 ……………………………… 70

第七章　助动词 ……………………… 72
 7.1　助动词概述 ……………………… 72
 7.2　基本助动词的用法 ……………… 72
 7.3　情态助动词概述 ………………… 75
 7.4　半助动词 ………………………… 87
 7.5　助动词的其他用法 ……………… 89
 巩固练习 ……………………………… 90

第八章　动词的时态 ………………… 94
 8.1　概述 ……………………………… 94
 8.2　一般现在时 ……………………… 95
 8.3　一般过去时 ……………………… 97
 8.4　一般将来时 ……………………… 99
 8.5　现在进行时 ……………………… 102
 8.6　过去进行时 ……………………… 104
 8.7　现在完成时 ……………………… 106
 8.8　过去完成时 ……………………… 109
 8.9　过去将来时 ……………………… 110
 8.10　将来完成时 …………………… 111

- 8.11 过去将来完成时 ·········· 112
- 8.12 将来进行时 ············· 113
- 8.13 过去将来进行时 ·········· 114
- 8.14 现在完成进行时 ·········· 115
- 8.15 过去完成进行时 ·········· 116
- 8.16 将来完成进行时 ·········· 117
- 8.17 过去将来完成进行时 ······· 117
- 巩固练习 ····················· 118

第九章 被动语态 122

- 9.1 被动语态的构成形式 ······· 122
- 9.2 被动语态的用法 ··········· 123
- 9.3 被动语态的形式 ··········· 123
- 9.4 主动结构表示被动意义的问题 ····················· 128
- 9.5 被动语态与系表结构的区别 ····················· 129
- 巩固练习 ····················· 130

第十章 虚拟语气 137

- 10.1 语气及其种类 ············ 137
- 10.2 虚拟语气的本质含义及表达形式 ····················· 137
- 10.3 虚拟语气的表达形式的用法 ····················· 137
- 巩固练习 ····················· 138

第十一章 不定式 141

- 11.1 非限定动词概述 ·········· 141
- 11.2 非限定动词的特点 ········ 141
- 11.3 非限定动词形式和语态的变化 ····················· 142
- 11.4 动词不定式 ·············· 142
- 巩固练习 ····················· 147

第十二章 动名词 153

- 12.1 动名词的意义和形式 ······ 153
- 12.2 动名词形式和语态的变化 ····················· 153
- 12.3 动名词的用法 ············ 153
- 12.4 动名词的否定结构 ········ 157
- 12.5 动名词的复合结构 ········ 157
- 12.6 动名词的形式 ············ 158
- 12.7 动名词的被动式 ·········· 158
- 巩固练习 ····················· 159

第十三章 分词 162

- 13.1 分词的概念 ·············· 162
- 13.2 分词的语法功能 ·········· 162
- 13.3 现在分词和过去分词的区别 ····················· 162
- 13.4 分词的用法 ·············· 163
- 13.5 分词的否定结构 ·········· 167
- 13.6 现在分词的形式 ·········· 167
- 13.7 现在分词的被动语态 ······ 167
- 13.8 独立主格结构 ············ 168
- 13.9 使用现在分词应注意的问题 ····················· 169
- 13.10 非谓语动词考点分析 ······ 169
- 巩固练习 ····················· 171
- 非谓语动词专练 ··············· 172

第十四章 形容词和副词 177

- 14.1 形容词 ·················· 177
- 14.2 副词 ···················· 181
- 14.3 形容词和副词的比较级和最高级 ····················· 184
- 巩固练习 ····················· 187

第十五章 连词 190

- 15.1 连词的定义和分类 ········ 190
- 15.2 并列连词 ················ 190
- 15.3 从属连词 ················ 192
- 15.4 一些特殊的从属连词的用法及区别 ····················· 194
- 巩固练习 ····················· 199

第十六章 介词 202

- 16.1 介词的定义和分类 ········ 202
- 16.2 介词短语 ················ 203

16.3 介词和其他词类的搭配 …………… 204
16.4 相似介词的辨析 …………… 206
巩固练习 …………………… 211

第十七章 感叹词 …………………… 214

17.1 感叹词的定义 …………… 214
17.2 常用的感叹词及其用法 …… 214

第十八章 句子类型 ………………… 217

18.1 按照句子的用途分类 ……… 217
18.2 按照句子的结构分类 ……… 223
巩固练习 …………………… 226

第十九章 直接引语和间接引语 …… 227

19.1 直接引语和间接引语的定义 ………………… 227
19.2 直接引语如何变为间接引语 ………………… 227
巩固练习 …………………… 232

第二十章 名词性从句 ……………… 233

20.1 概述 …………………… 233
20.2 名词性从句的引导词 ……… 233
20.3 名词性从句的种类 ………… 234
巩固练习 …………………… 240

第二十一章 定语从句 ……………… 243

21.1 概述 …………………… 243
21.2 关系词的分类 …………… 243
21.3 关系代词及其引导的定语从句 ……………… 243
21.4 关系副词及其引导的定语从句 ……………… 246
21.5 限制性定语从句和非限制性定语从句 ……… 247
巩固练习 …………………… 249

第二十二章 状语从句 ……………… 253

22.1 概述 …………………… 253

22.2 状语从句的种类 …………… 253
22.3 时间状语从句 …………… 253
22.4 地点状语从句 …………… 257
22.5 原因状语从句 …………… 257
22.6 条件状语从句 …………… 258
22.7 目的状语从句 …………… 258
22.8 结果状语从句 …………… 259
22.9 让步状语从句 …………… 260
22.10 方式状语从句 …………… 261
22.11 比较状语从句 …………… 261
巩固练习 …………………… 262

第二十三章 it 的用法 ……………… 265

23.1 代词 it 的用法 …………… 265
23.2 虚义 it 的用法 …………… 266
23.3 先行 it 的用法 …………… 267
23.4 分裂句引导词 it ………… 268
巩固练习 …………………… 270

第二十四章 一致 …………………… 273

24.1 主谓一致的三个基本原则 …………………… 273
24.2 以集体名词作主语的主谓一致 ……………… 274
24.3 表示确切数量的名词词组作主语时的主谓一致 ……………… 274
24.4 表示非确切数量的名词词组作主语时的主谓一致 ……………… 275
24.5 以 -s 结尾的名词作主语时的主谓一致 ……… 276
24.6 并列结构作主语时的主谓一致 ……………… 278
24.7 不定代词作主语时的主谓一致 ……………… 279
24.8 其他方面的主谓一致 …… 281
24.9 数词与名词的一致 ……… 282
巩固练习 …………………… 284

第二十五章　强调 ·········· 287
- 25.1　分裂句 ·········· 287
- 25.2　后置 ·········· 288
- 25.3　前置 ·········· 289
- 25.4　用 if 来表示强调 ·········· 290
- 25.5　强制性词语 ·········· 290
- 25.6　用破折号或黑体字表示强调 ·········· 291

巩固练习 ·········· 291

第二十六章　省略与倒装 ·········· 293
- 26.1　省略 ·········· 293
- 26.2　倒装 ·········· 298

巩固练习 ·········· 304

巩固练习参考答案 ·········· 309

参考文献 ·········· 318

第一章 语法概述

语法是组词造句的规则,是把合适的词放进合适位置的艺术,语法可分为词法和句法两部分。词法(Morphology)包括各类词的形态及其变化;句法(Syntax)主要论述句子的种类和类型、句子成分及遣词造句的规律。

1.1 词 法

词法以词为对象,研究各种词的形式和用法。

1.1.1 词 类

英语中的词可以根据词义、句法作用和形式分为十大词类(Parts of Speech)。这十类词又可分属实词(Notional Words)和虚词(Form Words)(又叫结构词)两个范畴。

1. 实词

实词具有一定的词汇意义,在句子中可独立担任句子成分。这类词包括名词、代词、形容词、动词、数词、副词。这六类词占英语词的绝大部分。

2. 虚词

虚词主要起结构作用,用来表明词与词或句子中各部分之间的关系或句子语气等。这类词包括冠词、介词、连词、感叹词。这类词的数量是有限的。

1.1.2 词的作用和语法功能

英语中的每个词类都有其特定的作用,在句子中的功能也各不相同。它们各自的作用及句法功能如下表所列。

	词类	缩写	意义和作用	句法功能	例词
实词	名词 noun	n.	人或事物的名称	担任主语、表语、宾语、定语等	Tom, Beijing, pen, water, time
	代词 pronoun	pron.	代替名词、形容词或数词	担任主语、表语、宾语、定语等	we, this, some, both, none
	形容词 adjective	adj. 或 a.	表示人和事物的性质和特征	担任表语、定语、补足语等	good, happy, large, old, healthy
	动词 verb	v.	表示动作或状态	担任谓语	read, take, come, laugh, go

(续)

	词类	缩写	意义和作用	句法功能	例词
实词	数词 numeral	num.	表示数量或顺序	担任主语、表语、宾语、定语等	two, ten, hundred, second, million
	副词 adverb	adv. 或 ad.	修饰动词、形容词及其他副词	担任状语	very, clearly, always, never
虚词	冠词 article	art.	用在名词前,表示名词的特指或泛指		a, an, the
	介词 preposition	prep.	表示名词或代词与句子中其他词的关系		in, of, from, between
	连词 conjunction	conj.	连接词、词组、从句或句子		and, when, or, if, but
	感叹词 interjection	interj. 或 int.	表示喜、怒、哀、乐等情感		oh, aha, hello, hush

注:(1) 同一个词有时可以属于几个词类但意思相同(如 since 自从,连词和介词;fast 快,形容词和副词等),而有些词不仅分属不同词类而且意思也不相同(如 well 井,名词;好,副词;健康的,形容词;涌出,动词;哦,那么,好吧,叹词);

(2) "介词"本身不能作句子成分,但与"名词性词语"构成"介词词组"后,可在句中作表语、定语、补足语、状语等成分;

(3) 虚词在句子中一律不能作为句子成分

1.1.3 词形变化

英语各类词(介词、连词和感叹词除外)都有一定的词形变化,如下表所列。

词类	变化内容	例词
名词	单、复数;所有格	boy(boys);ox(oxen); Jim(Jim's)
代词	单、复数;主格、宾格;所有格	he, they; she, her; ours, ourselves
数词	基数词和序数词	one, first
冠词	不定冠词、定冠词和零冠词(即不用冠词的场合)	a, an, the
形容词副词	原级、比较级、最高级	early, earlier, earliest
动词	人称;单、复数;时态;语态;语气	go, goes, going, went
	非谓语(不定式、现在分词、过去分词、动名词)	to do, doing, done

1.1.4 词组和从句

1. 词组或短语(Phrase)

词组是具有一定的意义但不构成从句或句子的一组词语。词组是按照一定语法规则围绕一定中心词结合起来的一组词。中心词所属词类决定着词组内部的结合方式,也决定着词组的类别。词组在句中可以单独作为一种句子成分。词组可分以下几类:

(1) 名词词组,以名词为中心词的词组。由中心词或中心词前后加修饰语构成。

① **all the college students** 全体大学生

② **the tall boy sitting in the corner** 坐在角落的高个子男孩

(2) 动词词组,是以主动词(也称实义动词)为中心词的词组。

① He **arrived** last night. 他昨晚到的。

② She **has told** him about it. 她把那件事告诉了他。

(3) 形容词词组,是以形容词为中心词的词组。

① The course is **pretty difficult**. 这课程相当难。

② That work is **too difficult for that child**. 那工作对于那个孩子来讲太难了。

(4) 副词词组,是以副词为中心词的词组。

① He spoke **loudly and clearly**. 他说话既洪亮又清晰。

② He lives **farthest from the station**. 他住的地方离车站最远。

(5) 介词词组,是以介词为中心词的词组。介词和其宾语(介词宾语也叫介词的补足成分)一起构成介词词组。介词词组前有时还可带修饰语。

① A friend **in need** is a friend indeed. 患难朋友是真正的朋友。

② Food has been scarce **since before the war**. 从战前食物就紧缺。

2. 从句

从句由连词、关系代词或关系副词引导,含有主语和谓语,但不能构成一个独立句子的一组词。从句构成句子的一个成分,如主语从句、表语从句、宾语从句、同位语从句、定语从句和状语从句(详见第二十章、第二十一章、第二十二章)。

1.2 句　法

句法以句子为研究对象,研究句子的形式和用法。

1.2.1 句子成分(Members of the Sentence)

句子是用一个或者多个单词组成的基本表意单位,也是最高一级的语法单位。英语的句子大都由主语部分和谓语部分构成。句子成分是句中起一定功用的一个组成部分。

英语句子有五个组成部分,根据它们的含义、作用、相互关系分别称它们为主语、谓语动词、宾语、补语、状语,也叫做五个主要的句子成分。

1. 主语 (Subject)

主语是句子的主体,是句子说明的主体和对象,描述的是"谁"或"什么"。主语通常由名词、代词、数词或由相当于名词作用的不定式、动名词或从句等担任,通常位于句首。

① **My father** likes to go on the Internet. 我爸爸喜欢上网。

② **Two plus three** is five. 二加三等于五。

③ **To become an artist** is his ambition. 成为一名艺术家是他的理想。

④ **Smoking** is harmful to health. 吸烟有害健康。

⑤ **What I shall do next** is not decided. 我还没有决定下一步做什么。

2. 谓语动词 （Predicate Verb）

谓语动词用于说明主语的动作、状态等内容，一般由动词或动词词组担任。一般紧跟主语后面。

① Tom **is running** outside. 汤姆正在外面跑步。

② Jane **is** very quiet. 珍妮很文静。

③ You **should pay attention to** your pronunciation. 你应该注意你的发音。

3. 宾语 （Object）

宾语表示及物动词的对象或内容。介词后面的名词或代词叫介词宾语。宾语通常由名词、代词、数词或与之相当的结构担任，位于及物动词或介词之后。

① I will write **100 books**. 我要写100本书。

② We help **each other** and learn from each other. 我们互相帮助互相学习。

③ I ask for **seven**. 我要7个。

④ Would you mind **coming earlier tomorrow**? 你介意明天来早些吗？

⑤ I don't know **why he has left**. 我不知道他离开的原因。

4. 补语 （Complement）

补语用来补充说明主语或宾语的动作、状态、身份、特征等内容，通常由名词、代词、形容词或具有相同性质的词语担任，位于主语或宾语的后面。补语分三种情况：表语、宾语补足语和主语补足语。

1) 表语

① He is **a lawyer**. 他是一名律师。

② The book is **hers**. 这书是她的。

③ My number is **two**. 我的号码是2。

④ She is **always careful**. 她总是很认真。

⑤ That was **what he said**. 那就是他所说的话。

2) 宾语补足语

① We call her **an angel**. 我们叫她天使。

② I found the room **empty**. 我发现房间是空的。

③ My aunt asked me **to call you**. 我姑姑让我叫你。

若宾语是不定式、动名词或从句，可用it作形式宾语代替其位置，而将其放到宾语补足语后面。

① I found it **difficult** to finish the task in time. 我觉得很难按时完成这个任务。

② Do you consider it **any good** sending more people there? 你认为派更多的人去那儿有用吗？

③ We made it **clear** that we disagreed. 我们明确表示我们不同意。

3) 主语补足语

含宾语补足语的句子改成被动语态时,原宾语和宾语补足语便分别成为主语和主语补足语。

We found him working in the office. 我们发现他正在办公室工作。

He was found **working in the office**.（被动语态）

5. 状语 （Adverbial）

状语用于修饰动词、形容词、副词或整个句子,说明谓语动作的时间、地点、速度、方式、程度、手段等内容,通常由副词或与之相当的结构担任。修饰形容词或副词的状语放在被修饰语之前;修饰动词的状语有的放在动词前,有的放在动词后。如动词有宾语,状语一般放在宾语之后。

① He has been in the hospital **for over a week**. 他已经在这医院一个多星期了。

② The girl is walking **slowly**. 这女孩正缓慢地走着。

③ **Arriving at the station**, he found the train gone. 他一到车站就发现火车已经开走了。

注：定语和同位语是名词的修饰语。

(1) 定语（Attribute）。修饰名词（代词、数词、-ing 式）的一种辅助成分,限定名词的性质、特征、数量、状态、类别等内容。定语有些放在被修饰的名词前,单词作定语一般放在被修饰名词前,即为前置定语；词组和从句作定语则放在被修饰名词的后边叫后置定语。

① There are **two large new** maps **of the world on the table**. 桌子上有两张巨大的新世界地图。

② The girl **playing the violin** is a fresher. 那正拉小提琴的女孩是新来的。

③ Those **who want to go** may leave now. 想走的人现在可以离开了。

(2) 同位语（Apposite）。位于名词或名词词组之后,说明名词或名词词组的内容。同位语通常由名词、名词性词组或从句担任。

① A year is divided into four seasons, **spring, summer, autumn and winter**. 一年分春、夏、秋、冬四季。

② They **each** have a dictionary. 他们每人都有一本词典。

③ Then aroused the question **where we were to get the machine needed**. 这时就产生了这样一个问题：我们到哪里去找所需要的机器。

1.2.2 基本句型及其转换与扩大

基本句型(Basic Sentence Patterns)

英语中千变万化的句子归根结底都是由五种基本句型组合、扩展、变化而来的。

① 主＋动(SV)

② 主＋动＋补(SVC)

③ 主＋动＋宾(SVO)

④ 主＋动＋间宾＋直宾(SVOiOd)

⑤ 主＋动＋宾＋补(SVOC)

基本句型都为陈述句、肯定句和主动句,这些句型可以转换为疑问句、否定句和被动句。基本句型及其转换形式可以通过不同的语法手段加以扩大,使之成为千变万化的句子,表达各种各样的思想。句型扩大的手段为并列、增加修饰成分和使用从句。现把基本句型举例分析如下：

(1) 主＋动(SV)。在这一句型中,动词为不及物动词(Intransitive Verb)。在有的句子中,不及物动词可以有状语修饰。

① The sun is rising. 太阳正冉冉升起。

② Did you sleep well?（well 作状语,修饰不及物动词 sleep）你睡得好吗？

③ The engine broke down. 这发动机坏了。

注意:在此句型中,有少数不及物动词表达被动含义。表达主语本身所具有的特性,不用被动语态。

① The book sells well. 这书很畅销。

② The window won't shut. 这窗户关不上。

③ The pen writes smoothly. 这笔写起来很滑。

④ Cheese cuts easily. 奶酪容易切。

(2) 主＋动＋补(SVC)。在这一句型中,谓语动词通常是连系动词(Linking Verb)。

① Mr. Brown is an engineer. （名词作表语）布朗先生是一名工程师。

② She looks cheerful and happy. （形容词作表语）她看起来很快乐幸福。

③ The machine is out of order. （介词短语作表语）这机器出故障了。

④ His plan is to keep the affair secret. （动词不定式作表语）他的计划是对此事保密。

⑤ The question is what you want to do. （从句作表语,即表语从句）问题是你想做什么。

(3) 主＋动＋宾(SVO)。在此句型中,谓语动词为及物动词(Transitive Verb),随后须跟宾语,带一个宾语的及物动词又叫"单宾语及物动词"(Mono-transitive Verb)。

① She treats them with patience。（名词或代词作宾语）她耐心对待他们。

② We can't afford to pay such a price. （不定式作宾语）我们付不起这个价格。

③ Would you mind waiting a few minutes? （动名词作宾语）你介意等几分钟吗？

④ I hope that I have said nothing to pain you. （从句作宾语,即宾语从句）我希望没说伤害你的话。

注:并不是所有的及物动词都可以接上述各种情况作宾语,不同的动词有不同的用法,所以在学习动词时,一定要掌握其用法。

(4) 主＋动＋间宾＋直宾(SVOiOd)。在此句型中,动词可以称作双宾语动词(Ditransitive Verb),其后面的宾语为间接宾语和直接宾语,其中间接宾语在前,一般表示人;直接宾语在后,一般表示物。这类句型有三种情况。

第一种情况,间接宾语可以改为 to 引导的短语。

① He handed me a letter. （可改为 He handed a letter to me.）他递给我一封信。

② She gave me her telephone number. （可改为 She gave her telephone number to me.）她把电话号码给了我。

第二种情况,间接宾语可以改为 for 引导的短语。

① She sang us a folk song. （可改为 She sang a folk song for us.）她给我们唱了一首民歌。

② She cooked us a delicious meal. （可改为 She cooked a delicious meal for us.）她给我们做了一顿美餐。

第三种情况,直接宾语可以由宾语从句充当。

① Tell him I'm out. 告诉他我出去了。

② Can you inform me where Miss Green lives? 你能告诉我格林小姐住哪儿吗？

(5) 主+动+宾+补(SVOC)。在此句型中,及物动词之后须跟宾语和宾语补足语,这种动词又叫复杂宾语及物动词(Complex Transitive Verb)。后面的宾语补足语是说明宾语的情况的,宾语和宾语补足语一起被称作复合宾语。这个句式是英语中比较复杂的一个句式,因为复合宾语的构成内容较多。

① He found his new job boring.（形容词作宾补）他觉得他的新工作很乏味。
② We elected Tom chairman.（名词作宾补）我们选汤姆为主席。
③ This placed her in a very difficult position.（介词短语作宾补）这使她陷入困境中。
④ We went to her house but found her out.（副词作宾补）我们去她家但是发现她出去了。
⑤ What do you advise me to do?（不定式作宾补）你向我提什么建议？

在这个结构中,可以出现用 it 作形式上的宾语,把真正的宾语放在宾语补足语的后面。在此结构中,宾语常常是动词不定式或宾语从句。

He felt it his duty to mention this to her. 他觉得向她提醒这事是他的责任。
分析:it 是形式宾语,his duty 是宾语补足语,to mention this to her 是真正的宾语。
I think it best that you should stay with us. 我认为你最好跟我们在一起。
分析:it 是形式宾语,best 是宾语补足语,that you should stay with us 是真正的宾语。

注:(1)习惯用语的使用。在英语中,有很多动词习惯用语,在学习的过程中,要注意它们的使用,不必分析单独每个词的使用。

① We are short of money.（be short of 中 short 作表语）我们缺乏资金。
② She is always making trouble for her friends.（trouble 作 make 的宾语）她总是给她的朋友找麻烦。
③ He has carried out our instructions to the letter.（our instructions 作词组 carry out 的宾语）他已经按信上我们的说明去执行了。
④ We are waiting for the rain to stop.（wait for 后面的 the rain 是宾语,to stop 是宾语补足语）我们在等雨停。

(2)在英语中,大多数动词既可以作及物动词又可以作不及物动词,而且还会有一些固定词组,因此一个动词可以用于几种句型。以动词 ask 为例说明。

① Did you ask the price?（接名词作宾语）你问价格了吗？
② She asked them their names.（接双宾语）她向他们问了名字。
③ I asked James to buy some bread.（接宾语加不定式作宾语补足语）我让詹姆士买了些面包。
④ I asked to speak to Fred.（接不定式作宾语）我要求同弗来德讲话。
⑤ He has asked for an interview with the President.（组成固定词组 ask for）他请求面见总统。

1.2.3 句子的种类

1. 按使用目的可分为陈述句、疑问句、祈使句和感叹句

(1) 陈述句(Declarative Sentences)。说明一个事实或陈述一种看法。
① Light travels faster than sound. 光速比声速快。（说明事实）

② The film is rather boring. 这部电影很乏味。（说明看法）

(2) 疑问句(Interrogative Sentences)。提出问题。有以下四种：

① 一般疑问句(General Questions)。

Can you finish the work in time? 你能按时完成工作吗？

② 特殊疑问句(W Questions；H Questions)。

What's the name of this tree? 这棵树的名字是什么？

How do you know that? 你怎么知道那件事？

③ 选择疑问句(Alternative Questions)。

Do you want tea or coffee? 你是要茶还是咖啡？

④ 反意疑问句(Tag-Questions)。

He doesn't know her, does he? 他不认识她,对不对？

(3) 祈使句(Imperative Sentences)。提出请求、建议或发出命令。

① Sit down, please. 请坐。

② Don't be nervous! 别紧张！

③ Let's go to the park. 我们去公园吧。

(4) 感叹句(Exclamatory Sentences)。表示说话人惊奇、喜悦、愤怒等情绪。

What good news it is! 多好的消息啊！

2. 按结构可分为简单句、并列句和复合句

(1) 简单句(Simple Sentences)。只包含一个主谓结构的句子叫简单句,个个成分都是单词或短语的句子。

① She has been very busy working hard every day. 她一直很忙,天天辛苦工作。

② I heard him singing in the hall. 我听到他在大厅唱歌。

(2) 并列句(Compound Sentences)。包含两个或两个以上主谓结构的句子叫并列句,句与句之间通常用并列连词或分号来连接；包含两个或更多互不依从的主谓结构,分句由并列连词 and,then,but,or,or else,so,for,while,when,both... and,either... or,neither... nor,not only... but also,as well as 等来连接。

① He is a basketball fan, and his wife is a volleyball fan. 他是足球迷而他妻子是排球迷。

② Honey is sweet, but the bee stings. 蜜甜蜂螫人。

③ Don't be late, for there is a meeting. 不要迟到,因为要开会。

④ Hurry up, or you'll be late. 快点,不然你就迟到了。

⑤ He works hard while his brother is a lazy bone. 他很用功而他哥哥是个懒虫。

(3) 复合句(Complex Sentences)。包含一个主句,一个或几个从句的句子叫复合句,复合句的主句往往可以独立存在,而从句则只作一个句子成分(如主语、宾语、表语、状语等),并且从句常常由从属连词引导。

① <u>She looks older</u> <u>than she really is</u>. 她看上去比实际年龄老。
   主句   状语从句

② <u>Do you see</u> <u>what I mean</u>? 你明白我的意思吗？
  主句 宾语从句

③ <u>I didn't understand</u> <u>what he meant.</u> 我不明白他的意思。
　　　主句　　　　　　从句

巩 固 练 习

请判断下列句子的结构类型。

1. He is running.
2. The loud voice from the upstairs made him angry.
3. The little boy is asking the teacher all kinds of questions.
4. She seemed angry.
5. My father bought me a beautiful present.
6. Why do you keep your eyes closed?
7. Will you tell us an exciting story?
8. We must keep our classroom tidy and clean.
9. I heard the baby crying in the sitting room.
10. Can you push the window open?
11. Cambridge is a university town.
12. They made Smith the president of the university.
13. A single spark can start a fire.
14. Bad news travels quickly.
15. Failure is the mother of success.
16. Doctors recognize Tom as a leading authority.
17. His teacher advised him to take up the piano.
18. The soup tasted delicious.
19. He gave me the facts in brief.
20. They left the children playing in the garden.

第二章 名 词

名词表示人、事物、地点或抽象概念的名称。在英语中,名词是最重要的词类之一。例如:desk 桌子,time 时间,life 生活,book 书本,room 房间,honesty 诚实,worker 工人,pencil 铅笔,computer 计算机等。

2.1 名词的分类

2.1.1 专有名词和普通名词

名词根据其意义可以分为专有名词(Proper Nouns)和普通名词(Common Nouns),专有名词主要是指人名、地名及某类人和事物专有的名称。

(1) 人名:Jack, Hannah, President Bush, Mrs. Hillary, Einstein。
(2) 地名:Beijing, Yangtze River, The Great Wall, Renmin Street。
(3) 某类人的名称:Chinese, Jews, Germans。
(4) 某些抽象事物的名称:Buddhism, Christianity, WTO。
(5) 月份周日名及节日名称:July, Monday, Easter, Christmas Day。
(6) 对家人等的称呼:Dad, Uncle, Auntie。
(7) 书名电影及诗歌的名称:*Gone with the Wind*, *Crouching Tiger, Hidden Dragon*。
注:专有名词的第一个字母要大写。

专有名词以外的名词都是普通名词。普通名词又可分为以下四类:
(1) 个体名词(Individual Nouns);
(2) 集体名词(Collective Nouns);
(3) 物质名词(Material Nouns);
(4) 抽象名词(Abstract Nouns)。

个体名词和集体名词可以用数目来计算,称为可数名词(Countable Nouns);物质名词和抽象名词一般无法用数目计算,称为不可数名词(Uncountable Nouns)。

归纳一下,名词的分类如下表所列。

类 别			用 法	例 词
普通名词	可数名词	个体名词	表示某类人或物中的个体	pen, student, desk
		集体名词	表示若干个个体组成的集合体	school, family, class

(续)

类别			用法	例词
普通名词	不可数名词	物质名词	表示无法分为个体的实物	tea, water, paper
		抽象名词	表示动作、状态、品质、感情等抽象概念	work, time, love
专有名词			某个(些)人、地方、机构等专有的名称	Shanghai, China, The Great Wall

2.1.2 简单名词与复合名词

名词还可以根据其形式分为简单名词与复合名词。简单名词由单个名词组成。如：
  poem 诗　　　　　　opinion 意见
  wine 酒　　　　　　work 工作
复合名词由单个名词加一个或一个以上的名词或其他词类组成。如：
  airman 飞行员　　　　sight-seeing 观光
  walking stick 拐杖　　woman worker 女工

2.1.3 可数名词与不可数名词

在英语中，区分可数名词与不可数名词非常重要。区分可数名词与不可数名词，单纯依靠常识(即数数的方法)并不十分准确。由于语言的差异，在名词的可数概念上，英语同汉语并不完全一致。例如英语中的 duty(责任)是可数的，但在汉语中往往是不可数的。反之，汉语中的"肥皂"是可数的，而在英语中 soap 则是不可数的。此外，有许多一般不可数的名词在一定的上下文中也可以用作可数名词。

  ① Do you want tea or milk? 您要茶还是牛奶？(不可数)
  ② Two teas, please. 请给两杯茶。(可数，等于 two cups of tea)

还有，抽象名词本应是不可数的，但英语中亦有不少是可数的，如：hope(希望)，experience(经历)等。

对名词可数性有疑问时，最可靠的方法是查阅标有[C](可数)和[U](不可数)的英英或英汉词典。

2.2 名词的数

数(number)是名词的语法范畴之一。英语名词可以分为单数和复数；单数(singular)表示"一"；复数表示"多于一"。一以下亦为单数，一以上即为复数(plural)，如 one half week（半周），one week（一周），one and a half weeks（一周半），two weeks（两周），one or two weeks（一两周）。

名词的数(作主语时)决定谓语动词的数。

2.2.1 名词复数的规则变化

情况	构成方法	读音	例词
一般情况	加-s	/p/,/t/,/k/,/f/,等清辅音后读/s/	map—maps
		浊辅音和元音后读/z/	bag—bags /car—cars
以 s,x,ch,sh 等结尾的词	加-es	读/iz/	bus—buses/ watch—watches
以 ce,se,ze,等结尾的词	加-s	读/iz/	license—licenses
以辅音+y结尾的名词（以-quy结尾的名词）	变 y 为 i 再加 es	读/z/	baby—babies soliloquy—soliloquies
以元音+y结尾的名词 以 y 结尾的专有名词	加-s	读/z/	toy—toys Mary—marys
以-f,或-fe 结尾的名词	变-f,-fe 为-ves	读/vz/	knife—knives
以辅音+o结尾的名词	加 -es	读/z/	tomato—tomatoes
以元音+o 或-oo 结尾的名词	加-s	读/z/	zoo—zoos bamboo—bamboos
以-th 结尾的名词	加-s	在长元音后，-ths 读作/ðz/	path—paths
		在短元音或辅音后-ths 读作/θz/	month—months

上述规则变化有一些例外：
(1) 只有一个/s/音结尾的名词,复数形式读作/ziz/,如:house—houses /hauziz/。
(2) 以-f-fe 结尾可变为-ves 的名词还有：
leaf—leaves 叶 thief—thieves 小偷 shelf—shelves 搁板
calf—calves 小牛 elf—elves 小精灵 half—halves 一半
life—lives 生命 loaf—loaves 一条面包 self—selves 自己

sheaf—sheaves 一捆 wife—wives 妻子 wolf—wolves 狼
还有的只加-s,读作/s/(个别可读作/fs/或/vz/)。如：
belief—beliefs 信条   chief—chiefs 首领   cliff—cliffs 悬崖   fife—fifes 横笛
grief—griefs 悲伤   gulf—gulfs 海湾   proof—proofs 证据   reef—reefs 礁石
roof—roofs(fs/fz) 屋顶   safe—safes 保险箱   strife—strifes 争斗
handkerchief—handkerchiefs(fs/fz) 手帕
有些这类名词有两种复数形式,如：
hoof—hoofs/hooves 蹄   dwarf—dwarfs/dwarves 矮子   scarf—scarfs/scarves 头巾
wharf—wharfs/wharves 码头   turf—turfs/turves 草皮
(3) 有些以辅音＋o 结尾的名词仍加-s/z/,如：
memo—memos 备忘录   kilo—kilos 千克   piano—pianos 钢琴   photo—photos 照片
solo—solos 独唱   quarto—quartos 四开本   dynamo—dynamos 发电机
Eskimo—Eskimos 因纽特人   Filipino—Filipinos 菲律宾人
有些这类名词有两种复数形式,如：
cargo—cargoes/cargos 货物   volcano—volcanos/volcanoes 火山
(4) 少数以-th 结尾的名词有两种读音,如：
truth—truths/truːθs/,/truːðz/ 真理
youth—youths/juːθs/,/juːðz/ 青年

2.2.2 名词复数的不规则变化

英语里有一些名词的复数形式不是以词尾加-s 或-es 构成,它们的不规则变化如下：
(1) 变内部元音。

child—children   foot—feet   tooth—teeth
mouse—mice   man—men   woman—women

注：由一个词加 man 或 woman 构成的合成词,其复数形式也是-men 和-women,如：an Englishman,two Englishmen。但 German 不是合成词,故复数形式为 Germans。Bowman 是姓,其复数是 the Bowmans。

(2) 单数复数同一种形式。

deer,sheep,fish,Chinese,Japanese ,li,jin,yuan,two li,three mu,four jin 等。但除人民币的元、角、分外,美元、英镑、法郎等都有复数形式。如：a dollar, two dollars; a pound, five pounds。

(3) 集体名词,以单数形式出现,但实为复数。

people,police,cattle 等本身就是复数,不能说 a people,a police,a cattle,但可以说 a person,a policeman,a head of cattle。the English,the British,the French,the Chinese,the Japanese,the Swiss 等名词,表示国民总称时,作复数用。

The English are reserved and modest. 英国人既保守又谦逊。

(4) 以 s 结尾,仍为单数的名词。

① maths,politics,physics 等学科名词,一般是不可数名词,为单数。
② news 为不可数名词。
③ the United States,the United Nations 应视为单数。

The United States was given real independence by the English in 1783.
美国在 1783 年获得独立。

④ 以复数形式出现的书名、剧名、报纸、杂志名也可视为单数。

Little Women is a very interesting novel.

《小妇人》是一本非常有趣的小说。

(5) 表示由两部分构成的东西,如 glasses（眼镜）, trousers, clothes 等,若表达具体数目,要借助数量词 pair(对、双), suit(套), a pair of glasses; two pairs of trousers 等。

(6) 另外还有一些名词,其复数形式有时可表示特别意思,如 goods 货物, waters 水域, fishes(各种)鱼。

2.2.3 不可数名词数的表示

不可数名词一般只有单数形式,没有复数形式。

(1) 物质名词属于不可数名词,一般没有复数形式。但以下情况例外

① 当物质名词转化为个体名词时,名词可数

Cake is a kind of food. 蛋糕是一种食物。（不可数）

These cakes are sweet. 这些蛋糕很好吃。（可数）

② 当物质名词表示该物质的种类时,名词可数。

This factory produces steel. （不可数）

We need various steels. （可数）

③ 当物质名词表示份数时可数。

Coffee is very popular with young people. 咖啡很受年轻人的欢迎。

Two coffees, please. 请来两杯咖啡。

(2) 许多抽象名词属于不可数名词,没有复数形式。但有些抽象名词则可用作可数名词,因而有复数形式。

change—changes 变化

hope—hopes 希望

four freedoms 四大自由

the four modernizations 四个现代化

(3) 物质名词和抽象名词可以借助单位词表一定的数量。

a glass of water 一杯水

a piece of advice 一条建议

2.2.4 集体名词的数

(1) 有些集体名词如 police, people, cattle 等,通常作复数。

The British police have very limited powers. 英国警察权力有限。

(2) 有些集体名词如 foliage, machinery, equipment 等,通常作不可数名词。

All the machinery in the factory is made in China. 这个工厂的机器都是中国制造的。

(3) 有些集体名词如:audience, committee, class, crew, family 等,即可作单数,也可作复数用。

① Her family was well known in their city. 她的家庭在她们的城市很有名。

② My family are waiting for me. 我的家人正在等我。

2.2.5 专有名词的数

专有名词具有"独一无二"的含义,因此只有单数形式。然而,专有名词"独一无二"的含义,只是相对来说的,有时也可有复数形式,例如,叫"汤姆"的人在一定范围内只有一个,但在更大的范围内可能有多个;拿姓氏来说,在英美国家,夫妻子女都是同一个姓,同姓的更多;叫"休斯敦"的地方在美国有六处;叫"剑桥"的地方在英国有两处,在美国有十处。

There are four Toms in our class. 我们班里有四个汤姆。

姓氏的复数之前加定冠词,表示一家人。例如:the Greens 格林一家人(或格林夫妇)。

2.2.6 不同国家的人的单复数

国 籍	总称(谓语用复数)	一个人	两个人
中国	the Chinese	a Chinese	two Chinese
瑞士	the Swiss	a Swiss	two Swiss
澳大利亚	the Australians	an Australian	two Australians
俄罗斯	the Russians	a Russian	two Russians
意大利	the Italians	an Italian	two Italians
希腊	the Greek	a Greek	two Greeks
法国	the French	a Frenchman	two Frenchmen
日本	the Japanese	a Japanese	two Japanese
美国	the Americans	an American	two Americans
印度	the Indians	an Indian	two Indians
加拿大	the Canadians	a Canadian	two Canadians
德国	the Germans	a German	two Germans
英国	the English	an Englishman	two Englishmen
瑞典	the Swedish	a Swede	two Swedes

2.3 名词的性

英语名词分四个性:阳性(Masculine Gender)表示男性的人或雄性动物;阴性(Feminine Gender)表示女性的人或雌性动物;通性(Common Gender)表示男女通用;中性(Neuter)表示无生命的物和抽象概念。

2.3.1 名词的阳性和阴性

阳性指男人、男孩和雄性动物(代词为 he/they),阴性指女人、女孩和雌性动物(代词为 she/they)。

阳性	阴性
king 国王	queen 王后
man 男人	woman 女人
monk 和尚	nun 尼姑
nephew 侄子	niece 侄女
sir 先生	madam 夫人
uncle 叔父	aunt 婶母

有些表示人的名词用后缀(个别用前缀)表示性别。如：

actor 男演员	actress 女演员
emperor 皇帝	empress 女皇、皇后
usher 男招待员	usherette 女招待员
widower 鳏夫	widow 寡妇
policeman 警察	policewoman 女警察
postman 邮递员	postwoman 女邮递员

注：(1) chairman(主席)等少数几个名词可表示阳性，亦可表示阴性。

(2) "man"指一般人时，包括 woman 在内；其代名词则用 he 表示。

Man does what he can, God (does) what he wills. ＝Man proposes, God disposes. 谋事在人，成事在天。

2.3.2　表示动物的名词的性

家禽、家畜和许多较大的野禽、野兽由不同的词来表示它们的性别。

bull 公牛	cow 母牛
cock 公鸡	hen 母鸡
dog 公狗	bitch 母狗
duck 公鸭	drake 母鸭
gander 公鹅	goose 母鹅

注：在一般的语境中，不必要指出动物的性别，可用阳性表示两性，如用 dog 表示 dog 和 bitch，或用另一个词表示两性，如用 horse 表示 stallion(雄马)和 mare(母马)。

在动物前可加 male, femal, he, she 之类的词来表示性别，如：

male frog 雄蛙	female frog 雌蛙
he-goat 公羊	she-goat 母羊

2.3.3　名词的中性

中性：指无生命的东西，不知性别的动物，有时也指不知性别的婴儿(代词为 it/they)。例外情况："baby" 婴孩和 "child" 小孩的性别不明时，则用中性氏名词 "it" 表示。

The child seems to have lost its way. 这孩子似乎迷了路。

1. 动物的性别中性

动物除按性别分别用 he，she 等外，可视为中性，概以 it, its 表示。

A fox caught a hen and killed her (or it). 一只狐狸捉到一只鸡，并将它咬死。

注：hen 常被认为是阴性名词。

2. 中性名词"拟人化"的性别

(1) 在文学上或口语里将无生命的东西或抽象的概念予以人格化的时候，都以一些强有力的、伟大的或恐怖的事物为阳性。

The sun drove away the clouds with his powerful rays.
太阳用他的强光驱散了乌云。

(2) 优美柔和的事物被看作阴性。

The moon shed her mild light upon the scene.
月亮以她的柔和光辉照在那片土地上。

(3) 轮船是阴性。有时对汽车或其他运载工具表示喜爱或尊重时，也认为它们是阴性。

① The ship sank with her crew on board. 船带着船上的水手沉入海底。

② The ship struck an iceberg, which tore a huge hole in her side. 船碰在一座冰山上，船帮被撞出一个大洞。

(4) 国名被看作阴性，但在地理上则为中性。

① Britain lost almost all her colonies during the Second World War. 第二次世界大战期间，英国几乎失去了她全部的殖民地。

② Britain is famous for its scenic spots. 英国以它的名胜而闻名。

③ Scotland lost many of her bravest men in two great rebellions. 在两次大起义中，苏格兰失去了许多极勇敢的男子汉。

2.3.4 名词的通性

这种名词有许多不分性别，既可表示阳性，亦可表示阴性。

  enemy 敌人   singer 歌唱家
  friend 朋友   teacher 教师
  musician 音乐家   typist 打字员

这些名词在使用代词时可根据实际指代的对象用 he 或 she 指代。

My teacher says he is moving his office.
我的老师说他将搬迁办公室。

英语大部分名词都分不出阴阳性。如果要表示一个人的性别，可以在这个名词前加 man 或 woman，如：

  a man doctor 男医生   a woman worker 女工

也可加 boy, girl 或 male, female 这类词，如：

  a boy friend 男朋友   a girl cousin 表姐妹
  a male model 男模特   a female singer 女歌手

2.4 名词的格

在英语中有些名词可以加"'s"来表示所有关系，带这种词尾的名词形式称为该名词的所有格，如 a teacher's book。名词所有格的规则如下：

(1) 单数名词词尾加"'s"，复数名词词尾没有 s，也要加"'s"，如：the boy's bag 男孩的书包，men's room 男厕所。

（2）若名词已有复数词尾-s，只加"'"，如：the workers' struggle 工人的斗争。

（3）凡不能加"'s"的名词，都可以用"名词＋of＋名词"的结构来表示所有关系(此形式多用来表示无生命的东西)，如：the title of the song 歌的名字。

（4）在表示店铺或教堂的名字或某人的家时，名词所有格的后面常常不出现它所修饰的名词，如：the barber's 理发店。

（5）如果两个名词并列，并且分别有's，则表示"分别有"；只有一个"'s"，则表示"共有"。如：John's and Mary's room(两间)，John and Mary's room(一间)。

（6）复合名词或短语，'s 加在最后一个词的词尾。如：a month or two's absence.

2.5 名词在句中的作用

名词在句中可以担任不同的成分。

作主语：Knowledge is power. 知识就是力量。

作表语：Running is my favourite sports. 跑步是我最喜欢的运动。

作宾语：Have you received my letter? 你收到我的信了吗？

作定语：We bought a new color TV. 我们买了台新彩电。

作同位语：You girls sit on this side. 你们女孩坐这边。

作呼语：Afternoon Mary. 玛丽，下午好。

作状语：We'll meet tomorrow. 我们明天碰头。

作介词宾语：He was devoted to pure science. 他专心致志于纯科学。

构成复合宾语(作宾语的补语)：He painted the door a brighter color. 他把门漆成了更鲜艳的颜色。

巩 固 练 习

一、给出下面名词的复数形式。

policeman	day	roof
tooth	wolf	monkey
leaf	lorry	watch
knife	gas	tomato
thief	ox	toy
fox	foot	boss
half	shelf	dish
aircraft	bus	mouse
piano	mosquito	hero
party	brush	life
child	box	branch
goose	kilo	lady

wife	glass	inch
baby	calf	photo
city	woman	class
fly	potato	wish

二、用名词填空。

1. He saw three _____ (sheep) in the field.
2. A flock of _____ (goose) are flying over our heads.
3. The cart was drawn by two _____ (ox).
4. He doesn't like eating with _____ (knife) and forks.
5. They saw a pack of _____ (wolf) in the distance.
6. He _____ (fisherman) were drawing the net.
7. The _____ (mouse) have eaten the cheese.
8. My bad _____ (tooth) are giving me a lot of pain.
9. Two _____ (policewoman) stopped him.
10. _____ (woman) tend to live longer than _____ (man).
11. Rain and snow are _____ (phenomenon) of the weather.
12. There he met people from different social _____ (stratum).
13. They shot down two enemy _____ (aircraft).
14. The man is six _____ (foot) tall.
15. They caught three small _____ (fish).
16. The grass was covered with _____ (leaf).

三、把下面句子译为英语。

1. 这家商店售卖男女服装。
2. 他们售卖婴儿服装吗？
3. 他在看狗的牙齿。
4. 这是一辆女式自行车。
5. 六月一日是儿童节。
6. 你可以在药房买阿司匹林。
7. 他有一个博士学位。
8. 春节我们有一周的假期。
9. 我买了十块钱的邮票。
10. 我到肉铺（面包坊、理发店）去。
11. 我们今晚在我姑姑家吃饭。
12. 我到约翰家去，但他在他姐姐家里。

第三章 冠　词

3.1　冠词的定义

冠词是置于名词之前、说明名词所表示的人或事物的一种虚词。冠词也可以说是名词的一种标志,它用在名词的前面,帮助指明名词的含义,它不能离开名词而单独存在。英语冠词有三种,即定冠词(Definite Article)、不定冠词(Indefinite Article)和零冠词(Zero Article)。

冠词总是与名词一起连用的。它的基本用法如下:
(1) 在单数可数名词前可用定冠词或不定冠词。
(2) 复数可数名词前可用定冠词或零冠词。
(3) 不可数名词前可用定冠词或零冠词。
专有名词前用零冠词。在特指时一般前面要加定冠词。
然而,由于名词的数形和数念都有不少特殊情况,以及历史、习惯等原因,在英语实践中,三种冠词几乎可用于各类名词。

3.2　冠词的位置

3.2.1　不定冠词位置

不定冠词常位于名词或名词修饰语前,但有一些例外。
(1) 位于 such,what,many,half 等形容词之后。
① I have never seen such an animal. 我从来没见过这样的动物。
② Many a man is fit for the job. 许多人适合这岗位。
③ What a pity! 多可惜!
(2) 当名词前的形容词被副词 as, so, too, how, however, enough 修饰时,不定冠词应放在形容词之后。
① It is as pleasant a day as I have ever spent. 我从未这么高兴过。
② So short a time. 如此短的时间。
③ Too long a distance. 距离太远了。
(3) quite,rather 与单数名词连用,冠词放在其后。但当 rather 后仍有形容词,不定冠词放其前后均可。
rather a cold day/a rather cold day
(4) 在 as,though 引导的让步状语从句中,当表语为形容词修饰的名词时,不定冠词放形容词后。
Brave a man though he is,he trembles at the sight of snakes. 他尽管勇敢,可见到蛇还是

发抖。

3.2.2　定冠词位置

定冠词通常位于名词或名词修饰语前，但放在 all，both，double，half，twice，three times 等词之后，名词之前。

① All the students in the class went out. 班里的所有学生都出去了。

② Both the boys were late for dinner. 两个孩子晚饭都来晚了。

both 后的定冠词常可省去。

③ Both(the)men were talking in low voices. 两个人在低声交谈。

all 后是否要用定冠词，由冠词的一般规则决定。

④ All children have to go to school one day. 所有孩子有一天都得去上学。（类指）

⑤ All the children of the boarding school were in bed. 寄宿学校的全体孩子都睡了。（特指）

3.3　冠词的用法

3.3.1　不定冠词的用法

不定冠词 a，an 与数词 one 同源，表示"一个"的意思。a 用于辅音音素前，一般读作/ə/，而 an 则用于元音音素前，一般读作/ən/。在强调时不定冠词 a 或 an 则须读作/ei/或/æn/。主要用在可数名词单数前，表示下列几种含义。

(1) 表示"一个"，意思接近 one；指某人或某物，意为 a certain。

A Mr. Ling is waiting for you. 有位姓凌的先生在等你。

(2) 代表一类人或物。

A knife is a tool for cutting with. 刀是切割的工具。

Mr. Smith is an engineer. 史密斯先生是工程师。

(3) 组成词组或成语。

a little / a few / a lot / a type of / a pile / a great many / many a / as a rule / in a hurry / in a minute / in a word / in a short while / after a while / have a cold / have a try /keep an eye on / all of a sudden 等。

3.3.2　定冠词的用法

定冠词 the 与指示代词 this，that 同源，有"那(这)个"的意思，但意义较弱，可以和一个名词连用，表示某个或某些特定的人或东西。定冠词 the 在强调时须读作/ðiː/。

(1) 特指双方都明白的人或物。

Take the medicine. 把药吃了。

(2) 上文提到过的人或事。

He bought a house. I've been to the house. 他买了幢房子。我去过那幢房子。

(3) 指世上独一无二的事物，如 the sun，the sky，the moon，the earth 等。

(4) 与单数名词连用表示一类事物，如 the dollar 美元；the fox 狐狸；或与形容词或分词连用,表示一类人:the rich 富人;the living 生者。

(5) 用在序数词和形容词最高级,及 only, very, same 等前面。

① Where do you live? I live on the second floor. 你住在哪？我住在二层。

② That's the very thing I've been looking for. 那正是我要找的东西。

(6) 与复数名词连用,指整个群体。

① They are the teachers of this school. 他们是这个学校的教师(指全体教师)

② They are teachers of this school. 他们是这个学校的教师(指部分教师)

(7) 表示所有,相当于物主代词,用在表示身体部位的名词前。

She caught me by the arm. 她抓住了我的手臂。

(8) 用在某些由普通名词构成的国家名称、机关团体、阶级等专有名词前。

the People's Republic of China 中华人民共和国

the United States 美国

(9) 用在表示乐器的名词之前。

She plays the piano. 她弹钢琴。

(10) 用在姓氏的复数名词之前,表示一家人。

the Greens 格林一家人(或格林夫妇)

(11) 用在惯用语中。

in the day, in the morning (afternoon, evening), the day after tomorrow

the day before yesterday, the next morning

in the sky (water, field, country)

in the dark, in the rain, in the distance

in the middle (of), in the end

on the whole, by the way, go to the theatre

3.3.3　零冠词的用法

零冠词是名词之前一种无形的冠词,即一般所谓的不用冠词(定冠词或不定冠词)的场合。零冠词的历史最为悠久。现在许多专有名词、抽象名词、物质名词都用零冠词。

(1) 国名、人名前通常不用定冠词:England, Mary。

(2) 泛指的复数名词,表示一类人或事物时,可不用定冠词。

They are teachers. 他们是教师。

(3) 抽象名词表示一般概念时,通常不加冠词。

Failure is the mother of success. 失败乃成功之母。

(4) 物质名词表示一般概念时,通常不加冠词,当表示特定的意思时,需要加定冠词。

Man cannot live without water. 人离开水就无法生存。

The water in the bottle is sweet. 这瓶里的水是甜的。

(5) 在季节、月份、节日、假日、日期、星期等表示时间的名词之前,不加冠词。

We go to school from Monday to Friday. 我们从星期一到星期五都上课。

(6) 在称呼或表示官衔、职位的名词前不加冠词。

The guards took the American to General Lee. 士兵们把这个美国人送到李将军那里。

(7) 在三餐、球类运动和娱乐运动的名称前,不加冠词,如 have breakfast, play chess。

(8) 当两个或两个以上名词并用时,常省去冠词。

I can't write without a pen or pencil. 没有钢笔和铅笔,我就写不了字。

(9) 当 by 与火车等交通工具连用,表示一种方式时,中间无冠词,如 by bus,by train。

(10) 有些个体名词不用冠词,如 school,college,prison,market,hospital,bed,table,class,town,church,court 等个体名词,直接置于介词后,表示该名词的深层含义。

go to hospital 去医院看病

go to the hospital 去医院(但若加上冠词并不是去看病,而是有其他目的)

(11) 不用冠词的序数词。His second wife is a nurse. 他第二任妻子是一名护士。

① 序数词前有物主代词。

② 序数词作副词。He came first in the race.

③ 在固定词组中。at (the) first/first of all/ from first to last

3.4 冠词的省略

有时名词前无冠词,但并非零冠词,而是省去了不定冠词或定冠词。在下列情况下冠词可省略。

(1) 避免重复。

The lightning flashed and thunder crashed.

电闪雷鸣。(thunder 前省去 the)

(2) 可省去句首的定冠词 the。

Class is dismissed.

下课了。

(3) 在 the next day(morning,etc.)等短语中,定冠词 the 常可省去。

(4) 新闻标题、通知说明、提纲、剧本提示、书名等常省去定冠词或不定冠词。

(A) Hotel Fire Disaster. 饭店大火成灾。

(The)Lift(is)out of order. 电梯坏了。

Exit into garden. 出去进入花园。

(The) BBC English Dictionary BBC 英语词典

注:冠词与形容词+名词结构。

(1) 两个形容词都有冠词,表示两个不同东西。

① He raises a black and a white cat. 他养了一只黑猫和一只白猫。

② The black and the white cats are hers. 这只黑猫和这只白猫都是她的。

(2) 如后一个形容词无冠词,则指一物。

He raises a black and white cat. 他养了一只花猫。

巩 固 练 习

一、单项选择。

1. When Linda was a child, her mother always let her have _____ bed.

   A. the breakfast in　　　　　　　B. the breakfast in the

  C. breakfast in   D. breakfast in the

2. He has promised to give up _____ hundreds of times.
  A. a tobacco   B. tobacco   C. the tobacco   D. tobaccos

3. _____ usually go to church every Sunday.
  A. The Brown   B. A Brown   C. Browns   D. The Browns

4. The train is running fifty miles _____.
  A. an hour   B. one hour   C. the hour   D. a hour

5. He can play almost every kind of music instrument but he is good _____.
  A. at the flute   B. at flute   C. at a flute   D. at that flute

6. The investigators found that more should be done for _____ in India.
  A. those poor   B. a poor   C. poor   D. the poor

7. You look in high spirit. You must have _____ during your holiday.
  A. wonderful time   B. a wonderful time
  C. the wonderful time   D. some wonderful time

8. The city assigned a policeman to the school crossing because _____ traffic there was so heavy.
  A. a   B. an   C. the   D. one

9. A new teacher was sent to the village in place of _____ one who had retired.
  A. a   B. the   C. an   D. its

10. Virtue and vice are before you; _____ leads you to happiness, _____ to misery.
  A. the former...latter   B. a former...a latter
  C. the former...the latter   D. former...latter

11. The children in the kinder-garden soon took _____ to their teachers.
  A. quite fancy   B. a quite fancy
  C. quite a fancy   D. the quite fancy

12. _____ tend to bemoan the lack of character in the young generation.
  A. The old   B. Old   C. Elderly   D. Older

13. A man suffering from a chock should be given _____.
  A. hot sweet tea   B. a hot sweet tea
  C. the hot sweet tea   D. one hot sweet tea

14. He answered my questions with _____ not to be expected of an ordinary schoolboy.
  A. his accuracy   B. a accuracy   C. the accuracy   D. an accuracy

15. If you go by train you can have quite _____ comfortable journey.
  A. the   B. one   C. a   D. that

16. We're going to _____ with _____ today, aren't we?
  A. the tea...the Smiths   B. tea...those Smiths
  C. a tea...a Smith   D. tea...the Smiths

17. I want an assistant with _____ knowledge of French and _____ experience of office routine.
  A. the...the   B. a...the   C. a...an   D. the...an

18. Ann's habit of riding a motorcycle up and down the road early in the morning annoyed the neighbors and _____ they took her to the court.
    A. in the end　　　B. at the end　　　C. in an end　　　D. in end
19. It is reported that today _____ president will have lunch with _____ President Omon.
    A. the;the　　　B. a;a　　　C. the;/　　　D. /;/
20. Tianan Men Square and _____ Great Wall are tow of the places everyone should see in _____ People's Republic of China.
    A. the;the　　　B. /;/　　　C. the;/　　　D. /;the
21. It has long been known that there is an electric field _____.
    A. inside the earth　B. inside earth　　C. inside an earth　　D. on earth
22. _____ much harder work, the volunteers were able to place the raging forest fire _____.
    A. By the means of;under the control　　B. By means of;under control
    C. By means of;under a control　　D. By a means of;under control
23. No sooner had the man departed than the tree began dropping coffee beans _____.
    A. by the thousand　B. by a thousand　C. by thousands　　D. by thousand
24. He expressed _____ of their having ever been married.
    A. the doubt　　　B. a doubt　　　C. doubt　　　D. an doubt
25. He saw through the little boy's tricks _____.
    A. at glance　　　B. at the glance　　　C. at some glance　　　D. at a glance
26. Their victory is _____, for they've lost too many men.
    A. out of question
    B. out of the question
    C. out question
    D. of question
27. Many a girl wants to become _____.
    A. some secretary　B. a secretary　　C. secretary　　D. secretaries
28. He grabbed me _____ and pulled me onto the bus.
    A. a arm　　　B. an arm　　　C. the arm　　　D. by the arm
29. I'll come in _____ minute; in fact I'll come _____ moment I'm through.
    A. /;the　　　B. a;the　　　C. the;a　　　D. /;/
30. This is one of _____ interesting books on your subject.
    A. the most　　　B. the most of the　C. most　　　D. most of the

二、在需要的地方填入冠词。
1. _____ Thailand is in _____ Southeast Asia.
2. _____ Japan and _____ United States are separated by _____ Pacific Ocean.
3. _____ Mount Everest is in _____ Himalayas on the border between _____ Nepal and _____ Tibet, which is part of _____ People's Republic of China.
4. _____ Suez flows through the north of _____ Egypt, connecting _____ Mediterranean, _____ Gulf of Suez and _____ Red sea.
5. While they were in London. they stayed at _____ Royal Hotel in _____ Abert Street near _____ Trafalgar Square.

6. After we visited _____ Houses of _____ Parliament and _____ Westminster Abbey. we had lunch at _____ Peking Restaurant.
7. _____ Yellow River originates in _____ Qinghai and flows into _____ Yellow Sea.
8. She swam _____ English Channel when she was sixteen, and planned to sail across _____ Atlantic in a yacht.

第四章 代　词

代词是代替名词以及起名词作用的短语、分句和句子的词。大多数代词具有名词和形容词的功能。英语中的代词,按其意义、特征及在句中的作用分为八类。

（1）人称代词(Personal Pronoun)。
① 主格 I,you,he,she,it,we,you,they。
② 宾格 me,you,him,her,it,us,you,them。
（2）物主代词(Possessive Pronoun)。
① 形容词性物主代词有 my,your,his,her,its,our,your,their。
② 名词性物主代词有 mine,yours,his,hers,its,ours,yours,theirs。
（3）反身代词(Reflexive Pronoun)有 myself,yourself,himself,herself,itself,ourselves,yourselves,themselves,oneself。
（4）相互代词(Reciprocal Pronoun)有 each other,one another。
（5）指示代词(Demonstrative Pronoun)有 this,that,these,those,it,such,same。
（6）疑问代词(Interrogative Pronoun)有 who,whom,whose,which,what。
（7）关系代词(Relative Pronoun)有 who,whom,whose,which,that,as。
（8）不定代词(Indefinite Pronoun)有 some,something,somebody,someone,any,anything,anybody,anyone,no,nothing,nobody,no one,every,everything,everybody,everyone,each,much,many,little,a little,few,a few,other,another,all,none,one,both,either,neither。

4.1　人　称　代　词

人称代词是表示"我"、"你"、"他"、"她"、"它"、"我们"、"你们"、"他们"的词。人称代词有人称、数、性和格的变化,如下表所列。

数	单 数		复 数	
格	主格	宾格	主格	宾格
第一人称	I	me	we	us
第二人称	You	you	you	you
第三人称 阳性	he	him	they	them
第三人称 阴性	she	her	they	them
第三人称 中性	it	it	they	them

例如：① He is my friend. 他是我的朋友。
② It's me. 是我。

4.1.1 人称代词的用法

(1) 人称代词的主格在句子中作主语或主语补语。

① John waited a while but eventually he went home. 约翰等了一会儿，最后他回家了。

② John hoped the passenger would be Mary and indeed it was she. 约翰希望那位乘客是玛丽，还真是她。

注：在复合句中，如果主句和从句主语相同，代词主语要用在从句中，名词主语用在主句中。

When he arrived, John went straight to the bank. 约翰一到就直接去银行了。

(2) 人称代词的宾格在句子中作宾语或介词宾语，但在口语中也能作表语，第一人称在省略句中，还可以作主语。

① I saw her with them; at least, I thought it was her. 我看到她和他们在一起，至少我认为是她。（her 做宾语，them 作介词宾语，her 作表语）

② — Who broke the vase? 谁打碎了花瓶？
— Me. 我。（me 作表语＝It's me.）

注：在上面两例中，her 和 me 分别作表语。现代英语中多用宾格，在正式文体中这里应为 she 和 I。

4.1.2 人称代词之主、宾格的替换

1. 宾格代替主格

(1) 在简短对话中，当人称代词单独使用或在 not 后，多用宾语。

— I like English.　　我喜欢英语。
— Me too.　　　　我也喜欢。
— Have more wine? 再来点酒喝吗？
— Not me.　　　　我可不要了。

(2) 在表示比较的非正式的文体中，常用宾格代替主格。但如果比较状语的谓语保留，则主语只能用主格。

He is taller than I/me.

He is taller than I am.

2. 主格代替宾格

(1) 在介词 but, except 后，有时可用主格代替宾格。如：No one but he can swim. 除了他大家都不会游泳。

(2) 在电话用语中常用主格。

— I wish to speak to Mary.　　　我想和玛丽通话。
— This is she.　　　　　　　　我就是玛丽。

注：在动词 be 或 to be 后的人称代词视其前面的名词或代词而定。

I thought it was she.　　　　我以为是她。　　　　（主格—主格）
I thought it to be her.　　　　我以为是她。　　　　（宾格—宾格）
I was taken to be she.　　　　我被当成了她。　　　　（主格—主格）

They took me to be her.　　　他们把我当成了她。　　（宾格—宾格）

4.1.3　人称代词的指代

顾名思义，人称代词表示人。然而，人称代词并不全指人，也指物。人称代词有三个人称，每个人称又分单数和复数（第二人称单数与复数同形），第三人称单数还有阳性、阴性和中性之分。人称代词的人称、数和性质取决于它所指代的名词，而人称代词的格则取决于它在句中的地位。

(1) 不定代词 anybody, everybody, nobody, anyone, someone, everyone, no one，及 whoever 和 person 在正式场合使用时，可用 he, his, him 代替。

Nobody came, did he?　谁也没来，是吗？

(2) 动物名词的指代一般用 it 或 they 代替，有时也用 he, she，带有亲切的感情色彩。

Give the cat some food. She is hungry.　给这猫一些吃的，她饿了。

① 第一人称单数 I 代表说话者，须大写。

That's what I mean.　这就是我的意思。

② 第一人称复数 we 代表说话者一方（两人或两人以上）。

We need one more book.　我们还需要一本书。

③ we 有时也包括听话者。

Let's go, shall we?　咱们走吧，行吗？

④ we 可以代表一个集体。

We should like to copy the order we sent you last month. 我们想复制一份我们上月给你们的订单。（we 代表公司或政府）

⑤ we 也可以用来泛指大家。

We all fear the unknown. 对于未知的事物我们都感到害怕。

We all get into trouble sometimes. 我们有时都会遇到麻烦。

(3) 第二人称单、复数 you 代表听话者或对方（复数 you 代表两人或两人以上）。

I choose you four; the rest of you can stay here. 我选你们四个。其余的可以留在这里。

① you 究竟是表示单数或复数，往往要根据句意和语境来确定。

Are you ready, Jack?　杰克，你准备好了吗？（you 表单数）

You must both come over some evening. 你们俩必须找个晚上过来一趟。（you 表复数）

② you 也可以用来泛指大家。

You never know what may happen. 谁也不知道会发生什么事。

(4) 第三人称单数阳性 he 代表已提到过的男人。

He is a good man.　他是个好人。

在一些谚语中 he 可以泛指大家。如：

He who hesitates is lost. 当断不断，必受其患。

He who laughs last laughs best. 谁笑到最后，谁笑得最好。

(5) 第三人称单数阴性 she 代表已提到过的女人。

She had a lively sense of humour. 她有一种很强的幽默感。

she 除了指"她"外，还可表示以下含义。

雌性动物：I stroked the cat and she rubbed against my leg. 我抚摸猫，她蹭我的腿。

船只，车辆：Nice car—how much did she cost? 好车——买她花了多少钱？

国家：England has done what she promised to do. 英国已履行了她的承诺。

(6) 第三人称单数中性 it 代表已提到过的一件事物。

I love swimming. It keeps me fit. 我喜欢游泳，它能使我保持健康。

① 当说话者不清楚或无必要知道说话对象的性别时，也可以用 it 来表示。

It's a lovely baby. Is it a boy or a girl? 宝宝真可爱，是男孩还是女孩？

② it 可用来指代团体。

The committee has met and it has rejected the proposal. 委员会已开过会，拒绝了这项建议。

③ it 常用来指代时间、距离、自然现象等。

It is half past two now. 现在是两点半钟。

It was very warm in the room. 房间里很暖和。

It's 112 miles from London to Birmingham. 从伦敦到伯明翰 112 英里。

④ it 有时非确指。

Take it easy. 不要紧张。

⑤ it 还常用于固定习语，it 所指为对方所熟知，故无必要明确指出。

cab it 乘车   come it 尽自己分内
walk it 步行   come it strong 做得过分
make it 办成   take it out of somebody 拿某人出气

(7) 第三人称复数 they(不分性别)代表已提到过的一些人或事物。

① —Where are the plates? 盘碟在哪儿？
— They are in the cupboard. 在碗橱里。

they 也可以用于一般陈述，泛指"人们"。

② They say that honesty is the best policy. 人们说诚实是上策。（they 泛指人们）

they 常用来指"当局"等。

③ They're putting up oil prices again soon. 当局即将再次提高油价。

(8) 人称代词一般出现在它所指代的名词之后，但有时也出现在它所指代的名词之前。

They tremble—the sustaining crags. 它们颤动了，这些支撑着的岩石。

(9) 人称代词有时有拟人化的作用，即用 it 指代的事物改用 he 或 she 以及相应的物主代词或反身代词指代。

She is a fine ship. 这是条很好的船。

(10) 人称代词有时亦可用作名词。

It's not a she, it's a he. 那不是个女孩，是个男孩。

4.1.4　并列人称代词的排列顺序

(1) 单数人称代词并列作主语时，其顺序为

第二人称＋第三人称＋第一人称

you ＋ he/she/it ＋ I

You, he and I should return on time. 你我和他应该按时返回。

(2) 复数人称代词作主语时，其顺序为

第一人称＋第二人称 ＋第三人称
we＋you＋they
注:在下列情况中,第一人称放在前面。
① 在承认错误,承担责任时。
It was I and John that made her angry. 是我和约翰惹她生气了。
② 在长辈对晚辈,长官对下属说话时,如长官为第一人称。
I and you try to finish it. 我和你尽力完成。
③ 并列主语只有第一人称和第三人称时。I and she will go there. 我和她要去那里。
④ 当其他人称代词或名词被定语从句修饰时。

4.1.5 人称代词的功用

人称代词在句中可用作主语、宾语、表语等。
(1) 人称代词主格在句中主要用作主语。
He majors in English. 他主修英语。
(2) 人称代词宾格在句中主要用作宾语,包括直接宾语、间接宾语与介词宾语。
① I saw you in the street。我在大街上看见了你。
② You don't need to thank me. 你不需要谢我。
③ This pen is bad. I can not write with it. 这支钢笔不好用,我没法用它写字。
两个人称代词分别用作间接宾语和直接宾语时,间接宾语前应加 to,并置于直接宾语之后。
④ I gave it to him. 我把这个给了他。
如其中一个为其他代词,则可采用间接宾语在前、直接宾语在后的形式。
⑤ I gave him some. 我给了他一些。
(3) 人称代词在句中作表语时一般用宾格。
① Oh, it's her. 啊,是她。
如跟有 who 或 that 引导的从句,则常用主格。
② It's I who did it. 是我做的。
(4) 人称代词单独使用时,一般不用主格而用宾格。
—I'd like to go back in here. 我想回到这里来。
—Me too. 我也想。
(5) 人称代词用于 as 和 than 之后,如果 as 和 than 用作介词,也往往用宾格。
① He's younger than me. 他比我年轻。
如果 as 和 than 用作连词,则须用主格。
② She's as old as I am. 她与我同岁。
(6) 在感叹疑问句中,人称代词宾格可用作主语,起强调作用。
Him go to the States! 他怎会去美国!
(7) we 和 you 可用作同位语结构的第一部分。
He asked you boys to be quiet. 他要你们男孩子安静些。

4.2 物主代词

物主代词是表示所有关系的代词,也可叫做代词所有格。物主代词分形容性物主代词和名词性物主代词两种,其人物和数的变化如下表所列。

数	单 数			复 数		
人 称	第一人称	第二人称	第三人称	第一人称	第二人称	第三人称
形容词性物主代词	my	your	his/her/its	our	your	their
名词性物主代词	mine	yours	his/hers/its	ours	yours	theirs

① I like his car. 我喜欢他的小汽车。
② Our school is here, and theirs is there. 我们的学校在这儿,他们的在那儿。

物主代词即是人称代词属格,表示"所有"。与人称代词一样,也分第一人称、第二人称和第三人称,每个人称分单数和复数,第三人称单数还分阳性、阴性和中性。物主代词有形容词性(my, your 等)和名词性(mine, yours 等)两种。

物主代词既有表示所属的作用又有指代作用。

③ John had cut his finger; apparently there was a broken glass on his desk. 约翰割破了手指,显而易见,他桌子上有个破玻璃杯。

形容词性物主代词相当于形容词,置于名词之前。它们的人称、数和性取决于它们所指代的名词或代词。

④ Mike has cut his finger. 麦克把手指割破了。

名词性物主代词相当于名词,不能用于名词之前,说话时要加重语气。它们的形式取决于它们指代的名词或代词。

⑤ Their classroom is larger than ours. 他们的教师比我们的大。

(1) 形容词性物主代词在句中只能用作定语,并可与形容词 own 连用表示强调。

① She turned away her eyes. 她把她的目光移开。
② I saw it with my own eyes. 那是我亲眼看见的。(与 own 连用表示强调)
③ I'd love to have my very own room。我喜欢有一个完全属于我自己的房间。(如进一步强调则可加 very)
④ I have nothing of my own. 我自己一无所有。(这种结构还可以与 of 连用)

有时可由定冠词 the 代替。

⑤ She received a blow on the head. 她头上挨了一击。(the=her)

(2) 名词性的物主代词在用法上相当于省略了中心名词的-'s 属格结构。

Jack's cap   意为   The cap is Jack's.
his cap   意为   The cap is his.

名词性物主代词的句法功能:

① 作主语（多用于正式文体）。
May I use your pen? Yours works better. 我可以用一用你的钢笔吗？你的比我的好用。
② 作宾语。
I love my motherland as much as you love yours. 我爱我的祖国就像你爱你的祖国一样深。
③ 作介词宾语。
You should interpret what I said in my sense of the word, not in yours. 你应当按我所用的词义去解释我说的话，而不能按你自己的词义去解释。
④ 作主语补语。
The life I have is yours. It's yours. It's yours. 我的生命属于你，属于你，属于你。
⑤ 用作表语。
This garden is ours. 这个花园是我们的。
⑥ 用作礼貌用语。
Yours sincerely(truly,faithfully)您的忠诚的（忠实的、可以信赖的）（这是书信落款的英国用法，美国多将 yours 放在 sincerely 等之后）
注：物主代词不可与 a, an, this, that, these, those, some, any, several, no, each, every, such, another, which 等词一起前置、修饰一个名词，而必须用双重所有格。公式为 a, an, this, that ＋名词＋of ＋名词性物主代词。
He is a friend of mine. 他是我的一个朋友。

4.3 反 身 代 词

1. 反身代词概述

反身代词是一种表示反射或强调的代词。表示"我自己"、"你自己"、"他自己"、"我们自己"、"你们自己"和"他们自己"等的代词。它由第一人称、第二人称形容词性物主代词和第三人称人称代词宾格，加词尾 self 或 selves 而成，如下表所列。

数	单 数			复 数		
人称	第一人称	第二人称	第三人称	第一人称	第二人称	第三人称
人称代词	I	you	he/she/it	we	you	they
反身代词	myself	yourself	yourself/herself/himself	ourselves	yourselves	themselves

另外：one 的反身代词为 oneself，例如：
She was talking to herself. 她自言自语。
反身代词的基本含义是：通过反身代词指代主语，使施动者把动作形式上反射到施动者自己。因此，反身代词与它所指代的名词或代词形成互指关系，在人称、性、数上保持一致。

2. 反身代词的功用

反身代词在句中可用作动词宾语、表语和同位语等。

1) 作宾语

（1）有些动词需有反身代词，如 absent，bathe，amuse，blame，dry，cut，enjoy，hurt，introduce，behave 等。

① We enjoyed ourselves very much last night. 我们昨晚玩得很开心。

② Please help yourself to some fish. 请你随便吃点鱼。

（2）用于及物动词＋宾语＋介词，如 take pride in，help oneself to sth. 等。

I could not dress(myself)up at that time. 那个时候我不能打扮我自己。

2）作表语

有些反身代词可作表语，如结构 be oneself。

I am not myself today. 我今天不舒服。

3）作同位语

The thing itself is not important. 事情本身并不重要。

4）某些情况下的特殊用法

在不强调的情况下，but，except，for 等介词后宾语用反身代词或人称代词宾格均可。

No one but myself(me)is hurt.

注：(1) 反身代词本身不能单独作主语。

（错）Myself drove the car.

（对）I myself drove the car. 我自己开车。

（2）但在 and，or，nor 连接的并列主语中，第二个主语可用反身代词，特别是 myself 作主语。

Charles and myself saw it. 查尔斯和我看见了这件事。

4.4 相 互 代 词

表示相互关系的代词叫相互代词，有 each other 和 one another 两组，它们的形式如下表所列。

宾 格	属 格
each other 相互	each other's 相互的
one another 相互	one another's 相互的

1. 相互代词的使用环境

它们表示句中动词所叙述的动作或感觉在涉及的各个对象之间是相互存在的，所指代的名词或代词必须是复形或两个以上。虽然按照传统语法指二者时用 each other，指二者以上时用 one another，但是在语言的实际运用时却很少有这种界线。一般认为，它们在文体上却存在一些差别：each other 多用于非正式文体，而 one another 则多用于较正式文体。

① They love each other. 他们彼此相爱。

② They looked at one another. 他们相互对望。

③ It is easy to see that the people of different cultures have always copied each other. 显而易见，不同文化的人总是相互借鉴的。

两组词交替使用的实例也很多。
④ He put all the books beside each other/one another. 他把所有书并列摆放起来。
⑤ Usually these small groups were independent of each other. 这些小团体通常是相互独立的。

2. 相互代词的句法功能
(1) 作动词宾语。
People should love one another. 人们应当彼此相爱。
(2) 可作介词宾语。
Dogs bark, cocks crow, frogs croak to each other. 犬吠、鸡鸣、蛙儿对唱。
(3) 相互代词属格用作定语。
The students borrowed each other's notes. 学生们互借笔记。
(4) each 和 other 可分开使用。
Each of the twins wanted to know what the other was doing. 这对孪生兄弟都想知道对方在干什么。

4.5 指示代词

指示代词是用来指示或标识人或事物的代词。

1. 指示代词的形式
指示代词分单数(this / that)和复数(these / those)两种形式,既可作限定词又可作代词,如下表所列。

	单 数	复 数
近 指	this(student)这个(学生)	these(students)这些(学生)
远 指	that(student)那个(学生)	those(students)那些(学生)

其他还有:such 这样的,same 同样的,so 这样,it(指人用)等。

2. 指示代词的句法功能
(1) 作主语。
This is the way to do it. 这事儿就该这样做。
(2) 作宾语。
I like this better than that. 我喜欢这个甚于那个。
(3) 作主语补语。
My point is this. 我的观点就是如此。
(4) 作介词宾语。
① I don't say no to that. 我并未拒绝那个。
② There is no fear of that. 那并不可怕。
注:(1) 指示代词在作主语时可指物也可指人,但作其他句子成分时只能指物,不能指人。
(对)That is my teacher. 那是我的老师。(that 作主语,指人)
(对)He is going to marry this girl. 他要和这个姑娘结婚。(this 作限定词)

（错）He is going to marry this. （this 作宾语时不能指人）

（对）I bought this. 我买这个。（this 指物,可作宾语）

(2) that 和 those 可作定语从句的先行词,但 this 和 these 不能;同时,在作先行词时,只有 those 可指人,试比较:

（对）He admired that which looked beautiful. 他赞赏外表漂亮的东西。

（对）He admired those who looked beautiful. 他赞赏那些外表漂亮的人。（those 指人）

（错）He admired that who danced well. （that 作宾语时不能指人）

（对）He admired those who danced well. 他赞赏跳舞好的人。（those 指人）

（对）He admired those which looked beautiful. 他赞赏那些外表漂亮的东西。（those 指物）

4.5.1 this(these)与 that(those)的用法

this(these)指近的事物,that(those)指远的事物。

(1) 指空间的远近。

This is a map of China. That is a map of the World. 这是一张中国地图。那是一张世界地图。

(2) 指时间的前后。

① Life was hard in those days. 在那些日子里,生活很苦。

② Life is much easier(in)these days. 这些日子,生活好过多了。

(3) 指叙述事物的前后,that 指前,this 指后。

Virtue and vice are before you; this leads to misery, that to peace. 善与恶都在你面前;后者导致不幸,前者导致安宁。

4.5.2 such 的用法

指示代词 such 意为"这样",亦具有名词和形容词的性质,在句中可用作主语、宾语、补语、定语等。

(1) 用作主语。

Such is life. 生活就是这样。

(2) 用作宾语。

Take from the drawer such as you need. 从抽屉里拿你所需要的东西吧。

(3) 用作表语(常与 as 和 that 从句连用)。

The book is not such that I can recommend it. 这样的书,我是不能介绍的。

(4) 用作宾语补语。

If you are a man, show yourself such. 如若你是男子汉,就显出男子汉的气概来。

(5) 用作定语。

① He was a silent, ambitious man. Such men usually succeed. 他是个沉默寡言而有进取心的人。这种人通常能成功。

修饰单数可数名词时,可与不定冠词连用,并须置于其前。

② He is such a bore. 他是这样一个讨厌的人。

(6) 常与 as 或 that 连用。

① Associate with such as will improve your manners. 要和有助于你礼貌修养的人交往。

② He shut the window with such force that the glass broke. 他关窗户用力太大,玻璃都被震破了。

注:such 后的 as 是关系代词,that 是连词。

4.6 疑问代词

(1) 疑问代词有 who(谁,主格),whom(谁,宾格),whose(谁的,属格),what(什么),which(哪个,哪些)等。其中 who,whom,whose 只能指人,what 和 which 可指人或物。它们可具有单数概念或复数概念。疑问代词引导的疑问句为特殊疑问句。它们一般都在该疑问句句首,并在其中作为某一句子成分(如主语、宾语、表语等)。疑问代词还可以引导间接疑问句。

① Tell me who he is. 告诉我他是谁。

② Do you know what his name is? 你知道他叫什么名字?

疑问代词 who,what,which 后可加 ever 以加强语气。

③ Who ever are you looking for? 你到底找谁?

④ What ever do you mean? 你究竟是什么意思?

⑤ Which ever do you want? 你究竟要哪个?

(2) 疑问代词在句中应位于谓语动词之前,没有性和数的变化,除 who 之外也没有格的变化。what,which,whose 还可作限定词。试比较下列句子。

疑问代词:

① Whose are these books on the desk? 桌上的书是谁的?

② What was the directional flow of U. S. territorial expansion? 美国的领土扩张是朝哪个方向的?

限定词:

③ Whose books are these on the desk? 桌上的书是谁的?

④ What events led to most of the east of the Mississippi River becoming part of the United States? 哪些事件使密西西比河以东的大部分土地归属于美国?

注:① 无论是作疑问代词还是限定词,which 和 what 所指的范围不同。what 所指的范围是无限的,而 which 则指在一定的范围内。

a. Which girls do you like best? 你喜欢哪几个姑娘?

b. What girls do you like best? 你喜欢什么样的姑娘?

② whom 是 who 的宾格,在书面语中,它作动词宾语或介词宾语,在口语中作宾语时,可用 who 代替,但在介词后只能用 whom。

a. Who(m) did you meet on the street? 你在街上遇到了谁?(作动词宾语)

b. Who(m) are you taking the book to? 你要把这书带给谁?(作介词宾语,置句首)

c. To whom did you speak on the campus? 你在校园里和谁讲话了?(作介词宾语,置介词后,不能用 who 取代。)

(3) who 与 what 的区别:who 多指姓名、关系等,what 多指职业、地位等。who 对人数有限制,what 对人数未加限制。

(4) 疑问代词用于对介词宾语提问时,过去的文体中介词和疑问代词通常一起放在句首,现代英语中,疑问代词在句首,介词在句末。

① For what do most people live and work? 大部分人生活和工作的目的是什么？（旧文体）

② What are you looking for? 你在找什么？（现代英语）

(5) 疑问代词还可引导名词性从句。

① I can't make out what he is driving at. 我不知道他用意何在。

② Can you tell me whose is the blue shirt on the bed? 你能告诉我床上的蓝衬衣是谁的吗？

③ Much of what you say I agree with, but I cannot go all the way with you. 你说的我大部分同意,但并不完全赞同。

4.7 关 系 代 词

关系代词有 who, whose, whom, that, which, as 等,是用作引导定语从句的关联词。它们在定语从句中可作主语、表语、宾语、定语等；另一方面它们又代表主句中为定语从句所修饰的那个名词或代词（通称为先行词）。

He is the man whom you have been looking for. 他就是你要找的那个人。（关系代词 whom 在从句中作宾语,它的先行词是 man, whom 在口语中一般可略去）

(1) 关系代词用来引导定语从句。它代表先行词,同时在从句中作一定的句子成分。

The girl to whom I spoke is my cousin. 跟我讲话的姑娘是我表妹。（该句中 whom 既代表先行词 the girl,又在从句中作介词 to 的宾语）

(2) 关系代词有主格、宾格和属格之分,并有指人与指物之分。在限定性定语从句中, that 可指人也可指物,如下表所列。

	指 人	指 物	指人或指物
主 格	who	which	that
宾 格	whom	that	that
属 格	whose	of which/whose	of which/whose

① This is the pencil whose point is broken. 这就是那支折了尖的铅笔。（whose 指物,在限定性定语从句中作定语）

② He came back for the book which he had forgotten. 他回来取他忘记取的书。（which 指物,在限定性定语从句中作宾语,可以省略）

说明:非限定性定语从句中,不能用 that 作关系代词。

(3) 关系代词 which 的先行词可以是一个句子。

① He said he saw me there, which was a lie. 他说在那儿看到了我,纯属谎言。

说明:关系代词在从句中作宾语时可以省略。另外,关系代词 that 在从句中作表语时也可省略。

② I've forgotten much of the Latin I once knew. 我过去懂拉丁语，现在大都忘了。
③ He is changed. He is not the man he was. 他变化很大，已不是过去的他了。

4.8 不定代词

不指明代替任何特定名词或形容词的代词叫不定代词。不定代词表示各种程度和各种类型的不定意义。它们在逻辑意义上是数量词，具有整体或局部的意义。不定代词可分为以下几种。

1. 普通不定代词

(1) some, any, no。

(2) somebody, anybody, nobody, someone, anyone, no one（不连写）, something, anything, nothing。

(3) one, none。

2. 个体代词

(1) all, every, each; other, another, either, neither, both, half。

(2) everybody, everyone, everything。

3. 数量代词

many, much, few, little, a few, a little, a lot of, lots of, a great deal, a great many。

4.8.1 some 的用法

不定代词 some 具有名词和形容词的性质，既可指人，亦可指物。

(1) 通常用于表示不定数或不定量，修饰复数可数名词或不可数名词，表示"几个"、"一些"。

① There are some children outside. 外面有几个孩子。（修饰复数可数名词）

② Give me some water, please. 请给我一些水。（修饰不可数名词）

(2) 用于修饰单数可数名词，意为"某个"。

He's living at some place in East Asia. 他住在东亚的某个地方。（修饰单数可数名词）

(3) 用于表示对比，须重读。

I enjoy some music, but not much of it. 我喜欢一些音乐，但不多。

(4) 相当于形容词时，在句中作定语（例句见前）；用作名词时，在句中作主语和宾语。

① Some are wise and some are otherwise. 有些人聪明，有些人愚笨。

② If you have no money, I will lend you some. 如果你没有钱，我愿借给你一些。

相当于名词时，还可后跟 of 短语。of 的宾语用复数可数名词，表示复数；of 的宾语用不可数名词，表示单数。

③ Some of her opinions were hard to accept. 她的一些观点难于接受。（of 的宾语为复数可数名词）

of 的宾语如用单数可数名词，则表示"部分"。

④ Some of the loaf has been eaten. 一条面包已吃了一些。（＝part of the loaf）

(5) 一般用于肯定句。

① The mother is doing some washing now. 妈妈正在洗衣服。

如果句中包含 some 的部分具有肯定意义,那么也可用于否定句或疑问句。
在否定句中,some 表示"一些"、"部分"。

② I could not answer some of his questions. 我不能回答他的某些问题。

含有 some 的疑问句大多表示"请求"或"建议",希望回答 yes(同意)。

③ Will you get me some matches? 给我几根火柴好吗?

some 有时表示反问。

④ Didn't he give you some money? 难道他没有给你一些钱吗?

(6) 用于修饰数词,表示"大约"。

It happened some twenty years ago. 这事发生在大约 20 年前。

4.8.2　any 的用法

不定代词 any 具有名词和形容词的性质,既可指人,亦可指物。

(1) 与 some 一样,any 也表示不定数或不定量,修饰复数可数名词或不可数名词,意为"一些"、"什么",常用于疑问句。

① Haven't you any work to do? 你没有工作做吗?(修饰不可数名词)

有时可修饰单数可数名词。

② Do you know any good doctor? 你认识什么好大夫吗?

(2) 常用于否定句或从句中,常与 never,without,seldom,hardly 等连用。

There isn't any water. 没有一点水。

(3) 用于由 if 或 whether 引导的宾语从句。

① I wonder if you have met any of these people before. 我不知道你以前是否见过这些人。

any 也可用于条件从句。

② If there are any new magazines in the library, take some for me. 图书馆如果来了新杂志,替我借几本。

(4) 亦用于肯定句,意为"任何",通常重读,修饰单数可数名词和不可数名词。

① Any time you want me, just send for me. 什么时候需要我,就给我个信儿。

any 有时修饰复数可数名词。

② We had no idea that any serious losses had been inflicted on the company. 我们不知道公司受到什么严重损失。

(5) 用作形容词,在句中作定语(例句见前)。用作名词时,在句中作主语和宾语,可表示单数或复数。

Did she give you any? 她给了你一些没有?

(6) 用作名词时,还可后跟 of 短语,of 之后用复数可数名词或代词。

I don't expect to see any of them at the concert. 我不期望在音乐会见到他们中的任何人。

(7) 用于表示"程度",意为"些微",用作状语。

He was too tired to walk any further. 他太累了,不能再往前走了。

(8) 用于固定习语。

At any rate, we decided to follow Bob's suggestion. 不管怎样,我们决定照鲍勃的意见去

做。

4.8.3　no 的用法

不定代词 no 只有形容词性质，在句中作定语。no 表示否定，意为"没有"、"不是"，可修饰单形、复数可数名词和不可数名词。

(1) 用于 there is(are),have,have got 之后，等于 not any。
① There are no letters for you today. 今天没有你的信。
② I've got no home. 我没有家。
(2) 用于连系动词之后，等于 not a，但语气很强。
He is no friend of mine. 他才不是我的朋友哩。
(3) 用于其他动词之后。
I took no part in these negotiations. 我没有参加这些谈判。
(4) 用于修饰其他句子成分。
I am in no mood for jokes. 我没有情绪开玩笑。
(5) 用于警告、命令等标识。
No parking! 禁止停车！
(6) 用于表示程度(＝not any)，用作状语，修饰形容词原级、比较级和词比较级。
He went no further. 他不再往前走了。
(7) 用于固定习语。
Men are no longer at the mercy of nature. 人类已不再任凭大自然摆布了。
(8) not 与 no 的比较：not 可用于否定动词，no 则没有这种功能。no 是具有形容词性质的不定代词，只能与名词或相当于名词的词连用。
no time(没有时间),no telephone(没有电话),"No spitting"(不许随地吐痰)
no 等于 not any,因此不能用于 a,the,all,both,every 等词之前；这些词之前必须用 not。
not a chance(毫无机会),not the least(一点都不),not all of us(不是我们全体),not everyone(不是每一个人),not enough(不够)。
其次,no 也不与姓名、副词、介词等连用,但 not 可与以下一些词连用。
me,not George(是我,不是乔治);not wisely(不聪明);not on Sundays(不在星期天)。

4.8.4　复合不定代词的用法

不定代词 some,any,no 与 -one,-body,-thing 可组成九个复合代词：someone, anyone, no one(或 no-one), somebody, anybody, nobody, something, anything, nothing。

这些复合代词均只有名词性质。
(1) 第二部分为 -one 和 -body 的复合代词只用于指人。它们形式上是单数,但可用复形代词 they 或 them 指代。
① There is someone in his office. Do you hear them talking? 他办公室里有人,你听见他们说话了吗？(them 指代 someone)
② Nobody can help him under the circumstances. 在这种情况下没有人能帮助他。
(2) 第二部分为 -one 和 -body 的复合代词可有 's 属格形式。
① Everybody's business is nobody's business. 事关大家无人管。

41

第二部分为-one 和-body 的复合代词如后跟 else,'s 属格则移至 else 之后。

② His hair is longer than anyone else's. 他的头发比谁都长。

(3) 第二部分为-one 和-body 的复合代词如有形容词修饰,形容词须后置。

I want someone reliable to do this work. 我需要一个可靠的人来做这件工作。

(4) 一般认为,第二部分为-one 的复合代词与第二部分为-body 的复合代词的功能和意义完全相同,可以互换,只是前者较后者文雅些。但也有人认为,前者侧重指个体,后者侧重指集体。

① This is a letter from someone interested in the job. 这是一封某个对这工作感兴趣的人的信。(＝some person,one person)

② Nobody knew about her arrival. 没有人知道她的到来。(＝no people)

因此,第二部分为-body 的复合代词不后接 of 短语,而第二部分为-one 的复合代词则有时可后跟 of 短语。

(5) 第二部分为-thing 的复合代词只用于指物,没有属格。

I'll do anything for you. 我愿意为你做任何事。

(6) 第二部分为-thing 的复合代词和第二部分为-one 或-body 的复合代词一样,其形容词亦须后置。

Is it something important? 事情重要吗?

4.8.5　one 的用法

不定代词 one 指代可数名词,既可指人,亦可指物。one 具有名词和形容词性质,在句中可用作主语、宾语、定语等。用作名词时,它有复数形式 ones 和属格形式 one's,而且还有相应的反身代词 oneself,用作形容词时形式无变化。

(1) 相当于名词,泛指"人们"、"一个人"、"任何人",无修饰词语。

① One would think I had agreed to her going. 人们会认为我同意她走的。

one 可以和 one's 或 oneself 一起使用。

② One shouldn't be too hard on oneself. 一个人不应该太难为自己。

(2) 相当于名词,意指"一个人"。

① There was a look in his eyes of one used to risking his life. 从他的目光中可以看出,他是个惯于冒生命危险的人。

one 还可后跟 of 短语,短语中用复数可数名词或代词。

② I've made some cakes. Would you like one of them? 我做了几块蛋糕,你吃一块好吗?

(3) 用于与 the other,another 表示对比,在这种情况下有数的含义。

One man's meat is another's poison. 对甲有利未必就对乙也有利。(谚语)

(4) 用作替代词,即代替前面刚提到过的名词,以免重复。仅用于可数名词,复数用 ones,指人指物均可。

① A hateful person is one that arouses feelings of hatred in you. 可憎之人就是会使你产生憎恨之情的人。

替代词可用复数形式 ones。

② I prefer red roses to white ones. 我喜欢红玫瑰胜过白玫瑰。

替代词如有修饰词语,则须加冠词。

③ My shoes are similar to the ones you had on yesterday. 我这鞋跟你昨天穿的那双差不多。

替代词可用其他代词或序数词修饰。

④ My house is the first one on the left. 我的房子是左边第一家。

the one 有"唯一"的含义。

⑤ She is the one who grumbles. 就是她常发牢骚。

在某些情况下可不用替代词。

⑥ I won't go by your car. I use my own. 我不搭你的车,我用我自己的。(own 之后)

⑦ Of all the runners my brother was the swiftest. 在所有赛跑选手中我弟弟是跑得最快的。(形容词最高级之后)

⑧ I have only one bike but you have two. 我只有一辆自行车,可你有两辆。(基数词之后)

另外,正式文件和学术文章应避免用替代词。

(5) 相当于形容词时和相当于名词时一样,也可意为"唯一"。

It was her one great sorrow. 那是她唯一的大憾事。

(6) 与时间名词连用,表示某种不确定的时间。

One summer evening I went for a stroll in the park. 一个夏天的夜晚,我去公园散步。(表过去)

(7) 用于固定习语。

The little ones always know a good man from a bad one. 孩子们总是分得出好人和坏人。

4.8.6　none 的用法

不定代词 none 通常只有名词性质,在句中作主语、宾语等。none 与 no 性质不同,no 只有形容词性质。二者意义相同,皆意为"没有(人或物)",既可指人,亦可指物。

(1) 用于指代单形、复数可数名词和不可数名词。

① None have arrived yet. 还没有人来。

none 常后跟 of 短语,其后用复数可数名词或不可数名词。作主语时谓语动词可用单数或复数形式。

② None of the dogs was(were) there. 没有一条狗在那儿。

(2) 用作主语、宾语、表语、同位语等。

① None of them spoke English except Tom. 除了汤姆,他们中没有人会说英语。(主语)

② Apart from the dizziness, I had none of the true signs of the disease. 除了头晕,我没有此病的任何真实症状。(宾语)

③ That's none of your business! 那与你不相干!(表语)

④ We none of us said anything. 我们中没有人说什么。(同位语)

(3) 用于固定习语。

It's none other than Tom! 这正是汤姆!

注:no one 与 none 的区别。

(1) no one ＝nobody 只指人,是绝对意"没有任何人,任何人都不"的意思,后面不能跟 of 短语。

(2) none 可以指人,也可以指物,后可跟 of + n. 是相对意思,有范围,如：none of the students "学生当中没有人",none of these books "这些书当中没有……"。

None of the students failed the examination.

没有学生考试不及格。(强调都及格了)

none 的强调口气更强烈。

① 一点儿也没；一个也没（+of）。

a. I wanted some more cold meat but there was none left. 我想再吃些冷盘肉,可是一点也不剩了。

b. He had none of his brother's boldness. 他一点都不像他哥哥那样有魄力。

② 没有任何人（或物）（+of）.

a. None of the telephones are/is working. 所有的电话都坏了。

b. None of them speak(s) English. 他们都不会讲英语。

③ 无一人,无一个。

None would take the risk. 谁也不愿冒此风险。

④ 毫不,决不。

He spent two weeks in hospital but he's none the better for it. 他在医院住了两星期,但未见好转。

(3) 在回答疑问句时,who 提问用 no one 回答,how many 提问用 none 回答,但有时可通用。

How many students has been in the classroom?（none（no one）均可使用）

4.8.7 all 的用法

个体代词 all 具有名词和形容词性质,在句中作主语、宾语、定语等。两个以上的人或物（指两个用 both）。

(1) 相当于名词,指人,意为"大家",等于 everybody,在句中作主语和宾语。它有复数概念,作主语时谓语动词须用复数形式。

It is hard to please all. 众口难调。

(2) 相当于名词,指物,意为"一切",等于 everything,在句中作主语和宾语。它表示单数概念,作主语时谓语动词须用单数形式。

① All is not lost. 一切都没丢。

注意：All...not...有时等于 Not all...。

② All is not gold that glitters. 发光的并不总是金子。

(3) 相当于名词时,在美国英语中常与 of 连用（在英国英语中一般不与 of 连用）。all of 的意思与 all 相同。

① All of these books are expensive. 所有这些书都很贵。

亦可后跟不可数名词,表示单数。

② All of that money you gave them has been spent. 你给他们的那些钱全花完了。

有时亦可后跟单数可数名词,但只有 all of 之后才可跟人称代词宾格。

③ All of us were disappointed by him. 他使我们大家都失望了。

(4) 用作主语同位语时有不同的位置。

① They all found the lectures helpful. 他们大家都觉得讲这些课有帮助。(谓语动词之前)

② We are all extremely fond of her. 我们大家都非常喜欢她。(谓语动词之后)

③ The villages have all been destroyed. 这些村庄全部被摧毁了。(谓语动词短语之中)

(5) 相当于形容词,在句中作定语,可修饰单数、复数可数名词以及专有名词。

All roads lead to Rome. 条条大路通罗马。

(6) 用作定语从句的先行词。

All I desired was leisure for study. 我的全部希望就是有空学习。

(7) 用于固定习语。

First of all you must be frank. 首先你必须坦诚。

4.8.8 every 的用法

every 只有形容词性质,在句中作定语。常用于修饰单数可数名词,述说对象至少有三个(如为两个则用 each)。every 还可构成复合代词 everyone,everybody,everything。

(1) 用于单数可数名词,意为"各个"。

① He knew by heart every word in her letter. 他牢记她信中的每一个词。

every 有时意为"一切"。

② I shall do my best to help you in every way. 我将尽最大努力用一切方法帮助你。

(2) 用于固定习语。

When the police arrived, the crowd started running every which way. 警察到达时,人群开始四处逃散。

(3) everyone 和 everybody 只有名词性质,用于指人,二者同义,意为"每人",表示单数。但可用复数物主代词 they,them,their 指代。作主语时谓语动词须用单数形式。

① Everybody had some weak spot. 人人都有某种弱点。

这两个词可有属格形式。

② He is sure of everyone's consent. 他确信大家都会同意。

注意:everyone 与词组 every one 的区别,前者的重音模式是ˈeveryone,后者是 everˈone 或ˈeveryˈone;前者只能指人,后者既可指人,也可指物。关于 every one 的实例如下:

③ Every one of us will be present. 我们大家都将出席。

(4) everything 只有名词性质,用于指物,意为"每件事"、"一切",表示单数,没有属格。

Money isn't everything. 金钱不是一切。

4.8.9 each 的用法

个体代词 each 具有名词和形容词性质,在句中作主语、宾语、定语。既可指人,亦可指物,描述对象至少有两个。

(1) 相当于名词,意为"每个",在句中作主语、宾语和同位语。

① Each went his way. 各走各的路。(主语)

② He gave two to each。他给了每人两个。(宾语)

③ They were each sentenced to thirty days. 他们每人被判 30 日徒刑。(同位语)

④ I told them what each was to do in case of an emgency. 我告诉他们在紧急情况下各

自要做的事。（指物）

⑤ "Toasts,"cried George,in furious cheerfulness,and the end of each threw his glass into the fireplace. "干杯，"乔治欣喜若狂地叫道，而且每干一次就把玻璃杯扔进炉子。（指事）

有时可后跟 of 短语，其后须用复数可数名词或复数人称代词。

⑥ I'll send each of them some seeds in the autumn. 秋天我将送给他们每人一些种子。

(2) 相当于形容词，修饰单数可数名词，在句中作定语。

He gave each boy a present. 他给了每个男孩一件礼物。

注：each 与 every 的区别，each 可用作名词和形容词，every 只用作形容词；二者用作形容词时，意义相同，但 each 着重于个别性，其构成成分有特性；every 则着重于整体性，其构成成分有共性。

① Each student contributed to the fund. 每一个学生都为基金会捐了款。（学生至少两人）

② Every student contributed to the fund. 各个学生为基金会捐了款。（学生至少三人）

each and every 短语则既有个性又有共性。

③ Each and every student contributed to the fund. 各个学生都为基金会捐了款。

4.8.10 other 和 another 的用法

个体代词 other 具有名词和形容词性质，既可指人，亦可指物。other 不确指，因此常与定冠词组成 the other。不定冠词 an 与 other 连用则组成 another，another 亦具有名词和形容词性质。

(1) other 相当于名词时，意为"另一个"，在句中作主语、宾语。

① He held a sword in one hand and a pistol in the other. 他一手握着剑，一手拿着手枪。

other 可用其他代词修饰。

② It's none other than Tom! 这正是汤姆！

other 有复数形式 others。

③ We should not think only of our own children, there are others to be cared for also. 我们不应该只想到我们自己的孩子，还有别的孩子需要照顾。

other 有时可有属格形式。

④ Each looked after the other's bag. 两人相互照料对方的包。（两人）

⑤ She thinks only of others' good. 她只想到别人的美德。（几个人）

(2) other 用作形容词，修饰复形名词，意为"另外的"、"其他的"，在句中作定语。

① I have no other friends but you. 除你以外我没有其他朋友。

the other 后跟单形名词，意为"另一个"。

② This seat is free, the other seat is taken. 这个座位空着，另一个座位有人。

the other 亦可后跟复形名词，意为"另外的"、"其他的"。

③ Jack is here, but where are the other boys? 杰克在这儿，但其他男孩在哪儿？

用作形容词的 other 亦可为其他词所修饰。

④ We have no other business before us. 我们手头没有别的事。

(3) another 用作名词，意为"另一个"，在句中作主语、宾语。

① One is blind, another is deaf, and a third is lame. 一个是瞎子，另一个是聋子，又一个

是瘸子。(主语)

② Ah,where can we find another like her? 啊,我们哪里还能找到像她这样的姑娘?(宾语)

有时可后跟 of 短语。

③ It was only another of her many disappointments. 这只是她许多失望外的又一个失望。

(4) another 用作形容词,意为"另一个",在句中作定语,通常修饰单数名词或代词 one。

① We went into another room. 我们进入另一个房间。

② Tell them I am not very well. I will go and see them another day. 告诉他们我不大舒服,过几天我会去看他们的。(another day 指未来,the other day 则指过去)

(5) other,another 可与 one 组合。one... the other 指两个人或物构成的一组中的个体。

① He held a book in one hand and his notes in the other. 他一手拿着书,一手拿着笔记。

one... another 指同一组内的两个个体。

② One person may like to spend his vacation at the seashore,while another may prefer the mountains. 一个人会喜欢在海滨度假,而另一个人会喜欢在山里度假。

还可用 still another 引进第三者。

③ One person may like to spend his vacation at the seashore,another may prefer the mountains,while still another may choose a large metropolis. 一个人也许喜欢在海滨度假,而另一个人也许喜欢在山里度假,还有人也许喜欢在大都市度假。

4.8.11　either 和 neither 的用法

either 和 neither 是一对意义相反的代词,具有名词和形容词性质。

(1) either 相当于名词时,意为"(二者之中)任何一个",在句中作主语、宾语,表示单数概念,作主语时谓语动词须单数形式,后常跟 of 短语。其后用复形名词或复数代词,但意义明确时可省略 of 短语。

Either of the plans is equally dangerous. 这两个计划中,不论哪一个都同样有危险。

(2) 用作形容词,修饰单形名词,在句中作定语。

Take either half; they're exactly the same. 随便拿哪一半,它们完全一样。

(3) neither 同 either 用法相同,意义相反,意为"(二者之中)哪个也不"。

—Which will you have? 你要哪一个?

—Neither,thank you. 哪个也不要,谢谢。

4.8.12　both 的用法

个体代词 both 意为"两个(都)",具有名词和形容词性质,在句中可作主语、宾语、定语等,既可指人,亦可指物。它表示复数,但只能指"两方"。

(1) 相当于名词,在句中作主语和宾语。

both 常后跟 of 短语,其后用复形名词或复数代词;后接复形名词时 of 省略,后接复数代词时 of 则不能省略。

She invited both of us to the party. 她邀请我们二人都参加聚会。

(2) 相当于名词时,在句中还用作同位语,与复形名词或复数代词在句中的位置取决于谓语动词的形式。作主语同位语时,如谓语为简单动词,both 位于主语之后、谓语动词之前。

① We both had a haircut. 我俩都理了发。

如谓语部分为系表结构,both 则位于连系动词和表语之间。

② These children are both mine. 这两个孩子都是我的。

如谓语为含有助动词或情态动词的动词短语,both 则位于助动词或情态动词之后。

③ You must both come over some evening. 你俩必须在哪天晚上都过来。

但在作简短回答时,both 须位于助动词或情态动词之前。作宾语同位语时,位于宾语之后。

(3) 相当于形容词,在句中作定语。

The club is open to people of both sexes. 这个俱乐部对男女都开放。

(4) each 与 both 的比较:each 表"一分为几",both 表"合二为一"。

① Each of us won a prize. 我们每人都得了一个奖。

② Both of us won a prize. 我们俩都得了奖。

both 相当于名词时,为复数。

③ Both are good. 二者均好。

each 相当于名词用作主语时,一般表单数概念。

④ Two boys entered. Each was carrying a suitcase. 两个孩子进来,每人都提着手提箱。

但用作复数名词(代词)的同位语时,谓语须与主语一致,用复形动词。

⑤ They each have beautiful daughters. 他们每个人的女儿都漂亮。

4.8.13 many 和 much 的用法

表数量的不定代词 many 和 much 具有名词和形容词性质,在句中可用作主语、宾语、定语等,都意为"许多"、"大量";它们的不同在于 many 只能指代或修饰复数可数名词,much 一般只能指代或修饰不可数名词。

(1) 常用于疑问句、否定句,或 if 或 whether 引导的宾语从句。

Did you have much rain of your holidays? 你休假时遇上很多雨吗?

(2) 用于肯定句,仅限于正式英语。

① I know many who would not agree with you. 我知道有很多人不会同意你的意见。

在日常英语中,则用 a lot of, lots of, plenty of, a great deal of, a large number of, a good many 和 a great many 等来代替。

② A great many mistakes have been made by nearly everybody. 几乎人人都做错了很多。

(3) 当 many 和 much 用作主语或用以修饰主语时,有时也可用于肯定句。

① Many of the workers were at the meeting. 许多工人在开会。

② Much of the time was spent on learning. 学习上花了许多时间。

当 many 和 much 有程度副词 so, too, as, how 等修饰时,亦可用于肯定句。

③ I've got so many jobs to do today. 今天我有这么多活要干。

(4) many 和 much 相当于名词时，常后跟 of 短语。

Much of the time was wasted. 很多时间浪费掉了。

(5) many 和 much 有共同的比较级形式 more 和最高级形式 most。

① Most work was done in my father's office. 大多数工作是在我父亲办公室干的。

② Most of his money came from selling his landscapes. 他的大多数钱来源于出卖他的风景画。

4.8.14 (a)few 和(a)little 的用法

a few 和 a little 是一对用作表数量的不定代词的固定词组。它们具有名词和形容词性质，在句中可用作主语、宾语、定语等，意为"少数"、"少量"，其意义是肯定的。a few 指代或修饰复数可数名词，a little 指代或修饰不可数名词。

表数量的不定代词 few 和 little 与 a few 和 a little 的用法基本相同，但具有否定意义，意为"几乎一点没有"，等于 not... many 或 hardly... any。

(1) a few 和 a little 相当于名词时，在句中作主语和宾语。

① Just put a little on each plate. 每只盘里放一点儿。

这两个词组常后跟 of 短语。

② Only a few of the children can read. 只有少数孩子能认字。

(2) a few 和 a little 相当于形容词时，在句中作定语。

There was a chill in the air and a little fresh wind. 寒气袭人，清风几许。

(3) few 和 little 相当于名词时，在句中作主语和宾语。

① You have done very little for us. 你为我们做的很少。

few 和 little 有时可后接 of 短语。

② I see very little of him。我不常看见他。

(4) few 和 little 相当于形容词时，在句中作定语。

① Few words are best. 少说为佳。

② There is little change in his appearance. 他的外貌没什么变化。

(5) few 可有比较级 fewer，最高级 fewest，little 可有比较级 less，最高级 least。

① Who made the fewest mistakes? 谁的错误最少？

② The more haste, the less speed. 欲速则不达。

③ Least talk, most work. 少说多干。

在非正式英语中，few 的比较级和最高级，亦可用 less 和 least。

④ There used to be more women than men in the country, but now there are less. 这个国家过去女多男少，但现在则是女少男多。

⑤ That's the least of my anxieties. 那是我最不焦急的事。

(6) 固定搭配。

only a few (=few), not a few (=many), quite a few (=many), many a (=many)。

① Many books were sold. 很多书都被卖了。

② Many a book was sold. 卖出了许多书。

巩 固 练 习

一、单项选择。

1. There are several pretty girls standing under the tree, but _____ are known to me.
   A. neither B. none C. no one D. all
2. In one year rats eat 40 to 50 times _____ weight.
   A. its B. and C. their D. theirs
3. You'd better continue to use the same spelling of your name as _____ you used in your application.
   A. one B. the one C. any D. some one
4. The little baby was left alone, with _____ to look after it.
   A. someone B. anyone C. not one D. no one
5. John can play chess better than _____ else.
   A. the one B. no one C. any one D. another
6. The weight of something is another way of describing the amount of force exerted on _____ by gravity.
   A. it B. them C. that D. one
7. It is one thing to enjoy listening to good music, but it is quite _____ to perform skillfully yourself.
   A. other B. another C. some D. any
8. Children should be taught how to get along with _____.
   A. another B. other C. others D. any other
9. The poor man lived on wild berries and roots because they had _____ to eat.
   A. nothing else B. anything else C. something other D. nothing other
10. I go to the cinema _____ day, Tuesdays, Thursdays, and Saturdays.
    A. each other B. every other C. this and the other D. all other
11. One of the properties of light is _____ traveling in wave form as it goes from one place to another.
    A. it B. it's C. its D. their
12. _____ in the world has been asked to do his duty for the human society.
    A. Each of the tramps B. Every of the tramps
    C. The each tramp D. The every tramp
13. In some restaurants, food and service are worse than _____ used to be.
    A. they B. it C. them D. that
14. Let the porter take all the baggage out and put _____ in the lobby.
    A. it B. they C. them D. its
15. Everyone who comes to the party is given a wooden apple with _____ own names cut in it as a souvenir.

    A. his   B. her   C. their   D. our
16. Everybody in the class must give in _____ exercise book within the given time.
    A. their   B. our   C. his   D. her
17. During the journey, the boys and girls entertained _____ with songs and games.
    A. themselves   B. theirselves   C. himself   D. itself
18. You'd better buy _____ some fruits when you go on a trip.
    A. youself   B. myself   C. yourself   D. you
19. The boys in this town like to bully _____.
    A. one another
    C. each other
    B. one and other
    D. one and the other
20. One common family name is Black, _____ is Anderson.
    A. another   B. the other   C. others   D. none other
21. I have two novels: one of the two is "Gone with the Wind", and _____ is "the Tale of Two Cities".
    A. another   B. other   C. none other   D. the other
22. All girls wear beautiful clothes. Some are dressed in red; _____ in green.
    A. other   B. another   C. others   D. none other
23. She can't seem to help herself. And _____ can help her, either.
    A. none else   B. no one else   C. not any   D. somebody else
24. Children can usually dress _____ by the age of five.
    A. him   B. them   C. hiself   D. themselves
25. The gold watch had belonged to me for years, but the police refused to believe it was _____.
    A. me   B. my   C. mine   D. I's
26. Mother would not let Mary and _____ attend the hockey game.
    A. I   B. my   C. me   D. we
27. In a news conference this afternoon, the university announced that _____ intends to make several important changes in next year's budget.
    A. he   B. it   C. she   D. they
28. _____ but a fool can make such a mistake.
    A. Everyone   B. No other   C. Not all   D. None
29. The poem by Browning is so observed that I cannot grasp _____ meaning.
    A. its   B. it's   C. their   D. that
30. The mayor felt that the police, in spite of the reports, had done _____ best.
    A. its   B. their   C. his   D. our

二、在空格中填入适当的关系代词。

1. The girl _____ spoke at the meeting is our monitor.
2. Is that the girl _____ you talked about yesterday?
3. This is the boy _____ bicycle I borrowed.
4. This is the train by _____ I came.

51

5. The man from _____ I got the information is a journalist.

6. Nancy, _____ mother lives in Beijing, sent us these pictures.

7. She was annoyed by something _____ I had said.

8. The man from _____ I bought it told me how to operate it.

9. The film is about a spy _____ wife informs against him.

10. This is the best hotel _____ I know.

11. Joe, _____ had been driving all day, suggested stopping for a rest.

12. Her sons, both of _____ work abroad, are coming back to see her.

13. China has hundreds of islands, the largest of _____ is Taiwan.

14. We arrived at noon, by _____ time the demonstration was over.

三、把下面句子译为汉语。

1. All of them have become scientists.

2. Everyday something pleasant happened.

3. There are buses to the station every ten minutes.

4. The film is not as good as the one we saw last week.

5. She gave me two big ones.

6. None of us paid much attention to her.

7. There are many sheep and goats.

8. There's so much here that I can write about.

9. There are a few bottles on this shelf.

10. Little is known of Raphael's childhood.

11. This story is more interesting than the other two.

12. One was a lawyer. Another was a pilot.

第五章 数　词

表示数目多少或顺序多少的词叫数词(Numeral)，数词与不定代词很相似，其用法相当于名词与形容词。数词分为基数词和序数词。表示数目多少的数词叫基数词(Cardinal Numeral)，如 one, ten, fifty-two 等。表示顺序的数词叫序数词(Ordinal Numeral)，如 first, tenth, fiftieth 等。

5.1　基　数　词

5.1.1　基数词的表示法

(1) 1～12 的基数词是：

one	1	seven	7
two	2	eight	8
three	3	nine	9
four	4	ten	10
five	5	eleven	11
six	6	twelve	12

13～19，皆由 3～9 加后缀-teen 构成，即

thirteen	13	seventeen	17
fourteen	14	eighteen	18
fifteen	15	nineteen	19
sixteen	16		

(注意 thirteen, fifteen, eighteen 的拼法)

20～90 等十位数均由 2～9 加后缀-ty 构成，即

twenty	20	thirty	30
forty	40	seventy	70
fifty	50	eighty	80
sixty	60	ninety	90

(注意 twenty, thirty, forty, fifty, eighty 的拼法)

21～29 由十位数 20 加个位数 1～9 构成，中间须有连字符"-"，即

twenty-one	21	twenty-six	26
twenty-two	22	twenty-seven	27
twenty-three	23	twenty-eight	28
twenty-four	24	twenty-nine	29
twenty-five	25		

其他的十位数照此类推，如：

 thirty-one 31 seventy-five 75

 forty-two 42 eighty-six 86

 fifty-three 53 ninety-seven 97

 sixty-four 64

（2）百位数由1～9加hundred构成，如包含十位数及个位数，中间用and连接，也可以不用；如只包含个位数，即十位数为零时，则and不可省。

 a（one）hundred 100

 two hundred 200

 seven hundred and six 706

 a（one）hundred（and）twenty-five 125

 twelve hundred 1,200

（英语中从1,100～1,900之间的整数常用hundred表示）

（3）千位数由1～9加thousand构成，其后的百、十、个位数构成方法同前。

 a（one）thousand 1,000

 two thousand 2,000

 six thousand eight hundred 6,800

 a（one）thousand one hundred（and）forty-nine 1,149（此处hundred之前不可用a）

 three thousand five hundred（and）thirty-seven 3,537

英语里没有"万"这一单位，万也用thousand表示。如：

 ten thousand 10,000

 ten thousand one hundred 10,100

 forty thousand seven hundred（and）eighty-five 40,785

十万的说法是：

 a（one）hundred thousand 100,000

 one hundred and one thousand 101,000（此处thousand之前不可用a）

 three hundred forty thousand five hundred 340,500

 four hundred sixty-two thousand seven hundred（and）eighty-nine 462,789

（4）百万的说法是：

 a（one）million 1,000,000

 three million 3,000,000

 three million four hundred twenty-one thousand five hundred 3,421,500

 four million five hundred thirty-five thousand six hundred（and）fifty-nine 4,535,659

千万及千万以上的说法是：

 sixty million 6千万

 five hundred million 5亿

 eight thousand million 80亿（等于美国英语eight billion）

 thirty thousand million 3百亿（等于美国英语thirty billion）

 a（one）hundred thousand million 1千亿（等于美国英语a(one) hundred billion）

注：英国英语的billion＝1,000,000,000,000，即10^{12}，等于美国英语的trillion。现在英国

也有人采用美国用法,故英国计量局认为最好避免使用 billion,trillion(美制 10^{12},英制 10^{15})和 quadrillion(美制 10^{15},英制 10^{18})。

(5) 基数词相当于名词,可有复数形式,其构成方法及读音与名词相同,hundred,thousand 和 million 的复数形式常后接 of 短语,表示不确定数目。如:

  two threes 两个三

  hundreds and hundreds of times 成百倍

  thousands upon thousands people 成千成万的人

注:million 的名词性较强,故亦可说 a million of times(百万倍),two million of people(2百万人)等,如 hundreds,thousands 与 millions 的意义清楚时,其后的 of 短语可省去。

① Millions were watching the performances at the moment. 当时成百万人在观看表演。

表示数量的 dozens 与 scores 的用法和 hundreds,thousands 相似。

② Amy bought dozens of of eggs in the supermarket. 艾米昨天在超市买了几十个鸡蛋。

5.1.2 基数词的功用

(1) 基数词在句中可用作主语、表语、宾语、定语、同位语和状语等。

① Two twos are four. 二二得四。(主语)

② The boy is ten. 这男孩十岁了。(等于 ten years old)(表语)

③ I need four hundred. 我需要 400。(宾语)

④ She has been to Beijing a hundred and one times. 她已去过北京很多次了。(状语)

⑤ They three joined the school team. 他们三人参加了校队。(同位语)

⑥ Sitting down thirteen at dinner is deemed unlucky in the western world. 在西方,坐在 13 号用餐,被认为是不吉利的(状语)。

(2) 基数词一般是单数形式,但下列情况,常用复数。

① 与 of 短语连用,表示概数,不能与具体数目连用,如 scores of people 指许多人。

② 在一些表示"一排"或"一组"的词组里。

They arrived in twos and threes. 他们三三两两地到达了。

③ 表示"几十多岁",in one's twenties。

④ 表示"年代",用 in+the+数词复数。in the 1990s(1990's) 在 20 世纪 90 年代。

⑤ 在乘法运算的一种表示法里,如 3×5=15 Three fives are fifteen.

5.2 序 数 词

5.2.1 序数词的构成

英语序数词第 1~19 除 first,second 与 third 有特殊形式外,其余均由基数词加后缀-th 构成。现将第 1~19 的序数词(包括其缩写式)列出如下:

  first 1st   eleventh 11th

  second 2nd   twelfth 12th(twelf 加 th)

  third 3rd   thirteenth 13th

  fourth 4th   fourteenth 14th

fifth 5th(fif 加 th)　　fifteenth 15th
sixth 6th　　　　　　　sixteenth 16th
seventh 7th　　　　　　seventeenth 17th
eighth 8th(后只加 h)　　eighteenth 18th
ninth 9th(nin 加 th)　　nineteenth 19th
tenth 10th

十位数的序数词的构成方法是：先将十位数的基数词的词尾 ty 中的 y 变为 i,然后加后缀-eth。

twentieth 20th　　fortieth 40th
thirtieth 30th

十位数的序数词如包含 1～9 的个位数时,十位数用基数词,个位数用序数词,中间须有连字符"-"。

twenty-first 21st　　fouty-fourth 44th
thirty-second 32nd　　eighty-seventh 87th

百、千、万等的序数词由 hundred,thousand 等加-th,前面加有关的基数词构成。

(one) hundredth　　100th
(one) thousandth　　1,000th
ten thousandth　　10,000th
(one) hundred thousandth　　100,000th
(one)millionth　　1,000,000th
ten millionth　　10,000,000th
(One)hundred millionth　　100,000,000th
(one)billionth　　1,000,000,000th

注意：序数词 hundredth, thousandth, millionth, billionth 之前的"一"只可用 one,不可用 a。

这种多位数序数词的后位数如包含 1～9 时,后位数用序数词,前位数同基数词,中间出现零时,须用 and 连接。

two hundred and first 201st
three thousand two hundred(and)twenty-first 3,221st

序数词亦可有复数形式,其构成方法及读音与名词相同。

5.2.2　序数词的功用

序数词在句中可用作主语、表语、宾语、定语、同位语和状语等。

① The first is better than the second. 第一个比第二个要好。（主语）

② His name is the fourth on the list. 他的名字在名单上排第四。（表语）

③ He was among the first to arrive in Wen Chuan. 他是首批到达汶川的。（宾语）

④ Mother's Day is on the second Sunday of May. 五月的第二个星期日是母亲节。（定语）

⑤ Who is that girl, the second in the long queue? 排在那个长队里面的第二个女孩是谁？（同位语）

⑥ My student Mary came first in the speech contest. 我的学生在演讲比赛中获得了第一名。(状语)

5.3 倍数、分数、小数和百分数的表示法

1. 表示倍数的方法

(1) 主语＋谓语＋倍数(或分数)＋as＋*adj.*＋as

I have three times as many as you. 我有你三倍那么多。

(2) 主语＋谓语＋倍数(分数)＋the size (amount, length...) of...

The earth is 49 times the size of the moon. 地球的体积是月球的49倍。

(3) 主语＋谓语＋倍数(分数)＋形容词(副词)比较级＋than...

The grain output is 8 percent higher this year than that of last year. 今年比去年粮食产量增加8%。

(4) 还可以用by＋倍数，表示增加多少倍。

① The total income of her family has incereased by three times this year. 今年她家的总收入增加了三倍。

表示三以上的倍数用 times，但表示两倍(汉语中的一倍实际上也指两倍)时则用 twice。

② This room is twice as large as that one. 这个房间有那个房间两个大。

表示倍数也可用 again, double, triple, quadruple fold 等词。

③ My uncle is as old again as I am. 我叔叔的年龄比我大一倍。

④ The top-brand cigarettes are often sold at double the normal price here. 这里名牌香烟售价经常比正常价高一倍。

表示增加多少倍可用百分比。

⑤ The students in our college has increased by 200% in the past two years. 在过去的两年内我校的学生增加了200%。

如表"增加"用 times 与 fold，则须注意英语要多说一倍，如说"增加了三倍"，则须用 four times 或 fourfold。

⑥ The private cars in this city is three times as many as that of last year. 这个城市的私家车比去年增加了两倍。

2. 分数表示法

构成：基数词代表分子，序数词代表分母。分子大于1时，基数词用单数，分母序数词用复数。

1/3 读作 one-third；3/4 读作 three quarters(或 fourths)，但是1/2须读作 a(one) half(不读作 one second)。

数学中可都用基数词读，1/2读作 one over two，2/3读作 two over three，11/20读作 eleven over twenty。

尤其是较复杂的分数多用此读法，如27/283应读作 twenty seven over two hundred (and) eighty-three。

整数与分数之间须用 and 连接。如 $7\frac{2}{5}$ 读作 seven and two fifths。

分数相当于名词时,用不用连字符皆可。如:three-quarters(three quarters)of a mile 四分之三英里,a three-quarter majority 四分之三的多数(用单形 quarter)。

分数用作前置定语时,注意下列写法与读法:a one-third mile 三分之一英里(用 one,后有连字符)。

3. 小数的读法

小数点的读法是:小数点前的基数词与前面所讲的基数词读法完全相同,小数点后则须将数字一一读出。如 1.25 读作 one point two five。

4. 百分数中的百分号(％)的读法

百分数中的百分号(％)读作 percent。

5％ 读作　five percent。

0.5％读作　(naught)point five percent。

300％读作　three hundred percent。

0.009 读作　(naught)(美国用 zero)point naught naught nine。

0.56 读作　(naught)(美国用 zero)point five six。

5.4　算式表示法

关于加、减、乘、除算式的读法。

2＋2＝4　读作 Two plus two equal(s)four.

10-3＝7　读作 Ten minus three is seven.

9×6＝54　读作 Nine multiplied by six is fifty-four.

20÷4＝5　读作 Twenty divided by four is five.

注:通常说"加"可用 and,如 Two and two are four(2＋2＝4)。说"减"可用 from,如 One from four leaves three(4-1＝3)。说 3×4＝12 可用 Four times five is twenty。说"除"可用 into,如 Four into twenty goes five(20÷4＝5)。

关于比例与乘方、开方的读法。

3∶2　读作 the ratio of three to two.

12∶3＝4　读作 The ratio of twelve to three equals four.

3^2　读作 three squared.

$3^3＝27$　读作 Three cubed is twenty seven.

$x^4＝y$　读作 The fourth power of x is y.

$\sqrt{9}＝3$　读作 The square root of nine is three.

$\sqrt[3]{27}＝3$　读作 The cubic root of twenty-seven is three.

$(17-\sqrt{9}+65/5)-(4\times 3)＝15$ 应读作 Seventeen minus the square root of nine,plus sixty-five over five, minus four times three, equals fifteen.

表示面积常用 by,如说一个房间的面积是 3′×6′(3 英尺×6 英尺)应说 three feet by six feet;如房间为 6 英尺见方,则可说 six feet by feet,也可以说 six feet square,其总面积为 thirty-six square feet。

5.5 编号表示法

编号可用序数词或基数词表示,序数词位于名词之前,并加定冠词,基数词位于名词之后。

the second part＝Part Two 第二部分

the eighth lesson＝Lesson Eight 第八课

由于基数词简单,所以用基数词的情况较多。

Number 6 第 6 号(读作 number six,缩写式为 No. 6)

Line 4 第 4 行(读作 line four,缩写式为 L. 4)

Page 10 第 10 页(读作 page ten,缩写式为 p. 10)

Room(No.)101 第 101 房间(读作 Room(number)one o one)

No. 10 Downing Street 唐宁街 10 号

Platform (No.)5 第 5 站台

Bus(No.)332 第 332 路公共汽车

Tel. No. 801－4609 电话号码 801-4609 读作 telephone number eight oh one four six oh nine,在 eight,oh,one 之后应稍加停顿。

Postcode(或 zip code)100081 邮政编码 100081

注:(1) 电话与门牌号码中的 0 多读作 o。

(2) 帝王称号"第几"用序数词,如 Henry Ⅷ 是 Henry the Eighth 的缩写式,当今英国女王 Elizabeth Ⅱ 是 Elizabeth the Second 的缩写式。

5.6 年、月、日表示法

请看下列各例:

1949 1949 年读作 nineteen forty-nine 或 nineteen hundred and forty-nine

1900 1900 年读作 nineteen hundred

1908 1908 年读作 nineteen and eight 或 nineteen hundred and eight

1960s(1960's) 20 世纪 60 年代(读作 nineteen sixties)

450 B. C. 公元前 450 年(读作 four fifty B. C. 或 four hundred and fifty B. C.)

476 A. D. (A. D. 476)公元 476 年(读作 four seventy-six A. D. 或 four hundred and seventy-six A. D. (A. D. 在不会误解的情况下常可省略)

February 7(th) (7(th)February)

2 月 7 日读作 February the seventh(或 February seven 或 February seventh)

7(th)February 则读作 the seventh of February

February7,1986 1986 年 2 月 7 日,可缩写成 7/2/86(或 7,2,86)(英式)或 2/7/86(或 2,7,86)(美式)。

下面是各个月份及其缩写式:

January Jan.

February Feb.
March Mar.
April Apr.
May May.
June Jun.
July Jul.
August Aug.
September Sept.
October Oct.
November Nov.
December Dec.

5.7　时刻表示法

请看下列各例：

(at)six o'clock(或 at six)a.m.(或 am) (在)上午六时

half past six p.m.(或 pm) 下午六时半

(a)quarter past six a.m.(或 am) 上午六时一刻

(a)quarter to eight p.m.(或 pm) 下午八时差一刻

five to eight p.m.(或 pm) 下午八时差五分

注：美国英语可用 after 代替 past，用 of 代替 to。除用文字外，还可用阿拉伯数字表示时刻。如：

6.00(英式)6:00(美式)(读作 six)

6.25(英式)6:25(美式)(读作 six twenty-five)

还有一种以 24 小时时制的表示法。如：

06.00 或 06:00(读作 zero six hundred hours)

21.25 或 21:25(读作 twenty-one twenty-five)

5.8　币制表示法

关于英国币制的说法见下列各例：

1 p　1 便士(读作 one penny 或 one p)

5 p　5 便士(读作 five pence 或 five p)

£5.86　5 英镑 86 便士(读作 five pounds eighty-six pence)

关于美国币制的说法见下列各例：

1 ¢　1 美分(读作 one cent 或 one penny)

$1.25　1 美元 25 美分(读作 one dollar twenty five 或 one twenty-five)

美国硬币除 penny 外，还有 nickel(＝five cents)，dime(＝ten cents)，quarter(＝twenty-five cents)，half-dollar(＝fifty cents)等。

巩 固 练 习

一、单项选择。

1. _____ martyrs have heroically laid down their lives for the people.
   A. Thousand upon thousand of   B. Thousand and thousands of
   C. Thousands upon thousands of   D. Thousand and thousand of

2. They received _____ of letters about their TV programs.
   A. dozen   B. dozen and dozen   C. score   D. dozens

3. Who is that man, _____ in the front row?
   A. one   B. the one   C. first   D. the first

4. We have produced _____ this year as we did in 1993.
   A. as much cotton twice   B. as twice much cotton
   C. much as twice cotton   D. twice as much cotton

5. The earth is about _____ as the moon.
   A. as fifty time big   B. fifty times as big
   C. as big fifty time   D. fifty as times big

6. The population of many Alaskan cities has _____ in the past three years.
   A. more than doubled   B. more doubled than
   C. much than doubled   D. much doubled than

7. The moon is about _____ in diameter as diameter as the earth.
   A. one-three as large   B. one three as large
   C. one-third as large   D. one third as large

8. Five hundred yuan a month _____ enough to live on.
   A. is   B. are   C. is being   D. has been

9. _____ of the buildings were ruined.
   A. Three fourth   B. Three four
   C. Three-fourths   D. Three-four

10. Consult _____ for questions about earthquakes.
    A. the six index   B. index six   C. sixth index   D. index numbering six

11. She went to the countryside _____.
    A. in the morning at nine/on June first,1968
    B. on June first, 1968/in the morning at nine
    C. at nine in the morning/on June first,1968
    D. on June first,1968/at nine inthe morning

12. Three-fourths of the surface of the earth _____ covered with water.
    A. are   B. is   C. were   D. be

13. This month the production of stainless steel in our steelworks has increased _____ 2,000 tons.
    A. with   B. in   C. on   D. by

14. With the miniaturization of the structural components the weight of these electric devices has decreased _____ 30 percent.
    A. as   B. with   C. in   D. by
15. The Olympic Games are held _____.
    A. every four years   B. every four year
    C. every fourth years   D. every four-years
16. As he is not in good health, he goes to his factory only _____ just to learn something about the progress of experiment.
    A. once a week   B. one week
    C. one time a week   D. one a week
17. Three students _____ in this university come from the South.
    A. of ten   B. out of in ten   C. out of ten   D. in tens
18. Strings of the same thickness made of nylon are _____.
    A. five times stronger than those   B. five time stronger than those
    C. five times strong than those   D. five times stronger as those
19. the wheels of the old wagon are nearly _____ those of a modern car.
    A. twice the size of   B. twice size of
    C. twice sizes of   D. twice the size of
20. One day on the moon is _____.
    A. two Earth week long   B. two Earth weeks long
    C. two Earth weeks longer   D. two Earth weeks length

二、把下列词组译为英语。
(一)
1. 三月八日   2. 八月一日   3. 十二月二十五日   4. 十月一日
5. 四月十二日 6. 九月三十一日 7. 六月二十一日   8. 七月三十日
(二)
1. 1949 年   2. 2008 年   3. 1804 年   4. 1600 年
5. 公元前 658 年 6. 公元前两千年 7. 公元后 720 年   8. 2010 年
(三)
1. 第三部分   2. 第 67 节   3. 第 12 章   4. 第四册
5. 第 108 航班 6. 第 5 号车厢   7. 103 路公共汽车   8. 23 频道
(四)
1. 上午八点   2. 九点一刻   3. 两点半   4. 五点三刻
5. 一点差五分 6. 早上七点   7. 下午两点一刻   8. 晚上十一点零五分
(五)
1. 2194-0730   2. 3720-2277   3. 009 分机   4. 137 分机

第六章 动 词

6.1 概 述

6.1.1 动词的定义

动词(Verb)是表示动作或状态的词。如：study（学习），play（玩），smile（笑），cry（哭），climb（爬），walk（走），sleep（睡），choose（选择），give（给），sell（卖），look（看）等。

6.1.2 动词的分类

动词可根据不同的特征分为下面几类。

1. 助动词(Auxiliary Verb)和实义动词(Lexical Verb)

根据动词在句中的用途，动词可分为助动词和实义动词。

实义动词是句子中表示有关主语的动作或状态的主要动词（也叫主动词）。如：study（学习），write（写），jump（跳）等。

① You go first and I will follow you. 你先走，我跟着你。

② They told me how they studied to improve their professional competence. 他们给我讲了他们是怎样学习来提高业务水平的。

助动词是和实义动词一起构成不同时态、语态或语气以及否定和疑问结构的词。英语的助动词分三类：基本助动词(Primary Auxiliary)、情态助动词(Modal Auxiliary)和半助动词(Semi-Auxiliary)。

三个最基本的助动词 do，have，be，只在动词词组中起语法作用或者说只表示语法意义，如助动词 be 通常用来协助主动词构成进行时或被动态。

① They are playing at the Capital Theatre tonight. 他们今晚在首都剧场演出。

② The thief **was caught** in the parking lot. 那小偷是在停车场被抓住的。

助动词 do 通常用来协助主动词表示否定意义或构成疑问句，还可用来加重语气。

① **Does** he have coffee with his breakfast? 他吃早饭时喝咖啡吗？

② **Don't** be so careless. 不要如此粗心大意。

③ **Did** he carry out the experiment in his laboratory yesterday? 昨天，他在实验室做这个实验了吗？

④ **Do** you like my new dress? 你喜欢我的新衣服吗？

助动词 have/has 通常用来协助主动词构成完成时或完成进行时。

① She has gown so that she is even a little taller than her mother. 她长得比她妈都高一点了。

② I **have been working** here for 20 years. 我已在这里工作 20 年了。

情态助动词共有 13 个，其中包括一些过去形式。它们是 shall，should，will，would，

can, could, may, might, must, ought to, dare, need, used to。情态动词表示情态意义,其过去时形态并不一定就表示过去时间。情态助动词不能重叠使用,随后的主动词是不带 to 的不定式,即动词原形。

① It **may** snow this night. 今晚可能下雪。

② **Would** you let me use your car? 我能用一下你的车吗?

③ They didn't come. They **might** not have got our notice. 他们没有,可能没接到我们的通知。

半助动词有 have to, seem to, happen to 等,它们兼有主动词和助动词的双重特征。如:

① He **didn't seem to** love her. 他看起来并不爱她。

② I **have to** buy a new house. 我得买一栋新房子。

2. 及物动词(Transitive Verb)、不及物动词(Intransitive Verb)和系动词(Link Verb)

根据动词能否有宾语,可将动词分为及物动词、不及物动词和系动词。及物动词是指动词所表达的动作能有一个接受动作的对象,即后面能跟宾语的动词。及物动词又可分为单宾语及物动词(Mono-transitive Verb)、双宾语及物动词(Di-transitive Verb)和复合宾语及物动词(Complex-transitive Verb)。

单宾语及物动词是指只能接直接宾语的动词。

May I **use** your pen? 我可以用你的钢笔吗?(use 是单宾语及物动词,your pen 是直接宾语)

双宾语及物动词是指除了直接宾语外,还有一个间接宾语,间接宾语用来表明动作是"向谁"或"为谁"而发出的。

They have **sent** me some pictures of Guilin. 他们寄给我几张桂林的图片。(send 是双宾语及物动词,me 是间接宾语,some pictures of Guilin 是直接宾语)

复合宾语及物动词是指需跟复合宾语的动词。复合宾语是指直接宾语和宾语补语。

They **selected** Mr. Smith president. 他们选史密斯先生做总统。(select 是复合及物动词,Mr. Smith 是直接宾语,president 是宾语补语)

不及物动词是指后面不能跟宾语的动词。

I couldn't get a seat on the bus, so I had to **stand**. 在公共汽车上,找不到座位,只好站着。(stand 是不及物动词)

上述及物动词和不及物动词的用法可概括为:

主语+不及物动词

主语+及物动词+宾语

主语+双宾动词+间宾+直宾

主语+宾补动词+宾语+宾补

系动词是指本身有词义,但不能单独作谓语,必须和表语一起构成谓语的动词。英语单词中有许多系动词,但最为常见的一个是"be",几乎所有其他的系动词都来自于实义动词。一方面,它们具有自己的含义,另一方面,它们还可以用作系动词。如:become, get, turn, seem, feel, grow, look, appear, smell, fall, keep, remain, stand, come, go, run 等。

① I **am** a teacher and you **are** students.

我是老师,你们是学生。(am, are 是系动词;teacher, students 是表语。)

② His argument **sounded** reasonable.

他的论点听起来是合理的。(sound 是系动词，reasonable 是表语。)

3. 限定性动词(Finite Verb)和非限定性动词(Non-finite Verb)

根据动词能否作句子的谓语，动词可分为限定性动词和非限定性动词。限定性动词形式要受主语的限制，要和主语在人称和数上保持一致，因此常称为动词的限定形式(Finite Forms of the Verb)，这种一致性主要表现在以下几方面：

(1) 人称(Person)：指谓语动词要和主语在人称上一致。

① Gearge smokes a cot. 乔治烟抽得厉害。(第三人称)

② Now we supply power to nine-tenths of the citys homes. 现在我们问这个城市十分之九的家庭提供电力。(第一人称)

③ You are a good student. 你是好学生。(第二人称)

(2) 数(Number)：指谓语动词要和主语在数上保持一致。

① He **helps** me a lot. 他帮了我很多忙。(第三人称单数)

② They **help** me a lot. 他们帮了我很多忙。(第三人称复数)

(3) 时态(Tense)：指动词要通过词尾变化或相关助动词来表示动作的发生时间。

① I met your sister in WanyFuJing Street the other day. 前几天我在王府井大街见到了你妹妹。(过去时)

② I **will meet** you in my office tomorrow morning. 明天我会在我的办公室见你。(将来时)

(4) 语态(Voice)：指动词要通过某种特殊形式来表示主语是动作施事者还是受事者。

① He **sent** this letter. 他送的这封信。(施事者)

② This letter **was sent** by him. 这封信是他送的。(受事者)

(5) 语气(Mood)：指动词通过某种特殊的形式表示说话人对所说事物的态度，即认为这句话是事实，是要求做的事还是假想虚拟的事。

① He gave me some suggestions. 他给了我一些建议。(陈述事实)

② Give me some suggestions. 给我一些建议。(提出要求)

③ I wish he would give me some suggestions. 我希望他给我一些建议。(表示愿望)

非限定性动词是指动词不受主语限制的形式。非限定性动词指动词不定式、-ing 分词和 -ed 分词。它们没有"时"的区别，不能独立充当句子的谓语动词，所以也不受主语的人称和数的制约。它们除了能与一定的助动词结合构成进行式、完成式和被动语态外，还可在句中充当主语、宾语、补语、定语、状语等。

4. 规则动词(Regular Verb)和不规则动词(Irregular Verb)

根据动词过去式与过去分词的变化是否规则，动词可分为规则动词和不规则动词。

规则动词的过去式与过去分词都以-ed 结尾，而不规则动词的变化是没有规律的。有的不规则动词，无论是原形、过去式或过去分词，形式都相同，如 cost, cost, cost; cast, cast, cast 等。有的是后两种形式相同，如 make, made, made; buy, bought, bought 等。有的是三者形式都各异，如 bite, bit, bitten 等。

5. 单词动词(Single-word Verb)和短语动词(Phrasal Verb)

根据词的构成，动词可分为单词动词和短语动词。动词大多是单词动词，但有些动词是由"动词＋副词"（如 pick up, put down 等）、"动词＋介词"（如 call on)或"动词＋副词＋介词"（如 catch up with, do away with 等)构成。这些多词动词又可统称为短语动词(Phrasal

Verb)。除短语动词外,常见的如"动词＋名词＋介词"(如 do damage to, put emphasis on 等)也是多字动词。

① He **was carried away** by his enthusiasm. 热情使他的头脑不够冷静。(动词＋副词)

② Everything we used **was made from** natural materials. 我们所用的一切都是由天然材料做成的。(动词＋介词＋介词宾语)

③ This morning I **hung up** all the shirts to dry out. 今天早上,我把所有的衬衣都挂起来晾干。(动词＋副词＋宾语)

④ They has **deprived** him **of** all his political rights. 他们剥夺了他所有的政治权利。(动词＋间接宾语＋介词＋介词宾语)

⑤ We are all **looking forward to** Beijing 2008 Olympic Games. 我们大家都期盼着北京2008年奥运会。(动词＋副词＋介词＋介词宾语)

"动词＋副词"这类短语动词有的可用作及物动词,有的可用作不及物动词。

1) 用作及物动词

① He **brought up** his children strictly. 他教育孩子很严。

② He **brought** his children (them) **up** strictly. 他教育孩子很严。

③ He **called up** the man. 他给那人打了电话。

④ He **called** him (the man) **up**. 他给他打了个电话。

从以上四例可以看出,当短语动词的宾语是名词时,它可以置于短语动词之后,亦可以置于短语动词之中,但若宾语由代词担任时,则只能置于短语动词之中。

2) 用作不及物动词

① Mind your head. **Look out.** 小心你的头。留神。

② Don't **give in.** 不要屈服。

有的短语动词可以兼作及物动词和不及物动词。

① He **took off** his hat when he entered the office. 他进办公室后脱下帽子。(及物动词)

② The plane **took off** at seven sharp. 飞机七点整起飞。(不及物动词)

③ I **rang up** Lao Li to ask about the time of the meeting. 我给老李打电话问他开会的时间。(及物)

④ If you can't come, please **ring up** and let us know. 你如果来不了,请来电话告诉我们。(不及物)

上述第一类短语动词中的介词与第二类短语动词中的副词有时形式完全一样,它们之后又都有名词作宾语。这时辨别介词与副词的方法通常有两种。一是看动词的性质,如果动词是及物动词,其后即是副词;反之,其后即是介词。

① The wind **blew** up the valley. 清风吹过山谷。

② The guerrillas **blew up** the bridge. 游击队员炸掉了那座桥。

例①中的 blew 意为"吹刮",显然是不及物动词,故 up 是介词;例②中的 blew 意为"炸毁",显然是及物动词,故 up 是副词。

二是看宾语的位置。如宾语只能放在短语动词之后,则动词之后必然是介词。

Come **off** it！别胡闹！(off 是介词)

如宾语可放在短语动词中间,宾语之后必然是副词。

I hate to see you **off**. 我真不愿意你走。(off 是副词)

6. 动态动词(Dynamic Verb)与静态动词(Stative Verb)

动词根据其词义可分为动态动词与静态动词。

1) 动态动词大致可分为四类

(1) 无限动词,即动作历时无限的词,如 drink, eat, read, write, play, talk, live, work, study, walk, run, rain, snow, fly 等。

(2) 有限动词,即表示动作历时有限的动词,如 bind, produce, build, make, create, mend 等。

(3) 瞬间动词,即表示动作极为短暂的动词,如 hit, jump, tap, knock 等。

(4) 重复动词,即表示动作不断重复的动词,如 giggle, struggle, pooh-pooh 等。

2) 静态动词亦大致可分为四类

(1) 表示内心活动的动词,如 want, know, think, believe, forget, understand, expect, consider, hope, imagine, mean, mind, notice, prefer, remember, suggest, suppose, wish 等。

(2) 表示情感的动词,如 care, detest, envy, fear, hate, like, love, regret 等。

(3) 表示感觉或知觉的动词,如 feel, ache, hurt, see, hear, smell, taste 等。

(4) 表示各种关系的动词,如 be, belong, compare, concern, contain, cost, deserve, differ, equal, exist, have, hold, interest, involve, fit, lack, matter, measure, owe, own, possess, resemble, weigh 等。

静态动词与动态动词之间有时是相通的,有些静态动词亦可用作动态动词。

① He is **having** dinner. 他正在吃晚饭。

② He **felt** in his pocket for some money. 他在口袋里摸了摸,想找一些钱。

动态动词之间亦可相通,如无限动词 sit, stand, read 在下列句子中即变成有限动词:

① Stand up. 起立。

② Sit down. 坐下。

③ I read a book yesterday. 我昨天读了一本书。

6.2 动词的基本形式

英语动词有五种基本形式,即动词原形(Verb Stem)、第三人称单数形式(Third Person Singular Tense Form)、过去式(Past Tense Form)、过去分词(Past Participle)和现在分词(Present Participle)。这五种形式和助动词一起构成动词的各种时态、语态和语气。

6.2.1 动词原形

动词原形是前面不加 to 的动词不定式形式,也就是在词典词目中所用的动词形式,如 make, take, work, study, smile, leave 等。

6.2.2 第三人称单数形式

第三人称单数形式是指当主语是第三人称单数,时态是现在一般时的动词形式。第三人称单数形式一般是在动词原形后加-s,具体变化如下表所列。

单词形式	词尾变化	例词
一般动词	加-s	take—takes, lend—lends, pick—picks, work—works, grow—grows
以-ch, -sh, -s, -x, -o 结尾的动词	加-es	finish—finishes, pass—passes, teach—teaches, mix—mixes, do—does
以"辅音字母＋y"结尾的动词	变-y 为-i 再加-es	carry—carries, study—studies, try—tries

第三人称单数形式词尾-s 的读音如下表所列。

单词词尾读音	读法	例词
清辅单[p][t][k][f]后	[s]	helps, hits, takes, laughs
在[s][z][ʃ][tʃ][dʒ]等音之后	[iz]	faces, guesses, washes, touches, urges
其他情况	[z]	flies, moves, knows, sings

6.2.3 过去式和过去分词

规则动词的过去式和过去分词都以-ed 结尾,而不规则动词的变化是没有规律的。规则动词的过去式和过去分词加-ed 的方式如下表所列。

词尾情况	变化方式	例词
一般情况	加-ed	talk—talked, work—worked, end—ended, borrow—borrowed, want—wanted, kill—killed
以 e 结尾	加-d	agree—agreed, arrive—arrived, hope—hoped
辅音字母＋y	去 y 加-ied	study—studied, apply—applied, cry—cried
重读闭音节	双写最后一个辅单字母再加-ed	admit—admitted, beg—begged, drop—dropped, pat—patted, zip—zipped, permit—permitted

注:以-r 音节结尾的词,双写 r 字母,再加-ed,如 prefer- preferred, refer-referred。
构成动词的过去式和过去分词的词尾-ed 的读音,如下表所列。

动词词尾的读音	ed 的读音	例词
在辅音[t]和[d]后	[id]	rested, patted, included, needed
清辅音(除[t]外)	[t]	hoped, liked, washed, reached, mixed
元音和浊辅音(除[d]外)	[d]	moved, allowed, called, alarmed, smoothed

少数双音节动词,尽管重音在第一个音节,仍双写末尾的辅音字母,然后再加-ed(现在分词亦如此),如 travel-travelled, program-programmed, worship-worshipped 等。但美国英语不双写辅音字母,如 travel-traveled。

注:panic, traffic, picnic 等动词的过去式和过去分词分别为 panicked, trafficked 和 picnicked。

不规则变化:英语中有些动词的过去式和过去分词形式变化不规则,可分为五种情况。

(1) 动词原形、过去式和过去分词完全同形,如 cut(切),hit(打),cast(扔),hurt(伤害),put(放),let(让),shut(关),cost(花费),set(放),rid(清除)等动词。

(2) 过去式与过去分词完全同形。

原形	过去式	过去分词
find(找到)	found	found
leave(离开)	left	left
lend(借出)	lent	lent
meet(遇见)	met	met
keep(保持)	kept	kept

(3) 动词原形与过去分词同形。

原形	过去式	过去分词
come(来)	came	come
run(跑)	ran	run
become(成为)	became	become

(4) 动词原形、过去式、过去分词形式完全不同。

原形	过去式	过去分词
give(给)	gave	given
fly(飞)	flew	flown
drink(喝)	drank	drunk

(5) 过去式和过去分词有两种形式。

原形	过去式	过去分词
burn(燃烧)	burned,burnt	burned,burnt
learn(学习)	learned,learnt	learned,learnt
smell(闻)	smelled,smelt	smelled,smelt

注:(1) beat 的过去式与原形同形:beat(打击),beat(过去式),beaten(过去分词)。

(2) lie 有规则变化和不规则变化两种,含义不同:lie, lied, lied(说谎);lie, lay, lain(躺,位于)。

(3) hang 有规则变化和不规则变化两种,含义不同:hang, hanged, hanged(处绞刑);hang, hung, hung(挂,吊)。

(4) welcome(欢迎)一词是规则动词,不可误用为不规则动词:welcome, welcomed, welcomed(正);welcome, welcome, welcome(误)。

6.2.4 现在分词

动词的现在分词由动词原形加-ing 构成,具体变化如下表所列。

词尾情况	变化方式	例 词
一般情况	加-ing	play—playing, work—working, go—going, fly—flying
以不发音的 e 结尾(注:当将 e 去掉会引起发音变化时,最后的 e 应保留)	去 e 加-ing	come—coming, take—taking, use—using, write—writing, (**agree—agreeing**)
重读闭音节	双写最后一个辅音字母再加-ing	sit—sitting, run—running, dig—digging, stop—stopping, swim—swimming, forget—forgetting, plan—planning, permit—permitting, begin—beginning

注:动词的-ing 形式还有以下特殊情况。

(1) 少数几个以-ie 结尾的单音节动词,须变-ie 为-y,再加-ing,如 die—dying, tie—tying, lie—lying。

(2) 动词结尾的-e 前为元音时,-e 也应保留,如 hoe—hoeing, dye—dyeing, toe—toeing。

(3) panic, traffic, picnic 等动词的现在分词分别为 panicking, trafficking, picnicking。

巩 固 练 习

1. Taking pictures _____ very interesting.
   A. is   B. are   C. to be   D. be
2. So far as I am concerned , I prefer reading _____ .
   A. than meat   B. for joy
   C. instead of sleeping   D. to drinking
3. It goes without _____ that knowledge is important.
   A. talking   B. telling   C. saying   D. mentioning
4. We are looking forward _____ our friends next week.
   A. to see   B. to seeing   C. to be seeing   D. shall see
5. He spent a lot of money _____ books and magazines.
   A. buy   B. buying   C. to buy   D. bought
6. The silkworm is an insect worth _____ .

A. to know   B. knowing   C. to be known   D. being known
7. The curious student kept on _____ questions.
   A. asks   B. asking   C. to ask   D. asked
8. When she heard the bad news, she burst _____.
   A. into crying   B. out to tears   C. crying   D. out crying
9. Scientists succeed _____ protein out of old newspapers.
   A. to make   B. at making   C. making   D. in making
10. I became _____ after watching too much television.
    A. bored   B. boring   C. bore   D. bores
11. I felt _____ by his interest in my new invention.
    A. encourage   B. to encourage   C. was encouraged   D. encouraged
12. The heavy rain kept us _____ for two hours.
    A. wait   B. waited   C. waiting   D. to wait
13. They got their car _____ at the garage.
    A. be washed   B. washed   C. being washed   D. to have been washed
14. Thousands of products _____ from coal are now in daily use.
    A. made   B. make   C. making   D. to make
15. The United States has developed into a modern nation in a very short time _____ with many other countries.
    A. compares   B. comparing   C. to compare   D. compared
16. None of us objected to _____ George to the birthday party.
    A. invite   B. inviting   C. have invited   D. invited
17. Her son, to whom she was _____, went abroad ten years ago.
    A. loved   B. cared   C. devoted   D. affected
18. —Why haven't you bought any butter?
    —I _____ to but I forgot about it.
    A. liked   B. wished   C. meant   D. expected
19. I'm planning to hold a party in the open air, but I can make no guarantees because it _____ the weather.
    A. links with   B. depends on   C. connects to   D. decides on
20. Can you make a sentence to _____ the meaning of the phrase?
    A. show off   B. turn out   C. bring out   D. take in

第七章 助动词

7.1 助动词概述

助动词(Auxiliary Verb)本身没有词义,只是用来帮助主要动词构成各种时态、语态、语气、否定和疑问结构以及表示说话人说话时的各种情态。英语的助动词分三类:基本助动词(Primary Auxiliary):be (is, am, are, was, were, being, been), do (did, does), have (has, had);情态助动词(Modal Auxiliary):shall, should, will, would, may, might, can, could, must, need, dare, ought to, used to 共十三个和半助动词(Semi-Auxiliary)。在否定结构中,not 须放在助动词之后,助动词加 not 一般都有简略式。

7.2 基本助动词的用法

7.2.1 助动词 be 的用法

1. be 的形式

be 的形式如下表所列。

形 式		肯定式	否定式
现在式	第一人称单数	am	am not
	第三人称单数	is	is not
	第二人称单复数和第一、第三人称复数	are	are not
过去式	第一、第三人称单数	was	was not
	第二人称单复数和第一、第三人称复数	were	were not
现在分词		being	not being
过去分词		been	not been

2. 基本用法

(1) 与现在分词构成进行时态。

① He **is telling** an interesting story to his son. 他正在给他儿子讲一个有趣的故事。(现在进行时)

② I'll **be waiting** for you there then. 我到时在那儿等你。(将来进行时)

(2) 与 have 及现在分词构成完成进行时态。

We **have been preparing** well for this greatest sports meeting. 我们已经为这次体育盛会做好了准备。

(3) 与过去分词构成被动语态,可以是现在时、过去时或将来时。

① This book **is** largely **read** by children. 这本书主要是儿童读的。(一般现在时的被动式)

② I **was invited** to the concert. 我应邀参加了音乐会。(一般过去时的被动式)

③ This matter **will be looked** into in the future. 这件事将来是要查明的。(一般将来时的被动式)

(4) be 有时可代表整个谓语,以避免重复前面的话(这时后面也可以跟 so,但不跟语气更强一些)。

① "Is he ill?" "He **is** (so)."

"他生病了吗?" "是的,他生病了。"

② "John was defeated." "He **was** (so)."

"约翰被击败了。" "是的,被击败了。"

③ "Mary will be a good nurse." "She **has been** (so)."

"玛丽将成为一名好护士。" "她已经是了。"

但在 to be 和 being 后必须跟 so,表示"这样"的意思。

My son is proud, but I don't want him to be **so**. 我儿子很自豪,可我不想让他这样。

7.2.2 助动词 have

1. have 的形式

have 的形式如下表所列。

	形　式	肯定式	否定式
现在式	第一、第二人称单数及复数	have	have not
	第三人称单数	has	has not
过去式		had	had not
现在分词		having	not having
过去分词		had	

2. 基本用法

(1) 与过去分词构成各种完成时态。

① **Have** you visited the exhibition? 你看过这个展览会吗?

② He has left for London. 他已去了伦敦。

(2) 与 been+现在分词构成各种完成进行时态。

① What **have** you **been doing** these days? 你这些天干什么来着?

② We **have been living** here for nearly 10 years. 我们住在这里有 10 年了。

(3) 与 been ＋过去分词构成完成式被动语态。

English **has been taught** in China for many years. 中国教英语已经多年。

注:have 还可用作使役动词和实义动词(表示"有"、"吃"等意义)。

① Let's **have** a good rest under the tree. 让我们在树下好好休息一下。(实义动词)

② Mary does not **have** much patience. 玛丽没有多少耐心。(实义动词)

③ Did you **have** some bread at your breakfast? 你早餐吃面包了吗？(实义动词)

7.2.3 助动词 do

1. do 的形式

do 的形式如下表所列。

形　式		肯定式	否定式
现在式	第一、第二人称单数及复数	do	do not
	第三人称单数	does	does not
过去式		did	did not

2. 基本用法

(1) 助动词 do 本身无词义，它用在实义动词前，构成疑问结构和否定结构，与动词原形连用。

① I **don't** want to change my job in such short time. 我不想在如此短的时间内换工作。

② Did you remember to call on them when you were there? 在那里时，你记住去看望他们了吗？

③ He **doesn't** like American novels. 他不喜欢美国小说。

(2) 构成简略问答及反意疑问句的简短问句。

① —**Did** John fail in this examination? 约翰考试失利了吗？

—Yes, he **did**. 是的。

② —She got lost yesterday. 她昨天迷路了。

—**Did** she? 是吗？

③ You always help me whenever I have troubles, **don't** you? 你总是在我有困难的时候帮助我，不是吗？

(3) 表示强调。在肯定句中，位于谓语动词之前表示强调。

① **Do** come to my office this morning. 今早，请务必到我的办公室来一下。

② But I **do** want to go! 可是我确实想去。

③ That's exactly what he **did** do. 他就是那样做的。

(4) 用于倒装语序的句子中表示强调。

① Not until late that night **did** they get back. 他们那天夜里很晚才赶回来。

② Under no circumstances **does** he lose his heart. 任何情况下他都不灰心。

注：用来替代前面出现过的动作，避免重复，有"时"和"人称"的区别。

① He hopes to get the first prize, but can he **do** it (=get the first prize)? 他希望得第一名，但他能做到吗？

② He didn't have a rest after a long run. Neither **did** I. 长跑以后，他没休息，我也没休息。

(5) 在一些以否定副词如 never, rarely, scarcely, only 等为首的句子中，如果实义动词是现在时或过去时,助动词 do,does 和 did 可以构成主谓倒装。

① Never **did** he tell a lie to us. 他从来没对我们撒过谎。

② Rarely **does** anyone visit him. 很少有人去看他。

③ Only after a short delay **did** they come. 只耽搁了不久他们就来了。

(6) 用于恳求。

① **Do** come to the party tonight. 请今晚一定来参加晚会。

② **Do** help yourself. 请随意呀。

7.3　情态助动词概述

情态助动词有词义,但不完全。用来表示说话人的说话方式,表达说话人对谈到的情况所持的态度。

情态助动词一般没有第三人称带-s 的后缀形式,也没有非限定动词形式。它们只有两种时态形式:现在式和过去式(如 may 和 might)。这两种时态形式可后接动词原形(如 may/might offer),亦可后接动词进行式(如 may/might be offering),动词完成式(如 may/might have offered),或动词被动式(如 may/might be offered)。

(1) 英语中的情态助动词主要有:can,could,may,might,must,ought to,shall,should,will,would,need,dare,used to 等。

(2) 情态助动词的特征。情态助动词有其自身的词汇意义,表示或暗示某种情绪或态度,表示可能、建议、愿望、必要、允许、能力等。情态动词在句中不能单独作句子的谓语,必须和实义动词一起组成复合谓语。所有的人称均可与情态助动词连用,情态助动词本身不随主语的不同而变化,其后要跟动词原形。情态助动词多半一词多义,在肯定句、否定句或疑问句中,意义不尽相同;而且现在时情态助动词不一定表示现在时间,过去时情态助动词也不一定表示过去时间,各有其用法上的特殊性。

7.3.1　can 的用法

can 本身表示能力或可能性,用于指现在或将来。

(1) 表示能力。

① I **can** speak English. 我会说英语。

② If you shut your eyes, you **can't** see. 如果闭上眼睛就看不见东西。

③ Two eyes **can** see more than one. 两只眼比一只眼看得真。(谚语)

(2) 表示可能性。

① Han Mei **can't** be in the classroom. 韩梅不可能在教室里。

② **Can** he come here today, please? 请问他今天能到这里来吗?

注:在疑问句中表示"可能",须用 can 而不用 may。

(3) 表示请求或允许,多用于口语中,意为"可以、能"等。

① **Can** you sing an English song for us? 你可以为我们大家唱一首英语歌吗?

② You **can** go home now. 现在你可以回家了。

(4) 用于否定句、疑问句中,表示猜测、怀疑或不肯定。

① — Where **can** it be? 它可能会在哪儿?

— It may be in your pencil-box. 也许在你的文具盒里。

② **Can** I have a cup of tea, please? 请问我可以喝一杯茶吗?

注:can't 在口语中代替 mustn't 时,表示禁止或不准。

You **can't** play football in the street. 不准在马路上踢足球。

7.3.2　could 的用法

情态动词 can 的过去式 could 本身表示能力或可能性,多用于指过去,也可以用于指现在,指现在时通常表示虚拟或作为 can 的委婉形式。

(1) 表示能力。

I could run pretty fast when I was a boy. 我小时候跑得相当快。

注:(1) could(能)和 was/were able to 都表示过去一般具有某种能力。

(2) was (were) able to 可以表示过去某时有某种具体的能力并且实际上可以做到,但 could 表示过去的习惯能力。

He **was able to** translate the article without a dictionary. 他可以不用词典翻译那篇文章。(具体做某一件事的能力)

(2) 用于表示试探性或礼貌。

① I **could** be wrong. 我也许错了。

② **Could** you come over here? 你能到这边来吗?

(3) 表示许可。

① He asked if he **could** smoke in the hall. 他问可不可以在大厅里吸烟。

② Father said I **could** swim in the river. 爸爸说我可以在河里游泳。

(4) 表示可能性。

① **Could** it be Henry? 可能是亨利吗。

② Where **could** he have gone? 他可能上哪去了?

(5) 表示惊异、怀疑等,在表示这种意义时,could 和 can 可以互换,用 could 时语气较婉转。

① It seems incredible that he **could** have finished the work so soon. 似乎令人不可相信,他竟很快完成了这项工作。

② She **couldn't** have left so soon. 她不可能这么快就走了。

(6) 用于虚拟句中。

① How I wish I **could** go with you! 我多么希望和你们一道去!

② If you had worked harder, you **could** have succeeded. 如果你工作再努力些,你原本是可以成功的。

7.3.3　may 的用法

(1) 表示可能性,常用于肯定和否定句中,指现在或将来的可能性。

① He **may** not be at home. 他可能不在家。(现在的可能性)

② She **may** come this evening. 他今晚可能来。(将来的可能性)

注：(1) 在否定句中一般不用 may not，常用 can't 表示"不可能"。

He **can't** be at home tonight. 今晚他不可能在家。

(2) may 表可能可用进行式、完成式或完成进行式。

① She **may** be waiting for you in the entrance hall. 他可能正在门厅等你。

② She **may** have missed her train. 他可能误火车了。

(2) 表示"许可、准许、请求、许可"，此时与 can 同义，可以互换使用。

① You **may** / **can** go to the cinema this evening. 你今晚可以去看电影。

② **May** I ask you a question? 我可以问你个问题吗？(比 **Can** I ask you a question? 更礼貌)

注：许可对方时，其答语可以用 Yes, you may. 但由于用 may 作肯定回答，语气显得生硬、严肃，因而一般常用 Yes, please. / Certainly. / Of course. 等。这些肯定答语显得热情、客气。

— **May** I use your ruler? 我可以用一下你的尺子吗？

— **Certainly.** Here you are. 当然可以。给你。

拒绝对方时，其答语可以用 No, you mustn't. / No, you can't. 或 Sorry, you can't. / No, please don't. 等说法。

— **May** I watch TV now? 现在我可以看电视吗？

— No, you **mustn't/can't.** 不，不可以。

注：may not 表示一般的"不许可"，即根据一般规定的"不许可"，而不是说话人不许可。

Students **may not** take out of the library more than 2 books at a time. 学生们不可以一次从图书馆借出超过两本书。

表示"不许可"还可以采用其他比较委婉的说法。

— Could I smoke here?

— No, **I'm afraid not.**

此外，may not 表示"不许可"的过去时形式并不是 might not。如：

He may not go. (＝I don't permit him to go.)

He might not go. (＝Possibly he will not go.)

若要表示过去的"不许可"，通常要说：

He was not allowed to go. 或 I didn't permit him to go.

(3) 用于特殊疑问句中，表示不确定，常可译为"会"。

Who **may** call me at night? 谁会在晚上给我打电话呢？

(4) 表示希望、祈求、祝愿，常可译为"祝愿"。

① **May** you have a good time. 祝你过得愉快。

② May the friendship between our two peoples last forever! 视两国人民的友谊万古长青。

(5) 在表示目的或让步的状语从句中构成谓语。

① Come what **may**, we'll always stand together. 不管发生什么情况，我们将永远站在一起。

② Phone her at once so that she **may** know in time. 马上给他打电话使他能及时知道情况。

(6) 与 well, as well 或 just as well 连用,表示"完全有理由"或"还是……的好"。

① You **may** well say so. 你完全可以这样说。

② You **may** as well stay where you are. 你们最好就待在现在的地方。

7.3.4　might 的用法

1. 表示可能

① He **might** never come. 他可能永远不来了。（比 He may never come. 的可能性更小）

② He **might** have some fever. 他可能有点发烧。

2. 表示请求、允许

表示请求允许(即请求别人允许自己做某事)，两者都可用，只是 might 表示的语气较委婉(但并不表示过去)。

① **May**(**Might**) I sit here? 我可以坐在这里吗？

② I wonder if I **might** ask you a favor? 不知能否请你帮个忙？

3. 表示推测

(1) 后接动词原形,表示对现在或将来的推测。

① You **may** (**might**) be right. 你可能是对的。

② He **may**(**might**) tell his wife. 他也许会告诉他妻子。

(2) 后接动词进行式,表示动作正在进行或将要发生。

① He **may** /**might** be writing a letter. 他可能在写信。

② They **may** /**might** be going abroad next month. 他们可能在下个月出国。

(3) 后接动词完成式,表示对过去可能发生的事进行推测。

① She **may** /**might have read** it in the papers. 她可能在报上已读到过此事。

② He **may** /**might have gone to** have his hair cut. 他可能理发去了。

might 后接动词的完成式,除表示对过去的推测外,还有以下用法(不用 may)：

A 表示过去某事可能发生而实际上却并没发生。

① A lot of men died who **might have been saved**. 很多人本来可以获救的却死了。

② It was really very dangerous. I **might have killed** myself. 那真的是太危险了,我差点没命了。

B 表示委婉的批评或责备。

① You **might have made** greater progress. 你的进步本来可更大一些的。

② You **might** at least **have answered** my letter. 你至少可以回我一封信嘛。

4. 用于虚拟句中

It **might** help a little if you would only keep clean. 如果你愿意保持干净,情况也许会好一些。

5. 用于表示委婉

用于 might (just) as well... 意为"不妨"、"还是……为好"、"有理由"等,用 might 比用 may 语气更委婉。

① I'm ready, so I **might as well** go now. 我已准备好,因此不妨现在就走。

② There's nothing to do, so I **may**(**might**)**as well** go to bed. 既然没什么事可做,我还是去睡觉为好。

注：might as well 还可用于指过去的情况或用于比较两个令人不愉快的情况。

This holiday isn't much fun; we **might as well** be back home. 这个假日过得真没意思，我们还不如待在家里。

7.3.5 must 的用法

1. 表示必须

must 表示现在或将来必须做某事，这种必须多是出于义务、责任或强制命令。

① You **must** go and see the doctor. You're not looking well. 你一定要去看医生，你气色不好。

② You **must** hand in your homework today. 你今天必须把作业交来。

2. mustn't 表示禁止

must 只用于肯定句中，表示"一定、肯定"。其否定 mustn't 表"不准、禁止、不可以"等。

① You **mustn't** leave here. 你不许离开这。

② Cars **mustn't** be parked in front of the entrance. 车不能停在入口处。

3. 由 must 引起的疑问句的回答

肯定回答要用 must 或 have to，否定回答要用 needn't 或 don't have to，意思是"不必"。

—**Must** I finish the task right now? 我现在必须完成这个工作吗？

—Yes, you **must**. / Yes, you **have to**. 是的。

(—No, you **needn't**. / No, you **don't have to**. 不，不必。)

4. 表示肯定的猜测

常用于肯定句中，意思为"一定是，必然……"。

注意：must 表示推断或猜测的几种情况。

① Your sister **must be** a doctor in this hospital. 你姐姐一定是这家医院的医生。（现在的猜测）

② It **must have rained** last night, for the ground is wet. 昨晚一定下雨了，因为地面上是湿的。（过去的猜测）

③ He **must be reading** newspapers in the reading room now. 他此刻一定正在阅览室读报。（正在进行的猜测）

注：如果表示对目前状态的否定猜测，则用 can't be(不可能……)。

① The light is off. Mary **can't** be in. 灯关着，玛丽不可能在里面。

② It **can't be** Mr. Li. He has gone to Beijing. 那肯定不是李先生，他已到北京去了。

5. 表示"偏偏"这个意思

① The car **must** break down just when we were about to start off. 我们正要出发时偏偏车又坏了。

② At a time when everyone was in bed, he **must** turn his radio on. 大家都上床睡觉了的时候他偏偏把广播打开了。

6. must 与 have to 用法

(1) 在表示"必须"这个意思时，must 多表主观意志，have to 则往往强调客观需要。

① I **must** wash the clothes. 我该洗衣服。（主观想法）

② I **have to** wash the clothes. 我必须洗衣服。（客观想法）

③ This is an awful party— we really **must** go. 这个晚会真够呛——我们确实该走了。

④ This is a lovely party, but we **have to** go because of the baby-sitter. 这个晚会真好，但因为要替换那临时看孩子的人，我们必须回去。

(2) 二者的否定含义大不相同。

① You **mustn't** go. 你可不要去。

② You **don't have to** go. 你不必去。

(3) 询问对方的意愿应用 must。

Must I clean all the rooms? 这些房间我都得打扫吗？

(4) have to 的疑问式和否定式常用 do ＋ 主语 ＋ have to...? 和 do ＋ not have to (needn't)...?

① **Did** he **have to** work? 他得工作吗？

② He **doesn't have to** be here. 他无须待在这儿。

(5) must 没有"时"的不同形式，have to 有"时"的各种形式，如 had to, have/has/had had to, 并能与一些助动词如 shall/should, will/would, may/might 等连用。

过去时为 had to, 如：

① We **had to** return home at 4 o'clock yesterday. 昨天我们在4点钟就得回家。

② He **had to** work hard when he was young. 他很小的时候就得去辛苦地工作。

将来时为 shall (will) have to, 如：

① I **shall have to** go to the clinic today for my bad cough. 我咳嗽很厉害，今天得去卫生室去。

② If you don't catch the last bus, you **may/will have to** walk home. 如果你赶不上末班车，你可能得走回去。

完成时为 have (has) had to 与 had had to, 如：

① We **have had to** discuss several of our plans with the chief. 我们不得不跟主任讨论了我们的一些计划。

② Such was the story which she **had had to** tell. 这就是他不得不讲出来的情况。

进行时为 be having to, 如：

As a matter of fact, he's **having to** sell his house. 事实上，他现在得卖房子了。

非限定形式为 to have to, having to, 如：

① I hate **to have to** get up in the morning. 我真不愿意早上非得起来不可。

② **Having to** obey, he went. 他不得不服从，于是他走了。

have to 与 have got to 常可以互换。如：

① You **haven't got to** work tomorrow. 明天你不用上班。（got 可省去）

② **Have** you **got to** work tomorrow? 你明天得上班吗？（got 可省去）

7.3.6 ought to 的用法

(1) 表义务。ought to 表示出于责任、义务、道德等方面的要求而该做的事。

① Such things **ought not to** be allowed. 这种行为是不允许的。

② You **ought to** be earning your living at your age. 你这个年龄应该自食其力的。

(2) 表可能性。

① John **ought to** know how to use the machine. 约翰可能知道怎么用这个机器。

② There is a fine sunset. It **ought to** be a sunny day tomorrow. 天有晚霞，明天可能是个晴天。

(3) ought to 与 should 的区别。在很多情况下 ought to 与 should 两者意义相同,只是口气有些不同而已。

① You **shouldn't** speak to your mother like that. 你不应当这样和你妈妈说话。

② You **oughtn't to** speak to your mother like that. 你不应该这样和你妈妈说话。

在表示义务时,ought to 和 should 意思相近,但它们也有一些差别,要表示因责任、任务等该做的事情时,常用 ought to；在表示某件事宜于做时,多用 should。在下面的句子中这两个词不宜换用：

① You are his father. You **ought to** take care of him. 你是他父亲,应该照顾他。

② We **should** not use too many big words in our everyday speech. 在日常生活中我们不宜说过多大话。

7.3.7　shall 的用法

(1) shall 的形式。肯定式为 shall,否定式为 shall not(缩略式为：shan't)。shall 和 should 用作时态助动词时,表示"预见"即表示"单纯将来"。should 是 shall 的过去式；shall 用来构成将来时,在表示一般将来情况时,shall 用于第一人称(在现代英语中,shall 常用 will 替代)。

① I **shall** be in touch with you again shortly. 不久,我将再和你联系。

② I **shall have repaired** it by the end of the week. 我将于本周末把它修好。

③ We **shall** finish our homework at 12. 我们将于 12 点完成家庭作业。

用作情态动词时,shall 和 should 是两个不同的词。shall 用作情态动词时常用第二、第三人称,指说话人的情态。

(2) shall 表意愿,用于第二、第三人称。这时。shall 所表示的意愿不是句子主语的意愿,而是说话人的意愿。

You **shall** stay with us as long as you like. (＝I'm willing to let you stay with us as long as you like.)你想和我们待多长时间就待多长时间。

(3) 在当代英语中,shall 多用于正式法律文字。

The vendor **shall** maintain the equipment in good repair. 卖方须完好地维护设备。

(4) shall 有时在从句中相当于 must。

It has been decided that the proposal **shall** not be opposed. 已经决定不得反对这项提议。

(5) shall 表示许诺,用于第二、第三人称,用于肯定句和否定句。

① You **shall** have my answer tomorrow. 你明天可以得到我的答复。

② If you work well, you **shall** get a chance of promotion. 你要是好好干,就有提升的机会。

(6) shall 表征询意见,用于第一、第三人称,并用于疑问句。

① **Shall** I get you some coffee, Miss Fleure? 费勒小姐,我给您点儿咖啡好吗？

② What **shall** he do next? 他下一步干什么呢？

(7) 表示命令,用于陈述句,与第二人称或第三人称连用,表示允诺、命令、警告和强制,或表示说话人的决心等。

① We **shall** do what we are told. 我们必须要按所吩咐的去做。

② You **shall not** get it so easily next time. 你下次就不会轻易得到它。

③ He **shall** be punished if he disobeys. 他若不服从就要受到处罚。

7.3.8　should 的用法

（1）表示"应该"，should 用于所有人称，表示常理认为是对的事或适宜做的事。

① You **should** do what your parents tell you. 你应该照你父母的话去做事。

② You **shouldn't** be sitting in the sun. 你不应该坐在阳光下。

（2）用于第一人称疑问句，表征询意见。

Should I open the window? 我可以开窗户吗？

（3）should 表推测，暗含很大的可能。

① It's 4:30. They **should** be in New York by now. 现在是 4 点半，他们应该到达纽约了。

② Three weeks **should** suffice. 三个星期应该足够了。

（4）should + have done sth. 用在肯定句中表示本应该做而未做的事情，译为"本应该"；用在否定句中表示过去本不应该做却做了的行为，可译为"本不应该"，含有委婉的批评、责备之意。

① Mr. White **should have arrived** at 8:00 for the meeting, but he didn't show up. 怀特先生本应该 8 点就到会的，但他没来。

② You **shouldn't have told** your mother this bad news. 你本不应该把这个坏消息告诉你妈妈。

（5）用在名词性从句中，表示惊异、意外、惋惜、忧虑、欢欣或惊讶等情绪。

① It's pity that you **should** leave so soon. 很遗憾，你这么快就要走了。

② Well, I could never imagine an honest boy like John, **should** cheat in the exam! 想不到像约翰这样诚实的人也会在考试中作弊。

（6）should 可在某些从句中，表虚拟语气。

① I suggest that you **should stay** here as if nothing had happened. 我建议你应该待在这儿，好像什么事也没有发生一样。

② She was terrified lest they **should go on** talking about her. 她感到害怕，唯恐他们再说她的事。

③ If he **should drop in**, give him my message. 他若来访，就将我的消息给他。

（7）should 表感情色彩，常用在以 why, how 开头的疑问句中。

① Why **shouldn't** you invite him? 为什么你不邀请他？

② I don't see why we **shouldn't** make friends. 我不明白为什么我们竟不能成为朋友。

7.3.9　will 的用法

（1）will 作情态助动词时，表示客气地请求、邀请，常用于疑问句。

① **Will** you come and help me? 你过来帮我一下好吗？

② **Won't** you have some milk? 喝点牛奶吧？

will 用于第二人称请求句时，为了缓和可能含有的命令语气，可在 Will you 后增添礼貌性词语。

① Will you **please** open the door for me?

② Will you **kindly** help me?

表示客气的请求还可用 Would you...? 但表示接受请求时,要用 will,而不用 would。

—**Would you** give me some suggestions about that problem? 你能就这个问题给我提些建议吗?

—Certainly, I **will**. 当然,可以。

(2) will 表示现在或将来的意愿、允诺或决心。

① If you **will** help me now, I'll surely help you sooner or later. 要是你现在愿意帮我,我迟早也会帮你。

② They **will** do it themselves. 他们要自己干。

③ I **won't** agree with you. 我不会同意你的。

(3) will 表示现在的习惯、倾向。

① Why **will** you always turn a deaf ear to what I tell you? 我给你说的事你怎么老当成耳旁风?

② Swallows **will** come in spring and fly away in autumn. 燕子春天来秋天去。

(4) will 表示现在的功用、能力。

① Oil **will** float on water. 油浮于水。

② This room **will** (＝can) hold 60 people. 这个房间能容纳 60 人。

(5) Will / Won't you...? 与 Would / Wouldn't you...? 都可表示现在或将来的请求、建议,但 would 表示的语气更委婉。

① Will /Would you please stand there? 请你站在那里好吗?

② **Won't** you come here? 你过来好吗?

(6) will 的否定意义表示拒绝。

① Nothing **will** stop them. 无法阻止他们。

② I **won't** accept your advice. 我不会听你的。

(7) will 的特殊用法:可用于第二人称陈述句,表示说话人的建议、命令,有"应该、必须"之意。

You **will** act at once. 你应该马上行动。

(8) 除用 should, ought to, must 外,还可用 will, would 表示"推测",其口气的肯定程度仅次于 must,若用 would,则口气的肯定程度又次于 will。

① They **should / ought to be** home now. 他们现在该到家了。

② They **would be** home by now. 他们现在大概到家了。

③ They **will be** home by now. 我估计他们现在一定到家了。

④ They **must be** home by now. 他们现在一定到家了。

7.3.10 would 的用法

(1) would 作情态助动词时,表示主观意志、可能性、有倾向或有条件性的习惯,用于所有人称。

① We **would** rather die than go there. 我们宁死也不愿去那儿。

② Whenever he comes across a new word, he **would** consult the dictionary. 他一遇到生

词就查词典。

(2) would 作情态助动词还可表示客气的请求或征求意见。

① **Would** you like a cup of tea? 喝杯茶吗？

② I **would** like you to fetch that document for me now. 我想请你现在就帮我把那份文件取来。

(3) 表示过去的习惯、功用、能力、意愿。

① Most often we **would** find him lying on bed, reading. 我们经常看到他躺在床上看书。

② After supper in summer we **would** go swimming when in the country. 在农村时，我们夏天晚饭后就去游泳。

(4) 用在虚拟语气中。

① I wish you **would** stay. 真希望你能留下。

② If I **hadn't** taken your advice, I **would have made** a mistake. 如果不是听了你的建议，我就犯错误了。

③ If it were not for the sun, there **would** be nothing living. 如果没有太阳就不会有生命。

④ Could I fly, I **would fly** immediately. 如果我会飞，我就会马上飞起来。

(5) 用于构成 would like, would rather, would sooner 等表达。

① **I'd rather not** go there. 我宁愿不去那里。

② I **would rather** you came tomorrow than today. 我倒是想让你明天来，别今天来。

(6) "would have＋过去分词"还可表示过去未曾实现的愿望，有"本想……（却没有……）"之意。

I **would have helped** you, but I was too busy. 我本想帮你，可我太忙了。

(7) would you mind ＋ doing 句型通常用于表示请求对方做一件有一定麻烦的事情，语气一般都非常客气。注意回答时通常是肯定的，以表示愿意做所要求的事情。

① **Would** you mind filling in this form? 请您填一下这张表。

② **Would** you mind repeating what you just said? 请你把你刚才说的话重复一遍好吗？

注：情态动词后面加动词完成式，有不同意义。请参看虚拟语气(10.3.2)。

7.3.11　need 的用法

need 既可用作情态动词，亦可用作实义动词。用作情态动词时，它只是一种形式，后跟不带 to 的动词不定式，只用于否定句和疑问句，或用于由 if 或 whether 引导的宾语从句中，一般不能用于肯定句。只要 need 后面跟的是动词原形，它就是情态动词。这时，变否定句，只需在其后加 not；变为疑问句，只需把它移到主语的前面。

(1) 表必要性，多用于疑问句、否定或否定意味的疑问句中。

① **Need** I repeat it? 需要我重复吗？

② There is enough time. You **needn't** hurry. 有的是时间，你不必着急。

③ The president wondered whether he **need** send more soldiers. 总统不知道他是否要增兵。

情态动词的句子改成一般疑问句时，一般把情态动词提前放在句首，其他语序不变。要注意的是，must 表示"必须"，否定回答是用 needn't，而 mustn't 表示不许可，禁止。

—**Must** I hand in my homework tomorrow? 我必须明天一早就交作业吗？

—No, you **needn't.** You can turn it in the day after tomorrow. 不必，你可以后天交上来。

(2) 用于虚拟句中。

① They Needn't have been punished so severely. 他们本不必受到这么严厉的惩罚的。

② You **needn't have come.** 你本不需要来。

(3) need 可作实义动词，用作实义动词时，need 后面的宾语可以是名词、动名词、动词不定式或代词，这种情况下，need 既可用于肯定句，也可用于否定句和疑问句，构成否定句和疑问句时要借助于助动词 do 或 does。它有动词的全部形式，即现在时单数第三人称 needs，现在分词 needing 以及过去式和过去分词 needed，后跟带 to 的不定式，可用于任何句式。

① need sth. ，这是 need 最常见的用法之一，其后的宾语可以是名词，也可以是代词。

a. We **need** a great deal of money now. 我们需要很多钱。

b. **Does** your father **need** any help? 你爸爸需要帮助吗？

② need doing 与 need to be done。need 后面可跟动名词作宾语，这种情况下应注意两点：主动形式的动名词 doing 具有被动的含义；该动名词可以改为其动词不定式的被动形式而句子的意义不变。

a. The door **needs** painting.

= The door **needs to be** painted. 那扇门需要油漆一下。

b. Your car **needs** repairing.

= Your car **needs to be** repaired. 你的车需要维修了。

③ need to do sth. 。作为实义动词，need 后面需要接带 to 的动词不定式，表示有义务或责任去做某事。

① What **do** we **need to** take for the picnic? 野餐我们需要带些什么？

② **Will** we **need to** show our passports? 我们需要出示护照吗？

③ I **don't need to** get up early this morning. 今天不用早起。

④ We shall **need to know** how things are with you. 我们将有必要知道你们的情况。

7.3.12　dare 的用法

(1) dare 既可用作情态动词，也可用作实义动词。用作情态动词时，它只有一种形式，后跟不带 to 的动词不定式，表示"胆敢"，指现在或过去，多用于疑问句、否定句、条件句或表示判断的句子。

① I **dare** say he will come. 我敢说他会回来的。

② He said he **dare not** tell her the bad news. 他说他不敢告诉她这个坏消息。

③ Dare you go home alone? 你敢自己回家吗？

(2) dare 还可用作实义动词，在现代英语中 dare 和 need 一样，用作及物动词的时候更多一些，作实义动词时，它有动词的全部形式，后面要跟带 to 的不定式。

① **Does** Tom **dare to** go to school alone? 汤姆敢自己去上学吗？

② I **have** never **dared to** tell him about it. 我怎么也不敢告诉他这件事。

③ He didn't **dare to** do it because he was under inspection. 因有人监视，他不敢做这件事。

7.3.13　used to 的用法

(1) used to(只有过去时形式,没有现在时形式)表示过去习惯动作或状态,表示此种情况现已不复存在。

① He **used to** smoke a lot, but he has long given up smoking. 过去他常常吸很多烟,现在他已戒烟很久了。

② He **used to** live in Shanghai, usedn't he? 过去他常常住在上海吗?

(2) used to 的否定形式一般是 usedn't to,在否定陈述句和否定疑问句中,用 didn't use to 或 usedn't to 均可。

① He **didn't use to** smoke cigarettes.(＝He usedn't to smoke cigarettes.)他过去不常吸烟。

② **Didn't** she **use to** have a walk in the park? (＝Usedn't she to have a walk in the park?)她过去不常去公园散步吗?

(3) 在肯定疑问句中也有两种形式。

Used you **to** preview the text before the class? (＝**Did** you **use to** preview the text before the class?)过去你经常课前预习课文吗?

7.3.14　情态助动词表示的"推测性"和"非推测性"意义

情态助动词表示的意义可归纳为"推测性"(Epistemic)和"非推测性"(Non-epistemic)两类。

① He **couldn't** help you yesterday. 他昨天不能帮你。

② He **couldn't** get there in 10 minutes. 他不可能 10 分钟到达那里。

③ We **must** keep silence now. 现在我们必须保持安静。

④ He **must be** a warm-hearted person. 他一定是个热心人。

上述①③句中的情态助动词是指现实情况,属于"非推测性用法",然而②④句中的情态助动词是指说话人的主观看法,属于"推测性用法"。

1. 能做推测性用法的情态助动词

能做推测性用法的情态助动词有九个,即表示"可能"的 might/ may/ could/ can,表示"推测"的 will/ would 以及表示"必然"的 should/ ought to/ must。这九个情态助动词实际上表示各种不同程度的可能性,他们按可能性程度的高低可分为三个等级:第一级是表示"可能"的 might/ may/ could/ can,第二级是表示"很有可能"的 should/ ought to/ would/ will,第三级是表示"最有可能的"的 must。一般来说,might 表示的可能性程度最低,must 表示的可能性程度最高。"可能性"由低到高的排列顺序为 might→ may could→ can→ should→ ought to→ would→ will→ must。如:

That might/ may/ could/ can/should/ ought to/ would/ will/ must be Tom. (可能性由低到高)

2. 能做推测性用法的情态助动词的句法特征

(1) 其后的不定式可以采用完成体形式。

① They **must have finished** their homework. 他们一定完成了作业。

② The little boy **must have been** excited after he received such good birthday present. 收到这么好的生日礼物,这个小男孩一定非常兴奋。

(2) 其后的不定式可以采用进行体形式。

① He **must be working** overnight. 他一定工作了一晚上。

② She **might be making** a joke of you. 她可能在跟你开玩笑。

③ She **should be reading** in the library by now. 现在她应该在阅览室读书。

(3) 可以用于 there－存在句。

① There **must be** a good fortune for us. 我们一定有好机遇。

② There **must have been** some good chances for us. 我们当时一定有很多好机会。

(4) 其后的不定式为一般形式（即非完成体或进行体形式）时通常是静态动词。

① He **must be** there. 他一定在那里。

② He **must know** the truth. 他一定知道真相。

(5) 主语可以是表示无生命物的名词词组。

It **must be** Tom. 一定是汤姆。

注：以上五个句法特征不是作非推测性用法的情态助动词都具备的。

7.4 半 助 动 词

7.4.1 半助动词的类型

半助动词是指在功能上介于主动词和助动词之间、本身带有词义的一类结构。可分为三类：①以 be 为中心成分，如 be about to, be going to, be bound to, be (un)able to, be due to, be apt to, be certain to, be (un)likely to, be liable to, be obliged to, be supposed to, be to, be (un)willing to, be meant to, be sure to 等；②以 have 为中心成分，如 had better/best, have got to, have to 等；③以 seem 等动词为中心成分，如 seem to, turn out to be, appear to, fail to, chance to, come to, get to, happen to, tend to 等。

7.4.2 半助动词的用法

半助动词既可以是限定形式（体现时态，语态特征），也可以是非限定形式（不定式或现在分词）。它们可与主动词搭配构成复杂动词词组并表示情态意义，有时也可与助动词搭配。半助动词后的主动词都用带 to 的不定式，这种不定式可以是一般形式、进行式或完成式。

① He **appears to** have many friends. 看起来他有很多朋友。

② He **seems to be enjoying** himself at the party. 看起来他在晚会上过得很愉快。

③ You **are supposed to have finished** your term paper by Sunday evening. 周日晚上之前你应该完成你的学期论文。

1. 半助动词 be to 的情态意义

(1) 表计划，只用于肯定句和疑问句。

① When **is** the meeting **to** be? 会议什么时候举行？

② He **is to** go to New York next week. 他下周要去纽约。

(2) 表命令，只用于肯定句和否定句。

① You **are to** explain this. 对此你要做出解释。

② He **is to** come to the office this afternoon. 要他今天下午来办公室。

(3) 表可能,多用于被动结构。

① Her father **was** often **to** be seen in the bar of this hotel. 在这家旅馆的酒吧经常可见到他的父亲。

② Where **is** he **to** be found? 在哪里可以找到他?

(4) 表示"应该",多用于现在式。

① How **am I** to answer him? 我该怎样答复他?

② Who **is to** go there? 谁该去那儿呢?

(5) 表示"注定",多用于过去式。

① He **was to** be my teacher and friend for many years to come. 在后来许多年里,他是我的老师和朋友。

② From that day on, he knew that he **was** never **to** make such foolish mistakes. 从那一天起,他就知道他再也不会犯那种愚蠢的错误了。

(6) 用于条件从句。

If we **are to** succeed, we must make great efforts. 要想成功必须努力。

(7) be 后接 going to, about to, on the point of 等表示将来时间或根据计划、意图等将要发生的事。

① It's **going to** rain. 快要下雨了。(将来时间)

② We **are going to** have a meeting tomorrow. 明天我们要开个会。(根据计划将要发生的事)

③ He **is about to** leave. 他正要走。(将来时间)

④ He **is on the point of** telling us the truth. 他正要告诉我们实情。(将来时间)

2. 半助动词 had better, had best, had rather 等词组的情态意义

had better 和 had best 是"最好还是……"或"还是……好"的意思。在 had better 中 had 不表示过去时间,不能用 have 或 has 代替 had better,后可接不带 to 的不定式或接进行式、完成式或被动语态。

① You had better work hard.

= I advise you to work hard. 你最好努力工作。

② I had better **have tried** again. 假如我再试一次就好了。

③ You had better not make such jokes.

你最好别开这种玩笑。(had better 的否定式是 had better not)

④ I had rather be poor and happy. 我想过虽然穷但很快乐的生活。

⑤ I had better **be paid back** now. 最好现在就把欠款还我。

⑥ You'd better **be working** now. 你最好现在就工作。

7.4.3 半助动词的其他用法

(1) 带有半助动词作为动词词组的组成部分的句子,有的可以转换为"It…that 分句"结构,而有的却不可以。从这个角度看,半助动词可分为两类。

一类是可以作上述转换的,其中包括 be certain to, be(un)likely to, appear to, happen to, seem to, chance to, turn out to 等。

① They are certain to win the game. 他们肯定会在比赛中获胜。

→**It is certain that** they will win the game.

② He is likely to let you down. 他可能使你失望。

→**It is likely that** he will let you down.

③ He appears to have many friends. 看来他有许多朋友。

→**It appears that** he has many friends.

上述两个句型的转换中,不定式是采取主动态还是被动态,是采取一般形式、进行体形式还是完成体形式,取决于 that-分句的限定动词词组形式。

另一类半助动词不可以作上述转换,这一类包括 be about to,be bound to,be going to,be to,had better,have to,have got to,tend to 等。

He is about to arrive. 他即将到达。

He is bound to win. 他一定会获胜。

The boy tended to be late. 这孩子老是迟到。

不可以转换为下列句子:

＊It is about that he will arrive.

＊It bound that he will win.

＊It tended that the boy was late.

(2) 半助动词也可用于 there-存在句。

① There's **sure to** be some rain tonight. 今晚一定有雨。

② There's **likely to** be a large audience. 观众人数可能很多。

③ There **are bound to** be obstacles for us to get over. 一定会有障碍需要我们去克服。

凡是能够作上述句型转换的半助动词,在 there-存在句中,也可作类似的转换。现在,再从相反的方向来看这种转换关系。

① It seems that there's a widespread change of attitude. → There **seems to be** a widespread change of attitude. 看起来,态度有全面的转变。

② It appears that there's no doubt about it. → There **appears to be** no doubt about it. 此事似乎毫无疑问。

(3) 如果"It...that＋there-存在句"的主句谓语动词是 is said,is believed 等被动语态,那么转换过来的 there-存在句的谓语动词也应是被动态。

It is said that there's trouble at the factory. 据说厂里有麻烦。

→There's **said to** be trouble at the factory.

7.5 助动词的其他用法

(1) 放在陈述句末的简短问句(Tag Question)一般也需用助动词。这时陈述句若为肯定结构,后面问句多为否定结构;若为否定结构,后面问句多用肯定结构。此"问句"只要听者赞同,无需答案,说时用降调,句末用问号或句号。

① John will do it, **won't** he? 约翰会做的,对吧?

② He must speak up, **mustn't** he? 他必须说出来,对吗?

③ Nobody should come, **should** they? 没人应该来,对吗?

(2) 在对别人的话作出反应时,有时也需用助动词(说时通常用升调)。

① "I am tired."—"**Are** you?""我累了"——"是吗?"(陈述句为肯定句时,后面问句也用肯定结构。)

② "I don't see it."—"**Don't** you?"(陈述句为否定句时,后面问句也用否定结构。)

(3) 助动词还可用在"主要动词＋主语＋强调式助动词"这种结构的句子中。

① While I may see beautiful things, see them I **will**. 我会看到美丽的事物,一定会看到。

② He wanted to go and go he **did**. 他很想去,他确实去了。

(4) 有强调性的否定副词开始的倒装句也需要用助动词。

① Never **can** I understand what she wants. 我一点也不明白她想要什么。

② Seldom **has** he been at home. 他一直很少在家。

③ Only from newspapers **do** I learn about the world affairs. 我只通过报纸了解世界大事。

在把否定的宾语提到句首加以强调时,也需要用助动词。

① Very little care **does** he take of his children. 他照顾孩子不太周到。

② Only (＝No more than) two persons **did** I meet in the desert. 我在沙漠中只见了两个人。

(5) 在"so＋主语＋助动词＋(被省略及物动词)＋新的宾语"这种结构中,助动词也是必不可少的,这时对前面句子的谓语加以重复,但把主要动词加以省略,只留下助动词。

The situation makes me worried. 这种情况让我担忧。So it **does** everybody. 我们大家都是。

(6) 在"主语＋助动词(＋被省略及物动词)＋宾语"这种结构中,助动词也是必不可少的,这时用一个新的主语代替前句中的主语,用一个新的宾语代替前句中的宾语。

He fondled the cat as a mother (新主语) **would** (fondle) her child(新宾语)。他就像妈妈轻抚孩子一样轻抚着这只小猫。

(7) There be 与情态助动词连用。There be 句型中的谓语动词 be 可与各种情态动词连用,表示"一定有"、"可能有"、"应该有"等含义。

① He felt that **there must be** something wrong. 他感到一定是出了错儿。

② **There might be** drinks if you wait a bit. 如果你等一会儿,可能会有酒。

③ **There can't have been** much traffic so late at night. 这么晚了,街上的车辆不会太多。

④ **There oughtn't to be** too great discrepancy in our views. 我们的看法不应该有太大的分歧。

巩 固 练 习

1. The possible _____ often proved impossible.
　　A. have　　　　B. has　　　　C. are　　　　D. will
2. Neither you nor I am mad, _____?
　　A. are you　　　B. aren't I　　　C. am I　　　D. are we
3. You don't think I am wrong, _____?
　　A. don't you　　B. do you　　　C. aren't　　　D. am I
4. It was Lin Song who broke the rules of the school, _____?
　　A. wasn't it　　B. didn't he　　C. was it　　　D. did he

90

5. Bruce must have been in China for a long time, _____?
   A. hasn't he   B. mustn't he   C. isn't he   D. wasn't he
6. What the teacher has said is true, _____?
   A. has he   B. hasn't he   C. is it   D. isn't it
7. It must have snowed last night, _____?
   A. isn't it   B. haven't he   C. mustn't it   D. didn't it
8. It's the first time that Xiao Qing has been to Tianjin, _____?
   A. has she   B. is it   C. hasn't she   D. isn't it
9. The trousers _____ fit for him.
   A. is   B. are   C. must   D. do
10. He rather than Li Ying and Wang Ping _____ praised by the teacher.
    A. are   B. is   C. were   D. was
11. Where is my pen? I _____ it.
    A. should have lost   B. must have lost
    C. would have lost   D. might lose
12. A computer _____ think for itself; it must be told what to do.
    A. can't   B. couldn't   C. may not   D. might not
13. We _____ last night, but we went to the concert instead.
    A. must have studied   B. might study
    C. should have studied   D. would study
14. I didn't hear the phone, I _____ asleep.
    A. must be   B. must have been
    C. should be   D. should have been
15. Be sure to write to us, _____?
    A. will you   B. aren't you   C. can you   D. mustn't you
16. I didn't see her in the meeting-room this morning. She _____ at the meeting.
    A. mustn't have spoken   B. shouldn't have spoken
    C. needn't have spoken   D. couldn't have spoken
17. There is plenty of time. She _____.
    A must have hurried   B. needn't have hurried
    C. need not hurry   D. couldn't have hurried
18. You don't _____ to go there if you have no time.
    A. need   B. want   C. must   D. ought
19. Sir, you _____ be sitting in this waiting-room. It is for women and children only.
    A. oughtn't to   B. can't   C. won't   D. don't
20. Tom ought not to _____ me your secret, but he meant no harm.
    A. have told   B. tell   C. be telling   D. having told
21. It's nearly seven o'clock. Jack _____ be here at any moment.
    A. must   B. need   C. should   D. can
22. Your coat is dirty, _____ it for you?

91

    A. Am I washing   B. Will I wash
    C. Am I going to wash   D. Shall I wash
23. No one _____ that to his face.
    A. dare say   B. dare to say   C. dares saying   D. dares said
24. There used to be a church in the east of the town, _____?
    A. didn't there   B. usen't to there   C. used there   D. usedn't to there
25. _____ you be happy!
    A. Can   B. May   C. Must   D. Would
26. —Could I borrow your dictionary?
    —Yes, of course you _____.
    A. might   B. will   C. can   D. should
27. —Shall I tell John about it?
    —No, you _____. I've told him already.
    A. needn't   B. wouldn't   C. mustn't   D. shouldn't
28. —There were already five people in the car, but they managed to take me as well.
    —It _____ a comfortable journey.
    A. can't be   B. shouldn't be
    C. mustn't have been   D. couldn't have been
29. The fire spread through the hotel very quickly, but everyone _____ get out.
    A. could   B. would   C. was able to   D. had to
30. I told Sally how to get here, but perhaps I _____ for her.
    A. had to write it out   B. must have written it out
    C. should have written it out   D. ought to write it out
31. That young man has made so much noise that he _____ not have been allowed to attend the concert.
    A. could   B. must   C. would   D. should
32. —Can I help you, sir?
    —Yes, I bought this radio here yesterday, but it _____.
    A. didn't work   B. couldn't work   C. can't work   D. doesn't work
33. If you don't like to swim, you _____ stay at home.
    A. should as well B. may as well   C. can as well   D. would as well
34. _____ my guest have forgotten my address?
    A. Might   B. May   C. Could   D. Would
35. The box is too heavy, _____ give me a hand?
    A. would you mind   B. would you please
    C. will you like to   D. will you please to
36. There _____ a war between his heart and his head.
    A. being   B. appeared to be   C. to be   D. were
37. Uncle Jesse, why? _____ poor people like those?
    A. are there have to be   B. do there have to be

    C. have there to be   D. there have to be

38. _____ more difficulties than you thought.
    A. It is likely   B. It is likely to be
    C. There is likely   D. There are likely to be

39. _____ just twenty-eight pounds.
    A. There remained   B. It remained
    C. There were remained   D. That remained

40. You wouldn't want _____ another war.
    A. there be   B. there to be
    C. to be   D. there being

第八章 动词的时态

8.1 概 述

在英语中,不同时间以不同方式发生的动作或存在的状态要用不同的动词形式来表示,动词的这种不同形式称为动词的时态。

时态从时间上划分,可分为四大类:现在时、过去时、将来时和过去将来时,每一类从行为上又可分为四种形式:一般时、进行时、完成时和完成进行时。这样,英语的动词共有十六种时态,这些时态中最常用的有五个,即一般现在时、现在进行时、现在完成时、一般过去时和一般将来时,还有些时态用得比较多一些,如过去进行时、过去完成时、过去将来时、现在完成进行时等,其他时态用得比较少,有的时态则很少用到。下面以 study 为例列出各个时态的形式,如下表所列。

时态	一般时态	进行时态	完成时态	完成进行时态
现在	study studies 一般现在时	am/is/are studying 现在进行时	has/have studied 现在完成时	has/have been studying 现在完成进行时
过去	studied 一般过去式	was/were studying 过去进行时	had studied 过去完成时	had been studying 过去完成进行时
将来	shall/will study 一般将来时	shall/will be studying 将来进行时	shall/will have studied 将来完成时	Shall/will have been studying 将来完成进行时
过去将来	should/would study 一般过去将来时	should/would be studying 过去将来进行时	should/would have studied 过去将来完成时	should/would have been studying 过去将来完成进行时

在口语中,很多时态都有紧缩形式(Contracted Forms)。如:

what's ＝what is　　who's＝who is　　that's＝that is
he's＝he is 或 he has　won't＝will not　where's ＝where is
she'll＝she will　　his name's＝his name is

8.2 一般现在时

8.2.1 一般现在时的构成

实义动词的一般现在时的肯定形式(除单数第三人称由动词原形加词尾-s 或-es 构成外)与动词原形相同。否定式由助动词 do not 或 does not＋动词原形构成,疑问式由助动词 do 或 does＋主语＋动词原形构成,动词 be 和 have("有")有自己的构成方式。

动词 be 和 have 及行为动词(以 study 为例)的一般现在时的肯定式、疑问式和否定式的构成形式如下表所列。

动词	肯定式	疑问式	否定式
be	I am... He/She/It is... We/You/They are...	Am I...? Is he/she/it...? Are we/you/they...?	I am not... He/She/It is not... We/You/They are not...
have	I have... He/She/It has... We/You/They have...	Have I...? Has he/she/it...? Have we/you/they...?	I have not... He/She/It has not... We/You/They have not...
study	I study... He/She/It studies... We/You/They study...	Do I study...? Does he/she/it study...? Do we/ you/ they study...?	I don't study... He/She/It doesn't study... We/You/ They don't study...

8.2.2 与一般现在时连用的时间状语

与一般现在时连用的时间状语有:always, often, usually, sometimes, seldom, ever, never, every day (week, month, year etc.), once a year, now and then, from time to time 等。

8.2.3 基本用法

1. 表示现在时间内的习惯性动作或经常性动作

这一用法通常用于表示动作的动词,并常与表示频率度的时间状语连用,有时可与表示现在一段时间的状语连用,也可不用时间状语。

① I **leave** home for school at 7 every morning. 我每天早上 7 点离开家去学校。

② We **volunteer** to teach the children in that remote village these years. 这些年,我们志愿教这些偏远山区的孩子们学习。

2. 表示现在时间的状况或特征

这种用法多用于表示状态的动词。

① She **continues** in good condition. 他的健康状况仍然良好。

② He **speaks** English as well as he speaks French. 他的英语说得和法语一样好。

3. 表示状态和感觉

有些表示状态和感觉的动词常用一般现在时。

① Sugar **tastes** sweet. 糖是甜的。

② This material **feels** soft. 这种料子摸上去柔软。

③ She **resembles** her sister in appearance but not in character. 她同她妹妹外貌上相像，但性格上不像。

这类动词有：be, love, like, hate, want, hope, need, prefer, wish, know, understand, remember, believe, recognize, guess, suppose, mean, belong, think（以为）, feel, envy, doubt, remain, consist, contain, seem, look（看起来）, see, fit, suit, owe, own, hear, find, suggest, propose, allow, show（说明）, prove, mind（在意）, have（有）, sound（听起来）, taste（尝起来）, matter, require, possess, desire 等。

4. 表示客观真理，格言或警句，科学事实及客观存在

① The earth **moves** around the sun. 地球围着太阳转。

② Shanghai **lies** in the east of China. 上海在中国的东部。

③ A just cause **enjoys abundant** support. 得道多助。

注：此用法如果出现在宾语从句中，即使主句是过去时，从句谓语也要用一般现在时。如 Columbus proved that the earth is round.

5. 用于时间和条件状语从句中

一般现在时常用在时间和条件状语从句中代替将来时，在 when, while, until, before, after, as soon as, if 等从属连词引导的状语从句里，主句用将来时态，从句用一般现在时。

① I shall come to help you if I **am free** tomorrow. 如果明天我有空就来帮你。

② When I **meet** a new word, I'll look it up in the dictionary. 当我遇到生词时，就会查字典。

6. 表示已决定或计划要做的事

表示按规定要发生的未来动作，或按自然规律会发生的事。常用于这类情况的动词有：arrive, be, begin, close, come, depart, end, go, leave, open, stop, start 等。

① It's only seven o'clock and the train **leaves** at ten. 现在刚七点，列车一般十点开出。

② School **begins** next week. 学校下周开学。

③ The plane **takes off** at 4 p.m. 飞机下午4点起飞。

7. 用于新闻标题或文章题目

① An earthquake **attacks** Sichuan of China at 14:28 on May 12 in 2008.（文章题目）

② We **stay** with you. 你我同在。（文章题目）

③ Roads crashes **kill** five. 公路车祸，五人丧生。（新闻标题）

8. 用于对过去事件进行生动描述

① I waited about 15 minutes and out he **comes**. 我等了大约十五分钟，他出来了。

② My mother **calls** me in low voice "Get up, honey, get up…" in the morning, and several minutes later we all **sit down** by the lake shore to see the sunrise when I was 10 years old. 我十岁大的时候，清早总被妈妈轻声唤醒，然后和她一起去看日出。

9. 电视节目直播解说

① Now Radio Beijing **presents** Music from China. 现在北京电台开始播送"中国音乐"。

② Johnson **passes** to Roberts, Roberts to Brown, Brown **takes** it forward, oh, he **slips** past the centre beautifully, he **shoots**. 约翰把球传给罗伯茨,罗伯茨又传给布朗,布朗往前带,噢,他巧妙地绕过了中卫,射门。

10. 表最近的将来

说话人说话时动作尚未开始,但即将开始。

① Here I **give** you some more examples. 这里我再给大家举几个例子。

② He **gets** his reward on Tuesday. 他将于下周二领奖。

11. 一般现在时用于表将来的从句

这种从句有状语从句、宾语从句和定语从句。

(1) 状语从句。

① Have something before you **go**. 吃点东西再走。(用于时间状语从句)

② I'll thank you if you **give** me a lift. 如果你能让我搭你的车,我就谢谢你了。(用于条件状语从句)

③ Next time I hope you'll go where I **tell** you to. 下次我希望你去我告诉你去的地方。(用于地点状语从句)

(2) 宾语从句。

① Tomorrow at this time we'll know who **is elected**. 明天这个时候我们就会知道谁当选了。

② Let's see who **gets** there first. 让我们看看谁先到达那里。

(3) 定语从句。

① I'll give you anything you **ask for**. 你要什么我都给你。

② Everyone who **takes part in** this game will get a souvenir. 任何参加活动的人都会得到纪念品。

8.3 一般过去时

8.3.1 一般过去时的构成

规则的行为动词的一般过去时的肯定式是由动词原形加词尾-ed构成,否定式由助动词did not＋动词原形构成,疑问式由助动词did＋主语＋动词原形构成,动词be和have有自己的构成方式。动词be和have及行为动词(以study为例)的一般过去时的肯定式、疑问式和否定式的构成形式如下表所列。

动词	肯定式	疑问式	否定式
be	I was... He/She/It was... We/You/They were...	Was/I/he/she/it...? Were we/you/they...?	I/He/She/It was not... We/You/They were not...

(续)

动词	肯定式	疑问式	否定式
have	I/He/She/It/We/You/They had...	Had I/he/she/it/we/you/they...?	I/He/She/It/We/You/They had not...
study	I/He/She/It/We/You/They studied...	Did I/he/she/it/we/you/they study...?	I/He/She/It/We/You/They didn't study...

8.3.2 与一般过去时连用的时间状语

与一般过去时连用的时间状语有以下几类：

(1) yesterday, last night(week, year, month, Sunday), then, at that time, at that moment, just now, a few days(weeks, months, years)ago 等；

(2) 由 after, before, when, while 等引导的表示过去的时间状语从句；

(3) 一般过去时也可以与 today, this week(month, year)等时间状语连用,但这些时间状语应指过去。

8.3.3 基本用法

(1) 表示过去的动作或状态。一般过去时在表示这个意义时多有明确的表过去时的时间状语,或有说话场合及上下文的暗示。

① At 5 o'clock (As soon as he received the telegram), he **drove to** the station. 他5点(他一收到电报)就开车去了车站。

② He **died** 5 years ago. 他5年前去世了。

③ The heavy storms **destroyed** a good part of our crops. 几场暴雨把大部分庄稼都毁掉了。

(2) 表示过去的习惯动作。

① He **took a walk** every morning last year. 去年她经常早上散步。

② When he was in Beijing, he **came to** see me every week. 他当初在北京时,每周都来看我。

(3) 用于描述一些发生时间不清楚但肯定是过去发生的事情。

① I **was** happy to hear from you. 很高兴收到你的来信。

② The last Ming emperor **hanged** himself from this tree. 明朝最后一个皇帝就是在这棵树上吊死的。

(4) 可用于表示现在情况,体现委婉客气的语气。

① **Did** you **want** anything to drink? 你想要点喝的东西吗?

② I wondered if you **could help** me to mail this letter? 不知你能否帮我寄这封信?

(5) 用于转述原本为一般现在时的直接引语。

① They told me that the rats **were** a real problem around here. 他们告诉我说这里老鼠成灾了。

② He said that he **was** very tired. 他说他很累。

(6) 用于虚拟语气中,表示现在或将来时间的动作或状态。

① It's high time we **went**. 是我们该走的时候了。

② It seems as if I **were** a fool. 好像我是个傻瓜似的。

③ I would buy the car if I **had** the money. 我要是有那笔钱就买下那辆车。

(7) 用于 since 从句。

主句的谓语动词如用现在完成时,其后接的 since 引导的从句一般需用一般过去时。

① You haven't changed much since we last **met**. 从我们上次见面以来你变化不大。

② It's been over a year since I **came** back from the countryside. 我从乡下回来已经一年多了。

如果 since 从句的谓语动词是静态动词的一般过去时,则仍表动作或状态的结束,并无持续性。

① It's a long time since I **lived** here. 我不住在这里已经好久了。(lived here 已结束,说话人说话时已不住在这里)

② It is 10 years since I **was** a teacher. 我不当教师已有 10 年了。(was a teacher 的状态已结束)

8.4 一般将来时

8.4.1 一般将来时的构成

一般将来时由动词 shall(第一人称),will(第二、第三人称)＋动词原形构成。美语则不管什么人称,一律用 will。在口语中,所有人称都可以用 will。但在第一人称的疑问句中,经常用动词 shall。

① He **will come** next week. 他下星期来。

② Where **shall** we go? 我们该去哪儿?

动词（以 study 为例）的一般将来时的肯定式、疑问式和否定式的构成形式如下表所列。

人称	肯定式	否定式	疑问式
第一人称	I/ We will/ shall study...	I/We will/ shall not study...	Will/ Shall I/ we study...?
第二人称	You will study...	You will not study...	Will you study...?
第三人称	He/ She/ It/ They will study...	He/ She/ It/ They will not study...	Will he/ she/ it they study...?

8.4.2 与一般将来时连用的时间状语

常与一般将来时连用的时间状语有:tomorrow, next week (month, year),in a few days (months, year)等。

8.4.3　基本用法

（1）一般将来时常用来表示将来时间的动作或状况。

① There **will be** no rain tomorrow. 明天不会有雨。

② He **will be** twenty next year. 他明年就 20 岁了。

③ You and I **will work** in the same factory. 你和我将在同一个工厂工作。

（2）一般将来时用于真实条件句和时间状语从句的主句中表示将来的情况。

① **I'll give** him the message as soon as he goes back home. 他一回来我就告诉他这个消息。

② We **shall go** unless it rains. 除非下雨，我们是要去的。

③ He **will help** you if you ask him. 你提出请求他就会帮助你。

（3）will，shall 除可表示单纯的将来时，还可以带有意愿的色彩，仍指的是将来。

① **I'll buy** you a bicycle for your birthday. 你过生日时，我给你买一辆自行车。（表示允诺）

② **Will** you **open** the door for me please? 请你帮我开门好吗？（表示请求）

③ **Shall I get** your coat for you? 我可以为你拿外套吗？（表示提议）

（4）一般将来时可用来表示一种倾向或习惯性动作。

① Bus No. 11 **will arrive** at our station until 9. 11 路车 9 点会到站。

② Children **will be** children. 孩子就是孩子。

（5）将来时其他表示方法。

8.4.4　一般将来时的其他结构

一般将来时还可以由其他一些结构来表示。

1. be going to＋动词原形

（1）表示打算或准备好要做的事或有迹象表明要发生的天气变化等情况。表示说话人根据现在已有的迹象，判断将要或即将发生某种情况。这类句子的主语可以是人，也可是物。

① When are we going to discuss the matter? 我们什么时候讨论这件事？

② I feel terrible. I think **I'm going to** die. 我感到难受极了，我想我快不行了。

③ Look at those black clouds! It's **going to** rain. 看看那些乌云！天快要下雨了。

（2）表示主语现在的意图或现已作出的决定，即打算在最近或将来进行某事。这种意图或决定往往是事先经过考虑的。

① He **isn't going to** see his elder brother tomorrow. 他明天不准备去看他哥哥。

② Mary **is going to** be a teacher when she grows up. 玛丽决定长大了当一名教师。

（3）只是单纯地预测未来的事，此时可与 will 互换。

I think it **is going to**/will rain this evening. 我认为今晚要下雨。

注：be going to 和 will 在含义和用法上略有不同：be going to 往往表示事先经过考虑的打算；will 多表示意愿、决心，两者有时不能互换。

① He is studying hard and **is going to** try for the exams. 他正努力学习，准备参加考试。（不能用 will 替换）

② —Can somebody help me? 谁能帮我一下吗？

—I **will**. 我来。（不能用 be going to 替换）

在 if 之后，通常不用 will 表示预言，但可以用 be going to 表示意图。

If you **are going to** go to the cinema this evening, you'd better take your coat with you. 你若今晚去看电影，最好带着外套。

(4) be going to 也常可以用于 there be 句型之中。

If you invite Jack, there's **going to** be trouble. 如果你邀请杰克，那就要惹麻烦了。

2. 现在进行时（be＋现在分词）

有些动词的现在进行时可以表示将要发生的动作，表示按计划或安排即将发生的事。

表示位置转移的动词（如 go, come, leave, start, arrive, return, send, move, travel, fly 等）和其他几个动作动词（如 do, begin, work, spend, play, stay, happen, have, finish, join, eat, die, meet 等）常与现在进行时和表示将来的时间状语连用，表示在最近将要发生某事，这些事是事先安排好的。

① The Browns **are coming to** dinner tomorrow. 明天布朗夫妇要来吃晚饭。

② What **are** you **doing** tomorrow? 明天你做什么？

③ The train **is arriving** at nine o'clock. 火车将在 9 点钟到。

在特定的上下文中，这类动词有时也可不带时间状语。

—Come to school in your old clothes tomorrow. 明天穿你的旧衣服来上学。

—Why? What's **happening**? 为什么？有什么事？

3. 一般现在时表将来

(1) 动词 be，表示位置转移的动词（如 go, come, arrive, leave, return 等）和表示"开始，结束"的动词（如 start, begin, open, finish, end, close 等）与一般现在时和表示将来的时间状语连用，表示时间表、节目单或日程表上所安排好的动作或事情将要发生，日程不易改变，口气肯定。

① School **finishe**s on January 18th. 学期 1 月 18 日结束。

② **Are** you **free** next Tuesday evening? 下周二晚上你有空吗？

③ The party **starts** at four thirty, doesn't it? 晚会四点半开始，是吗？

(2) 在由 when, before, as soon as, until/till 引导的时间状语从句和由 if 引导的条件状语从句中，常用一般现在时表示将来。

① If it **doesn't** rain tomorrow, we'll go to the East Lake. 如果明天不下雨，我们就去东湖。

② I must finish my homework before my mother **returns**. 我必须在妈妈回来之前做完家庭作业。

(3) 在 hope 后接表示将来时间的宾语从句中，也可用一般现在时代替一般将来时，hope 的主语往往是第一人称。

① I hope you **have**（will have）a good holiday. 我希望你假日愉快。

② I hope he **comes**（will come）. 我希望他会来。

4. be＋不定式表将来

be＋不定式表将来，用于表示按计划或正式安排将发生的事。

① We **are to discuss** the report next Saturday. 我们下星期六讨论这份报告。

② **Are** we **to go on with** this work? 我们继续干吗?
③ The boy **is to go to school** tomorrow. 这个男孩明天要去上学。

5．be about to ＋不定式

be about to ＋不定式意为马上做某事。

① He **is about to** leave for Beijing. 他马上要去北京。
② The vocation **is about to** start. 假期即将开始。

注：be about to do 不能与 tomorrow，next week 等表示明确将来时的时间状语连用。

8.5 现在进行时

8.5.1 现在进行时的构成

现在进行时由助动词 be 的现在式(am，is，are)＋现在分词(动词原形＋ing)构成。现以动词 study 为例，将现在进行时的肯定式、否定式和疑问式列表如下：

人称	肯定式	否定式	疑问式
第一人称	I am studying... We are studying...	I am not studying... We are not studying...	Am I studying...? Are we studying...?
第二人称	You are studying...	You are not studying...	Are you studying...?
第三人称	He/She/It is studying... They are studying...	He/She/It is not studying... They are not studying...	Is he/ she/ it studying...? Are they studying...?

8.5.2 与现在进行时连用的时间状语

常与现在进行时连用的时间状语有 now，at this moment，at present 等。

8.5.3 基本用法

(1) 表示现在进行的动作。现在(说话的瞬间)正在进行或发生的动作，强调"此时此刻"。

① He **is reading**. 他正在读书。
② We **are developing** nuclear weapons to do away with such weapons. 我们发展核武器是为了消灭核武器。
③ We **are waiting** for you. 我们在等你。

(2) 由 look，listen 等引出的句子中通常要用现在进行时。

① Listen! She **is singing** in the room. 听！她在房间里唱歌。
② Look! They **are reading** over there under the tree. 看！他们在那边的树底下看书。

(3) 表示现阶段正在进行的动作。通常有表示现阶段的时间状语，如 today，this week，this month，this year，this term，now 等。

① They **are compiling** a dictionary now. 他们在编写一本词典。

② He **is writing** a novel this year. 今年他在写一部小说。

③ We **are working** in a factory these days. 这几天我们在一家工厂工作。

(4) 表示某种感情色彩，表示反复发生的动作或持续存在的状态，往往带有说话人的主观色彩。这一用法常与 always, constantly 等词连用。

① She **is** always **repeating** the same mistake. 他总是在重复同一个错误。

② His classmates **are** forever **laughing** at him. 他的同学总是嘲笑他。

③ Why **are** you always **changing** your mind? 为什么你总是改变想法？

(5) 表示按计划或已安排好要做的事。这一用法只适用于某些动词，如 go, come, leave, start, arrive, return, spend, sail, meet, fly 等。

① **I'm leaving** by train tonight. 我今晚坐火车走。

② **Are** you **going abroad** next year? 明年你要出国吗？

③ The plane **is taking off** an hour later. 飞机将在一小时后起飞。

(6) 表示在刚刚过去的时间内发生的事。

① What he **is telling** you is not the truth. 他刚才告诉你的不是事实。

② I don't know what they **are talking** about. 我不知道他们刚才说什么？

(7) 习惯进行。表示长期的或重复性的动作，说话时动作未必正在进行。

① Mr. Green **is writing** another novel. 格林先生在写另一部小说。（说话时并未在写，只处于写作的状态。）

② She **is learning** piano under Mr. Smith. 她在跟史密斯先生学钢琴。

(8) 有的动词用于现在进行时表示"逐渐"的含义。此种用法除了偶尔和 now 连用外，一般不和其他时间副词连用。表示渐变的动词有：get, grow, become, turn, run, go, begin 等。

① The leaves **are turning** red. 树叶都变红了。

② It's **getting** warmer and warmer. 天越来越暖和了。

③ Our study **is becoming** more interesting. 我们的学习变得越来越有趣了。

(9) 有时通过上下文可以判断出应采用何种时态。

① It's four o'clock in the afternoon. The children **are playing** football on the sports ground. 现在是下午4点，孩子们在操场上踢足球。

② Hurry up! We **are** all **waiting for** you. 快点！我们大家都等着你。

③ Where is Kate? She **is reading** in the room. 凯特在哪里？她在房间里看书。

(10) 有的现在进行时句子和一般现在时同义，用现在进行时表示问者的关切心情。

① How **are** you **feeling** today? (How do you feel today?) 你今天感觉如何？

② I am **looking** (look) forward to your next visit. 我盼望你下次再来。

③ Why **are** you **looking** (do you look) so sad? 为什么你看起来这么愁眉苦脸的样子呢？

注：(1) 在不少情况下，表示正在进行的动作的汉语句子，并没有"正在"这样的字，但在译为英语时必须用进行时态。

① How **are** you **getting on with** your classmates? 你和同学相处的如何？

② It's **raining** heavily. 下大雨了。

③ How **is** everything **going**? 事情进展如何？

(2) 有些动词通常不能用进行时,不能用进行时的动词有三种。表示感觉或情感的词,如 hear, see, smell, taste, feel, seem, notice, hate, love, like, want, wish, refuse, prefer, forgive 等;表示存在或所属的词,如 exist, stay, remain, obtain, have, own, form, contain 等;表示认识或理解的词,如 understand, know, remember, forget, believe, doubt 等。

8.6 过去进行时

8.6.1 过去进行时的构成

过去进行时由"was(were)+现在分词"构成。现在以动词 study 为例,其过去进行时的肯定式、否定式和疑问式如下表所列。

人称	肯定式	否定式	疑问式
第一人称	I was studying... We were studying...	I was not studying... We were not studying...	Was I studying...? Were we studying...?
第二人称	You were studying...	You were not studying...	Were you studying...?
第三人称	He/ She/ It was studying... They were studying...	He/ She/ It was not studying... They were not studying...	Was he/ she/ it studying...? Were they studying...?

一般过去时与过去进行时的用法比较:

① We **built** a bridge last winter. 去年冬天我们修了一座桥。(全过程,桥已修好)

② We **were building** a bridge last winter. 去年冬天我们在修一座桥。(片断,修完与否未知)

③ She **wrote** a letter to her friend last night. 她昨晚给她的朋友写了封信。(信写完了)

④ She **was writing** a letter to her friend last night. 她昨晚一直在给她的朋友写信。(信不一定写完)

一般过去时往往表示某一动作已经完成,而过去进行时却表示动作在持续或未完成。

8.6.2 与过去进行时连用的时间状语

过去进行时的时间状语往往是表示过去某一点时间的短语或句子,如 at that time/moment, (at) this time yesterday (last night/Sunday/week...), at+点钟+yesterday (last night / Sunday...),when sb. did sth. 等时间状语从句等。

过去进行时的时间状语也可以是表示过去一段时间的短语,如 at night, yesterday, this morning, last week (month/year...)等。

8.6.3 基本用法

(1) 表示过去某时正在发生的动作。

① It **was raining** at 6 o'clock this morning. 今天早晨六点钟天正下雨。

② As I walked on, some binds **were singing** in the woods. 我朝前走着林子里有些鸟在鸣叫。

③ They **were watching** TV when I entered the room. 我进入房间时,他们正在看电视。

(2) 表示过去某段时间内持续的动作,一般要有表示过去时间的状语。

① At that time she **was working** in Oxford. 那时,她正在牛津大学工作。

② I **was helping** my mother in the kitchen all day yesterday. 我昨天一天都在厨房帮妈妈干活。

③ He was reading a newspaper while we **were having** the meeting. 我们在开会的时候,他在看报纸。

(3) 表示与过去某个动作同时发生的动作。

① The children **were playing** with their toys while I **was eating** my dinner. 我吃饭的时候,孩子们在玩他们的玩具。

② While he **was waiting** for the bus, he **was reading** a newspaper. 他边等车边看报。

③ He **was cleaning** his car while I **was cooking**. 他擦车时我在做饭。

(4) 过去进行时可与 soon, the next moment, in minutes, minutes later 等时间状语连用,表示一个新的动作刚刚开始。

Soon the whole town **was talking about** it. 不久镇上的人就都谈论起这种事了。

(5) 表示事情发生的背景。

① It was a sunny morning. Some people **were sitting** on the riverbank. Some **were walking** with their dogs. Several boys **were playing** football nearby... 一个阳光明媚的清晨。河堤上坐着几个人,有的人在溜狗,不远处有几个男童在踢足球……

② It was a dark night. The wind **was blowing** hard and the rain **was falling** heavily. A PLA man suddenly appeared on the river bank. He wanted to cross the river. 那是一个漆黑的夜晚,风刮得很厉害,雨下得很大,一个解放军战士突然出现在河岸上,他想过河去。

(6) 与某些动词连用时,代替过去将来时。

① He telephoned me, saying that his aunt **was coming** to see me soon. 他打电话给我,说他姨妈很快就要来看我了。

② I **was leaving** for Wuhan that day. 那天我正要去武汉。

③ He **was meeting** his mother at the airport the next day. 明天他要去机场接她妈妈。

这类动词有 come"来", go"去", leave"离开", start"开始", stay"逗留"等,主语必须是人。

(7) 过去进行时可表示过去未曾实现的愿望或打算,这时 be 动词 was/were 要重读。

① I **was writing** him a letter this morning and forgot all about it. 我本该今天早上给他写信的,后来全给忘了。

② I **was seeing** her tomorrow. 我本来打算明天会见她。

③ He **was watching** the play yesterday, but he was too busy. 他昨天本来要看那场戏的,可是太忙了。

(8) 和 always, constantly 等词连用表示赞美、厌烦等感情色彩时。

① John **was** always **coming** to school late. 约翰上学总是迟到。

② Lei Feng **was** always **doing** good deeds for the people. 雷锋总是为人民做好事。

(9) 一种婉转的语气和礼貌的态度。过去进行时表示婉转语气（只限于 want, hope, wonder 等动词），用以提出请求。

① I **was wondering** if you could help me. 我想知道你能否帮助我。

② I **was hoping** you could send me home. 我希望你能送我回家。

8.7 现在完成时

8.7.1 现在完成时的构成

现在完成时由助动词 have＋过去分词构成（第三人称单数形式为助动词 has＋过去分词），现以动词 study 为例，将现在完成时的肯定式、否定式和疑问式列表如下：

人称	肯定式	否定式	疑问式
第一人称	I/ We have studied...	I/ We have not studied...	Have I/ we studied...?
第二人称	You have studied...	You have not studied...	Have you studied...?
第三人称	He/ She/ It has studied... They have studied...	He /She/ It has not studied... They have not studied...	Has he/ she/ it studied...? Have they studied...?

8.7.2 与现在完成时连用的时间状语

现在完成时所表示的动作或状态是发生在现在以前的某个未明确指出的过去时间内，因此和它连用的时间状语就应该是指不具体的过去时间状语，而且这个状语还必须与现在时间有关，即包含现在时间在内。常与现在完成时连用的时间状语有以下几种：

(1) 表示不定的过去时间的词，如 already, yet, before, recently, lately, just, of late, in the past 等。

① **Have** you **finished** your work yet? 你已经完成你的工作了吗？

② I **have** never **heard** that before. 过去，我从未听说过那件事。

③ The train **has** just **left**. 火车刚刚离开。

④ I have forgotten much of what I learned. 我学的很多东西都忘了。

(2) 表示频度的词，如 often, sometimes, ever, never, once, rarely 等。

① **Have** you ever **sung** this English song? 你曾唱过这首英文歌吗？

② —**Have** you ever **been to** the Great Wall? 你曾经去过长城吗？

　　—I **have** never **been to** the Great Wall. 我从未去过长城。

③ How many times **have** you **been** there this year? 今年你去过那里多少次？

(3) 句型 It is/ will be the first (second, third...) time that... 的 that 从句中，谓语动词须用现在完成时，表示到说话时为止动作发生过几次。

① It will be the first time that I **have been** there. 这将是我第一次去那里。

② It's the first time that I **have seen** this kind of film. 这是我第一次看这样的电影。

在句型 It was the first（second，third...）time that... 的 that 从句中,谓语动词须用过去完成时,有时也用一般过去时;如果有明确的时间状语,而说话时这个时间尚未成为过去,偶尔也用现在完成时。

① It was the first time she **had been** to Beijing. 那是她第一次去北京。

② It was the first time this year he **hadn't worked** / **hasn't worked** on a Saturday. 这是他第一次周末不加班。

（4）包含有现在时间意义在内的词,如 now，just，today，this morning，this week，this month，this year 等。

① Now I **have finished** the work. 现在我已完成工作了。

② **Have** you **seen** Tom today? 今天你见过汤姆了吗?

③ There **has been** too much rain in San Francisco this year. 今年,洛杉矶下了很多雨。

（5）现在完成时常与 always，often，many times，every day 等时间状语连用,表示重复的动作。

① My mother **has** always **gone** to work on foot. 我妈妈一向步行上班。

② It's **rained** everyday this week. 这个星期天天下雨。

③ Five times he **has tried** and five times she **has failed**. 他试了五次,五次都失败了。

（6）由 since 引导的短语或从句,表示"自从……以来"的持续状态。

① He **has taught** here since 1981. 他自 1981 年就在这儿教书。（可能还要继续教）

② He **has lived** here since 1978. 自从 1978 年以来,他一直住在这儿。（动作起始于 1978 年,一直住到现在,可能还要继续住下去。）

③ I **haven't heard** from him since he left. 他走之后我还没接到过他的信。

（7）由 for＋表示一段时间的词,表示动作或状态持续了多久,常跟一个时间段,指某个动作到现在为止已持续了多长时间,如 for three years，for half an hour 等。

① I **have been** in the army for more than 5 years. 我在部队已经待了五年多了。（动作开始于五年前,一直延续至今,有可能还要继续下去）

② He **has been** in the League for three years. 他入团已经三年了。

③ I **haven't received** a letter from my father for two months. 我已经两个月没收到我爸爸的信了。

短暂性动词用于现在完成时中,不能和 for，since 等表示一段时间的状语连用。

①He has left America for 5 years. 他已离开美国。（此句不正确,短暂性动词不能和表示延续的时间连用）

② She **has been away** from America for five years. 她离开美国已达五年之久。（延续性动词可以和表示延续的时间连用）

非延续性动词虽然不能直接和 for 或 since 连用,但可以找一个相应的延续性动词或动词短语来替换这些非延续性动词,如:

come→be， come to→be in / at, go out→ be out, leave→be away,

begin→be on， stop→ be over， buy→ have， borrow→ keep，

open→be open， close→be closed， join→be a member of，

die→be dead， catch a cold→have a cold， get to know→know，

become a teacher →be a teacher, fall asleep→be asleep, fall ill→ be ill 等。

(8) 表示从某时到目前这段时间的状语,如 until now, so far, in the past two years, up to the present, all day, up to now 等。

① The friendly relations and cooperation between our two countries **have been enhanced** in the past few years. 在刚刚过去的几年中,我们两国之间的友谊加深了。

② I **have heard** nothing from him up to now. 到目前为止,我没有他的任何消息。

③ Peter **has written** six papers so far. 目前,彼得已经写了六篇论文了。

8.7.3 基本用法

(1) 表示动作或状况发生在现在以前的某个未经明确指出的过去时间内,目前已经完成结束,给现在留下了结果或造成了影响。

A. 已完成用法(影响性用法)

该用法的现在完成时表示一个过去发生的动作在过去已经完成,并且这个过去发生并完成的动作对现在有影响或结果,同时说话人强调的或感兴趣的就是这个影响或结果。

① He **has turned off** the light. 他已把灯关了。(动作结束于过去,但说明现在的情况是灯不亮了。)

② She**'s gone to** bed. 她睡觉了。(结果是她现在在床上)

③ **Have** you **seen** my key? 你看到我的钥匙了吗?(结果:你知道它在哪里吗?)

④ He **has eaten** nothing today. 他今天什么也没吃。(结果:他现在一定很饿。)

B. 未完成用法(持续性用法)

该用法的现在完成时表示一个过去发生的动作并未在过去完成,而是一直持续到现在,并且有可能继续下去(也可能到此结束)。

① **Have** you **waited** long? 你等了很久吗?

② We **have been** busy this afternoon. 今天下午我们一直很忙。

③ I've **waited** a week for your answer. 等你的回答我等了一个星期。

(2) have been to 和 have gone to 的特殊用法。

① have been to 到……去过,关键是到过某地,而且又已经离开了那个地方。

Mr. Chen is back home from holiday. He **has been to** Beijing. 陈先生度假回来了,他去了北京。

② have gone to 到……去了,关键是人已离开出发地,至于到达目的地了没有则无从知道。

Jack is away on holiday. He **has gone** to France. 杰克去度假了,他到法国去了。

两者均可后接地点,前者表示去过某地,通常可与表示次数的状语连用;后者表示到某地去了,强调说话的当时去某地的人不在场,比较下面的例句。

① He **has been to** Beijing three times. 他去过北京三次。

② He **has gone to** Beijing. 他北京了。(即现在不在这儿)

③ —Where **have** you **been**? 你到哪里去了?

—I **have been to** the library. 我到图书馆去了。

(3) 可以在条件状语从句和在 when, before, after, until, as soon as 等引导的时间状语从句中。

① I'll go with you when /as soon as I **have made** the model plane. 我做完模型飞机就同

你一块去。

② They often go for a walk after they **have had** supper. 他们晚饭后经常去散步。

(4) 现在完成时可以用于 because 引导的状语中表示原因。

① We cannot cross the river because the water **has risen**. 因为河水涨了，我们过不了河。

② She can do it quite well now because she **has tried** many times. 他已经试过好多次了，因此他现在可以做得很好。

8.8 过去完成时

8.8.1 过去完成时的构成

过去完成时由助动词 had + 过去分词构成。现以动词 study 为例，其过去完成时的肯定式、否定式和疑问式如下表所列。

肯定式	否定式	疑问式
I/We/You/He/She/It/They had studied…	I/We/You/He/She/It/They had not studied…	Had/I/we/you/he/she/it/they studied…

8.8.2 与过去完成时连用的时间状语

过去完成时用于由 by, at, before, until, after, as soon as 等词引导的短语或从句，及与 already, yet, still, just, ever, never, hardly, scarcely 等词连用。

8.8.3 基本用法

(1) 表示过去某一时间或某一事件前已发生且已完成的动作或状态。

① We **had learned** 5,000 words by the end of last month. 到上个月底为止，我已经学了 5000 个单词。

② The farmers were in high spirits because they **had got** another good harvest. 农民们兴高采烈，因为他们又有了一次好收成。

③ I **had finished** the composition before supper. 晚饭前我就已经把作文写完了。

(2) 表示在过去某一时间或某一事件前已发生但尚未完成的动作或状态。

① He **had worked** in the factory for five years before he moved here. 在他搬到这儿以前，他已经在那家工厂工作了五年。

② I saw Li Ping yesterday. We **had not seen** each other since I left Beijing. 我昨天看见李平了。自从我离开北京，我们就没见过面。

(3) 用于宾语从句或间接引语中。

① I wondered who **had taken** the umbrella without permission. 我想知道谁不经允许就把雨伞拿走了。

② He told me that he **had passed** the exam. 他告诉我他已经通过考试。

③ She saw empty glasses and cups and realized that three people **had been** in the room.

她看到了空玻璃杯子和茶杯,知道房间里曾来过三个人。

(4) 用于对过去事实进行虚拟的条件句中。

① If you **had come** yesterday, you would have met him. 如果你昨天来的话,你就已经见到他了。

② She would have come if she **hadn't been** so busy. 要不是这么忙的话,她就已经来了。

(5) think,want,hope,plan,intend,mean 和 suppose 等词的过去完成时可以用来表示本来要做而没做或无法做的事,或没有实现的希望或意图。

① We **had hoped** that you would be able to visit us. 我们原本希望你去看我们。

② We **had hoped** to catch the early bus, but found it was gone. 我们本希望搭早班车,却发现车已开了。

③ They **had hoped** to be able to arrive before ten. 他们本来打算能在 10 点之前到达。

(6) 用于 wish 后的宾语从句中,表示对过去未做成的事情的某种感叹或愿望。

① I wish I **had been** there at that time. 那时候我要在那就好了。

② I wish I **had told** him about it. 我要是告诉他那件事就好了。

(7) 过去完成时还可表示过去某一时刻之前发生的动作或状态持续到过去某个时间或持续下去,常与 for,since 等词连用。

When Jack arrived, he learned Mary **had been away** for almost an hour. 当杰克到达时,他得知玛丽已经离开快一个小时了。

(8) 下列句式中常用过去完成时。

① hardly, scarcely, barely ＋ 过去完成时 ＋ when ＋ 过去时。

Hardly **had I got on** the bus when it started to move. 我刚上了汽车,它就开了。

② no sooner ＋ 过去完成时 ＋ than ＋ 过去时。

No sooner **had I gone out** than he came to see me. 我刚出去,他就来看我了。

8.9 过去将来时

8.9.1 过去将来时的构成

过去将来时由动词 should(第一人称),would(第二、第三人称)＋动词原形构成。美语则不管什么人称,一律用 would。

现以动词 study 为例,其动词的过去将来时的肯定式、疑问式和否定式的构成形式如下表所列。

人称	肯定式	否定式	疑问式
第一人称	I/We should study…	I/We should not study…	Should I/we study…?
第二人称	You would study…	You would not study…	Would you study…?
第三人称	He/She/It/They would study…	He/She/It/They would not study…	Would he/she/it/they study…?

8.9.2 基本用法

(1) 一般过去将来时表示过去某一时刻看来将要发生的动作,主要用于间接引语或宾语从句中。

① I rang up to tell my father that I **should (would) leave** for London. 我打电话告诉我父亲我要去伦敦。

② My brother told me he **would be** back on Saturday. 我哥哥告诉我,他要在星期六回来。

③ They never knew that population **would become** a big problem. 他们从来都不知道人口问题将会成为一个大问题。

(2) 一般过去将来时也可以用"was/were＋going to＋动词原形"表示过去将来时。

① I thought the film **was going to be** interesting. 我想这部电影将会很有趣。

② She said she **was going to start** at once. 她说她将立即出发。

③ I was told that he **was going to return** home. 有人告诉我他准备回家。

(3) 表示过去习惯性动作(不管什么人称都用 would)。

① Whenever he had time, he **would work** in the garden. 他一有时间就到花园劳动。

② Every evening I **would help** the students with their lessons. 每个晚上我都要帮助学生做功课。

(4) 表示"愿望"或"倾向",多用于否定句。

① She told me that the play **wouldn't** act. 他告诉我这戏没法上演。

② I knew he **would** never permit such a thing. 我知道他绝不会允许这样的事(发生)。

(5) 用于虚拟语气。

① If I had money, I **would** buy a car. 如果我有钱,我会买辆车。

② It is necessary that we **should** invite him. 很有必要请他来。

注:条件状语从句和时间状语从句中须用一般过去时代替过去将来时。

① I didn't know when she would come, but when she **came** I would let you know. 我不知道她什么时候来,但她来了我会告诉你。

② The teacher said that it would be very difficult to make progress if **I didn't work** hard. 老师说,如果我不努力学习,就很难取得进步。

8.10 将来完成时

8.10.1 将来完成时的构成

将来完成时由助动词 shall have＋过去分词构成(第一人称),will have＋过去分词构成(第二、第三人称)。

现以动词 study 为例,其将来完成时的肯定式、否定式和疑问式如下表所列。

人称	肯定式	否定式	疑问式
第一人称	I/We shall have studied...	I/We shall not have studied...	Shall I/we have studied...?
第二人称	You will have studied...	You will not have studied...	Will you have studied...?
第三人称	He/ She/ It/ They will have studied...	He/ She/ It/ They will not have studied...	Will he/ she/ it/ they have studied...?

8.10.2 基本用法

(1) 表示将来某时之前完成的动作,这一动作往往对将来某时产生影响,常与将来的时间状语或 never, have, soon 等词连用。

① On Monday he **'ll have been** in Britain for three years. 到星期一,他在英国就满三年了。

② He **will have finished** writing his novel by the end of next year. 到明年年底他就会写完他的小说了。

③ Before long he **will have forgotten** all about the matter. 不久他就会全然忘记这件事的。

(2) 表示推测,相当于"must have done"结构。

① You **will have heard** of this, I guess. 我想你已经听说过这件事了。

② I am sure he **will have got** the information. 我相信他一定得到了这个信息。

注:在表示时间或者条件的状语从句中,通常要用现在完成时来表示将来完成时,而不能直接使用将来完成时。

① I will go with you when I **have finished** my work. 等我完成工作之后我就同你一起去。

② When I **have finished** that, I shall have done all I am supposed to do. 等我做完这件事时,我就做完我该做的所有的事了。

③ Please don't get off the bus until it **has stopped**. 请等车停稳后再下车。

8.11 过去将来完成时

8.11.1 过去将来完成时的构成

过去将来完成时由助动词 should have+过去分词构成(第一人称), would have+过去分词构成(第二、第三人称)。

现以动词 study 为例,将过去将来完成时的肯定式、否定式和疑问式列表如下:

人称	肯定式	否定式	疑问式
第一人称	I/We should have studied...	I/We should not have studied...	Should I/we have studied...?
第二人称	You would have studied...	You would not have studied...	would you have studied...?

(续)

人称	肯定式	否定式	疑问式
第三人称	He/She/It/They would have studied...	He/She/It/They would not have studied...	Would he/she/it/they have studied...?

8.11.2 基本用法

(1) 表示在过去将来某时间以前发生的动作，并会对过去将来某一时间产生影响。

① He told me he **would have finished** it by 9. 他告诉我他将在9点钟的时候完成。

② She said she **'d have finished** her exams by then. 她说她那时已经考完试了。

③ I thought Sophia **would have told** you something. 我想索菲娅已经告诉你一些情况。

(2) 用于虚拟语气。

① If you had not helped me, I **would not have succeeded**. 如果你不帮我，我是不会成功的。

② There are a lot of things I **should have liked** to ask you. 有好些事我本想问你的。

③ If I had seen him this afternoon, I **would have told** him about it. 今天下午我要是见到他，我会告诉他那件事的。

8.12 将来进行时

8.12.1 将来进行时的构成

将来进行时由 shall be+现在分词（第一人称），will be+现在分词（第二、三人称）构成。

现以动词 study 为例，将将来进行时的肯定式、否定式和疑问式列表如下：

人称	肯定式	否定式	疑问式
第一人称	I/We shall be studying...	I/We shall not be studying...	Shall I/we be studying...?
第二人称	You will be studying...	You will not be studying...	Will you be studying...?
第三人称	He/She/It/They will be studying...	He/She/It/They will not be studying...	Will he/she/it/they be studying...?

8.12.2 基本用法

(1) 表示从现在着眼，从将来某时开始并且持续进行的动作。

① When I arrive at the airport, my whole family **will be waiting** for me. 全家人都会来机场迎接我。

② I **shall be traveling** this time next year. 明年的这个时候我正好在旅行。

③ Don't phone me between 5 and 6. We'**ll be having** dinner then. 五点至六点之间不要给我打电话,那时我们在吃饭。

(2) 表示预测或希望某事会发生。

① We **will be hearing** from them pretty soon. 我们不久就会接到他们的信。

② I hope it **won't** still **be raining** when we have to go to school. 我希望到非得去上学的时候不要还是在下雨。

(3) 用于询问别人的安排,特别是当想得到别人帮助的时候。

① **Will** you **be passing** the post office when you're out? 你出去的时候会不会经过邮局?

② **Will** you **be using** your bicycle tomorrow morning? 明天早上你会不会用自行车?

(4) 表示按计划或安排要发生的动作。

① I **will be seeing** you next week. 我下个星期来看你。

② I'**ll be taking** my holidays soon. 不久我将度假了。

③ We **shall be going to** London next week. 下周我们要去伦敦。

(5) 表示委婉的语气。

① **Will** you **be having** some tea? 喝点茶吧。

② **Will** you **be needing** anything else? 你还需要什么吗?

8.13 过去将来进行时

8.13.1 过去将来进行时的构成

过去将来进行时由 should be + 现在分词(第一人称),would be + 现在分词(第二、第三人称)构成。

现以动词 study 为例,其过去将来进行时的肯定式、否定式和疑问式如下表所列。

人称	肯定式	否定式	疑问式
第一人称	I/We should be studying...	I/We should not be studying...	Should I/we be studying...?
第二人称	You would be studying...	You would not be studying...	Would you be studying...?
第三人称	He/She/It/They would be studying...	He/She/It/They would not be studying...	Would he/she/it/they be studying...?

8.13.2 基本用法

表示在过去将来某一时间正在发生的动作。

① He asked me what I **should be doing** at six the next day. 他问我第二天 6 点钟干什么。
② They said that they **would be expecting** us the next week. 他们说他们下个星期等我们去。
③ He told me that he **would be living** in China some day. 他告诉我将来有一天会在中国居住。

8.14 现在完成进行时

8.14.1 现在完成进行时的构成

现在完成进行时由 have been＋现在分词(第三人称单数用 has been＋现在分词)构成。现以动词 study 为例,其现在完成进行时的肯定式、否定式和疑问式如下表所列。

人称	肯定式	否定式	疑问式
第一人称	I/We have been studying...	I/We have not been studying...	Have I/we been studying...?
第二人称	You have been studying...	You have not been studying...	Have you been studying...?
第三人称	He/She/It has been studying... They have been studying...	He/She/It has not been studying... They have been studying...	Has he/she/it been studying...? Have they been studying

8.14.2 基本用法

(1) 表示从过去某时开始一直持续到现在的动作,并且还将持续下去。
① The Chinese **have been making** paper for two thousand years. 中国有 2000 年的造纸历史。(动作还将继续下去)
② I **have been learning** English since three years ago. 自从三年前以来我一直在学英语。(动作还将继续下去)
③ Since that unfortunate accident last week, I **haven't been sleeping at** all well. 自从上周发生了那次不幸事故之后,我一直睡得很不好。(现在完成进行时的否定结构)

(2) 表示在说话时刻之前刚刚结束的动作。
We **have been waiting for** you for half an hour. 我们已经等你半个钟头了。(动作不再继续下去)

(3) 现在完成进行时有时表示根据直接或间接的证据得出的结论。
① She is very tired. She**'s been typing** letters all day. 她很累了,整天都在打信件。
② Her eyes are red. She **has been crying.** 她眼睛红了。她一直在哭。

(4) 有些现在完成进行时的句子等同于现在完成时的句子。
他们在这个城市已经住了 10 年了。
① They **have been living** in this city for ten years.

② They **have lived** in this city for ten years.

我在这里已经工作五年了。

① I **have been working** here for five years.

② I **have worked** here for five years.

(5) 大多数现在完成进行时的句子不等同于现在完成时的句子。

① I **have been writing** a book. 我一直在写一本书。（动作还将继续下去）

② I **have written** a book. 我已经写了一本书。（动作已经完成）

(6) 表示状态的动词不能用于现在完成进行时。

我认识他已经好几年了。

（错）I **have been knowing** him for years.

（对）I **have known** him for years.

I have been knowing...这类不能用于现在完成进行时的动词还有：love 爱，like 喜欢，hate 讨厌等。

注：现在完成进行时不用于被动语态，若要用可用现在完成时的被动语态代替。

① The **house has been painted** for a month. 这房子已漆了一个月。

② The problem **has been studied** for five days. 这个问题已被研究了五天。

③ They **have been repairing** the road. 他们这一阵一直在修这条路。此句的最近似的被动形式通常是 The road **has been repaired** lately.（这条路最近修过）。这是现在完成时的被动语态，但是这两个句子并不完全相同。

(7) 现在完成时通常只陈述事实，而现在完成进行时还可表示一种感情色彩。

① I **have waited for** two hours. 我等了两个小时。（陈述事实）

② I **have been waiting** for two hours. 我等了两个小时。（等得很辛苦）

8.15 过去完成进行时

8.15.1 过去完成进行时的构成

过去完成进行时由 had been＋现在分词构成。

现以动词 study 为例，其过去完成进行时的肯定式、否定式和疑问式如下表所列。

人称	肯定式	否定式	疑问式
第一人称	I/We had been studying...	I/We had not been studying...	Had I/we been studying...?
第二人称	You had been studying...	You had not been studying...	Had you been studying...?
第三人称	He/She/It/They had been studying...	He/She/It/They had not been studying...	Had he/she/it/they been studying...?

8.15.2 基本用法

(1) 表示过去某时以前一直进行的动作。

① It was now six and he was tired because he **had been working** since dawn. 现在是6点,他很累了,因为他从一大早就开始干活。
② He **had been trying to** get her on the phone just now. 他刚才一直在试着打电话找她。
③ **I had been looking for** it for days before I found it. 这个东西我找了很多天才找着。

(2) 过去完成进行时还常用在间接引语中。

The doctor asked what he **had been eating**. 医生问他吃什么来着。

8.16 将来完成进行时

8.16.1 将来完成进行时的构成

将来完成进行时由 shall have been+现在分词(第一人称),will have been+现在分词(第二、第三人称)构成。

现以动词 study 为例,将将来完成进行时的肯定式、否定式和疑问式列表如下:

人称	肯定式	否定式	疑问式
第一人称	I/We shall have been studying...	I/We shall not have been studying...	Shall have I/we been studying...?
第二人称	You will have been studying...	You will not have been studying...	Will you have been studying...?
第三人称	He/She/It They will have been studying...	He/She/It/They will not have been studying...	Will he/she/it/they have been studying...?

8.16.2 基本用法

将来完成进行时表示从某一时刻开始一直延续到将来某一时刻的动作。

① By the end of this year he'**ll have been acting** for thirty years. 到今年年底他当演员就满30年了。
② By the end of the month he **will have been living/working/studying** here for ten years. 到了月底他在这里居住/工作/学习就满十年了。

8.17 过去将来完成进行时

8.17.1 过去将来完成进行时的形式

过去将来完成进行时由 should have been +现在分词(第一人称),would have been+现在分词(第二、三人称)构成。

现以动词 study 为例,将过去将来完成进行时的肯定式、否定式和疑问式列表如下:

人称	肯定式	否定式	疑问式
第一人称	I/We should have been studying...	I/We should not have been studying...	Should I/we have been studying...?
第二人称	You would have been studying...	You would not have been studying...	would you have been studying...?
第三人称	He/ She/ It/ They would have been studying...	He/ She/ It/ They would not have been studying...	Would he/ she/ it/ they have been studying...?

8.17.2 过去将来完成进行时的用法

（1）过去将来完成进行时表示从过去某一时刻开始一直延续到过去将来某一时刻的动作。

He said he **would have been working** in this university for 20 years by the end of this year. 他说到今年年底他在这所大学任教就将 20 年了。

（2）过去将来完成进行时还可用于虚拟语气。

He **should have been working**, but he was otherwise engaged. 他本应该在工作，可是他却在干别的事。

巩 固 练 习

一、将所给单词的正确形式填入空格。

1. My mother often tells me _____ in bed. (not read)
2. I must take it back the day after tomorrow. You can only _____ it for 24 hours. (keep)
3. Why have you kept me _____ here for so long a time? (wait)
4. Please come to our meeting if you _____ free tomorrow. (be)
5. She _____ to the Great Wall several times. (go)
6. In his letter, he said that he _____ us very much. (miss)
7. The film _____ for nearly fifteen minutes when I got to the cinema. (be on)
8. He said he became _____ in physics. (interest)
9. This film is worth _____. (see)
10. He went to school instead of _____ home. (go)
11. In the old days it was difficult for the poor to _____ a job. (find)
12. It's cold outside, so you'd better _____ your coat. (穿上)
13. He is hungry. Please give him something _____. (eat)
14. Please don't waste time _____ TV every evening. You should work hard at English. (watch)
15. We found the window _____. (break)
16. Mother often tells me _____ too late. (not come home)
17. Great changes _____ in our country since 1978. (take place)
18. I _____ my daughter since last month. (hear from)

19. It _____ me two days to write the article. (take)
20. If I had arrived there earlier, I _____ him. (meet)
21. I didn't remember _____ her the book before. (give)
22. He called at every door, _____ people the exciting news. (tell)
23. Yesterday Mary couldn't finish her homework, so she has to go on _____ it this afternoon. (do)
24. We _____ football when it began to rain. We had to stop and go home. (play)
25. Xiao Lin _____ from here for about two hours. (be away)
26. Last night we _____ back home until the teacher left school. (not go)
27. Comrade Li Dazhao _____ in prison in 1927. (put)
28. We could not help _____ after we heard the story. (laugh)
29. Would you please _____ me an English-Chinese dictionary when you come? (bring)
30. He told me that he _____ the Great Wall the year before. (visit)

二、单项选择。

1. Here _____ the bus!
   A. is coming   B. comes   C. has come   D. has been coming
2. It's the third time I _____ him this month.
   A. had seen   B. see   C. saw   D. have seen
3. If you go to the western suburbs of the city, you _____ a lot of new buildings.
   A. will see   B. have seen   C. see   D. are going to see
4. She showed him the photo she _____ the day before.
   A. has taken   B. took   C. was taking   D. had taken
5. While Tom _____, his sister is writing.
   A. reads   B. has read   C. has been reading   D. is reading
6. By the time he was ten, Edison _____ experiments in chemistry.
   A. had already done   B. already had done
   C. was already doing   D. already did
7. I don't know if it _____ or not tomorrow.
   A. will snow   B. snows   C. has snowed   D. is snowing
8. He was sixty-eight. In two years he _____ seventy.
   A. was going to be   B. would be   C. had been   D. will be
9. Tom _____ for more than a week.
   A. has left   B. has gone away
   C. went away   D. has been away
10. He said that honesty _____ the key to success.
    A. was   B. will be   C. is   D. is being
11. We _____ each other since I left Shanghai.
    A. haven't seen   B. hadn't seen
    C. didn't see   D. wouldn't see
12. I'll return the book to the library as soon as I _____ it.

A. will finish B. am going to finish
C. finished D. have finished
13. _____ you _____ ?
A. Do ; marry B. Have ; married
C. Have; been married D. Are; married
14. She told me that her father _____ to the post office when I arrived.
A. just went B. has just gone
C. had just gone D. had just been going
15. Peter said that he _____ home the next day.
A. was going to B. will go C. would go D. had gone
16. They _____ to help but could not get here in time.
A. had wanted B. have wanted C. was wanting D. want
17. They will go to work in the countryside when they _____ school next year.
A. will leave B. will have leave
C. are leaving D. leave
18. I didn't know when they _____ again.
A. came B. were coming
C. had come D. had been coming
19. They _____ here for more than a month.
A. have arrived B. have reached
C. have come D. have been
20. We _____ a meeting from 2 to 4 yesterday afternoon.
A. had had B. would have C. were having D. had
21. If it _____ tomorrow, we won't go to the school farm.
A. is to rain B. will be raining C. will rain D. rains
22. _____ you _____ to the 6:30 broadcast?
A. Have; listened B. Did; listen C. Had; listened D. would; listen
23. I _____ Tom has made a mistake.
A. am thinking B. shall think
C. think D. have been thinking
24. He was taken into hospital last week. In fact he _____ ill for three months.
A. has been B. has got
C. had fallen D. had been
25. I'll look after your children after you _____ .
A. will go B. will have gone C. are gone D. went
26. The foreign friends _____ here just now.
A. left B. have left
C. have been away from D. had left
27. The teacher said that we _____ ten lessons by the end of this term.
A. should study B. have studied

C. were going to study D. should have studied
28. It _____ ten years since he left Shanghai.
    A. was   B. is   C. had been   D. will be
29. We _____ about two thousand English words by the end of last term.
    A. learned   B. have learned
    C. had learned   D. would learn
30. It _____ long before we celebrate the New Year's Day.
    A. isn't   B. hasn't been   C. wasn't   D. won't be
31. I _____ along the road when suddenly some patted me on the shoulder from behind.
    A. walked   B. had walked
    C. was walking   D. would walk
32. My brother _____ Tom quite well, they were introduced at a Party.
    A. is knowing   B. was knowing
    C. knows   D. had been knowing
33. Don't be late, Mary, the train _____ at 8 a.m.
    A. is starting   B. has started
    C. would start   D. starts
34. There will come a day when the people of the whole country _____ a happy life.
    A. live   B. will live   C. will have lived   D. are living
35. My father, who died fifteen years ago, _____ very kind to me.
    A. is   B. was   C. had been   D. would be
36. We _____ that you would be able to visit us.
    A. hope   B. were hoping   C. have hoped   D. hoped
37. By 1914 Einstein _____ world fame.
    A. gained   B. would gain
    C. had gained   D. was gaining
38. Comrade Wang _____ the Party for about three years.
    A. has attended   B. has joined
    C. has been in   D. has taken part in
39. The boy _____. A bullet _____ through his chest on the left side.
    A. had died; passed   B. died; had passed
    C. died; passed   D. had died; had passed
40. It _____ and the streets were still wet.
    A. had been raining   B. rained
    C. has rained   D. would rain

第九章 被动语态

被动语态是个语法范畴,是表示主语和动词之间语法和语义关系的动词形式。英语动词有主动和被动两种语态,当主语是动作的发出者时,动词用主动语态(Active Voice);当主语是动作的承受者时,动词要用被动语态(Passive Voice)。只有及物动词才有被动语态。

The same experiment **has been conducted** by the scientists for so many years, and now they **get** the results successfully. 多年来,科学家们一直在从事着这一相同的实验,现在,他们终于成功地得到了实验结果。

这句话中,experiment 是 conduct 的承受者,故 conduct 用被动语态。they 是 get 的发出者,故 get 用主动语态。

9.1 被动语态的构成形式

动词的被动语态是由助动词 be 加动词的过去分词构成的,时态由 be 体现。主动语态的句子结构与被动语态的句子结构如下所示:

主动语态:
动作的发出者+主动语态动词+动作的接受者
  主语   谓语   宾语
被动语态:
动作的接受者+被动语态动词(be+动词过去分词)+(by+动作的发出者)
  主语   谓语   宾语
下面以 keep 为例,说明各时态动词的被动语态形式:

现在范畴	一般现在时	am/is/are kept
	现在进行时	am/is/are being kept
	现在完成时	has/have been kept
过去范畴	一般过去时	was/were kept
	过去进行时	was/were being kept
	过去完成时	had been kept
将来范畴	一般将来时	shall/will be kept
	将来完成时	shall/will have been kept
	过去将来时	should/would be kept
	过去将来完成时	should/would have been kept

注:完成进行时态一般不用被动语态。

9.2 被动语态的用法

被动语态主要用于下面几种情况：

(1) 动作的发出者不必说出，不宜说出或没有具体的所指。

① The English evening has been put off till Saturday. 英语晚会已推迟到周六。

② Rice is chiefly grown in the south. 水稻主要生长在南方。

③ Visitors are requested not to touch the exhibits. 参观者不允许触摸陈列品。

(2) 需要强调动作的承受者，所表述的意义以动作的承受者为中心，这时如有必要可用 by 短语引出动作的执行者。

① Books and newspapers in the reading room mustn't be taken away. 任何人不许拿走阅览室中的书和报纸。

② The car is being cleaned by John. 约翰正清洗小汽车。

③ Great progress has been made in our work. 我们的工作已取得很大进步。

(3) 为了使语气婉转，避免提及自己或对方而使用被动语态；或由于修饰的需要，使用被动语态，避免中途变更主语，使句子得以更好的安排。

① The construction of the new lab must be completed by the end of next month. 新实验室的建设必须在下个月底前完工。

② Jack fought Mike in the men's singles（男子单打）and (Jack) was beaten. 杰克与迈克在男子单打中对决，但被击败了。

而有时是为了上下句紧密衔接而采用被动结构。

③ He visited the Great Wall in 2007. The Great Wall was built during Qin Dynasty. 他在 2007 年参观长城，长城是在秦朝建立的。

(4) 用于科技文章、新闻报道、书刊介绍等文体中，突出描述的客观性。

① It is the first time that genes have been linked with clone. 这是首次将基因与克隆联系起来。

② Over 60,000 people have so far been killed in the earthquakes sweeping across Sichuan. 在这次席卷四川的地震中，目前已有超过 6 万人丧生。

9.3 被动语态的形式

1. 含有情态动词的被动语态

构成：情态动词＋be＋过去分词。

① Children **should be given** enough freedom to develop their interests. 应该给予孩子们足够的空间去培养他们的兴趣。

② **Can** this work **be finished** at once? 这项工作能马上完成吗？

③ This book **shouldn't be taken** out of the library, should it? 这本书不应被带出图书馆，是吗？

2. 带有直接宾语和间接宾语的句子变为被动语态

带有直接宾语和间接宾语的句子变为被动语态时，只把一个宾语变为主语，另一个宾语保留在动词之后,如果保留的是间接宾语,要在间接宾语之前加上介词 to 或 for,这种句子可以有两个被动句。

① He **bought** me a pen. 他给我买了一支钢笔。

这个句子的被动句为 I **was bought** a pen by him. 或 A pen **was bought** for me by him.

② He sent me a birthday present. 他送给我一件生日礼物。

这个句子的被动句为 I **was sent** a birthday present by him. 或 A birthday present **was sent to** me by him.

③ She is making Tom a new coat. 她正在给汤姆做一件新衣服。

这个句子的被动句为 Tom is **being made** a new coat. 或 A new coat **is being made for** Tom.

3. 含有复合宾语的主动句变为被动句

含有复合宾语的主动句变为被动句时,将宾语变成主语,宾补仍保留在动词之后,成为主补。

① They **chose** Tom captain. 他们选汤姆为队长。

→Tom **was chosen** captain. 汤姆被选为队长。

② They **call** her XiaoLi. 他们叫她小李。

→She **is called** XiaoLi. 她被叫做小李。

③ She **saw** a man stealing a bike. 她看到一个人正偷自行车。

→A thief **was seen** stealing a bike. 有人发现一个贼正偷自行车。

4. 短语动词的被动语态

一般情况下,及物动词才能构成被动语态,但有些不及物动词组成短语后,也可构成被动语态。短语动词有三种基本形式,即"动词+介词"、"动词+副词"、"动词+副词+介词",当它们用作及物动词时,一般都可以变为被动态。此时,短语动词应视为一个及物动词,其后的介词或副词不可略去。

(1) 动词+介词,如 look after, look into, talk about 等。

① Parents should be well **looked after**. 应该好好照顾父母。

② Employment problems were **talked about** among the students. 学生之间讨论了就业问题。

③ Poor students were **looked down upon** by rich students. 有钱的学生看不起贫穷的学生。

(2) 动词+副词,如 put out, set up, bring about 等。

① The fire **had been put out** before the fire-brigade arrived. 在消防队赶来之前,大火就已经被他们扑灭了。

② A new public school **will be set up** here. 一座新的公立学校将在这里被建造。

③ A new study and research enthusiasm will soon **be brought about**. 新的学习和研究热情很快将被带动起来。

(3) 动词+副词+介词,如 do away with, put up with, look down upon 等。

① He **was looked down upon** because of his selfishness. 他因自私而受人冷落。

② That sort of thing **should be done away with**. 这种事情应该被废除。

③ Such a state of things **cannot be put up with**. 这种事态不能再被容忍了。

5. "动词+名词+介词"的被动态

除上述三种动词词组外,还有一种由"动词+名词+介词"构成的动词词组,如 take care of, make a mess of, pay attention to 等。这类动词词组由主动态转换为被动态时通常有两种形式,一种形式是把整个动词词组当作一个及物动词处理。

① The children **were taken good care of** in the orphanage. 孩子们在孤儿院受到了良好的照顾。

第二种形式是把动词词组看作"动词+宾语+介词词组"结构处理。

② **Good care was taken of** the children in the orphanage.

采用第二种形式时要把整个介词词组放到被动语态的后面去。

③ The house had been made a mess of. 房子被弄得一团糟。 →**A mess had been made of the house.**

6. 非限定动词的被动态

非限定动词包括不定式、-ing 分词和-ed 分词,其中不定式和-ing 分词有被动态。以 make 为例:to make 的被动态是 to be made,其完成体形式为 to have been made;making 的被动态是 being made,其完成体形式为 having been made。

(1) 不定式的被动态。

A. 当不定式的逻辑主语是动作的承受者时,不定式要用被动态。

① I don't want to **be criticized**. 我不想被批评。

② It is impossible for him **to be promoted**. 他不可能被提升。

③ The thing doesn't deserve **to be done**. 这件事不值得做。

④ I expect all my friends **to be invited** by you. 我希望你能邀请我所有的朋友。

当不定式的逻辑主语就是主句的主语时,这时逻辑主语不需要表示出来,如上述例 a、例 c 句;当不定式的逻辑主语不是主句的主语时,逻辑主语就需要表示出来,如上述例 b、例 d 句。

B. 在有些句子中,使用不定式的主动态和不定式的被动态,意义没有区别。

① There is so much work **to do** / **to be done**. 这儿有不少要做的工作。

② These books are not suitable **to use** / **to be used** as the students' textbook. 这些书不太适合做学生的教科书用。

注:在下面两句中,用不定式主动态和不定式被动态含义不同。

① There was nothing **to see**. 这儿没什么可看的。

② There was nothing **to be seen**. 在这儿没看见什么。

(2) -ing 分词的被动态。当-ing 分词的逻辑主语是动作的承受者时,要用-ing 分词的被动态。

① Although she is a teenager, Lucy could **resist being told** what to do and what not to do. 虽然露西是一个少年,但她能抵制住自己该做什么,不该做什么。

② I insist on **them being punished**. 我执意要求他们受到惩罚。

③ I wouldn't mind **being criticized**. 我不介意被批评。

④ The parents anticipated **their children being praised** highly by others. 父母都期望孩子受到他人的表扬。

当-ing 分词被动态逻辑主语就是主句的主语时,这时逻辑主语不需要表示出来,如上述例①、③句;当-ing 分词的逻辑主语不是主句的主语时,逻辑主语就需要表示出来,如上述例②、④句。

(3) 不定式的被动态和-ing 分词被动态用法比较。

不定式的被动态和-ing 分词被动态都可在及物动词之后作宾语,但有些动词只能与不定式搭配,有些只能与-ing 分词搭配,有时意义相同,有时则不同。

① I don't **want** to be misunderstood. 我不想被误解。
② He **enjoys** being praised. 他喜欢被表扬。
③ He **hates** to be disturbed. 他讨厌被打扰。
④ He **hates** being disturbed. 他讨厌被打扰。
⑤ He **remembered** to be interviewed. 他记得他要被采访。
⑥ He **remembered** being interviewed. 他记得他被采访过。

例①句不能改为 I don't **want** being misunderstood.（错）;例②句不能改为 He **enjoys** to be praised.（错）;例③、④句差别不大;例⑤、⑥句含义不同。

注:只能带不定式作宾语的动词有 allow, permit, encourage, help, want, expect, wish, intend, ask, hope, refuse, agree, decide 等;只能带-ing 分词作宾语的动词有 enjoy, anticipate, insist on, agree to, think about 等;能带不定式又能带-ing 分词作宾语的动词有 like, love, hate, remember, forget 等。

(4) 主动语态中的不带 to 的动词不定式作宾补变为被动语态时,要加上不定式符号 to。这类动词主要有 make, let, have, hear, watch, see, feel, notice, help 等。

① Mom helped me do my homework. →I **was helped to** do my homework by mum. 妈妈帮我做作业。
② My brother often made me do this and that when I was young. →I **was** often **made to** do this and that by my brother when I young. 小时候,我哥哥总让我做这做那的。
③ I heard her sing about in her room last night. → She **was heard to** sing in her room last night. 昨天晚上,我听见她在房间里唱歌。

(5) 主动语态中的宾语是从句,变成被动时有两种句型。

① We know that Britain is an island country. 我们都知道英国是一个岛国。(句型 I)
② It's **known** that Britain is an island country. 众所周知英国是一个岛国。(句型 I)

亦可把主动句中宾语从句的主语变为被动句的主语,宾语从句中的谓语部分变为不定式短语。

③ Britain **is known to** be an island country. (句型 II)

句型 II 的不定式结构形式取决于句型 I 中 that-分句的动词形式。主要有以下几种情况:

A. 当 that-分句谓语动词为表示将来时间的 will 结构或现在进行体时。

① **It is said** that he will study abroad. 据说他将在国外读书。
② **It is said** that he will be studying abroad.
③ **It is said** that he is studying abroad.

句型 II 的不定式结构一律转换为进行体形式,即 to be ＋-ing。

He is said **to be studying** abroad.

注:若主句主动词为 expect,句型 II 的不定式结构通常用一般形式,不用进行体形式。

It is expected he will study abroad. →He is expected **to study** abroad. 据估计他将在国外读书。

B. 当 that-分句谓语动词为表示现在时间的一般现在时时,句型 II 的不定式结构用一般形式。

It is thought that he drives badly. →He is thought **to drive** badly. 大家认为他驾驶技术差。

C. 当 that-分句谓语动词为表示过去时间的一般过去时或现在完成体时,句型 II 的不定式结构均转换为完成体形式。

It is known that we failed/ have failed in this match. →We are believed to have failed in this match. 大家知道我们这次比赛输了。

如果 that-分句谓语动词为过去进行体,那么句型 II 的不定式结构用完成进行体形式。

It is reported that he was speaking English fluently. → He is reported **to have been speaking** English fluently. 据报道他说一口流利的英语。

D. 当 that-分句谓语动词为被动态时,句型 II 用不定式的被动态结构 to be＋-ed 或 to have been＋-ed 的形式。

① It is known that paper was made in China first. →Paper is known **to be made** in China first. 大家知道纸是在中国最早制成的。

② It is reported that this problem has been solved. →This problem is reported **to have been solved.** 据报道这个问题已经解决了。

上述两个被动句型能否相互转换,与句型 I 的主句主动词有关。这类动词通常都是表示"估计"、"相信"等的动词,如 assume, believe, expect, fear, feel, know, presume, report, say think, understand 等。口语中常用的 suppose 也可归于此类。如:

① We suppose that this book has been translated into several languages. 我们认为这本书已经被译成了多种语言文字。

② It's supposed that this book has been translated into several languages. 据说这本书已经被译成了多种语言文字。

③ This book is supposed to have been translated into several languages. 这本书据说已经被译成了多种语言文字。

注:主动句与被动句相互转换的限制性。

并非任何一种主动句和被动句都可以相互转换,这首先与动词的类别有密切关系,如 own 和 have 都可表示所有关系,但前者可用于被动句而后者不可以。如:The house was owned by Bob.（此句正确）；The house was had by Bob.（此句错误）。还有一些类似 have(作"有"解)的静态动词通常也都没有被动态。

① The shoes fit(适合) me well. 这鞋很适合我。

② The girl resembles(像) her mother. 这女孩很像她母亲。

③ The meeting shall last(持续) 2 hours. 会议将开两小时。

④ Those children lack(缺乏) the sense of safety. 那些孩子缺乏安全感。

⑤ This classroom holds(容纳) about 200 students. 这教室能容纳大约 200 个学生。

当主动句的宾语是反身代词或相互代词时,这种主动句也不可以变为被动句,因为反身代词和相互代词通常不可以做主语。

① He hurt himself when he fell from the ladder. 他从梯子上摔下来摔伤了。

② We should help each other. 我们应该互相帮助。

9.4 主动结构表示被动意义的问题

英语的被动意义除了用及物动词的被动语态形式表示外,还可以用其他方法来表示,就像在汉语中并非一定要用"被"字来表示的被动意义一样。英语中有些结构是主动语态的形式,却表示被动的意义。

(1) 用某些不及物动词表示被动意义,这里有两种情况:一种情况是用这些动词(最常用的是一般现在时)表示被动意义,这类句子的主语(指物的居多)通常具有某些内在的特性,能够促使动词所表达的动作得以实现或难以实现,如 carry, cut, drive, iron, keep, lock, open, pick, read, sell, shut, tear, wash, wear, write, clean, draw, burn, cook 等。这类动词既能作及物动词,也能作不及物动词。作不及物动词时,形式上虽为主动,却表示被动意义。

① The shirt **washes** well. 这衬衫很好洗。

② His novel **sells** well. 他的小说很畅销。

③ The floor **cleans** easily. 地板很容易清洗。

④ Your pen **writes** quite smoothly. 你的笔写起来很滑。

另一种情况是用这类动词的进行体(主要是现在进行时)表示被动意义,这种句子的主语通常都是指物的,而且可以转换为相应的被动结构,如少数动词(bind, cook, do, owe, print)的进行时有时有被动意义。

① The magazine **is binding**(**printing**). 这本杂志正在装订(印刷)。

② He paid all that **was owing**. 欠的钱他都还了。

③ The meat **is cooking**. 正在火上炖肉。

注:当 break out, take place, shut off, turn off, work out 等动词表示"发生、关闭、制定"等意思时,也用主动形式表示被动意义。

① In China, great changes **have taken place**. 中国已发生了翻天覆地的变化。

② The war **broke out** between two countries. 战争在两国之间爆发了。

(2) 某些感觉动词(smell, taste, sound, prove, feel 等)的主动态表示被动意义。

① The course **tastes** delicious. 这道菜尝起来很好吃。

② The stone **feels** very smooth. 石头摸起来很光滑。

③ It **proves** right. 这证明是对的。

(3) 在 need(want, require, deserve, etc.)doing 句型中,动名词(doing)相当于动词不定式的被动式(to be done),在意思上没有多大差别。

① The flowers **need watering**. 或 The flowers **need to be watered**. 这些花需要浇水。

② The problem **requires** solving carefully. 或 The problem **requires to be solved** carefully. 这个问题需要仔细解决。

③ The floor of the classroom **needs/ wants/ requires cleaning**. 教室的地板需要打扫。

用法相似的结构还有 bear doing, stand doing, be worth doing,习惯上不用动词不定式。

① I can't **bear being laughed at**. 我不能忍受被嘲笑。

② The little girl can't **stand** criticizing. 小女孩经不起批评。

③ The book **is not worth** reading. 这本书不值得一读。

注:在 be worth doing 句型中,只能用动名词的主动式,而在 be worthy to be done 中,才能用动词不定式的被动式,两者不可混淆。

① His suggestion **is worthy to be** considered. 他的建议值得考虑。
② His work **is worthy to be** mentioned. 他的工作值得一提。

(4) 在某些性质形容词+动词不定式的句型中,其动词不定式的主动形式表示被动意义。

① The problem **is easy to** solve. 这问题容易回答。
② This story **is difficult to** understand. 故事很难懂。
③ This kind of water **isn't fit to** drink. 这种水不适合饮用。
④ The strict teacher **isn't easy to** get along with. 这个严厉的老师不易相处。

在这种句型结构中,动词不定式和主语的关系实际上是一种逻辑上的动宾关系,可以说是动词不定式作主语变换来的,相当于 It's easy to answer the question. 和 It's difficult to understand that book. 由于把动词宾语放在主语位置,所以和不定式的关系构成一种被动关系。

9.5 被动语态与系表结构的区别

英语中有些"be+过去分词"形式不表示被动意义,而是一个系表结构。大多数"be+过去分词"结构既可以表示被动语态,又可以表示系表结构。如果表示一个动作,则是被动语态;系表结构表示主语的特点或所处的状态,这一区分可以帮助决定用什么时态,如果是被动结构,它的时态一般要与相应的主动结构一致,如果是带表语的结构,用一般时态比较多,如下表所列。

带表语的句子	表被动语态的句子
The bridge is completed. 桥已修好。	The bridge was completed in 1968. 桥是 1968 年建成的。
The glass is broken. 玻璃杯破了。	The glass was broken by my sister. 玻璃杯是我妹妹打破的。
The truck is loaded. 卡车上满满的。	The truck is loaded with food. 卡车上装满了食物。
The door is locked. 门锁着。	The door is locked by his father. 门被他父亲锁上了。
The novel is well written. 这部小说写得很好。	The novel was written by a woman. 这部小说是一位妇女写的。
The man was offended. 那个人很生气。	The man was offended by the woman. 那个男人被那个女人激怒了。
He was annoyed with his son. 他对他儿子很生气。	He was annoyed by mosquitoes all night. 他整夜让蚊子搅得不得安宁。

这两种结构的主要差别还有：

（1）作为被动结构，他们都有相应的主动句（如 My sister broke the glass. His father locked the door. A woman wrote the novel. Mosquitoes annoyed him all night.），而系表结构没有。在被动结构中，助动词除 be 外还可用 get 取代，而在系表结构中，系动词除用 be 和 get 外，还可用 become，feel，look，seem，remain 等其他连系动词。

He is/ looks/ seems/ feels tired. 他是/看起来/似乎/感觉累了。

（2）在系表结构中，其中的过去分词相当于形容词，可被 very，quite，rather 等副词修饰，也能有比较级形式，而在被动结构中的-ed 分词不可以。

① This question is **very，very** complicated. 这个问题是非常非常复杂的。

② He was **badly** cut up at the news of his son's death. 他得知儿子的死讯后极为悲痛。

③ China's agriculture is getting **more and more** mechanized. 中国的农业越来越机械化了。

（3）系表结构中的-ed 分词既然已经形容词化，往往具有其固定的介词搭配关系，而且这个介词通常不是 by，而多用其他介词短语（如 in，at，with，about 等）。

① He is interested **in** painting. 他对画画感兴趣。

② We are all involved **in** the traffic accident. 我们都牵涉进了那场交通事故。

③ He is bent **on** the study of this mathematical problems. 他正专心致志于这个数学问题的研究。

④ I'm tired **of** his rude behaviors. 我受够了他粗鲁的行为。

巩 固 练 习

一、将下列句子变为被动语态，每空一词。

1. We can finish the work in two days.

   The work _____ _____ _____ in two days.

2. He paid much attention to the Chinese environmental protection.

   Much attention _____ _____ _____ the Chinese environmental protection.

3. The children will sing an English song.

   An English song _____ _____ _____ by the children.

4. You needn't do it now.

   It _____ _____ _____ by you now.

5. The little child's grandmother will look after him.

   The little child _____ _____ _____ _____ by his grandmother.

6. People use metal for making machines.

   Metal _____ _____ for making machines.

7. He made me do that for him.

   I _____ _____ _____ _____ that for him.

8. I have given this book to the library.

   This book _____ _____ _____ to the library.

9. Did they build a bridge here a year ago?

_____ a bridge _____ here by them a year ago?

10. We'll put on an English play in our school.

    An English play _____ _____ _____ on in our school.

11. People say that the murderer is hiding in the woods.

    The murderer _____ _____ _____ _____ _____ in the woods.

12. My brother often mends his watch.

    His watch _____ _____ _____ by my brother.

13. It is about time that we did away with all this obsolete machinery.

    It is about time all this obsolete machinery _____ _____ _____ _____.

14. Be careful so that you won't hurt yourself.

    Be careful so that you _____ _____ _____.

15. He made the farmers work for a long time.

    The farmers _____ _____ _____ _____ for a long time.

16. Did he break the window yesterday?

    _____ the window _____ _____ _____ yesterday?

17. They have sold out the light green dresses.

    The light green dresses _____ _____ _____ out.

18. We're turning out the new washing machines at the rate of fifty a day.

    The new washing machines _____ _____ _____ _____ at the rate of fifty a day.

19. You must not plant trees in very dry earth.

    Trees _____ _____ _____ _____ in very dry earth.

20. You can dig a hole in the earth.

    A Hole _____ _____ _____ in the earth.

二、用动词的正确语态填空。

1. The students _____ often _____ (tell) to take care of their desks and chairs.
2. That play _____ (put) on again sometime next month.
3. The old man is ill. He _____ (must send) to the hospital.
4. Vegetables, eggs and fruits _____ (sell) in this shop.
5. What _____ a knife _____ (make) of?

   It _____ (make) of metal and wood.
6. A Piano concert _____ (give) here last Friday.
7. _____ the magazine _____ (can take) out of the library?
8. The room _____ (clean) by me every day.
9. The stars _____ (can see) in the daytime.
10. Some flowers _____ (water) by Li Ming already.
11. These kinds of machines _____ (make) in Japan.
12. Apples _____ _____ (grow) in this farm.
13. Russian _____ _____ (learn) as the second language by some students in China.
14. Planes, cars and trains _____ _____ (use) by business people for travelling.
15. The cinema _____ _____ (build) in 1985.

16. The bike _____ _____ _____ _____ (must not put) here.
17. A beautiful horse _____ _____ _____ (draw) by John next day.
18. This kind of machine _____ _____ _____ (can make) by uncle Wang.
19. Mr. Green _____ _____ (open) two new school.
20. The PLA _____ _____ (found) on August 1st, 1927.

第十章 虚拟语气

10.1 语气及其种类

语气(Mood)是区别说话人以何种口气说话的动词形式,是陈述事实,还是发出命令,还是虚拟假设。语气是一种动词形式,随着说话人意图的不同,动词需要用不同的语气,英语中有三种语气。

1. 陈述语气

陈述语气表示所说的话是一种事实,动词可用各种时态。

① I think your idea is correct. 我认为你的想法对。

② She saw the man go into a room. 她看到那男人走进了一个房间。

2. 祈使语气

祈使语气表示说话人向对方提出请求或命令等,动词用原形。

① Don't make a noise. 别闹。

② Remember to e-mail me. 记着给我发邮件。

3. 虚拟语气

虚拟语气是一种特殊的动词形式,用来表示说话人所说的话并不是事实,而是一种假设、愿望、怀疑或推测。

① I wish I could have slept longer this morning, but I had to get up and come to class. 我真希望今天早上能多睡会儿,但是我不得不起床来上课。

② Mary is ill today. If she were not ill, she wouldn't be absent from school. 玛丽今天病了。如果她没生病,她不会缺课。

10.2 虚拟语气的本质含义及表达形式

虚拟语气是专门表达假设意义及其他非事实意义的动词形式。这种假设分为有可能实现的假设和与事实相反的假设。因此表示虚拟语气的动词形式可有两种:(should+)动词原形;主动词或情态助动词的过去时形式。可能实现的假设的动词形式为(should+)动词原形,与事实相反的用主动词或情态助动词的过去时。

10.3 虚拟语气的表达形式的用法

10.3.1 (should+)动词原形的用法

动词原形的用法包括三种情况。

1. 用来表示某事应该(或必须)去做的含义

凡表示"建议、命令、决定、愿望、要求"和此词义有关的动词、名词或句意为此含义的 that 引导的名词性分句中,用(should＋)动词原形,此时 should 可带可不带。有下列几种句型:

(1) 主语＋ suggest (advise, propose, recommend, insist, request, require, order, demand, decide, vote...)＋that clause(宾语从句)。

① My sister advised me that I (should) accept the invitation. 我姐姐建议我接受这个邀请。

② The expert proposed that TV should be turned off at least one hour every day. 这位专家提议每天关掉电视至少 1 个小时。

③ Experiments demand that accurate measurements be made. 实验要求精准的测量。

④ The board recommended that the company should invest in the new property. 董事会建议公司投资新领域。

注意:suggest 表示"建议"时其后的 that 从句用(should＋)动词原形,但表示"暗示,表明"讲时从句用陈述语气。insist 表示"坚决要求"时其后的 that 从句用(should＋)动词原形,但表示"坚持认为"讲时从句用陈述语气。

① What he said suggested that he didn't agree to the plan. 他的话表明了他不同意这个计划。

② She insisted that I should finish the work at once. 她坚持要求我立刻完成这项工作。

③ Tom insisted that he was right. 汤姆坚持认为他是对的。

(2) It is suggested (proposed, requested…)＋that clause (主语从句)

① It is suggested that the question be discussed at the next meeting. 有人建议这问题下次会上再议。

② It is desired that we get everything ready by tonight. 有人希望我们在今晚前准备好一切。

③ It has been decided that the sports meet be postponed till next Friday. 已经决定把运动会推迟到下周五。

(3) suggestion, proposal, requirement, decision, instruction, order 等名词之后的 that 分句(同位语从句或表语从句)中。

① They made the request that the problem should be discussed as soon as possible. 他们请求尽快讨论这个问题。

② His suggestion was that everyone should have a map. 他的建议是每人有一张地图。

(4) It is necessary (important, vital, impossible, advisable, essential, imperative)＋that clause(主语从句)。

① It is necessary that the work should be done. 做这项工作很必要。

② It is essential that we should tell her the news. 我们告诉她这个消息至关重要。

③ It is important that we close the window before we leave. 我们在离开前关上窗户非常重要。

(5) I think it necessary(important, etc.) that clause (宾语从句)。

① I thought it important that young people work hard. 我认为年轻人努力工作很重要。

② I thought it advisable that an armed guard stand in readiness. 我认为安排一名全部武装的警卫站岗是明智的。

2. 用来表示祝愿、诅咒、禁止等

这种虚拟语气常用在感叹句及某些公式化语句中，用动词原形。

① Heaven forbid! 天理不容!

② Long live the People's Republic of China! 中华人民共和国万岁!

③ Far be it from me to (我极不愿)spoil the fun. 我才不愿意扫别人的兴哩。

④ He will remain here if need be. 必要的话他会留在这儿。

3. 状语从句中的用法

以 lest, for fear that, in case 引出的状语从句中，谓语动词常用 should＋动词原形，should 可以省略。

① He handled the instrument with care for fear that it should be damaged. 他小心地操作仪器唯恐损坏了它。

② I'll keep a seat for you in case you should change your mind. 我会给你留个座位以防你改变主意。

10.3.2 主动词及情态助动词的过去时形式

此类用来表示不可能实现的愿望或假设的虚拟式。这种虚拟式主动词常用一般过去时和过去完成时。与现在相反或将来不可能实现的事用一般过去时表示，如果动词为 be 则多用 were；与过去事实相反用过去完成时表示。此类常见于 that 从句, if, though 从句中。

若含有情态助动词，与现在相反或将来不可能实现的事用一般过去时表示，即所用的情态助动词为 should, would, could, might。与过去事实相反用情态助动词的完成体表示，即 should, would, could, might ＋have ＋过去分词。常见于非真实条件句和含蓄条件句中。

常用句型如下：

1. it's (high/about) time ＋that clause

此句式含义为"该是……时间了"，是与现在相反的，所以只用过去式。

① It's high time we went home. 我们该回家了。

② It is about time you made up your mind. 是你下定决心的时候了。

2. I wish ＋that clause

① Tom is very short now. His mother wishes that he would be taller when he grows up. 汤姆现在很矮。他妈妈但愿他长大后会高一些。

② I wish I had enough money for a car. 但愿我有足够的钱买辆车。

③ I wish I hadn't said that. 但愿我没说过那些话。

3. I would rather(sooner) that clause

① I'm sure he is keeping something back. I'd rather he told me the truth. 我肯定他有事瞒着我们。我宁愿他给我讲真话。

② I could do it myself but I would sooner you did it. 我自己能做这事，但是我倒是希望你做。

③ She got drunk last night. I'd rather she hadn't drunk so much. 昨晚她喝醉了。我倒

宁愿她没喝那么多。

4. If only…

① If only I had the book. 我要是有这本书就好了。

② If only I could swim. 我要是会游泳就好了。

③ If only I had listened to the lecture. 我要是听了那个演讲就好了。

5. He acts/behaves as if(though)…

① He treats us as if we were all idiots. 他对待我们就像我们大家都是白痴。

② He talks as if he had done all the work himself, but in fact Tom and I did most of it. 他谈起来仿佛所有的工作都是他自己做的似的,但实际上是我和汤姆干了大部分。

③ The cheese looks as if rats had nibbled it. 这奶酪看起来好像老鼠咬过似的。

注：as if/as though 结构中的动词形式决定于说话人的语义意图。在某些语境中,如果不表示假设意义,就不必用过去时形式。

① The apple tastes as if it is sour. 这苹果味道有点酸。

② It seems as if we will have to go home on foot. 看来我们要步行回家了。

6. 非真实条件句

非真实条件句的现在时间、过去时间、将来时间的主要语法标记如下表所列。

	if 从句	主　句
与现在事实相反	were /一般过去时	would /should（could, might）+动词原形
与过去事实相反	过去完成时	would /should（could, might）+have +过去分词
与将来事实相反或将来不可能实现	were to+动词原形 should +动词原形 一般过去时	would /should（could, might）+动词原形

① If he were here now, I would explain to him myself. 如果他现在在这儿,我就亲自给他解释。

② If he had been here yesterday, I would have explained to him myself. 要是他昨天在这儿,我就亲自向他解释了。

③ If he were to come /should come /came here tomorrow, I would explain to him myself. 要是他明天来这,我就亲自给他解释。

注:非真实条件句中的 if-可以省略,此时条件句要部分倒装,即将谓语中的过去式 were, had 或 should 等移至主语之前。

① Were you in my position, what would you do? 假如你处在我的位置,你会怎么做?

② Were he to leave today, he would get there by Friday. 如果他今天动身,星期五前会赶到那儿。

③ Had some work been done, energy would have been applied. 如果做了一定量的功,就一定消耗了能量。

7. 含蓄条件句

含蓄条件句是指条件从句不表示出来的条件句。主要用法有两种(同虚拟条件句中主句的形式相同):

（1）Would /should（could，might）＋动词原形，表示说话人委婉的请求、愿望或推测。

（2）Would /should（could，might）＋have＋过去分词，表示与过去事实相反的主观设想。

① But for your help, I couldn't have achieved so much. 如果没有你的帮助,我不可能取得这么大的成绩。

② Anyone who should violate the law would be punished. 任何违反法律的人都要受到惩罚。

③ In different circumstances, I might have agreed. 换种情况我也许会同意。

④ Another half hour and all the people there would be killed. 再过半小时,那里所有的人就会被杀死。

注：(1) Expect, think, intend, mean（＝intend），want, suppose 等几个动词的过去完成体,表示过去未曾实现的希望、打算或意图：

① I had hoped that we would be able to leave tomorrow, but it's beginning to look difficult. 原本希望明天我们能离开,但是看来难了。

② I had intended to make a cake, but I ran out of time. 我本打算做蛋糕的,但是没时间了。

（2）情态助动词＋have＋动词的过去分词的特殊含义。情态助动词有推测性用法和非推测性用法,这里只谈非推测性用法中表示虚拟含义"与过去事实相反"的特殊用法。

① should＋have＋done 意思是"本来应该做某事,而实际没做。" shouldn't＋have＋done 表示本来不应该做某事,而实际做了,有指责对方或自责的含义。

a. Tom, you are too lazy. The work should have been finished yesterday. 汤姆,你太懒惰了,这项工作本来应该昨天就做完的。

b. Look, Tom is crying. I shouldn't have been so harsh on him. 看,汤姆哭了,我本来不应该对他如此严厉。

② ought to＋have＋done 表示过去应该做而实际并没有做,译成"理应做……",往往表示遗憾,与"should＋have＋done"用法基本一样。

a. I ought to have gone home last Sunday. 我理应上星期日回家。

b. You ought not to have given him more help. 你不应该帮助他那么多。

③ "need＋have＋done" 表示本来需要做某事而没有做;"needn't＋have＋done" 则表示"本来不需要做某事而做了"。

a. I needn't have bought so much wine—only five people came. 我本来没有必要买这么多酒,只来了五个人。

b. He need have hurried to the station. In that case, he wouldn't have missed the train. 他本来需要快点去车站,那样的话,他就不会误了火车。

④ would like to have done sth. 本打算做某事。

I would like to have read the article, but I was very busy then. 我本打算读那篇文章,但那时很忙。

⑤ "could(不能用 can)＋have＋done"表示对过去事情的假设,意思是本来能够或可以做某事而没有做。

注意:其否定形式 couldn't have done 没有虚拟语气的用法,couldn't have done 只能表推

测,相当于 can't have done,意为"过去不可能做了某事"。

  a. He could have passed the exam, but he was too careless. 本来他能够通过考试,但是他太粗心。

  b. I could have lent you the money. Why didn't you ask me? 我本来可以借给你钱的,你为什么没向我要?

 ⑥ might（不能用 may）have done 表示"过去本可以做某事却未做"。

  注意:其否定形式 might not have done 没有虚拟语气的用法,只能表推测,相当于 may not have done,意为"过去可能没有做某事。"

  You might have helped him even though you were busy at that time. 即使那时你很忙,你也本可以帮他一把的。

巩 固 练 习

1. The boy acted _____ he had never lived in Canada before.
 A. as though B. even if C. as D. since
2. _____ to the doctor right away, he might have been alive.
 A. If he went   B. Were he gone
 C. Should he have gone D. Had he gone
3. If you were older, I _____ you to go there yesterday.
 A. will allow   B. should allow
 C. would have allowed D. had allowed
4. The secretary suggested that they _____ the men in at once.
 A. had brought   B. should have brought
 C. brought   D. bring
5. I wish I _____ able to tell him all about it last night.
 A. was B. were C. had been D. should be
6. If we _____ here ten minutes earlier, we _____ the bus.
 A. arrived/would catch   B. arrived/would have caught
 C. had arrived/had caught D. had arrived/would have caught
7. If I _____ more time, I would have gone with him.
 A. had B. had had C. have had D. would have
8. He was very busy yesterday, otherwise he _____ to the meeting.
 A. would come B. came C. would have come D. had come
9. The Jade Emperor ordered that the Monkey King _____ right away.
 A. would be arrested   B. must be arrested
 C. be arrested   D. had to be arrested
10. Jane's uncle insisted _____ in this hotel any longer.
 A. not staying B. not to stay C. that he not stay D. staying not
11. Don't touch the sleeping tiger. If he woke up, he _____ you.
 A. would come to   B. would come at

C. would have come toward   D. will come to
12. Without electricity, human life _____ quite different today.
    A. is   B. will be   C. would have been   D. would be
13. How I wish I _____ to repair the watch! I only made it worse.
    A. had tried   B. hadn't tried   C. have tried   D. didn't try
14. He demanded that the laboratory report _____ immediately after the experiment was done.
    A. was written   B. be written
    C. must be written   D. would be written
15. The man insisted that he _____ there.
    A. should send   B. would be sent   C. sent   D. be sent
16. If he had not gone out in the storm, _____.
    A. he will be alive now   B. he would be alive now
    C. he would have been alive now   D. he will have been alive now
17. If it _____ tomorrow, what would we do?
    A. rains   B. were to rain   C. would rain   D. rain
18. It is required that you _____ at six.
    A. will arrive   B. arrive   C. arrived   D. would arrive
19. If only I _____ how to operate an electronic computer as you do.
    A. had known   B. would know   C. should know   D. knew
20. He spoke in a quiet, distinct voice, as though his thought _____.
    A. was far away   B. had been far away
    C. were far away   D. went far away.
21. If it _____ rain, we _____ get wet.
    A. is to, should   B. were to, would
    C. were going to, would   D. was going to, should
22. If he _____ to the teacher attentively, he _____ the answer to the problem now.
    A. had listened, would have known   B. listened, would know
    C. listened, would have known   D. had listened, would know
23. But for the party, he _____ of hunger 30 years ago.
    A. would have died   B. would die
    C. must have died   D. must die
24. _____ today, he would get there for holiday.
    A. Was he leaving   B. Were he to leave
    C. Would he leave   D. If he leaves
25. I would have come earlier, but I _____ that you were waiting for me.
    A. didn't know   B. hadn't know
    C. would have known   D. haven't known
26. It's high time that we _____ to school.
    A. would to   B. went   C. go   D. will go

27. It seems as if it _____ rain.
    A. will to   B. is going to   C. is to   D. were going to
28. I'd rather you _____ right away.
    A. leave   B. left   C. will leave   D. to leave
29. He is working hard for fear that he _____.
    A. fails   B. failed   C. would fail   D. fail
30. It is really strange that the girl _____ so early.
    A. has been married   B. has married   C. be married   D. would marry
31. Supposing I _____ this gift, what would he say?
    A. accept   B. accepted   C. should accept   D. would accept
32. The teacher agreed to the suggestion that the students _____ two weeks to prepare for the exam.
    A. give   B. should give   C. be given   D. would be given
33. I was busy yesterday, otherwise I _____ your birthday party.
    A. attended   B. had attended
    C. would attend   D. would have attended
34. He insisted that he _____ me before.
    A. see   B. should see   C. had seen   D. saw
35. The two strangers talked as if they _____ friends for years.
    A. were   B. would be   C. have been   D. had been
36. We _____ our lives had it not been for the policeman.
    A. would have lost   B. should lose   C. might lose   D. could have lost
37. —I thought you would come back tomorrow.
    —I would if I _____ to attend a meeting.
    A. don't have   B. didn't have
    C. will not have   D. would not have
38. He wishes _____ mistakes.
    A. he doesn't always make   B. he isn't always making
    C. he didn't always make   D. he wouldn't always making
39. It _____ very nice if only it were possible.
    A. will be   B. would be   C. is   D. were
40. Without your help, our team _____ the last match.
    A. won't win   B. will lose   C. wouldn't have won   D. can't win

第十一章 不定式

11.1 非限定动词概述

在句子中,不能作谓语,而是担任其他语法功能的动词,叫做非限定动词(the Non-finite Verb)。非限定动词包括动词不定式(the Infinite)、分词(the Participle)和动名词(the Gerund)。由于它们不能单独作谓语,口语中也称作"非谓语动词"。

11.2 非限定动词的特点

非限定动词虽然没有动词该有的功能,即不能作谓语,但仍具有动词部分的特征。非限定动词可以有自身的宾语,也可以用副词加以修饰。也就是说,它可以模仿动词,但却无法当真正的动词使用。非限定动词除了不能作谓语外,根据它的特性可在句中作其他成分。不定式相当于名词、形容词或副词的作用;分词具有形容词或副词的作用;动名词具有名词的作用。

非限定动词的语法功能列表如下:

担任成分 种类	主语	表语	宾语	介宾	宾补	定语	状语
不定式	√	√	√	限 but except √	√	√	√
分词		√			√	√	√
动名词	√	√	√	√		√	

① To see is to believe. 百闻不如一见。(to see 与 to believe 分别作主语和表语)
② He is fond of playing football. 他喜欢踢足球。(playing football 作介词宾语)
③ I have no choice but to leave. 我别无选择,只有离开。(to leave 作介词宾语)
④ The man sitting by the window is our teacher. 坐在窗户边的那个人是我们的老师。(sitting by the window 作定语)
⑤ She got him to turn down the TV. 她让他把电视机音量调低点。(to turn down the TV 作宾补)
⑥ He was surprised to hear the news. 听到这个消息,他感到很吃惊。(to hear the news 作原因状语)
⑦ Going into the room, he shut the door. 走进房子,他就关上了门。(going into the room 作时间状语)

⑧ I had my car repaired. 我让人把我的车修好了。（repaired 作宾补）

11.3　非限定动词形式和语态的变化

非限定动词形式和语态的变化如下表所列。

非限定动词	形式＼语态	主动	被动
动词不定式	一般式	to do	to be done
	进行式	to be doing	
	完成式	to have done	to have been done
	完成进行式	to have been doing	
现在分词和动名词	一般式	doing	being done
	完成式	having done	having been done
过去分词	一般式		done

11.4　动词不定式

11.4.1　动词不定式的意义和形式

　　动词不定式是动词的一种非限定形式,由"to＋动词原形"构成,其否定形式是"not to＋动词原形"。由于其功能多样,无法确切命名,所以叫不定式。动词不定式虽然不能作谓语动词,但仍保留着动词的特征,它可以带有所需要的宾语或状语而构成动词不定式短语,其形式的变化参见前表。

11.4.2　不定式的时态形式所表示的时间关系

1. 一般式

　　一般式表示的动作和谓语动词所表示的动作同时发生,或在谓语动作之后,或没有时间限制。

① They often watch us play table tennis. （与谓语动作同时）他们经常看我们打乒乓球。
② She hopes to go there again. （在谓语动作之后）她希望再次去那里。
③ The factory to make radios is over there. （无时间限制）生产无线电的工厂在那边。

2. 完成式

(1) 表示的动作在谓语动词所表示的动作之前。

① I'm sorry to have kept you waiting. 很抱歉让你一直等。
② We are happy to have visited so many historic places in Beijing. 在北京参观了那么多的名胜古迹,我们感到很开心。
③ She seems to have been a teacher for many years. 看来她当了许多年老师了。

④ I am sorry not to have come on Thursday. (= I am sorry that I didn't come on Thursday.) 我很遗憾星期四没来。

(2) 表示"非真实"的过去。用在表示打算、需要、计划等动词的过去时后面,表示过去本打算做但事实上没有实现的动作。这些动词有 mean, intend, think, plan, hope, wish, propose 等。

① I meant to have telephoned, but I forgot. 我本打算打电话的,但是我忘了。

② I planned to have visited you last night, but I was too busy. 我昨晚本来想去看你,但太忙了。

注:还可用以下两种结构表达同一意思:a. was/were to have done, would/should like to have done。b. 过去完成时＋to do。如:I was to have visited you last night. I had intended to visit you last night. 同样表示"我昨晚本来想去看你"的意思。

3. 不定式的进行式

(1) 正在进行的动作。通常用在 appear, happen, pretend, seem 等动词之后。如同进行时态那样,不定式的进行式用于描写人们谈论(现在或过去)正在继续的动作,或者与谓语动作同时发生的动作。

① He pretended to be sleeping when she came in. 当她进来时,他假装在睡觉。

② He happened to be singing in the room when I came in this morning. 今天早上我进来时碰巧他在房间唱歌。

③ He seems to be eating something. 他好像正在吃什么东西。

(2) 反复发生的一般性动作。因为进行时态可以表示一个最近一段时间内持续的一般性动作,同样,不定式的进行式也表示一种反复发生的一般性动作,此时带有很强的感情色彩。I'd rather read than watch television; the programs seem to be getting worse all the time. 比起看电视我倒宁愿读书;电视节目看来正变得更滥。

4. 不定式的完成进行式

不定式的完成进行式(较少用到)表示在谓语动作之前已经开始并且一直在持续进行的某一动作,即表示动作从过去开始并延续至说话的时候。

① They are said to have been collecting folk songs in Yunnan. 据说他们一直在云南收集民歌。

② The little girl seems to have been watching TV all this evening. 这个小女孩看来看了一整晚电视。

③ She is known to have been working on the problem for many years. 我们知道她研究这问题有好几年了。

11.4.3 不定式的语态

(1) 一般来讲,在句中若出现了不定式动作的执行者,则不定式用主动形式。若没有执行者或不定式所修饰的成分是不定式动作的承受者,则不定式用被动形式。

比较:He wants someone to take photos. 他想找人拍几张照片。(someone 执行 take 动作)

He wants photos to be taken. 他想拍几张照片。(不是他拍照,所以照片 be taken)

I have three letters to write today. 我今天要写三封信。(由 I 来执行 write 动作)

I want the letters to be typed at once. 我想找人立即把这些信件打印出来。

What is to be done is unknown. 还不知道做什么。(不强调谁去做)

The bridge to be bulit there is very long. 要在那里建的桥很长。

(2) 形容词后边的不定式通常用不定式的主动形式表示被动意义。

① English is difficult to speak. 英语难说。

② The box is too heavy to move. 这个箱子太重了而挪不动。

③ This magazine is interesting to read. 这本杂志读起来很有趣。

(3) to let(出租), to blame(责备)这两个短语是固定用法, 主动形式表示被动意义。

① You should be to blame for it. 你应该为此受到责备。

② The house is to let. 这所房子要出租。

11.4.4 动词不定式的分类

动词不定式分为带 to 不定式(To-infinitive)和不带 to 不定式(Bare-infinitive)。不定式通常带 to,但在某些搭配中不带 to,在另一些搭配中既可带 to 也可不带 to。下面就不定式不带 to 的使用场合归纳如下：

(1) 在情态助动词、半助动词及情态成语之后。

① He must do as you're told. 他必须按别人告诉你的那样去做。

② You needn't leave this evening. 你不必今晚离开。

③ You'd better have that bad tooth pulled out. 你最好把那颗坏牙拔掉。

在 would rather, would sooner, would (just) as soon(宁愿), may, might (just) as well (不妨,可以), cannot but, cannot help but (不能不,不由得)等情态成语(Modal Idiom)之后跟不带 to 的不定式。

① I'd rather not have eggs for breakfast. 早饭我不愿意吃鸡蛋。

② Since it's a fine day we might as well walk. 既然天气不错,我们不妨去散散步。

③ You can't help but respect them. 你不由得不尊敬他们。

rather than, sooner than (宁可……而不)置于句首时,跟不带 to 的不定式。当它们出现在句中其他位置,其后不定式可带也可不带 to。

① Rather than cause trouble, he left. 他宁可离开也不愿找麻烦。

② He decided to walk rather than drive. 他决定走路而不开车。

(2) 在感官动词(feel, hear, listen to, see, look at, watch, notice, observe)和使役动词(let, make, have)后的复合宾语中,不定式作宾语补足语,且不带 to。这些常用动词可归纳为 feel (一感); hear, listen to(二听); make, let, have(三让); see, watch, observe, notice, look at(五看); help (半帮助,可带 to 或不带 to)等。但改为被动语态时,不定式要加 to。

① I watched him eat his breakfast. 我看他吃早饭。

② They saw him enter the building. 他们看见他进了大楼。

③ He made her stay to tea. 他让她待下来喝茶。

④ He was seen to enter the building. 有人看见他进了大楼。

⑤ She was made to stay to tea. 有人让她待下来喝茶。

在 listen to, look at, help 后不定式可带也可不带 to。

① Would you like to listen to me (to) read the poem? 你愿意听我读这首诗吗?

② The teacher will help you (to) study English well. 老师会帮你学好英语。

（3）在 Do nothing/anything/everything but/except do 句型中。如果 except/but 之前有动词"do"的某种形式,其后通常不带 to 不定式,否则带 to。

① They did nothing except work. 他们除了工作之外什么都不做。

② They have no choice but to wait. 他们别无选择只能等待。

（4）在"主系表"句型中,如果主语部分有动词"do"的某种形式,则作表语的不定式既可带也可不带 to。

① What I could do then was(to) wait. 那时我能做的事只能是等待。

② All that I could do then was(to) wait.

（5）在 why (not)＋do? 句子中。Why do? 含有责怪之意,通常表明做某事是无意义或愚蠢的。Why not...? 表示建议。

① Why argue with him? 为什么和他争吵？

② Why not take a holiday? 何不去度个假？

（6）两个动词由 and, or. but 等连接时,为了避免重复而省去 to。

① I'd like to lie down and go to sleep. 我想躺下睡觉。

② Do you want to have lunch now or wait till later? 你想现在吃午饭还是等晚会儿？

但是,若两个不定式动词有对比之义时,则均须加 to。

① I came not to praise, but to scold you. 我来不是表扬你而是责备你的。

② He likes to be respected, not to respect others. 他喜欢受人尊重而不是尊重别人。

（7）在一些习惯用法中,如 come, go, try 后,如 come look（＝come and look）. Go post（＝go and post）a letter for me. 在一些固定搭配中,如 make believe(假装), make do(with/on)(凑合,靠……维持), let drop/ let fall(有意无意说出), hear tell (of)(听说)等中动词不定式不加 to。

① Let's make believe we have a million dollars. 我们假装我们有一百万美元。

② We hadn't time for lunch, but we made do with sandwiches. 我们没时间吃午饭,但是我们凑合吃了三明治。

11.4.5 动词不定式的用法

动词不定式具有名词、形容词和副词的特征,因此它在句中可用作主语、表语、宾语、宾语补足语、定语和状语。

1. 作主语

① To hesitate means failure. 犹豫不决就意味着失败。

② To talk with her is a great pleasure. 和她谈话是一件非常愉快的事。

③ To speak English well isn't an easy job. 说好英语不是一件容易的事。

动词不定式短语作主语时,为了保持句子平衡,往往用 it 作主语,而把动词不定式短语置于谓语动词之后。

① It is important **to master English grammar.** 掌握英语语法很重要。

② It was quite a difficult task to complete the 30 storied building in one year. 一年建成30层的大楼是很艰巨的任务。

注：此处形式主语 it 不能用 this 或 that 来替换。大多数情况下都可以用动名词替代,但有三种情况只用不定式作主语,不用动名词替代。

(1) 固定说法。To err is human. 人非圣贤，孰能无过。

(2) 表示强烈的对比（常为一对矛盾）。To love is to be loved. 爱别人就是被人爱。
To teach is to learn 教即是学。To forgive is to be forgiven. 原谅他人就是原谅自己。

(3) 某具体情况（即具体的或一次性的动作或事情）。To finish this job in one day is impossible. 在一天里完成这项工作是不可能的。

2. 作表语

① The most important thing for one's health is to have plenty of exercise. 对人的健康来说，最重要的是充足的锻炼。

② My only hope is to continue my study. 我唯一的希望是继续我的学习。

③ To live is to do something worthwhile. 活着就是要做一些有价值的事。

此时作表语的不定式短语与主语中心词没有任何逻辑关系（即没有逻辑上的主谓或动宾关系）。

注：注意和半助动词"be to"的比较。"be to"可表示安排、命令、决定、劝告、愿望、禁止等。

① We are to arrive there at five. 我们将在5点到达那个地方。

② You are to finish it by six. 你必须在6点前完成。

③ If you are to succeed, you must work hard. 如果你想成功，就必须努力工作。

④ Children are not to smoke. 禁止孩子吸烟。

3. 作宾语

有些及物动词常用动词不定式作宾语。这些动词常用的有：afford, agree, arrange, ask, attempt, beg, begin, care, choose, claim, consent, continue, contrive, dare, decide, decline, demand, deserve, desire, determine, endeavor, expect, fail, fear, forget, guarantee, happen, help, hesitate, hope, intend, learn, long, manage, mean, need, offer, plan, pledge, pray, prepare, pretend, promise, refuse, resolve, seek, swear, think, tend, threaten, undertake, venture, volunteer, want, wish 等。

① She failed to finish the assignment in time, and she was worried about it. 她没有及时完成任务，她很担心。

② I can't afford to live in a detached house. 我住不起独门独院的房子。

常跟疑问词+不定式作宾语的动词有：ask, consider, decide, discover, discuss, explain, find out, forget, inquire, know, learn, remember, show, tell, think, understand, wonder 等。

① I don't know what to do next. 我不知道下一步该做什么。

② Could you tell me how to ride a bike? 你能告诉我怎么骑自行车吗？

③ He found out where to buy fruit cheaply. 他打听出在哪儿买水果便宜。

动词不定式短语作宾语时，如果还带有宾语补足语，常把动词不定式短语放在宾语补足语之后，而用 it 作形式宾语。

① I find it interesting to study English. 我发现学英语很有趣。

② He feels it difficult to answer the question. 他觉得很难回答这个问题。

动词不定式一般不作介词的宾语（but, except 除外）。如：① He did nothing but play game. ② She did everything expect clean the floor.

但动词不定式之前如有疑问词时，就可作介词的宾语。

Professor Lee gave us some advice on how to learn a foreign language.

4. 作宾语补足语

动词不定式可用作复合宾语中的宾语补足语。常跟不定式作宾补的动词有 advice, allow, ask, beg, cause, compel, convince, command, direct, enable, encourage, expect, feel, force, get, hate, have, hear, help, hire, inspire, intend, invite, instruct, lead, let, listen to, look at, make, notice, observe, order, permit, persuade, press, remind, request, teach, tell, urge, want, watch, warn, wish 等。

① My English teacher advised me to buy a better dictionary. 我的英语老师劝我买一本更好的词典。

② Tell the children not to play in the street. 告诉孩子们不要在街上玩。

5. 作定语

(1) 不定式作主语的定语时,相当于一定语从句,表明动作即将发生。不定式一般式作定语时不定式是主动或被动形式要看与主语的关系,主谓关系用主动,动宾关系用被动。

① The man to come to help us is Mike. 要来帮我们的人是麦克。

② The meeting to be held tomorrow is put off. 明天要开的会推迟了。

(2) 当不定式作其他成分的定语时,当句中可找到不定式动作的执行者时,或听话者和说话者双方不言而喻知道动作执行者时,不定式用主动形式,否则用被动形式。

① He is not a man to tell lies. 他不是一个撒谎的人。

② He is a man to be trusted. 他是一个可以信赖的人。

③ His wife left him a lot of problems to solve. 他的妻子留给他许多要解决的问题。

④ I have a lot of things to deal with. 我有许多事要处理。

比较:

—"Do you have a letter to be typed, manager?"asked the typist. "你有要打的信吗？经理?"打字员问。

—"If you don't have any letter to type, please type it for me."said the manager. "如果你无信可打了,请把这个给我打一下"经理说。

(3) 若不定式为不及物动词,或不定式所修饰的名词或代词是不定式动作的地点、工具等,其后应有必要的介词。

① I have no chair to sit in. 我没有椅子坐。

② Do you have enough money to buy a TV with? 你有足够的钱买电视吗？

但是,不定式所修饰的名词如果是 time, place 或 way,不定式后面的介词习惯上可省去。

① You have only a short time to decide. (on)你们仅有很短的时间选定。

② There is no way to talk. (in)没办法谈。

6. 不定式作状语

动词不定式可用作修饰动词或形容词的状语,一般放在其修饰的动词或形容词之后,主要表示目的、结果和条件等。

1) 作目的状语

① Every morning he gets up very early to exercise. 每天早晨他都起很早锻炼。

② I went to the post office to mail a letter. 我去邮局寄了一封信。

③ To avoid criticism, do nothing, say nothing, be nothing. 为了避免批评,什么都不做,

什么都不说,什么都不是。

为了强调不定式所表示的目的时,可用 in order to(为了)或 so as to(以便)加动词原形。in order to 位于句首或句中均可,而 so as to 不能位于句首。其否定式为 in order not to,so as not to。

① We had better start early so as not to miss the train. 为了不错过火车,我们最好早些动身。

② In order to improve her English, she reads *China Daily* every day. 为了提高英语水平,她每天读《中国日报》。

2) 作结果状语

不定式作结果状语时,往往仅限于 learn, find, see, hear, make 等几个具有终止含义的动词。

① He returned home to learn his son had gone to the countryside. 他回到家就得知儿子已经去了乡下。

② A few years later we came to our home to find that our hometown had greatly changed. 几年后,我们回到家发现我们的家乡发生了很大变化。

不定式也可用 enough 和 too...to 结构来表示结果。

① He is not old enough to go to school. 他还没有到上学的年龄。

② He is too short to reach the top of the shelf. 他太矮了,够不着书架的顶层。

注:(1) 形容词 anxious, delighted, eager, easy, glad, kind, pleased, ready, surprised, willing 等在"too...to"结构中没有否定的含义,而表示肯定。

① He is too ready to find fault. 他老是爱挑毛病。

② She was too surprised to see how angry her father was. 看到父亲那么生气,她非常吃惊。

(2) 在 not, never, only, all, but 等后的"too...to"结构中,"too"的含义为"very",不定式没有否定含义。

① I'm only too pleased to help you. 我非常愿意帮助你。

② It's never too late to learn. 活到老,学到老。

(3) 动词不定式和 only 连用时,常表示未预料到的结果。

① I went to see my friend only to learn he was in hospital. 我去看我的朋友,不料他住院了。

② He went to the station hurriedly only to find the train had left. 他匆匆赶到车站,却发现火车已经离开了。

3) 作条件状语

当不定式表示条件时,句子谓语通常含有助动词,如 will, would, shall, should, must, can, could 等。

① You would be stupid not to ask for a raise. (= you will be stupid if you don't ask for a raise)如果你不要求涨工资,那真是愚蠢。

② I would have been happy to be invited to the party. 如果受到邀请去参加舞会,我会很高兴。

③ I would be happy to go with you. 如果和你一起走,我会很高兴。

7. 用作独立成分

动词不定式可用作独立成分，用来修饰整个句子，说明说话人的态度看法等。常见的有：to begin with, to tell the truth, to make a long story short, so to speak, to be brief/exact/frank/honest, to say nothing of(姑且不说), to say the least（至少可以这么说）。

① To tell the truth, I don't agree with you. 说实话，我不同意你的意见。

② To make a long story short, he is in hospital now. 长话短说，他现在住院了。

11.4.6 动词不定式的复合结构

（1）不定式的逻辑主语常见的是由"for＋名词或代词"引出，这里的名词或代词即为不定式的逻辑主语，来说明不定式动作的执行者或承受者。"for＋名词或代词＋动词不定式"又称为动词不定式复合结构。这种结构在句子中可充当主语、表语、宾语、定语和状语等。

① It is very common for him to be absent without leave. 不请假就擅自离开是他的一贯作风。（作主语）

② It is for you to decide. 这得由你决定。（作表语）

③ He will arrange for a car to take us back. 他将安排一部车送我们回去。（作宾语）

④ There are many books for you to read. 有许多书你们要读。（作定语）

⑤ The teacher spoke slowly for all the studuts to understand. 为了让所有学生理解，老师讲得很慢。（作状语）

（2）用来说明人的性格特征或行为表现的动态形容词与不定式连用时，用"of＋名词或代词"这一结构引出不定式的逻辑主语。这样的形容词主要有：brave, careful, careless, clever, cruel, foolish, generous, kind, modest, nice, polite, rude, selfish, silly, stupid, thoughtful 等。

① It's wise of you not to argue with your boss. 你很明智不和你老板争辩。

② It's generous of him to lend me his car. 他很慷慨地把车借给了我。

for 和 of 的使用规律是：看句子的表语形容词是着重说明人还是事。若是前者，用 of；若是后者，则用 for。且用 of 的句子，可以用人作主语将句子改写；用 for 的句子则不能。

① It is wise of you not to argue with your boss. 你很明智不和你老板争辩。

② You are wise not to argue with your boss.

注：不定式逻辑主语的省略。不定式的逻辑主语并非只有"for＋名词或代词"或是"of＋名词或代词"的形态。当不定式的逻辑主语在句子中可找到或泛指任何人时，即为其省略形式。

逻辑主语和句子的主语一致 I expect to succeed. ＝ I expect that I will succeed. 我期待成功。

逻辑主语和句子的宾语一致 I expect you to succeed. ＝ I expect that you will succeed. 我期待你成功。

逻辑主语为一般人 It is not easy to learn a foreign language. 学一门外语不容易。

巩 固 练 习

一、用括号中动词的适当形式填空(是否省去 to)。

1. The boy was made _____ (sing) the song once again.
2. Don't make children _____ (work) too hard.
3. They would rather _____ (die) than _____ (surrender).
4. He could not choose but _____ (love) her.
5. She could do nothing but _____ (change) her name under the circumstances.
6. He had his son _____ (play) the violin three hours a day.
7. There was nothing to do except _____ (escape).
8. He has no alternative but _____ (go) and ask his sister for help.
9. If he is not willing to be with you, why _____ (not, ask) somebody else?
10. Since he is only a kid, why _____ (make) fun of him?
11. All I did was _____ (give) him a little push.
12. He let _____ (drop) the suggestion that we should meet him in town.
13. You may _____ (take) the horse to the water, but you can't make him _____ (drink).
14. Rather than _____ (marry) that man, she would earn her living as a waitress.
15. Why don't you get your wife _____ (explain) it to you?

用括号中动词的适当形式填空(不定式时态)。

16. He hope to _____ (become) a university student this year.
17. They seem to _____ (make) much progress in their English study.
18. We are happy to _____ (visit) so many historic spots in Beijing.
19. My teacher happened to _____ (correct) my essay when I came in.
20. They are proud to _____ (win) the football match.
21. You look tired. You seem to _____ (work) too hard all day.
22. A: I thought Sam was sick.
    B: So did I. but he seems to _____ (recover) very quickly. He certainly doesn't seem to be sick now.
23. I am glad that my company sent me to another country to study. I am very pleased to _____ (give) the opportunity to learn about another culture.
24. They seemed to _____ (discuss) something important.
25. A: Do you believe that Tom did his best in the exam?
    B: Yes. He is said _____ (work) very hard.

用括号中动词的适当形式填空(不定式语态)。

26. This letter needs to _____ (send) immediately.
27. He asked to _____ (send) to work in Tibet.
28. It is easy to _____ (fool) by his lies.
29. I considered it an honor to _____ (invite) to address the meeting of world-famous scientists.
30. Don't all of us want to _____ (love) and _____ (need) by other people?
31. Jim wants us to tell him the news as soon as we hear anything. He wants to _____ (tell) about it immediately.
32. Give him some books to _____ (read).

33. The house is to _____ (let).
34. The reason is not far to _____ (seek).
35. The magazine is interesting to _____ (read).
36. It is necessary for us to _____ (constantly, remind) of our shortcomings.
37. The report is difficult to _____ (write).
38. Everyone hates to _____ (use).
39. They found the lecture hard to _____ (understand).
40. I have a lot of clothes to _____ (wash).

二、单项选择。

1. I need a piece of paper to _____.
   A. write on   B. write   C. be written   D. write with
2. He is the first _____ and the last _____.
   A. arriving; leaving   B. to arrive; to leave
   C. arrive; leave   D. for arriving; for leaving
3. His refusal _____ surprised us.
   A. of helping   B. with help   C. to help   D. of help
4. It is wise _____ the experiment that way.
   A. of him to do   B. for him to do
   C. of his doing   D. that he do
5. We will have to get the Dean _____ this form.
   A. to sign   B. sign   C. signed   D. signing
6. The teacher had the students _____ the text.
   A. recite   B. recited   C. to recite   D. reciting.
7. Charles Babbage is generally considered _____ the first computer.
   A. to invent   B. inventing
   C. to have invented   D. have invented
8. The patient was warned _____ oily food after the operation.
   A. to eat not   B. eating not   C. not to eat   D. not eat
9. Last summer I took a course on _____.
   A. how to make dresses   B. how dresses be made
   C. how to be made dresses   D. how dresses to be made
10. She pretended _____ me when I passed by.
    A. not to see   B. not seeing
    C. to not see   D. having not seen
11. John was made _____ the truck for a week as a punishment.
    A. wash   B. washing   C. to be washing   D. to wash
12. Little Jim should love _____ to the theatre this evening.
    A. being taken   B. to be taken C. to take   D. taking.
13. As time went on, the theory she had stuck _____ correct.
    A. proved   B. to proving   C. to proved   D. to prove

14. With some flowers dotted about the room it looked more comfortable _____.
    A. to live   B. to live in   C. to be lived   D. to be lived in
15. We found such people difficult _____.
    A. to deal with   B. to be dealt with
    C. to do away with   D. to be got on well
16. Tom kept quiet about the accident _____ lose his job.
    A. so not as to   B. so as not to
    C. so as to not   D. not so as to
17. Mr. Smith warned his daughter _____ after drinking.
    A. never to drive   B. to never drive
    C. never driving   D. never drive
18. The girl wasn't _____ to lift that bookcase.
    A. too strong   B. enough strong
    C. strong enough   D. so strong
19. Do let your mother know the truth. She appears _____ everything.
    A. to tell   B. to be told
    C. to be telling   D. to have been told
20. Would you please tell me _____ next?
    A. how to do   B. what to do   C. what do I do   D. how I should do

第十二章 动名词

12.1 动名词的意义和形式

动名词(the Gerund)是一种非限定动词,它兼有动词和名词的特征。动名词具有动词部分的特征,可以有自身的宾语,也可以用副词加以修饰。动名词加宾语或状语一起构成动名词短语。动名词具有名词的作用。

动名词和现在分词虽然功能不同,但变化形式相同,有的语法学家统称其为-ing 分词。动名词有一般式和完成式,并有主动语态和被动语态。

12.2 动名词形式和语态的变化

动名词形式和语态的变化如下表所列。

	语态 形式	主　动	被　动
动名词	一般式	doing	being done
	完成式	having done	having been done

12.3 动名词的用法

由于动名词具有名词的作用,因此在句中可作主语、表语、宾语和定语等。

12.3.1 作主语

① Fighting broke out between the South and the North. 南方与北方开战了。
② Seeing is believing. 眼见为实。
③ Talking is easier than doing. 说起来容易做起来难。
④ It's no use waiting here. 在这儿等没用。
注:动名词与不定式作主语的用法比较。
(1) 多数情况两者可以互换。
① Seeing is believing. =To see is to believe.
② Talking is easy and doing is difficult. =To talk is easy and to do is difficult.
(2) 如果表示一种具体、短期的行为,或表示将来的行为,宜用不定式;如果表示一般或抽象的多次行为,即经常性、习惯性的行为,一般用动名词。

① It took him two hours to finish the work. 完成这项工作花了他两小时。(短期)

② To be a scientist is his desire. (愿望)当一名科学家是他的愿望。

③ To play with fire will be dangerous. (指一具体动作)玩火会很危险。

④ It is not very good for you to smoke so much. 你抽这么多烟对你身体很不好。(具体)

⑤ Playing with fire is dangerous. (泛指玩火)玩火危险。

⑥ Smoking is prohibited here. 这里禁止抽烟。(抽象)

(3) 在 it is no use (good), not any use (good), useless 等后一般用动名词。

① It is no use arguing with him. 同他争论是没用的。

② It is no good learning English without practice. 学英语不练是不行的。

12.3.2　作宾语

① The young guy still denies having started the fire. 那个年轻人仍然否认自己放的火。

② He has given up smoking. 他已经戒烟了。

③ We often do our cleaning on Saturday afternoon. 我们经常在周六下午打扫卫生。

④ My shoes need mending. 我的鞋子需要修理。

1. 作动词宾语

有些动词后面不用不定式作宾语,而只用动名词作宾语。必须以动名词作宾语的动词有: admit(承认), appreciate(感激), avoid(避免), consider(认为), delay(耽误), deny(否认), detest(讨厌), endure(忍受), enjoy(喜欢), escape(逃避), excuse(原谅), fancy(想象), finish(完成), forbid(严禁), imagine(想象), mind(介意), miss(错过), permit(允许), postpone(推迟), practice(练习), quit(放弃), regret(后悔), resent(讨厌), risk(冒险), stop(停止), suggest(建议)。

请记住以下口诀:memepscarfi(音译成:妹妹不吃咖啡)。这里每个字母代表一个或几个单词:m—miss;e—enjoy;m—mind;e—escape;p—practise;s—suggest / stand; c—consider / complete; a—admit / allow /advise / appreciate / avoid; r—risk; f—finish ; i—imagine,常用的词都列在里面了。

① Would you mind turning down your radio a little, please? 你把收音机音量调小一点,好吗?

② Mike often attempts to escape being fined whenever he breaks traffic regulations. 每次违犯交通规则,迈克总能设法逃脱惩罚。

③ The girl avoided giving him any personal information. 这女孩避免给他任何个人信息。

④ We'd better postpone discussing it till next week. 我们最好把这事推迟到下星期讨论。

注:(1)有些动词跟不定式、动名词作宾语皆可,意义也差不多,主要有 can't bear, cease, dread, hate, like, love, neglect, omit, prefer, propose 等。如表示一般的行为,多用动名词;如表示特定的或具体的动作,则多用不定式。

① I can't bear living alone. 我受不了独居。

② I can't bear to see the child treated stupidly. 我不忍心看这孩子被愚弄。

③ Tom prefers doing it his way. 汤姆喜欢用自己的方式做事。

④ He prefers to go by train this evening. 他今晚愿意坐火车去。

⑤ I don't like watching television. 我不喜欢看电视。

⑥ I'd like to swim today. 我想今天游泳。

(2) 在 begin, start, continue 之后虽然既能跟不定式也能跟动名词,且意义相同,但当 begin, start, continue 已用于进行时态时,或者其后跟的是静态动词时,便只能用不定式。

① We begin to see what he meant. 我们开始明白他的意思了。

② She began to believe his story. 她开始相信他的故事了。

③ It's beginning to rain. 天开始下雨了。

④ I'm starting to work on my essay next week. 下周我要开始写论文了。

(3) 在 need, want, require, deserve 等动词之后,可用动名词的主动形式表示被动意义, 这相当于用不定式的被动态。

① The letter needs signing by the manager. 这封信需要经理签字。

= The letter needs to be signed by the manager.

② That boy deserves looking after. 那男孩应该得到照顾。

= That boy deserves to be looked after.

(4) 有些动词后跟不定式或动名词意义有明显差别,主要有 forget, remember, regret, stop, go on, mean, try。

forget to do sth. 忘记要做某事

forget doing sth. 忘记做过某事＝forget having done sth.

remember to do sth. 记住要做某事

remember doing sth. 记得做过某事

regret to do sth. 遗憾(要)做某事

regret doing sth. 懊悔做了某事

stop to do sth. 停下(原来的事)去做另某事(不定式作目的状语)

stop doing sth. 停止做某事

go on to do sth. 继续做不同的事

go on doing sth. 继续做相同的事

mean to do sth. 决意/打算做某事

mean doing sth. 意味/表明做某事

try to do sth. 努力/设法去做某事

try doing sth. 试图/尝试用某一方法做某事:

① I remember reading the book. 我记得读过这本书。

② I must remember to read the book. 我必须记住去读这本书。

③ The old lady forgot telling us the story and told us a second time. 那个老太太忘记给我们讲过这个故事,她又讲了一遍。

④ Don't forget to take an umbrella when you go out. 出去时别忘带雨伞。

⑤ Though they were all tired, they wouldn't stop working. 虽然他们都很累了,但是他们也不肯停止工作。

⑥ After walking for a long time, he stopped to have a rest. 走了很长时间后,他停下来休息。

⑦ Missing the train means waiting for another hour. 误了这趟火车意味着再等一个小时。

⑧ I mean to come early today. 我打算今天早些来。

2. 绝大部分短语动词后要求跟动名词

其后要求跟动名词的有 be fond of(喜欢)，can't help(禁不住)，can't stand(无法忍受)，feel like(想要)，give up (放弃)，keep on(继续)，insist on(坚持)，put off(推迟)。

① Do you feel like going out for dinner with me tonight? 你今晚想要和我一起出去吃饭吗?

② He gave up smoking on medical advice. 遵从医嘱，他戒烟了。

3. 作介词宾语

① He is against dancing all night. 他反对通宵跳舞。

② The college is a new type of college for training cadres. 这所大学是新型的培养干部的大学。

③ Through traveling, he became very well-informed. 他通过旅游增长了许多见识。

注：下列短语中的"to"是介词，而不是不定式符号，因此后面须接名词或动名词，如 in addition to (除外)，admit to(承认)，devote oneself to(献身于)，be equal to(能胜任)，be familiar to (对……熟悉)，find one's way to (设法达到)，get down to (着手做)，give way to (对……让步)，give one's mind to(专心于)，keep to (坚持)，look up to(尊敬)，lead to (导致)，look forward to (期望)，object to(反对)，be opposed to(反对)，pay attention to(注意)，point to(指向)，be reduced to(沦为)，give rise to(使……发生)，stick to(坚持)，stand up to (勇敢面对)，be sentenced to(被判刑)，see to(注意处理，照顾)，be/get used to (习惯于)，trust to (依靠)，turn to (求助于) 等。

① He is used to working on the night shift. 他已习惯了上夜班。

② We're so much looking forward to seeing you again. 我们非常盼望再见到你。

③ I have no objection to hearing your story again. 我不反对再听一遍你的故事。

12.3.3 作表语

作表语主要是对主语说明、解释。

① My hobby(爱好)is collecting stamps. 我的爱好是集邮。

② The real problem is getting to know the difficulties of the students. 现实的问题是了解学生的困难。

注：(1)动名词和不定式都可以作表语，但略有区别：表示比较抽象的一般行为时，多用动名词；表示某次具体的动作或具有将来时的意义时，多用不定式。

① Her job is washing, cleaning and taking care of the children. 她的工作是洗刷、清扫和照顾孩子。

② Her today's job is to teach you how to study English. 她今天的任务是教你如何学英语。

(2) 动名词和现在分词作表语的区别是：动名词作表语说明主语的内容，而且一般可以转换到句首作主语；现在分词作表语，表示主语的特征，其作用相当于形容词。

① His favorite sport is running. (＝Running is his favorite sport.) 他最喜欢的运动是跑

步。

② The film is very moving. 这部电影很感人。

（3）动名词作表语时不可与进行时态相混淆，进行时态说明动作是由主语完成的。动名词作表语，说明主语的性质或状况。试比较：

① He is collecting stamps. 他在集邮。（现在进行时）

② His hobby is collecting stamps. 他的爱好是集邮。（动名词）

12.3.4　作定语

① The teacher has many reading materials. 老师有很多阅读材料。

② Our teacher uses a very good teaching method. 我们老师的教学方法很好。

注：动名词作定语和现在分词作定语的区别：动名词作定语时，和它所修饰的名词在逻辑上没有主谓关系，即它不是该名词发出的动作，只是表明所修饰名词的"目的"或"用途"。现在分词作定语时则表明所修饰的名词与分词有逻辑上的主谓关系。

① a sleeping car（＝a car for sleeping）卧铺车厢（动名词作定语）

a sleeping boy（＝a boy who is sleeping）睡觉的男孩（现在分词作定语）

② a writing desk 写字台

③ a swimming pool 游泳池

有些动名词作定语，与所修饰的名词关系比较复杂。

① boiling point＝a temperature point at which something begins to boil 沸点

② a walking tractor＝a tractor which a driver can operate while he or she is walking behind it 手扶拖拉机

12.4　动名词的否定结构

动名词的否定结构由 not/no ＋动名词构成。

① No smoking. 禁止吸烟。

② He hated himself for not having worked hard. 他悔恨自己没有用功。

③ I'm sorry for not having telephoned you before. 很抱歉没有早给你打电话。

12.5　动名词的复合结构

形式为名词所有格＋动名词或形容词性物主代词＋动名词，如 Tom's /his coming。

一般情况下，动名词的逻辑主语为谓语动词的主语。如果动名词动作的发出者不是谓语动词的主语时，则需要有自己的逻辑主语。这样名词所有格或形容词性物主代词加动名词就构成了动名词的复合结构。这种结构在句中可作主语、宾语等。

1. 语法功能

（1）作主语。Your smoking too much will do harm to your health. 你抽烟太多会对你的健康有害。（动名词的复合结构在句首作主语时，只能用 sb's 的形式，此句中的 Your 不可改为 You）

(2) 作宾语。I don't like his/him staying with us. 我不喜欢他和我们在一起。

(3) 作表语。My joy is his winning the table tennis game. (his 不能改为 him)使我们高兴的是他赢了这次乒乓球比赛。

2. 动名词复合结构使用的一般规则

(1) 逻辑主语是有生命的名词:作主语时,必须用名词所有格或形容词性物主代词,作宾语时(尤其在口语中),也可用名词普通格或人称代词宾格代替。

① Tom's being late made the teacher angry. 汤姆迟到了,老师很生气。

② Do you mind my/me smoking? 你介意我抽烟吗?

(2) 逻辑主语是无生命的名词时,一般只用名词普通格。

Is there any hope of our team winning the match? 我们队有希望赢这场比赛吗?

(3) 逻辑主语是指示代词或不定代词 this,that,somebody,someone,nobody,none,anybody,anyone 时,只用普通格。

She was woken up by somebody shouting outside. 她被外面喊叫的人吵醒了。

12.6　动名词的形式

1. 动名词的一般式

动名词的一般式所表示的动作为一种时间性不强的或泛指的动作,或表示的动作与谓语动词所表示的动作同时发生,或是在谓语动词表示的动作之后发生。

① We are interested in collecting stamps. 我们对集邮感兴趣。

② His coming will be of great help to us. 他的到来将会给我们很大的帮助。

但在有些明确表示时间的 remember,forget,regret,excuse,apologize 等动词之后和介词 after,on,upon 或 for 之后,常用一般式代替完成式,表示动作发生在谓语动词动作之前。

① I shall never forget seeing the Great Wall for the first time. 我永远不会忘记第一次看到长城的情景。

② On hearing that bad news, she couldn't help crying. 一听到这个糟糕的消息,她就禁不住哭了起来。

③ After finishing his homework, he went out for a walk. 他做完作业后就出去散步了。

④ Thank you for giving us so much help. 感谢你给我们那么大帮助。

2. 动名词的完成式

动名词的完成式所表示的动作发生在谓语动词表示的动作之前。

① He regrets not having taken part in the work. 他很后悔没有参与这项工作。

② We were praised for having finished the work ahead of time. 我们因提前完成了这项工作而受到了表扬。

12.7　动名词的被动式

如果动名词的逻辑主语为动名词所表示动作的承受者,这个动名词就要用被动式。

① She is proud of being admitted into the university. 她为被大学录取而感到自豪。

② The meeting was put off without his having been consulted. 会议延期并未和他商量。

③ He doesn't mind having been criticized. 他不介意过去受到的批评。

动名词的完成被动式往往用一般被动式来代替,以免句子显得累赘。

I still remember being invited(代替 having been invited)by a famous artist when I was in Shanghai. 我仍然记得在上海时被一著名艺术家邀请的事。

巩 固 练 习

1. Just after putting away the dishes, _____.
   A. the doorbell rang loud   B. Nancy heard the door bell ring
   C. someone knocked at the door D. the doorbell was rung
2. Mr. Reed made up his mind to devote all he had to _____ some schools for poor children.
   A. set up   B. setting up   C. have set up   D. having set up
3. While shopping, people sometimes can't help _____ into buying something they don't really need.
   A. to persuade   B. persuading   C. being persuaded   D. be persuaded
4. How about the two of us _____ a walk down the garden?
   A. to take   B. take   C. taking   D. to be taking
5. —I must apologize for _____ ahead of time.
   —That's all right.
   A. letting you not know   B. not letting you know
   C. letting you know not   D. letting not you know
6. She looks forward every spring to _____ the flower—lined garden.
   A. visit   B. paying a visit   C. walk in   D. walking in
7. —You were brave enough to raise objections at the meeting.
   —Well, now I regret _____ that.
   A. to do   B. to be doing
   C. not to have done   D. having done
8. —The old lady has been sad since her husband died.
   —Yes, she needs _____.
   A. being comforted   B. comforting   C. be comforted   D. to comfort
9. It's no use _____ me at the office this week because I'm _____.
   A. to ring, on my leave   B. to ring, at leave
   C. ringing, in holidays   D. ringing, on holiday
10. On hearing the _____ result, all the teachers of Class Six couldn't help _____.
    A. satisfied, to jump   B. satisfactory, to jump
    C. satisfied, jumping   D. satisfactory, jumping
11. The farmer who admitted _____ the tiger was severely punished.
    A. to kill   B. killing   C. killed   D. to have killed
12. I realized we should do something to avoid _____ to death.

A. freezing   B. to freeze   C. to be frozen   D. being frozen

13. She used to _____ a girl who is used to _____ jokes.

    A. be, make   B. be, making   C. being, making   D. being, tell

14. A man can never accomplish if he always puts off _____ a decision.

    A. to make   B. making   C. in making   D. till making

15. They couldn't stand _____ by the host at the party.

    A. to be neglected   B. being neglected
    C. neglected   D. that they were neglected

16. They dare not tell the truth, for they are afraid _____.

    A. to be laughed   B. of laughing at
    C. of being laughed at   D. being laughed at

17. —What made his mother angry?
    —_____.

    A. Because he had lost the ticket   B. Because of his having lost the ticket
    C. As he had lost the ticket   D. Having lost the ticket

18. Did you have difficulty _____ the professor's house in the dark?

    A. to find   B. finding
    C. by finding   D. to have found

19. Trying without success is better than _____ at all.

    A. not to try   B. to not try   C. not trying   D. trying not

20. _____ the work in that way would cost much more time and money.

    A. If doing   B. Do   C. To be doing   D. Doing

21. We are looking forward to _____ you at our party, but we wouldn't mind _____ soon if you have to.

    A. have, you to leave   B. having, your leaving
    C. have, your leaving   D. having, your being left

22. We don't allow _____ in the school.

    A. smoking   B. to smoke   C. they smoking   D. anyone smoked

23. He was busy _____ his lessons.

    A. prepare   B. to prepare   C. preparing   D. prepared

24. Tired of the cold weather in New England, Mr. And Mrs. Smith are considering _____ to the south.

    A. to move   B. moving   C. move   D. to be moving

25. The _____ video games all day made his mother very angry.

    A. child's playing   B. child playing   C. child's play   D. child play

26. If you miss _____ for a couple of hours, no harm _____ to you.

    A. sleeping, will do   B. to sleep, will be done
    C. to sleep, will do   D. sleeping, will be done

27. How much time does he spend _____ piano every day?

    A. practicing playing   B. to practise playing the

C. practicing playing the   D. to practise playing
28. He suggested _____ to Beijing by plane and _____ without a word.
 A. going, left   B. to go, to leave   C. going, leaving   D. go, left
29. The discovery of new evidence led to _____.
 A. the thief having caught   B. catch the thief
 C. the thief being caught   D. the thief to be caught
30. At that time she was so angry that she felt like _____ something at him.
 A. to throw   B. throwing   C. to have thrown   D. having thrown

第十三章 分 词

13.1 分词的概念

分词是一种非限定动词,它具有动词的特征,同时具有形容词和副词的作用。分词可有宾语(仅限于现在分词)或状语,分词加宾语或状语一起构成分词短语。分词分为现在分词和过去分词两种,过去分词只有一种形式,现在分词则有:一般主动式 doing,一般被动式 being done,完成主动式 having done,完成被动式 having been done。

13.2 分词的语法功能

分词在句中作定语、表语、宾补、状语。

13.3 现在分词和过去分词的区别

1. 语态不同
现在分词表示主动概念,多用以描述事物对人的情感所具有的影响力或作用。及物动词的过去分词表示被动概念,多用以描述人物的情感,表达外界事物对人所产生的影响。
the moving film 动人的电影
the moved girl 受感动的姑娘
a running machine 一台转动的机器
a stolen car 一辆被盗的汽车
也有一些过去分词是由不及物动词变来的,它们只表示一个动作已经完成,没有被动的意味。
fallen leaves 落叶
the risen sun 升起了的太阳
escaped prisoners 逃犯
returned students 归国留学生
2. 时间关系上不同
现在分词常表正在进行的动作,过去分词往往表已经完成的动作。
a developing country 发展中国家
a developed country 发达国家
boiling water 正在开的水
boiled water 开水

13.4 分词的用法

13.4.1 分词作表语

1. 现在分词作表语

分词相当于形容词,可以被看作一个形容词,是形容词化的分词。

现在分词作表语,一般表示主动或主语的性质和特征,"令人……的",主语多数情况是物。

① The match is **exciting**. 比赛是令人兴奋的。

② That book was rather **boring**. 那本书相当乏味。

2. 过去分词作表语

过去分词作表语,表示主语的状态,且该状态通常是由外界因素引起的。一般表示被动或说明主语情感心理上的感受,"感到……的",主语多数是人。

① We were so **bored** that we couldn't help yawning. 我们厌烦得要命,禁不住打起了呵欠。

② They were very **pleased** with the girl. 他们很喜欢这姑娘。

注:(1)分词作表语时相当于形容词,不可与构成进行时态和被动语态中的分词混淆起来。它们形式一样,但可以从意义上予以区别。

现在分词作表语表示主语的性质与特征,进行时表示正在进行的动作。

① The film is **moving**. 这电影很动人。(表语,说明主语的性质)

② They are **moving** next Monday. 他们下周日搬家。(现在进行时,表示动作)

③ With the help of the teacher, the students **are practising** the idioms. (现在进行时) 在老师的帮助下学生们正练习成语。

过去分词作表语表示主语所处的被动状态或完成某动作的状态,而被动语态表示主语所承受的动作。

① The bookstore is now **closed**. 书店现在已经关门了。(表语,说明主语所处的状态)

② The bookstore is usually **closed** at 8:00 p.m. (被动语态,表示动作)书店经常晚上八点关门。

③ He is well **educated**. (过去分词作表语)他很有教养。

④ He has been **educated** in this college for three years. (被动语态)他接受过三年大学教育。

(2)表示心理状态的动词,即含有使动意,使人产生某种情感、心理变化的动词(如 surprise 使惊讶;interest 使感兴趣),它们的-ing 形式含主动意义,-ed 形式含被动意义。这些-ing 形式及-ed 形式也称为形容词化了的分词,皆可视为形容词,如 surprising 令人惊讶的,interesting 令人感兴趣的,surprised(因……)感到惊讶的,interested(因……)感到兴趣的。类似的心理状态的动词还有 astonish 使厌烦, delight, disappoint, discourage, encourage, excite, frighten, interest, move 使感动, please 使高兴, puzzle 使迷惑, satisfy 使满意, surprise, shock, tire 使疲劳, trouble, upset 使不安, worry。

下面的句子可显示两者的区别:

The film is so interesting that they are all interested in it. 这部电影很有趣,他们都很感兴趣。

She was much surprised at the surprising news. 她听到这个令人吃惊的消息很吃惊。

它们的-ing 形式多和物连用。

The news is pleasing/exciting. 这消息很令人满意/令人激动。

a boring report 一个令人厌烦的报告；a tiring walk 累人的步行。

它们的-ed 形式多和人连用,如 an excited girl(一个激动的女孩)；I'm tired(我累了).

另外,过去分词除修饰人以外,还可修饰表示神态、声音等的名词,说明主语的心理状态。

① He had a terrified look in his eyes. 他眼里流露出害怕的神情。
② The boy answered in a frightened voice. 这男孩用害怕的声音回答。
③ He looked at me with a puzzled expression. 他用一种迷惑不解的表情看着我。
④ She said in a frightened voice. 她用受了惊吓的声音说着话。

也有现在分词和人连用,如 an inspiring leader 一位有感召力的领袖,an amusing girl 一个讨人喜欢的女孩。

13.4.2 分词作定语

(1) 单个分词作定语一般放在其修饰的名词之前。

① That must have been a **terrifying** experience. 那准是一段可怕的经历。
② I found him a **charming** person. 我发现他是一个讨人喜欢的人。
③ **Polluted air** and water are harmful to people's health. 受到污染的空气和水有害于人们的健康。
④ She has a **pleased** look on her face. 她脸上现出高兴的神情。
⑤ The teacher gave us a **satisfied** smile. 老师向我们满意地笑了。

(2) 分词短语作定语时通常放在其修饰的名词之后。

① There are a few boys **swimming in the river**. (=who are swimming in the river)河里有几个游泳的男孩。
② There is a car **waiting outside**. (=that is waiting)一辆车正在外面等着。
③ What's the language **spoken in that country**? (=which is spoken in that country)那个国家讲什么语言?
④ The play **put on by the teachers** was a big success. (=which is put on by the teachers) 老师们表演的戏很成功。

注:(1)动名词与现在分词作定语的区别为,动名词作定语说明所修饰名词的用途;现在分词作定语,表示所修饰名词进行的动作。

a **walking** stick 拐杖(动名词,a stick for walking)
a **sleeping** car 卧铺车厢(动名词,a car for sleeping)
the **rising** sun 正在升起的太阳(现在分词)
the **changing** world 变化中的世界(现在分词)

(2) 现在分词与过去分词作定语的区别:现在分词作定语表示主动或进行的动作。现在分词的一般被动式表示一个正在发生的被动动作,过去分词作定语表示完成或被动的动作或没有时间性的状态。

① Do you see the hospital **being built** there? 你看见那边那个正在建造的医院了吗?

② Do you see the hospital **built** there? 你看见那边那个建好的医院了吗?

③ The continent **connected with Asia** at the Suez Canal is Africa. 在苏伊士运河处与亚洲相连的洲是非洲。(句中 connected 无时间性)

④ a piece of **disappointing** news (＝a piece of news which disappointed us) 一条令人失望的消息

⑤ in the **following** years (＝in the years that followed) 在以后的岁月

⑥ a well **dressed** woman (＝a woman who is dressed well) 穿着讲究的女子

⑦ a car **parked** at the gate (＝a car which was parked at the gate) 停在门口的车

13.4.3 分词作宾补

常跟分词作宾补的动词有：see(看见), hear(听见), find(发现), keep(使处于某状态), have(使,让), get(使得), make(使), feel(感觉到), leave(使处于某状态), want(想要), start(引起), notice(注意到), observe(观察), watch(注视), set(使处于某状态)等。用现在分词还是用过去分词做宾补，要看分词与宾语的关系，主谓关系用现在分词，动宾关系用过去分词。

① We heard him **singing** the song when we came in. 我们进来时听见他在唱歌。

② We have heard the song **sung** in Japanese. 我们听过用日语唱的这首歌。

③ How would you like your hair **cut**? 你喜欢把头发剪成什么式样?

④ Don't have the students studying all day. 不要让学生们整天学习。

⑤ When they get back home, they found the room **robbed.** 当他们回到家,他们发现房间被洗劫一空。

在 have 或 get 后面的复合宾语中,宾语补足语大多是过去分词,不用现在分词被动式或不定式被动式作宾补,且表示的动作往往是由别人完成的。

① I will have the clothes **washed** tomorrow. (别人洗的)明天我要把衣服让人洗了。

② I had my hair **cut.** (别人给我理的)我理发了。

③ I must get the television set **repaired.** 我必须让人修理一下电视机。

④ I'll have my hair **cut.** (cut 不能改为 being cut 或 be cut)我要理发了。

⑤ He got his watch **repaired.** (repaired 不能改为 being repaired 或 to be repaired)他让人把手表修了修。

但 have 的复合宾语的过去分词的动作有时不一定由别人来完成,而是表明自己的经历。

He had his arm **broken.** 他把手臂折断了。(不是别人弄折的,而是自己弄折的)

在 make, order, want, like, wish 等动词后,多用过去分词作宾补,少用现在分词被动式作宾补。

① The speaker couldn't make himself **heard.** (一般不说 being heard)讲演者无法让人听到他的声音。

② He wanted his house **painted.** (一般不说 being painted) 他想漆一下房子。

注：(1) 现在分词构成的复合宾语与不定式构成的复合宾语在意义上是有区别的。前者表示动作正在发生；后者着重说明动作的全过程,表示动作发生了(即动作全过程结束了)。

① I saw the girl getting on the bus. 我看见她在上公共汽车。

② I saw the girl get on the bus. 我看见她上公共汽车了。

(2) 如果宾语补足语是一系列动作,要用不定式。

I saw him **enter** the room, **unlock** a drawer, **take out** a document, photograph it and put it back. 我看他走进房间,打开抽屉,拿出一个文件,拍照后又放了回去。

13.4.4 分词作状语

一般来说,分词短语的位置为:时间、原因、条件、让步等分词短语多放在句首;而表结果、伴随的分词短语放在句尾。

现在分词作状语时,现在分词的动作就是主语的动作,它们之间的关系是主动关系;过去分词作状语时,及物动词的过去分词表示的动作是句子主语承受的动作,它们之间的关系是被动关系,分词作状语时可表示时间、原因、方式或伴随状况等。

时间状语相当于一个时间状语从句,有时为了突出时间,可在分词前加 when 或 while。

① Walking in the street, I saw him. (＝when I was walking in the street). 当我在街上走时,我看到他了。

② You must be careful **when crossing the road**. (＝when you cross the road)过马路时一定要小心。

③ **Seen from the hill**, the city looks magnificent. (＝when it is seen from the hill) 从山上看,这座城市非常壮观。

④ **When treated with kindness**, he was very amiable. (＝when he was treated with kindness) 当别人善待他时,他是非常和蔼可亲的。

分词短语还可以表示原因,相当于一个原因状语从句。

① **Not knowing her address**, we couldn't get in touch with her.

(＝Because we didn't know her address)因为我们不知道她的地址,没法和她联系。

② Being ill, she stayed at home.

(＝because she was ill)因为失业他没有很多钱。

③ **Encouraged by his heroic deeds**, they worked harder.

(＝Because they were encouraged by his heroic deeds)因为受到他的英雄事迹的鼓舞,他们工作更努力了。

注:方式状语、伴随状语及结果状语(意料中的结果),没有相当的状语从句可以代替。

① Tom stood at the school gate **waiting for Mary.** (伴随状况或方式)汤姆站在学校门口等玛丽。

② They came in, **followed by some children.** (伴随)他们走了进来,一些孩子跟随在后。

③ He came running all the way. (方式)她跑回来告诉我们这个消息。

④ The hunters fired, **shooting one of the wolves.** (结果)猎人们开枪射击,击中其中一只狼。

⑤ The bus was held up by the snowstorm, thus **causing the delay.** (结果)汽车被暴雪所阻,因此导致延误。

条件状语前面可带 if, unless 等从属连词,相当于条件状语从句。

① **If working hard**, you will succeed. (＝if you work hard)只要努力你就会成功。

② **If given another chance**, I would have done the job far better.
＝If I had been given another chance, I would have done the job far better. 如果再给我一次机会,我会把工作做得更好。

13.5　分词的否定结构

分词的否定式由"**not＋分词**"构成。
Not knowing where to go, she wanted to ask the police for help. 因为不知道去哪里,她想向警察求助。
过去分词表否定时,常借助 un- 等前缀来表示。
The boy was left uncared for. 那孩子无人照管。

13.6　现在分词的形式

(1) 现在分词的一般式表示的动作与谓语动词表示的动作同时发生,或在谓语动词表示的动作之后发生。
① She sat there **reading the text**. 她坐在那里读课文。
② **Going into the room**, he shut the door. 一走进房间他就关上了门。
(2) 现在分词的完成式表示的动作发生在谓语动词表示的动作之前,通常只作状语,表示时间或原因。
① **Having finished her homework**, she went to bed. 她写完作业后就上床睡觉了。
② **Having found the cause**, they continued the experiment. 他们找到原因后继续实验。
③ **Having lived in Beijing for many years**, she knew the city well. 因为在北京住了许多年,她对这个城市很了解。
注:现在分词完成式不能作定语修饰名词。
The builders **having completed the hotel** were given prizes. (误)
改为 The builders **completed the hotel** were given prizes. (正)完成了旅馆建设的建设者们得到了奖励。

13.7　现在分词的被动语态

(1) 一般式表示一个被动动作正在进行,或与谓语动词表示的动作同时进行,在句中作定语或状语。
① The building **being built** is our library. 那座正在施工的大楼是我们的图书馆。
② The question **being discussed** is of great importance. 正在讨论的问题是非常重要的。
(2) 完成式表示一个被动动作在谓语动词表示的动作之前已经完成了,在句中多作状语,不能作定语。
① **Having been warned by the teacher**, they didn't make such mistakes. 老师警告他们之

后,他们不再出这样的错误了。

② **Having been told many times**, he still did not know how to do it. (人家)已经告诉他多少次了,他还是不知道怎么做。

13.8　独立主格结构

分词短语作状语,其逻辑主语必须是主句的主语,如果分词的逻辑主语并不是主句的主语,而另有其逻辑主语,则应在分词前补上其逻辑主语,构成独立主格结构,简称独立结构。

独立主格结构在句中常作状语,用来表示条件、原因、伴随状况等,相当于一个状语从句,且多用于书面语中,口语中较为罕见。尤其用于文学体裁,独立结构能使句子结构紧凑,用词精炼,描写生动,形象具体,是文学语言常用的修辞手法。

① **The bell ringing**, we all stopped talking. (=When the bell rang, we all stopped talking.) 铃声一响,我们大家都停止了说话。

② **There being no bus**, we had to walk home. (=There was no bus, so we had to walk home.) 因为没有公共汽车,我们不得不走回家。

③ **His homework done**, Jim decided to go and see the play. (=After his homework done, Jim...) 吉姆做完功课后,决定去看那个剧的演出。

④ **Weather permitting**, we'll have an outing tomorrow. (=If weather permits) 如果天气允许,我们明天就去旅行。

⑤ **Winter coming**, it gets colder and colder. (=when winter comes) 冬天来临时,天气变得越来越冷。

还有一种用"with+名词或代词宾格+分词(或形容词、介词词组)"表示伴随状况的独立结构。

① He fell asleep **with the lamp burning**. 他开着灯睡着了。

② He sleeps **with the windows open** even in winter. 甚至在冬天他也是开着窗户睡。

③ She entered the train station, **with a bag in her hand**. 她手里提着一个包走进了火车站。

注:(1) 独立主格结构中的 being, having been 有时可以省去。

① The meeting (being) **over**, we all left the room. 开完会我们都离开了这个房间。

② Our work (having been) **finished**, we went home. 完成了工作之后我们就回家了。

(2) 有的分词已转换为介词或者已成了习惯用语,在句中没有逻辑上的主语。

① **According to** our records, he has been in prison six times. 根据我们的记录,他曾入狱六次。

② The band played many songs, **including** some of my favorites. 乐队演奏了许多歌曲,包括几首我最喜爱的。

③ **Considering** he's only just started, he knows quite a lot about it. 考虑到他只是刚刚开始,他对此的了解已经不少了。

④ Generally **speaking**, it's quite a fair settlement. 总起来说,这样解决很恰当。

13.9 使用现在分词应注意的问题

(1) 作状语用的现在分词,其逻辑主语必须同句中主语为同一人或同一事。

① **Standing** on top of the tall building, **we** could see the whole city. (正) (Standing = When we stood)站在这座高楼的楼顶,我们能看到整个城市。

Standing on top of the tall building, the whole city could be seen. (误)

② **Having found the cause**, **they** continued the experiment. (正) (Having found = After/When they had found)他们找到原因后继续实验。

Having found the cause, the experiment continued. (误)

(2) 短暂动词(即瞬间动词)的现在分词被动式不可作宾补或定语。

① He saw the old man **knocked down** by the car. 他看到那老人被这汽车撞倒了。

(knocked down 不可改为 being knocked down 或 having been knocked down)

② Do you like the dictionary **bought** by Zhang Ming? 你喜欢张明买的那本词典吗？

(bought 不可改为 being bought 或 having been bought)

(3) 作原因状语,现在分词被动式与过去分词可以互换。

Being led(=Led)by the Party, the Chinese people have won great victories. 在党的领导下,中国人民取得了伟大的胜利。

(4) 作方式或伴随状语,不用现在分词被动式,而用过去分词。

The soldiers lay on the ground, **covered with nothing**. 士兵们什么都没盖,躺在地上。

(5) 作时间状语,若动作先于句子的谓语动作,且有具体过去时间,不可用现在分词一般被动式或完成被动式。例如:**Built** in 1192, **the** bridge was very useful. 在1192年建的这座桥很有用。

如果没有具体过去时间状语,可用过去分词或现在分词完成被动式。例如:**Discussed**(=Having been discussed)many times, the problem was settled at last. 经过几次讨论后,这个问题最终得到了解决。

如果要强调分词状语的动作发生的时间在谓语动作之前,则宜用现在分词完成被动式,而不用过去分词。例如:**Not having been invited**, she had to stay at home. 因为没有受到邀请,她不得不待在家里。

13.10 非谓语动词考点分析

1. The Olympic Games, _____ in 776 B.C. didn't include women players until 1919.

  A. first playing   B. to be first played

  C. first played   D. to be first playing

 析:根据题干,必须选表示被动的选项,故排除 A、D;因 B 选项表示"将要被举行的"意断,不合题干之用,只有 C 选项(相当于 which was first played)才合用。

2. European football is played in 80 countries, _____ it the most popular sport in the world.

| A. making | B. makes | C. made | D. to make |

析：B、C是谓语动词，在此不可用；D项to make或表示目的，或表示"将要使得"，这都不合题干情景；只有A. making，可作状语，表结果。又如：The bus was held up by the snowstorm, causing the delay. 公共汽车被大风雪所阻，因而耽误了。

3. Little Jim should love _____ to the theatre this evening.

   A. to be taken　　B. to take　　C. being taken　　D. taking

   析：根据this evening，应选表示将来意的选项，C、D应排除。take后无宾语，必然要用被动式，故答案为A。

4. John was made _____ the truck for a week as a punishment.

   A. to wash　　B. washing　　C. wash　　D. to be washing

   析：根据be made to do sth.句式，可确定答案为A。

5. The patient was warned _____ oily food after the operation.

   A. to eat not　　B. eating not　　C. not to eat　　D. not eating

   析：根据warn sb. (not) to do sth.句式，可排除B、D两项；又根据非谓语动词的否定式not总是在首位的规律，又可排除A，而确定C。

6. —I usually go there by train.

   —Why not _____ by boat for a change?

   A. to try going　　B. trying to go　　C. to try and go　　D. try going

   析：此题可根据why not后直接跟原形动词规律而一举确定正确答案为D。若将B项改为try to go，则要根据其与try going意义之别来确定答案。依据题干对话内容，乙方是建议甲方尝试乘船变变花样，所以答案仍为D。

7. _____ a reply, he decided to write again. (NMET)

   A. Not receiving　　　　　　B. Receiving not
   C. Not having received　　　D. Having not received

   析：非谓语动词的否定式not应置于首位，B、D皆为错误形式。A项不能表达先于decided的动作，只有选C项才表示没收到信在先，决定再写信在后，所以C为正确答案。

8. Charles Babbage is generally considered _____ the first computer.

   A. to invent　　B. inventing　　C. to have invented　　D. having invented

   析：consider表"考虑"意时，其后动词用doing形式，此处不表示"考虑"，而表示"认为"，这时consider后作宾语补足语或主语补足语多为to do, to have done, to be等形式。据此可排除B、D两个选项。又因A表示"要发明"意，不合题用，只有C表示"发明了"之意，才合题用，故选C。

9. Most of the artists _____ to the party were from South Africa.

   A. invited　　B. to invite　　C. being invited　　D. had been invited

   析："被邀请参加晚会"，应选表被动意的选项，B不可用。D项少引导词who，也应排除。又因短暂动词的现在分词被动式不可作定语，C也应排除，只有A. invited (=who were invited)才是正确答案。

10. The murderer was brought in, with his hands _____ behind his back.

    A. being tied　　B. having tied　　C. to be tied　　D. tied

    析：B表主动意思，应排除。C表"将要被捆绑"，A表"正在被捆绑"都不合题意，只有D项填入空白才能表达"双手被反绑着"这一意思，符合题干情景。再看一类似例句：

He came in,(with)his head held high. 他昂首走了进来。

巩 固 练 习

1. At the shopping center, he didn't know what _____ and _____ with an empty bag.
   A. to buy; leave   B. to be bought; left
   C. to buy; left   D. was to buy; leave
2. The long and tiring talk, filled with arguments and quarrels, ended in disorder, _____ no agreement at all.
   A. arriving   B. arrived at   C. reaching   D. and getting to
3. Do you know the difficulty he had _____ five children at school?
   A. to keep   B. to have kept   C. keeping   D. having kept
4. —Let me tell you something about my Chinese teacher.
   — I remember _____ about her yesterday.
   A. telling   B. being told   C. to tell   D. having told
5. Having no money but _____ to know, he simply said he would go without dinner.
   A. not to want anyone   B. wanted no one
   C. not wanting anyone   D. to want no one
6. The old lady needed _____ as she was in her 80s.
   A. to look after   B. looking after   C. look after   D. being looked after
7. —Why are you always making me drink milk?
   — _____ enough calcium for you to grow tall and strong.
   A. Get   B. To get   C. Getting   D. To be getting
8. Many students _____ around, I explained the story into details.
   A. stood   B. standing   C. to stand   D. were standing
9. He has few friends and never mind _____ alone, playing by himself.
   A. leaving   B. having   C. to be left   D. being left
10. I explained the theory as clearly as possible, _____ to make it easy _____.
    A. hope; to understand   B. hoped; understood
    C. hoping; to understand   D. to hope; to be understood
11. The students listened carefully, with their eyes _____ the blackboard.
    A. fixing at   B. fixed at   C. fixing on   D. fixed on
12. _____ to go with the others made him rather disappointed.
    A. His not allowed   B. His not being allowed
    C. Not his allowing   D. Having not been allowed
13. I was very poor when young and had no toys _____.
    A. to play   B. to play with   C. with playing   D. playing with
14. He went to bed _____. The next morning he woke up only _____ himself lying on the floor.

A. drinking; to find B. drunk; to find
C. being drunk; finding D. to drink; finding

15. We can hardly imagine Peter _____ such rude words to you.
    A. say   B. to say   C. saying   D. to have said
16. I'd like my child _____ in a school of high quality.
    A. educating   B. to educate
    C. to be educated   D. being educated
17. My son pretended _____ when I came back.
    A. to sleep   B. sleeping   C. being sleeping   D. to be sleeping
18. Tom is thought _____ the good deed to the blind man.
    A. of doing   B. to do   C. to have done   D. of being done
19. The stranger has spent a whole week _____ in his room. No one knows what he is doing.
    A. locking   B. to lock   C. locked   D. being locked
20. The music of the film _____ by him sounds so _____.
    A. playing, exciting   B. played, excited
    C. playing, excited   D. played, exciting
21. _____ against the coming hurricane, they dared not leave home.
    A. Warned   B. Having warned   C. To warn   D. Warn
22. In _____ countries, you can't always make yourself _____ by speaking English.
    A. English-speaking, understand   B. English-spoken, understand
    C. English-speaking, understood   D. English-speaking, understood
23. After _____ the old man, the doctor suggested that he _____ a bad cold.
    A. examining, should catch   B. examined, had caught
    C. examining, had caught   D. examined, catch
24. _____, Tom jumped into the river and had a good time in it.
    A. Be a good swimmer   B. Being a good swimmer
    C. Having been a good swimmer   D. To be a good swimmer
25. _____ how to read the new words, I often look them up in the dictionary.
    A. Having not known   B. Not to know
    C. Don't know   D. Not knowing

非谓语动词专练

1. _____ more attention, the trees could have grown better.
   A. To give   B. Having given   C. Given   D. Giving
2. The first textbooks _____ for teaching English as a foreign language came out in the 16th century.
   A. to be written   B. written   C. being written   D. having written
3. The missing boys were last seen _____ near the river.

    A. to play   B. play   C. to be playing   D. playing

4. _____ in thought, he almost ran into the car in front of him.
    A. To lose   B. Lost   C. Having lost   D. Losing

5. When passing me he pretended _____ me.
    A. to see   B. not having seen
    C. to have not seen   D. not to have seen

6. The children insisted _____ there on foot.
    A. they going   B. they would go   C. on their going   D. going

7. He still remembers _____ to Shanghai when he was very young.
    A. taking   B. being taken   C. taken   D. having taken

8. _____ the railway station, we had a break, only _____ the train had left.
    A. Arriving at; to find   B. Coming to; discovering that
    C. On arriving at; finding out   D. Hurrying to; to have found out

9. With the boy _____ the way, we had no trouble _____ the way _____ to Zhongshan Park.
    A. leading; finding; leading   B. to lead; found; to lead
    C. led; finding; led   D. leading; found; led

10. _____ these pictures, I couldn't help thinking of those days when I was in Being and _____ from the top of a thirty-storeyed building, Bei jing looks more beautiful.
     A. Seeing; seen   B. Seen; seeing
     C. Seeing; seeing   D. Seen; seen

11. I can hardly imagine Peter _____ across the Atlantic Ocean in five days.
     A. to have sailed   B. to sail   C. sailing   D. sail

12. If you wave your book in front of your face, you can feel the air _____ against your face. (MET)
     A. moved   B. moving   C. moves   D. to move

13. _____ is known to all, China will be an _____ and powerful country in 20 or 30 years time.
     A. That; advancing B. This; advanced C. As; advanced   D. It; advancing

14. While shopping, people sometimes can't help _____ into buying something they don't really need.
     A. persuade   B. persuading
     C. being persuaded   D. be persuaded

15. There was terrible noise _____ the sudden burst of light.
     A. followed   B. following
     C. to be followed   D. being followed

16. Please excuse my _____ in without _____.
     A. come; permitted   B. coming; permitted
     C. coming; being permitted   D. to come; being permitted

17. _____ his head high, the manager walked into the room to attend the meeting _____

then.
   A. Holding; being held   B. Held; holding
   C. Having held; held   D. Held; to be held
18. —Did you hear her _____ this pop song this time the other day?
    —Yes, and I heard this song _____ in English.
    A. sing; singing   B. sung; sung
    C. sung; singing   D. singing; sung
19. The question _____ now at the meeting is not the question _____ yesterday.
    A. discussed; discussed   B. discussing; had discussed
    C. being discussed; discussed   D. discussing; discussing
20. With the cooking _____, I went on _____ some sewing.
    A. done; to do   B. being done; doing
    C. to be done; doing   D. to have done; doing
21. It is no use _____ your past mistakes.
    A. regretting   B. regret   C. to regret   D. regretted
22. Her husband died in 1980 and had nothing _____ to her, only _____ her five children.
    A. left; to leave   B. leaving; leaving   C. leaving; left   D. left; leaving
23. I am very busy. I have a very difficult problem _____.
    A. to work   B. to work out
    C. to be worked out   D. to work it out
24. I would appreciate _____ back this afternoon.
    A. you to call   B. you call   C. your calling   D. you're calling
25. Climbing mountains was _____, so we all felt _____.
    A. tiring; tired   B. tired; tiring   C. tiring; tiring   D. tired; tired
26. I saw some villagers _____ on the bench at the end of the room.
    A. seating   B. seat   C. seated   D. seated themselves
27. She was glad to see her child well _____ care of.
    A. take   B. to be taken   C. taken   D. taking
28. It is one of the important problems _____ tomorrow.
    A. to solve   B. to be solved   C. solved   D. solving
29. _____ maps properly, you need a special pen.
    A. Drawn   B. Drawing   C. To draw   D. Be drawing
30. There is a river _____ around our school.
    A. to run   B. run   C. running   D. to be running
31. How about the two of us _____ a walk down the garden?
    A. to take   B. take   C. taking   D. to be taken
32. I was fortunate to pick up a wallet _____ on the ground on the way back home, but unfortunately for me, I found my color TV set _____ when I got home.
    A. lying; stolen   B. laying; stealing   C. lay; stolen   D. lying; stealing
33. With the kind-hearted boy _____ me with my work, I'm sure I'll be able to spare time

_____ with your work.
   A. to help; help you out
   B. helping; helping you
   C. helped; to help you out
   D. to help; to help you

34. Greatly moved by her words, _____.
   A. tears came to his eyes
   B. he could hardly hold back his tears
   C. tears could hardly be held back
   D. his eyes were filled with tears.

35. —I hope the children won't touch the dog.
   —I've warned them _____.
   A. not   B. not to   C. not touch   D. not do

36. I would love _____ to the party last night but I had to work extra hours to finish a report.
   A. to go   B. to have gone   C. going   D. having gone

37. When _____ why he walked in without permission, he just stared at us and said nothing.
   A. been asked   B. asked   C. asking   D. to be asked

38. The man kept silent in the room unless _____.
   A. spoken to   B. spoke to   C. spoken   D. to speak

39. He was often listened _____ in the next room.
   A. sing   B. sung   C. to sing   D. to singing

40. Rather than _____ on a crowded bus, he always prefers _____ a bicycle.
   A. ride; ride   B. riding; ride   C. ride; to ride   D. to ride; riding

41. The boy wanted to ride his bicycle in the street, but his mother told him _____.
   A. not to   B. not to do   C. not do it   D. do not to

42. What's troubling them is _____ enough experienced workers.
   A. that they have to
   B. they have not
   C. their not having
   D. not their having

43. _____ his telephone number, she had some difficulty getting in touch with Bill.
   A. Not knowing
   B. Knowing not
   C. Not having known
   D. Having not know

44. Bamboo is used _____ houses in some places.
   A. to build   B. to building   C. to be built   D. being built

45. Go on _____ the other exercise after you have finished this one.
   A. to do   B. doing   C. with   D. to be doing

46. The day we looked forward to _____.
   A. come   B. coming   C. has come   D. have come

47. Whom would you rather _____ the work?
   A. to have to do   B. to have do   C. have to do   D. have do

48. Do you think it any good _____ with him again
   A. to talk   B. talking   C. to talking   D. having talked

49. Sometimes new ideas have to be tested many times before _____.

A. accepting fully	B. being fully accepted
C. fully accepting	D. fully being accepted

50. The government forbids _____ such bad books.

A. published	B. to publish	C. publish	D. publishing

第十四章 形容词和副词

14.1 形容词

14.1.1 形容词的定义和分类

形容词是用来描写或修饰名词或代词,说明人或事物的归属性质、状态、大小或数量的词。按照不同的分类标准,形容词可以分为以下几类。

1. 按构成形式分类

按构成形式可以分为简单形容词和复合形容词。

1) 简单形容词

简单形容词是指由一个词素构成的形容词。简单形容词又可以分为以下几类:

(1) 由不带词缀的单一单词构成。

bright 明亮的 fresh 新鲜的 good 好的 young 年轻的

(2) 由带有词缀的单一单词构成(词缀分为前缀,后缀或者是前后缀)。

impatient 不耐烦的 unimportant 不重要的 suitable 合适的

(3) 由现在分词构成的单一形容词。

interesting 有趣的 charming 有魅力的 exciting 令人激动的 fascinating 吸引人的

(4) 由过去分词构成的单一形容词。

amazed 感到惊讶的 bored 感到厌倦的 conceited 自负的 satisfied 满意的

2) 复合形容词

复合形容词是指由两个或者是两个以上的词构成的形容词,复合形容词可以分为下面几类:

(1) 名词+形容词。

home-sick 想家的 world-famous 世界有名的 fat-free 低脂的 duty-free 免税的

(2) 名词+现在分词。

labor-saving 省工的 mouth-watering 令人垂涎的 peace-loving 热爱和平的

(3) 名词+过去分词。

weather-beaten 饱经风霜的 heart-felt 由衷的 man-made 人工的

(4) 形容词+现在分词。

good-looking 好看的 easy-going 随和的 high-sounding 夸张的

(5) 形容词+名词。

large-scale 大规模的 first-class 头等的,上等的 low-cost 低成本的

(6) 形容词+名词+-ed。

red-haired 红头发的 good-tempered 好脾气的 warm-hearted 热心的

(7) 形容词+形容词。

bitter-sweet 苦乐参半的   icy-cold 冰冷的   red-hot 炙热的

（8）副词＋现在分词。

fast-moving 快速移动的   far-seeing 目光远大的   hard-working 努力工作的

（9）副词＋过去分词。

well-informed 消息灵通的   wide-spread 大面积的   out-spoken 直言的

（10）数词＋名词＋ed。

one-legged 独脚的   three-headed 三个头的   five-sided 五个边的   two-storied 两层楼的

（11）由短语构成的形容词。

down-to-earth 实际的，不加渲染的   hard-to-please 难以取悦的

2. 根据与所修饰的名词的关系分类

根据与所修饰的名词的关系，形容词可分为限制性形容词和描述性形容词。

1）限制性形容词

所谓限制性的形容词是指描述事物本质的形容词，它与名词紧紧相连，这些形容词如果去掉会严重影响名词的意义，如 a French table 一张法国造桌子，a Catholic church 天主教教堂。

2）描述性形容词

描述性形容词又称非限制性形容词，置于名词之前，常对名词进行描述，省略之后也不会影响所修饰名词的本义。

a smooth French table 一张平滑的法国造桌子（smooth 是非限制性形容词）

an impressive Catholic church 一座令人难忘的天主教教堂（impressive 是非限制性形容词）

3. 按照语法功能来分类

按照语法功能可以分为定语形容词和表语形容词

（1）大多数形容词既作表语又作定语。

① It is a beautiful city. 这是一座美丽的城市。

② The city is beautiful. 这座城市美丽。

（2）有些形容词总是作表语而不作定语，这就是表语形容词。

① Birds are alike in many ways. 鸟在许多方面相似。

② Scientists found these birds alike in many ways. 科学家发现这些鸟在许多方面相似。我们不说：The alike birds. ...。

许多表语形容词以 a-开头，如 ablaze 着火的，afire 燃烧的，aglow 发红的，afraid 害怕的，alike 相像的，alive 活着的，alone 孤单的，ashamed 惭愧的，asleep 睡着的，astir 活动的，averse 反对的，awake 醒着的，aware 意识到的，awash 被波浪冲打的，awry 歪的等。其他的表语形容词有：content 满足的，glad 高兴的，ill 生病的，likely 可能的，ready 准备好的，sorry 遗憾的，sure 肯定的，unable 无能的，unlikely 不可能的，well 健康的等。

（3）另一些形容词又只作定语，不作表语，如 atomic energy 原子能，而不说 The energy is atomic.

常见的定语形容词还有：countless, cubic, digital, east, eastern, eventual, existing, federal, indoor, institutional, introductory, investigative, lone, maximum, nationwide, neighbouring, north, northern, occasional, outdoor, phonetic, remedial, reproductive, south, southern, supplementary, underlying, west, western, woollen 等。

（4）形容词作表语或定语还与词义有关，如 ill 作"生病的"讲，一般作表语。我们说 The man was ill. 我们不说 the ill man。ill 作"有害的、坏的"讲又只作定语。我们说 The war had many ill consequences. 战争造成了很多恶劣后果；我们不说 The war consequence was ill. 又如"His wife was late."是"他的妻子迟到了。"而 his late wife 则是"他的已故妻子"。

14.1.2　形容词在句中的作用

形容词可以在句子中担当下列的成分：

1. 作定语

① Shanghai is a big industrial city. 上海是一座大工业城市。

② We lived in a beautiful village. 我们住在一座美丽的村子里。

2. 作表语

① We could see that he was very handsome. 我们可以看出他非常英俊。

② Don't feel bad. Everything will be all right. 不要难过，一切都会好的。

3. 作补语

（1）宾语补语（构成复合宾语）。

① We found him asleep on the sofa. 我们发现他在双人沙发上睡着了。

② Who left the door open? 谁让大门敞开着？

（2）主语补语。

He was born poor. 他出身贫寒。

4. 作状语

① They came over, eager to help. 他们跑了过来，急于帮忙。

② Afraid of the hardships, they stopped half-way. 由于害怕困难，他们中途停了下来。

5. 作同位语或独立成分

① He read all kinds of books, ancient and modern, Chinese and foreign. 他看了各式各样的书，古今中外都有。（作同位语）

② Strange to say, he did pass the exam after all. 说也奇怪，他考试竟然及格了。（作独立成分）

注意：有个别形容词通常作表语，作定语时常有特别意思。

① She is fond of children. 她喜欢孩子。

② I have very fond memories of my time in Spain. 对我在西班牙的岁月，我有亲切的回忆。

14.1.3　形容词的位置

一般情况下，单个形容词修饰名词时放在名词之前，这也是形容词最常见的用法。

① He is a **handsome** boy. 他是一个英俊的男孩。

② Mary is my **best** friend. 玛莉是我最好的朋友。

在下列情况下，形容词应放在被修饰词的后面。

（1）修饰 something, anything, everything, nothing 等不定代词时。

① Is there anything **important**? 有什么重要的事吗?

② I have nothing **new** to tell you. 我没有什么新鲜事要告诉你。

(2) 形容词短语作定语时。

① The old fisherman drew in an old basket **full of sand**. 老渔夫拖上来一只旧篮子,篮子里面全是沙子。

② Antarctica is a continent very **difficult to reach**. 南极洲是一块很难到达的大陆。

(3) 用 and 或 or 连接的两个形容词通常放在被修饰名词的后面,形容词前面和后面的成分一般用逗号与形容词隔开。

① People in that area, **young and old**, were very friendly. 在那个地区的人们,无论老幼,都非常友好。

② Every country, **big or small**, must be respected in the international affairs. 无论大国还是小国,在国际事务中都应该得到尊重。

(4) 带前缀 a- 的形容词通常作表语用,但这些形容词作定语时,需要后置。常见的这类形容词有 afraid, alive, along, alike, ashamed, asleep, ablaze, awake 等。

Who is the greatest poet **alive**? 谁是当今世界上最伟大的诗人?

多个形容词修饰名词时,其先后顺序如下:限定词(this, these...) ＋ 数词(two, three...) ＋描述性形容词(beautiful, great...) ＋大小(big, small) ＋长短(long, short) ＋高低(tall, short) ＋形状(round, square) ＋新旧(new, old) ＋颜色(red, blue...) ＋国家(Chinese, American...) ＋材料(silk, stone...) ＋用途(hunting, writing...) ＋名词,即描＋大＋新＋颜＋国＋材＋用＋名词。如:

① We have visited **two old Chinese stone** bridges. 我们参观了两个古老的中国石桥。

② Can you see that **beautiful new white French sports** car? 你能看到那辆漂亮的崭新白色法国跑车吗?

14.1.4 名词化的形容词

在英语中,一些形容词与定冠词 the 连用,在句子中起到名词的作用,这种现象叫做名词化的形容词。其主要用法有以下几种:

(1) 形容词与定冠词 the 连用表示一种抽象的概念,作主语时,谓语多用单数形式。

The new is going to replace the old. 新事物将取代旧事物。

(2) 形容词的比较级和最高级与 the 连用,起到名词的作用,作主语时,谓语动词多用单数形式。

① The older of the two men is my uncle. 那两个人中年龄较大的是我的叔叔。

② Tom is in trouble, but the worst is that he has nothing. 汤姆身陷逆境,但最糟糕的是他一无所有。

(3) 表示人的特征、状态或条件的形容词与 the 连用,表示一类人,作主语时,谓语动词可用复数形式也可用单数形式,视情况而定。

① The young should respect the old. 年轻人应该尊敬老人。

② There are two strangers in the office, the old is Mr Li, the young is Mr Li's son. 办公室里有两个陌生人,年纪大的是李先生,年轻的是李先生的儿子。

(4) 少数表示国籍的形容词与 the 连用,相当于名词,作主语,指整体时,谓语动词用复数,指个体时,谓语动词用单数。

① The Chinese are very friendly. 中国人是非常友好的。
② There are two men looking for you, the Chinese is Wang Laowu. 有两个人找你，其中那个中国人叫王老五。

14.2 副　词

14.2.1 副词的定义和分类

副词是一种用来修饰动词、形容词、副词或全句的词，说明时间、地点、程度、方式等概念。

1. 按构成分类

1) 简单副词

just 刚刚；well 好；back 在后；near 在附近；very 很；enough 足够

2) 复合副词

somehow 不知怎么地，nowhere 无处，therefore 因此，somewhat 有点。有的常用于书面，如 whereupon 因此，hereby 特此，herewith 顺此，whereto 向那里。

3) 派生副词

派生副词，是指在某些词后加上副词后缀而派生出的副词。

(1) 许多副词由形容词和分词后加后缀-ly 而成。

odd→oddly 奇怪的→奇怪地，interesting→interestingly 有趣的→有趣地。

具体的变法如下：

① 以辅音+y 读作/i/结尾的形容词变为副词时，须将 y 变为 i，再加-ly，如 easily，happily 等。② 以-ll 结尾的形容词变为副词时，只加-y，如 chilly，fully 等。③ 以辅音+le 结尾的形容词变为副词时须省去 le，再加-ly，如 ably，idly，singly，simply（supplely 例外），subtly 等。④ 以-ue 结尾的形容词变为副词时，须省去-e，再加-ly，如 truly，duly 等。⑤ 以-ic 结尾的形容词变为副词时，须加-ally，如 heroically，domestically，tragically 等。（但 public 的副词形式须作 publicly）。⑥ 此外，shy 和 sly 的副词形式常作 shyly 和 slyly，gay 和 dry 则有两种副词形式，分别为 gaily，gayly 和 drily，dryly。

注：有些形容词一般并没有派生副词形式，如 difficult，big，future，以及以 a-起首的 awake，alive，asleep 等。除由形容词和分词派生的副词外，还有从其他词语变来的副词，如 weekly（名词+ly），firstly（数词+ly），mostly（不定代词+ly），overly（介词+ly）等。

(2) 副词除常用的后缀-ly 外，还有一些其他后缀。

-wise：clockwise 顺时针方向地

-ward(s)：northward(s) 向北方

-fashion：schoolboy-fashion 学生式

-ways：sideways 斜着

-style：cowboy-style 牛仔型

(3) 有些副词带有前缀 a-，如 abroad 在国外，ahead 在前面，around 在周围，aloud 大声，alike 相像、同样，alone 独自。

2. 按意义分类

(1) 时间和频度副词，如 now, then, often, always, usually, early, todaylately, next, last,

already, generally, frequently, seldom, ever, never, yet, soon, too, immediately, hardly, finally, shortly, before, ago, sometimes, yesterday。

(2) 地点副词, 如 here, there, everywhere, anywhere, in, out, inside, outside, above, below, down, back, forward, home, upstairs, downstairs, across, along, round, around, near, off, past, up, away, on。

(3) 方式副词, 如 carefully, properly, anxiously, suddenly, normally, fast, well, calmly, politely, proudly, softly, warmly。

(4) 程度副词(放在被修饰词之前), 如 much, little, very, rather, so, too, still, quite, perfectly, enough, extremely, entirely, almost, slightly。

(5) 疑问副词(一般放在句首), 如 how, when, where, why。

(6) 关系副词(一般放在句首), 如 when, where, why。(引导定语从句)

(7) 连接副词, 如 how, when, where, why, whether。(引导名词性从句)

14.2.2 副词在句子中的作用

1. 作状语

副词在句子中主要作状语, 可以修饰动词、形容词、副词, 有时修饰整个句子。

1) 修饰动词

I can hardly agree with you. (hardly 修饰 agree)

2) 修饰形容词

Her pronunciation is very good. (very 修饰 good)

3) 修饰副词

He works quite hard. (quite 修饰 hard)

4) 修饰整个句子

(1) Unfortunately, he wasn't at home when I came. 不幸的是, 当我回去的时候他不在家。(unfortunately 修饰整个句子)

(2) Luckily, she wasn't injured in the accident. 幸运的是, 她在这场事故中没有受伤。(luckily 修饰整个句子)

2. 作表语

(1) Is he in? 他在家吗?

(2) Time is over. 时间到了。

(3) The light is on. 灯亮着。

(4) He is back. 他回来了。

3. 作定语

(1) People there are very friendly. 那里的人们很友好。(there 作定语修饰 people)

(2) China today is very strong. 今日之中国非常强大。(today 作定语修饰 China)

14.2.3 副词的位置

副词的位置比较灵活, 可以在句首、句中或句尾, 不同类型的副词会有不同的位置, 而同一个副词也会有不同的位置。

1. 时间副词

时间副词(now,then,recently,soon, just now,right away 等)可以放在整个句子或从句之前或之后,并通常放在句末。其中 then,recently 可以放在动词之前;still 常放在动词之前或系动词、助动词、情态动词之后;而 yet 常放于句末,并且句子常用否定形式。

① I'll **then** turn to my classmates for help. 那么我去找我的同学帮忙。(then 在动词 turn 之前)

② When all the students finished the morning exercise,he was **still** asleep. 当所有的学生都做完早操的时候,他还在睡觉。(still 放在系动词 was 后面)

③ We haven't finished the work **yet**. 我们还没有完成这项工作。(yet 在句尾,并且常用于否定形式)

2. 地点副词

地点副词(here,there,down,anywhere,everywhere,inside 等)常放在及物动词宾语之后,或不及物动词之后。其中 here,there,up,down 等副词与不及物动词 go,come,stand,walk,lie 等词连用时,副词可置于句首。如句子主语是名词或名词短语时,句子需用完全倒装语序。

① We looked for the lost wallet **here and there**,but in vain. (副词 here and there 放在动词宾语 wallet 之后)

② **There** stands the tower. 那座塔矗立在那里。(句子主语是名词 the tower,副词 there 放在句首并且句子完全倒装)

③ **Down** came the rain. (与上面的例子用法相同)

3. 程度副词

程度副词(very,quite,almost,fairly, nearly,just,extremely,hardly 等)常放在被修饰词之前,但当 very 修饰动词时,常与 much 连用并置于句末。

① I like her **very much.** 我非常喜欢她。

② With one false movement,he **nearly** loses the whole game. 一步走错,他差点输掉整个比赛。(nearly 放在 lose 前面)

4. 频度副词

频度副词(ever,never,often,always, seldom,sometimes 等)常放在所修饰的动词之前,但如果句子里有系动词、助动词或情态动词,频度副词通常放在第一个这类动词之后,其中 sometimes 也常置于句首。

(1) I have **never** been to America. 我从没去过美国。(never 在助动词 have 之后)

(2) **Sometimes** he phones me,and sometimes he writes to me. 他有时给我打电话,有时给我写信。(sometimes 常在句首)

5. 副词 only

副词 only 的位置比较灵活,可以修饰名词、代词、动词、形容词、副词等,但不同的位置会引起某些语义变化,句子可能有几种含义,这就得靠上下文的意思来正确理解。

① It was **only** an coincidence. 这仅仅是巧合。(only 用来强调 coincidence)

② They **only** have coffee in the morning. 他们早上只喝咖啡。(only 用来强调 coffee)

③ They have coffee **only** in the morning. 他们只在早上喝咖啡。(only 强调 morning)

④ **Only** they have coffee in the morning. 只有他们在早上喝咖啡。(only 强调 they)

6. 副词 enough

enough 作副词位于它所修饰的形容词或副词之后。

① He is clever **enough** to answer this question. 他够聪明了，能回答这个问题。(enough 在形容词 clever 后面)

② Tom didn't look at the picture carefully **enough**. 汤姆没有足够认真来看这幅画。(enough 在副词 carefully 之后)

注：(1)当程度副词与频度副词同时在句子中出现时，程度副词通常前置修饰频度副词。

① He hardly ever leaves his house all the day. 他几乎一天都没出门。(hardly 在 ever 前面)

② The president of our university is nearly always occupied. 我们的大学校长几乎总是很忙。(nearly 在 always 前面)

(2)当时间、地点、程度与方式副词同时在句子中出现时，常把程度副词放在最前面，方式副词放在地点副词之前，时间副词放在最后。但是，句中动词是动态动词（go，come，leave，arrive等）时，则常把地点副词放在方式副词之前。

① They performed pretty well in the city hall last night. 他们昨晚在市政厅表演得很精彩。

② She went home quickly. 她很快回家了。

(3)用作定语的副词(here，there，back，ahead，abroad，below，above，yesterday，before等)通常放在被修饰名词之后。

① We will see a beautiful picture about the country in the years ahead. 在未来我们会看到这个国家的美丽画卷。(ahead 在它修饰的名词 years 之后)

② The atmosphere here is seriously polluted. 这里的空气被严重地污染了。(here 在 atmosphere之后)

14.3 形容词和副词的比较级和最高级

英语里形容词和副词有三个比较等级，即原级（Positive Degree）、比较级（Comparative Degree）和最高级（Superlative Degree）。

14.3.1 原级的构成和用法

(1) 构成：形容词、副词的原级形式是形容词、副词的原形。

(2) 用法：表示双方在程度、性质、特征等某方面相等时，用"as＋原级形容词或副词＋as"的结构；表示双方不相等时，用"not so（as）＋原级形容词或副词＋as"的结构；表示一方是另一方的若干倍时，用"倍数＋as＋原级形容词或副词＋as"的结构。

① This building looks not so (as) high as that one. 这座楼看起来没有那座高。

② Ms. Sun speaks English as fluently as you. 孙女士英语和你说得一样流利。

③ This room is three times as large as that one. 这个房间是那个房间的三倍。

14.3.2 比较级与最高级的构成和用法

1. 比较级与最高级的构成

(1) 单音节形容词以及少数以- er,- ow 结尾的形容词和副词后面加"er"，"est"。如：

great　greater　greatest　narrow　narrower　narrowest

fast　　faster　　fastest　　clever　　cleverer　　cleverest

(2) 以 e 结尾的单音节形容词和副词后以及少数以-ble,-ple 结尾的双音节形容词和副词后,加"r","st"。如:

large　　　larger　　　largest
able　　　abler　　　ablest
simple　　　simpler　　　simplest

(3) 以一个辅音结尾的单音节形容词,其前的元音字母发短元音时,该辅音字母要双写,然后加"er","est"。如:

hot　　　hotter　　　hottest

(4) 以辅音加 y 结尾的形容词和少数不是形容词加 ly 构成的副词要将 y 改为 i,再加"er","est"。如:

easy　　　easier　　　easiest
early　　　earlier　　　earliest
happy　　　happier　　　happiest

(5) 一般双音节、多音节形容词和副词在原级前加 more 或 most。如:

beautiful　　more beautiful　　most beautiful
carefully　　more carefully　　most carefully

(6) 少数单音节形容词也加 more 和 most 构成比较级和最高级。如:

tired　　more tired　　most tired　　pleased　　more pleased　　most pleased

(7) 下列形容词、副词的比较级和最高级有两种构成方法:

cruel	crueler	cruelest
	more cruel	most cruel
often	oftener	oftenest
	more often	most often
strict	stricter	strictest
	more strict	most strict
friendly	friendlier	friendliest
	more friendly	most friendly

(8) 下列形容词、副词的比较级和最高级的构成不规则。

good, well	better	best
bad, badly, ill	worse	worst
many, much	more	most
little	less	least
far	farther	farthest
	further	furthest
old	elder	eldest
	older	oldest

2. 比较级的用法

(1) 双方比较,表示一方超过另一方时,用"比较级＋than"的结构表示。

This pen is better than that one. 这支笔比那支好。

(2) 表示一方不及另一方时,用"less+原级+than"的结构表示。

This room is less beautiful than that one. 这个房间没那个房间漂亮。

(3) 表示一方超过另一方的程度或数量时,可在比较级前加表示程度的状语,如 even, a lot, a bit, a little, still, much, far, yet, by far 等修饰。He is much fatter than his father.

(4) 表示一方随另一方的程度而变化时,用"the +比较级(主语+谓语),the+比较级(主语+谓语)"的结构。

The harder he works, the happier he feels. 他工作越努力越感到幸福。

(5) 不与其他事物相比,表示本身程度的改变时,用"比较级+ and +比较级"的结构。

① The weather is getting colder and colder. 天气变得越来越冷。

② The girl becomes more and more beautiful. 这姑娘越长越漂亮。

(6) 某些以 or 结尾的形容词进行比较时,常用 to 代替 than。这些词有 inferior, superior, junior, senior, prior 等。

He is superior to Mr. Wang in mathematics. 在数学方面,他比王老师更胜一筹。

(7) 在比较从句中为了避免重复,我们通常用 that(those), one(ones)代替前面出现的名词。that 指物,one 既可指人,也可指物。that 可代替可数名词单数和不可数名词,而 one 只能代替可数名词。

① The book on the table is more interesting than that on the desk. (that 指 the book)桌子上的这本书比课桌上那本更有趣。

② A box made of iron is stronger than one made of wood. (one 指 a box)铁制的盒子比木制的更结实。

③ The soup you made tasts better than that I did. (that 指 the soup)你做的汤比我做的味道更好。

(8) 表示倍数的比较级有如下几种句型:

① A is three(four, etc.) times the size(height, length, width, etc.) of B. 如:

The new building is four times the size(the height) of the old one. 这座新楼是那座旧楼的四倍大(四倍高)。或:这座新楼比那座旧楼大三倍(高三倍)。

② A is three(four, etc.) times as big(high, long, wide, etc.) as B. 如:

Asia is four times as large as Europe. 亚洲是欧洲的四倍大。(亚洲比欧洲大三倍。)

③ A is three(four, etc.) times bigger(higher, longer, wider, etc.) than B. 如:

Your school is three times bigger than ours. 你们的学校比我们的学校大三倍。(你们的学校是我们学校的四倍大。)

用 times 表示倍数,一般只限于表示包括基数在内三倍或三倍以上的数,表示两倍可以用 twice 或 double。

3. 最高级的用法

(1) 三者或三者以上相比,表示最高程度时,用"the+最高级"的结构表示。这种句式一般常有表示比较范围的介词短语。

Zhang Hua is the tallest of the three. 张华是他们三个中最高的。

(2) 最高级可被序数词以及 much, by far, nearly, almost, by no means, not quite, not really, nothing like 等词语所修饰。

This hat is by far/much/nearly/almost/not nearly/by no means/not quite/nothing like the biggest. 这项帽子是最大的。

How much did the second most expensive hat cost? 第二个最贵的帽子花了多少钱?

（3）表示"最高程度"的形容词，如 excellent, extreme, perfect 等,这些词没有最高级，也不能用比较级。

（4）形容词最高级修饰作表语或介词宾语的名词、代词时，被修饰的词往往省略。

He is the tallest(boy) in his class. 他是他班里最高的（男生）。

（5）作状语的副词最高级前可以不加定冠词。

Of all the boys he came(the) earliest. 在所有男孩中他来得最早。

注：(1) 英语的比较级前如无 even, still, 或 yet 等时，译成汉语时可用"较"或"……一些"或不译出，一般不可用"更"。

She is better than she was yesterday. 她比昨天好些了。

Please come earlier tomorrow. 请明天早点来。

（2）by far 通常用于强调最高级。用于比较级时，一般放在比较级的后面，如在前面，应在二者中间加" the"。

He is taller by far than his brother. 他比他弟弟高很多。

He is by far the taller of the two brothers. 他比他弟弟高很多。

巩 固 练 习

一、改错题。

1. Well, how could I afford so an expensive car?
2. The dish is delicious, at least it's not worse than the one we had yesterday.
3. The Olympic Games in Greece were the biggest lively sports events in the world.
4. We are glad to see our motherland getting more and more developing.
5. After two days he arrived at last, tired and hungrily.
6. She said that her son worked happy there every day.
7. The bus stop is two miles far from here.
8. This is a most beautiful park. I have never seen a best one before.
9. The scientists presented today are mostly from Asia.
10. The best time to go to Australia is latest autumn.

二、单项选择。

1. — How can I get to New York in three hours?
   — You can't get there _____ by air.
   A. more than   B. other than   C. rather than   D. less than

2. I didn't even speak to him, _____ discuss your problems with him.
   A. much more   B. less   C. more   D. much less

3. — Is Mr. White out of danger?
   — No, _____ than before, I'm afraid.
   A. no better   B. a little better   C. not worse   D. no worse

4. Mary's biology is _____ than _____ in the class.

A. a lot of better; anyone else's   B. far better; anyone else's
   C. much better; anyone else   D. a lot better; anyone else
5. — The disease he suffers is not easy to cure.
   — I know, but is he _____ better?
   A. much   B. rather   C. any   D. little
6. You can speak _____ in front of him, but you can't eat _____ in his restaurant.
   A. freely; freely   B. free; freely   C. freely; free   D. free; free
7. Tom will not be at the picnic, _____ to the family's disappointment.
   A. much   B. more   C. too much   D. much more
8. — I have seen so little of Mike _____. Is he away on business?
   — Oh, no. He just leaves for his office early and comes back very _____.
   A. later; lately   B. later; later   C. lately; late   D. late; lately
9. From his _____ voice on the phone I know everything is well under way.
   A. satisfactory   B. satisfying   C. satisfied   D. satisfaction
10. — He is _____ a brave man.
    — We can't admire his courage _____.
    A. actually; very much   B. indeed; too a lot
    C. really; too much   D. truly; a bit
11. — Why did she spend so much time searching shop after shop only for a blouse?
    — Oh, she was very _____ about her clothes.
    A. pleased   B. particular   C. worried   D. curious
12. I might fail, but _____ I insist on doing it. I don't mind.
    A. however   B. anyhow   C. yet   D. meanwhile
13. — Could you tell Lucy about the meeting when you see her?
    — Sure, I will _____ I see her.
    A. certainly   B. fortunately   C. probably   D. immediately
14. His voice was quite ordinary, and not _____ angry.
    A. a little   B. very much   C. a bit   D. plenty of
15. Oh, boy, why are you killing your time this way? Can't you find something else _____ doing at all?
    A. useful   B. valuable   C. worth   D. good
16. — Hi, I hear you're going to World Park this weekend.
    — _____, I was going to, but I have changed my plans.
    A. Usually   B. Finally   C. Actually   D. Normally
17. — Mum, we've got to be _____ and buy only what we need.
    — Oh, I'm glad to hear that.
    A. practical   B. content   C. familiar   D. actual
18. Mr. Smith was _____ with the boys who had picked flowers in his garden without his permission.
    A. strict   B. gentle   C. delighted   D. cross

19. — If you're free tonight, I'd like to invite you to a football match.
    — That's nice of you, but are you _____?
    A. rich   B. careful   C. serious   D. true
20. Attention please, everybody! Please keep _____ for a moment. And let me take a photo.
    A. calm   B. still   C. silent   D. quiet
21. Fred is second to none in maths in our class, but believe it or not, he _____ passed the last exam.
    A. easily   B. hardly   C. actually   D. successfully
22. — How is your sister now?
    — She is not very _____ after her illness.
    A. strong   B. tough   C. powerful   D. healthy
23. It's true that the old road is less direct and a bit longer. We won't take the new one, _____, because we don't feel as safe on it.
    A. somehow   B. though   C. therefore   D. otherwise
24. _____, more than 200 houses and buildings are heated by solar energy, not to mention the big cities.
    A. Alone in the small town   B. In the small alone town
    C. In the alone small town   D. In the small town alone
25. That night I felt especially tired and went to bed _____ earlier than usual.
    A. quite   B. rather   C. fairly   D. so
26. — She seems a _____ waitress.
    — Yes, each of us always feels _____ with her good manners and service.
    A. pleased; pleased   B. pleasant; pleasant
    C. pleased; pleasant   D. pleasant; pleased
27. Sending short messages by mobile phones has become a _____ way to send festival greetings in recent years in China.
    A. welcome   B. popular   C. general   D. simple
28. While tidying the room, Jim found the _____ toy bought for him as a birthday present.
    A. fine plastic small   B. plastic fine small
    C. small fine plastic   D. fine small plastic
29. — The young man is good at a lot of things but you can't say he is _____.
    — I agree with you. Actually no one is.
    A. wonderful   B. splendid   C. perfect   D. complete
30. The number of people present at the concert was _____ than expected. There were many tickets left.
    A. much smaller B. much more   C. much larger   D. many more

第十五章 连 词

15.1 连词的定义和分类

连词(Conjunction)是连接单词、短语或句子的一种虚词,在句中不单独作句子成分,一般不重读。

连词按其构成可分为以下几类:

(1) 简单连词(Simple Conjunction),如 and,or,but,if,because 等。

(2) 关联连词(Corelative Conjunction),如 both...and..., not only...but also... 等。

(3) 分词连词(Participal Conjunction),如 supposing,considering,provided 等。

(4) 短语连词(Phrasal Conjunction),如 as if,as long as,in order that 等。

连词按其性质又可分为两类:

(1) 并列连词(Coordinative Conjunction),这种连词是用以连接并列的单词、短语、从句或分句的,如 and, or, but, for 等。

(2) 从属连词(Subordinative Conjunction),这种连词是用以引导名词性从句和状语从句的。前者如 that, whether 等,后者如 when, although, because 等。

15.2 并 列 连 词

并列连词主要有 and、but、or、so、nor、yet,以及 not only...but (also)...、both...and...、neither...nor...、either...or... 几对关联并列连词。此外还有几个近似并列连词,介乎并列连词与从属连词或复杂介词之间的语法结构。这样的词有 as well as、as much as、rather than、more than、for 等。并列连词是构成英语并列句的桥梁,英语中两个或两个以上的互不依从的对等句子通常都是通过并列连词来连接的。并列连词的用法主要有:

1. 表示增补关系

这类并列连词通常是 and,both...and...,not...nor...,so,not only...but (also)...,neither...nor...,as well as... 等。

(1) and 可用来连接两个或两个以上的单词、短语或句子,表示一种顺接的关系。

① My deskmate and I have the same hobby. 我和同桌有共同的爱好。

② We are studying and they are talking. 我们在学习,他们在说话。

(2) so 表示肯定的增补,而 neither、nor 表示否定的增补,三者常位于句首,要求主谓倒装。

① Tom likes painting. So does Mike. 汤姆喜欢画画,迈克也是。

② I can't sing, neither can John. 我不会唱歌,约翰也不会。

(3) both...and... 可用来连接两个并列的主语、谓语、宾语、表语和状语等。当连接两个并列的主语时谓语动词通常用复数形式。

① Both Lucy and Lily are studying hard. 露西和莉莉都在努力学习。

② I can both sing and dance. 我既会唱歌也会跳舞。

(4) not only...but (also)...,neither...nor...这两个并列连词和 both...and...的共同特征是都连接两个相同的句法单位,如主语、谓语、宾语、表语和状语等。其不同之处主要是它们连接两个并列主语时谓语动词用就近原则。

① Not only the teacher but also the students give the money to our school. 不仅那位老师为我们学校捐了款,而且学生也捐了款。

② Neither I nor he is right. 我不对,他也不对。

(5) 注意 not only...but (also)...强调的是后者,而 as well as...强调的是前者。当 as well as...引导并列主语时,谓语动词与前面的主语保持一致。如:

He as well as his students gets up at six o'clock. 不仅他的学生们而且他也是六点钟起床。

2. 表示选择关系

这类并列连词通常是 or,either...or...等。

(1) 这两个连词主要表示一种选择关系,注意的是 either...or...通常引导两个相同的句法单位,当连接两个并列主语时谓语动词用就近原则。

① He is either at home or at school. 他或者在家或者在学校。

② Either I or he is wrong. 不是我错就是他错。

(2) or 有时表示"否则",前面的祈使句通常表示条件,后面的简单句表示结果。

Hurry up or you will be late. 快点,否则你会晚的。

3. 表示一种转折、因果、对比或并列的关系

这类并列连词主要有 but,yet,for,so,while,whereas 等。

① I have a pen but no pencil. 我有钢笔,但没有铅笔。(but 表示转折)

② He is good at math for he studies harder than others. 他擅长数学,因为他学习比别人努力。(for 表示原因)

③ He is ill so he can't go to school today. 他病了,所以今天不能去上学。(so 表示结果)

④ My parents want to live in town, whereas I myself would rather live in the country. 我的父母想住在城市,而我却宁愿住在乡下。(whereas 表示对比)

⑤ I am fat, while my elder sister is slender. 我很胖,但我的姐姐却很苗条。(while 表示对比)

注:(1) not only...but (also),neither...nor,either...or 都可以位于两个分句句首构成并列句,而 both...and 却不能这样来使用。

① Not only is he good at painting, but all his students are beginning to like it. 不仅他擅长画画,他所有的学生也开始喜欢了。

② Neither has he gone to school, nor will he do so. 他既没有去学校,也不想去。

③ Either you ask for my help, or you do it by yourself. 你或者是让我来帮你,或是自己来做这件事。

(2) neither 或 either 出现在主要动词之前,随后的 nor 或 or 既可以带主要动词,也可以不带。

① He neither likes dancing nor (likes) singing. 他既不喜欢跳舞,也不喜欢唱歌。

② She has either gone to the movies or (gone) to the theatre. 她不是去了电影院,就是去了剧院。

(3) neither 或 either 经常引导的是述谓成分,而 nor 或 or 却能引导整个分句。

① He neither likes dancing nor does he like singing. 他既不喜欢跳舞也不喜欢唱歌。

② She has either gone to the movies or she has gone to the theatre. 她不是去了电影院,就是去了剧院。

而 both... and... 和 not only... but (also) 通常没有这样的用法。下面的句子是错误的:

① He both likes this book and that one.

② He not only likes dancing but (also) singing.

③ He both likes dancing and singing.

15.3 从 属 连 词

从属连词主要用来把从属分句和主句连接起来,它用来引导状语从句和名词性从句。不同的从属连词用来连接不同的从句。

15.3.1 引导状语从句的连词

1. 引导时间状语从句的从属连词

(1) 表示"当……时候"或"每当"的时间连词,主要有 when, while, as, whenever 等。

① I was eating when the teacher came in. 老师进来时,我正吃着。

② We listened while the teacher read. 老师朗读时我们听着。

③ The doorbell rang just as I was sleeping. 我刚睡,门铃响了。

(2) 表示"在……之前(或之后)"的时间连词。主要有 before, after 等。如:

① Turn the lights off before you leave. 离开前请关灯。

② He found a job after graduation. 毕业后他找到了一份工作。

(3) 表示"自从"或"直到"的时间连词,主要有 since, until, till。

① He has lived here since he got married. 他结婚后就一直住在这儿。

② The mother didn't leave until the child fell asleep. 孩子睡着了母亲才离开。

(4) 表示"一……就"的时间连词,主要有 as soon as, the moment, the minute, the second, the instant, immediately, directly, instantly, once, no sooner... than, hardly... when 等。

① Tell him to see me immediately you see him. 你一见到他就告诉他来见我。

② I recognized her the moment (that) I saw her. 我一看到她就认出她来了。

③ It rained the minute I left home. 我一出门就下雨了。

④ I went home directly I had finished work. 我一干完活就回家了。

⑤ Once he arrives, we can start. 他一来我们就可以开始。

(5) 表示"上次"、"下次"、"每次"等的时间连词。主要有 every time(每次),each time(每次),(the) next time(下次),any time(随时),(the) last time(上次),the first time(第一次)。

① Last time I saw him, he looked ill. 上次我见到他的时候,他好像有病。

② Do look me up next time you're in London. 你下次到伦敦来，一定来找我。

③ Every time I call on him, he is out. 我每次去访问他，他都不在。

④ You can call me any time, if you need help. 如果需要帮忙，随时给我打电话。

注：every time，each time，any time 前不用冠词，(the) next time，(the) last time 中的冠词可以省略，而 the first time 中的冠词通常不能省略。

2. 引导条件状语从句的从属连词

这类连词主要有 if，unless，as(so) long as，in case 等。

① If anyone calls, tell them I'm not at home. 要是有人打电话来，就说我不在家。

② You won't pass the exam unless you work hard. 你若不努力学习就不能通过考试。

③ As (So) long as you work hard, you can get a good mark. 只要你努力，就可以得高分。

④ In case there is fire, ring the bell. 如遇火情，请按警铃。

注：在条件状语从句中，通常要用一般现在时表示将来意义，而不能直接使用将来时态。不过，有时表示条件的 if 之后可能用 will，但那不是将来时态，而是表示意愿或委婉的请求（will 为情态动词）。

If you will wait a moment, I'll fetch the money. 请等一下，我就去拿钱。

3. 引导目的状语从句的从属连词

这类连词主要有 in order that，so that，in case，for fear 等。

① We used the computer in order that we can know more about the world. 我们使用计算机是为了更多地了解世界。

② Speak slowly so that we can follow you. 说慢些，以便人们能跟上你。

③ Be quiet in case you should wake the baby. 安静些，免得把婴儿吵醒。

④ He is working hard for fear he should fail. 他努力工作以免会失败。

4. 引导结果状语从句的从属连词

这类连词主要有 so that，so...that，such...that 等。

① We're all here now, so that the meeting can begin at last. 我们现在都到齐了，终于能开会了。

② It's such cold weather that we were not willing to go out. 天很冷，我们不愿出去。

③ He shut the window with such force that the glass broke. 他关窗户用力很大，结果玻璃震破了。

注：so that 中的 that 在口语中通常可以省略。

5. 引导原因状语从句的从属连词

这类连词主要有 because，as，since，seeing (that)，now (that)，considering (that) 等。

① He dare not go home because he didn't pass the exam. 他不敢回家，因为考试不及格。

② Since everybody is ready, let's set out. 既然大家都准备好了，我们出发吧。

③ Seeing that it is 8 o'clock, we'll wait no longer. 由于时间已到 8 点，我们将不再等了。

④ Now that you are here, you'd better stay. 你既然来了，最好还是留下吧。

6. 引导让步状语从句的从属连词

这类连词主要有 although，though，even though，even if，while，however，whatever，whoever，whenever，wherever 等。

① Although (Though) he is poor, he is well contented. 他虽穷却能知足常乐。

② Though (Even though) it's hard work, I enjoy it. 尽管是苦活,但我乐意干。

③ Even if you don't like wine, try a glass of this. 即使你不喜欢喝酒,也尝尝这杯吧。

④ While we don't agree, we continue to be friends. 尽管我们意见不同,但我们还是朋友。

⑤ However you start the machine, it won't work. 不管你怎么启动机器,它都不工作。

⑥ Whatever you say, I believe you. 无论你说什么,我都相信你。

⑦ Whoever telephones, tell them I'm out. 不管是谁打电话,都说我出去了。

⑧ Whenever you come, you are welcome. 你什么时候来,我们都欢迎。

⑨ However much he eats, he never gets fat. 无论他吃多少,他都不发胖。

7. 引导方式状语从句的从属连词

这类连词主要有 as, like, as if, as though, the way 等。

① Do it as (like) he does. 像他那样做。

② It seems as if it is going to rain. 看起来好像要下雨了。

③ They have loved me as though I were their son. 他们爱我,就好像我是他们的儿子。

④ Nobody else loves you the way(＝as) I do. 没有人像我这样爱你。

8. 引导地点状语从句的从属连词

这类连词主要有 where, wherever, everywhere 等。

① This is the place where I lived. 这是我过去居住过的地方。

② Sit wherever you like. 你想坐在哪儿就坐在哪儿。

③ Everywhere they went, they were warmly welcomed. 他们每到一个地方都受到热烈欢迎。

9. 引导比较状语从句的从属连词

这类连词主要有 than 和 as...as。

① It's easier said than done. 说起来容易,做着难。

② They are as often wrong as they are right. 他们错对各半。

15.3.2 引导名词性从句的从属连词

引导主语、宾语、表语或同位语从句的连词主要有 that, whether, if 三个。

① The reason(why)he was dismissed is that he was careless and irresponsible. 他被解雇的原因是他粗心又没责任心。(that 引导表语从句)

② That Einstein was a great scientist is a well-know fact. 爱因斯坦是伟大的科学家,这是一个众所周知的事实。(that 引导主语从句)

③ She didn't say if he was still alive. 她没说他是否还活着。(if 引导宾语从句)

④ The news that Tom has passed the examination makes his parents very happy. 汤姆通过考试的消息让他的父母很高兴。(that 引导同位语从句)

15.4 一些特殊的从属连词的用法及区别

1. while, when 和 as

当 while, when, as 引导时间状语从句时的区别有以下几方面:

(1) while 引导的状语从句中动词必须是持续性的,谓语动词多为进行时,或状态动词的一般时。while 的这些用法可用 when 代替,等于 "at the time that", "during the time that"。

Please keep quiet while (when) others are studying.

(2) when 除可指一段时间外,还可用来指一点时间,等于"at the time",也就是说 when 引出的时间状语从句中的谓语动词可以是终止性的,也可以是延续性的。因此主句和从句的谓语可以是一般时、进行时或完成时。

① When the teacher came in, the students were talking. 老师进来时,学生们正在说话。(when 不能换成 while)

② He often makes mistakes when he is speaking English. 他说英语的时候经常出错。(when 可以换成 while)

(3) as 常可与 when, while 通用,但强调"一边,一边"。

As (when, while) I was walking down the street, I noticed a police car in front of number 37. 我正沿着街道走的时候,注意到在 37 号门前有一辆警车。

(4) when 引导的状语从句中的主语与主句主语一致,主、谓是"主语+系动词"结构时,这时主语和系动词可以省略。

① When I was little, I always went to the park. 我小时候经常去公园。

② Give me a call when you need help. 需要帮助时,给我打电话。

(5) when 有时代替 if,引导条件句,意为"如果"、"假如"。

I'll come when (if) I'm free. 如果我有时间我就会来。

2. before

before 作连词时一般表示时间,意为"在……之前",但有些句子中这样翻译并不合适。

① He almost knocked me down before he saw me.

应译为"他几乎把我撞倒才看见我。"

② Before I could get in a word he had measured me.

应译为"我还没来得及插话,他已经给我量好了尺寸"。

3. till, until

till, until 作为介词式从属连词引导时间状语短语或状语从句,用于否定句时,结构为 not... until (till),主句谓语动词延续与非延续皆可,意为"直到……才……"。用于肯定句时,只与延续性动词连用,表示"到……为止"。

① They played volleyball until (till) it got dark. 他们打排球一直到天黑。

② They talked(延续性动词)until (till) the teacher came. 直到老师来了他们才停止说话。

③ He didn't go to bed(非延续性动词)until (till) his father came back. 直到他爸爸回来他才去睡觉。

注意:(1) until 可以放在句首,till 则不行。

① Until the last minute of the match we kept on playing. 我们一直玩到比赛结束。

② Not until he finished his work did he go home. (倒装)他直到做完工作才回家。

(2) till, until 表示"直到……"时只用于时间。

4. because, since, as, now that, seeing that

because, since, as, now that, seeing that 引导原因状语时注意使用上的区别:

(1) 如果原因构成句子的最主要部分，一般用 because，因此 because 引导的从句往往放在句末。用 why 提问的句子，一定用 because 回答。

① He had to study hard because he was afraid to fail the exam. 他必须努力学习因为他怕考不及格。

② —Why are you late? 你为什么迟到？
—Because my car is broken on the way. 因为我的车半路坏了。

(2) 如果原因已为人们所知，或不如句子的其他部分重要，就用 as 或 since。since 比 as 更正式些，并且 as 和 since 引导的从句一般放在句子的开头。

① As you are tired, you had better rest. 既然你累了，你最好休息一下。

② Since everyone is here, now let's begin. 既然人都到齐了，咱们开始吧。

(3) now that 引导的从句如果是现在时，可以与 since，as 及 seeing that 互换，但是从句如果是过去时，就不能用 now that，只能用 since，as 或 seeing that 来引导。并且在口语中 now that 和 seeing that 中的 that 可以省略。

① Seeing that/Since/As he was ill yesterday, he didn't go to school. 由于他昨天生病了所以没去上学。

② Now (that)/Seeing (that) I am here, I'd better tell you the truth. 既然我来了，我最好把真相告诉你。

5. although 和 though

although 和 though 引导让步状语从句往往用法一样，但注意以下区别：

(1) although 用于各种文体，而 though 则多用于非正式的口语或书面语中。由 although，though 引导的从句后，主句不能用 but，但可用副词 yet，still。

Although/Though it rained all the morning, they still went on working.（或 yet they went on working）虽然整个上午都在下雨，他们还是坚持继续工作。

(2) though 常与 even 连用，even though 表示强调，意为"即使"，"尽管"，但不能说 even although。

Even though I didn't understand a word, I deeply smiled. 尽管我一句话都没听懂，我还是放声大笑。

(3) though 可用作副词，在非正式文体中作连接性状语，意为"然而"，常用逗号与句子分开。although 则不能这样使用，它只作连词。

It was a quiet party, I had a good time, though. 这是个很安静的聚会，然而我玩得很开心。

6. once

once 作副词意为"曾经"。作为连词意为"一旦"，引导时间状语从句，含条件意味，相当于 if 的加强形式。

① I don't believe he was once a thief. 我不相信他曾经是个小偷。（once 是副词）

② Once bitten, twice shy. 一朝被蛇咬，十年怕井绳。（once 是连词）

7. unless

unless 引导真实条件状语从句等于 if... not...，如果引导非真实条件句时有时不能用 if... not... 代替。

① He'll accept the job unless the salary is too low. 他会接受这份工作的，除非薪水太低。

等于：He'll accept the job if the salary is not too low. 如果薪水不是很低，他会接受这份工作。

② I couldn't afford this car unless I were rich. 除非我有钱，否则我是买不起这辆车的。
不等于：I couldn't afford this car if I were not rich.

8. as if

在用 as if 引导的方式状语从句及表语从句中，根据情况要使用虚拟语气。

① He talks as if he knew all about it. 他说话的口气好像他知道这件事似的。

但有时也可用直陈语气。如：

② It looks as if it is going to rain. 天看起来要下雨了。

9. whether, if 引导从句的用法区别

(1) 引导主语从句、表语从句或同位语从句时，只能用 whether，不用 if。

① Whether he will come or not doesn't matter. 他来不来关系不大。

② My question is whether people can live on the moon someday. 我的问题是人们是否有一天能在月球上生活。

③ The question whether we will take part in the physics contest has not been decided. 我们是不是参加物理竞赛还没有确定。

(2) whether 可接不定式，而 if 则不可。

I haven't decided whether to leave or not. 我还没有确定是走是留。

(3) whether 可以置于句首表示强调，而 if 则不可。

① Whether you can succeed depends on how hard you work. 是否能成功取决于你的努力程度。

② Whether he will come, I am not sure. 我不确信他是否会来。

(4) whether 和 if 均可引导宾语从句，whether 引导的宾语从句一般都是肯定句，if 引导的宾语从句可以是肯定的，也可以是否定的（此时不能用 whether）。

① I wonder whether/if you have got any letters for me? 我想知道你是否为我取来了信件。

② I wonder if it doesn't rain. 我不知道是否会下雨。

(5) 引导宾语从句的 whether 和 if 常可与 or not 连用。连用时要注意 or not 的位置，它一般与 whether, if 分开使用，有时它可与 whether 合起来使用，但不能与 if 合起来使用。

① I don't care whether/ if your car breaks down or not. 我不介意你的车是否坏了。

② He asked whether or not I wanted to insure my luggage. 他问我是否想为我的行李买保险。

(6) if 可用来引导条件状语从句，译为"如果"，whether 则不行。

If you work hard, you are sure to succeed. 如果你努力工作，肯定会成功。

10. as 作从属连词可引导多种状语从句

(1) as 引导时间状语从句，意为"当……时"。

① As (he was) a young man, he was a storekeeper and later a postmaster. 当他年轻的时候，他先是一个店老板，后来成为了一名邮政所长。

② He sang as he worked. 他工作的时候还唱着歌。

(2) as 引导方式状语从句，意为"像……一样"。

We must do as the Party teaches us. 我们要按照党教育我们的去做。

（3）as 引导原因状语从句。意为"由于"，"既然"。

As you are tired, you had better rest. 既然你累了,最好休息休息。

（4）as 引导让步状语从句。意为"虽然"、"尽管"。

① Young as he is, he knows a lot. 尽管他年龄小,他懂很多。

等于：Although he is a child, he can do it well.

另外,as 作为关系代词还可以引导定语从句,如：

② I am of the same mind as you are about this. 我和你对这件事上有同样的想法。

11. as 和 like 的区别

as 与 like 是英语中常见的两个词,他们的语义和用法很多。在语义上两个词都可以当"像……","正如……"讲,说明人与人、物与物、动作与动作、状态与状态之间的相似之处。但其语法结构却不一样。

（1）当"像"讲时,as 是连接词,它引导比较状语从句和方式状语从句,而且这两种从句通常为省略句,like 则是介词。

① She is a fine singer, as her mother used to be. 她和她母亲一样都唱歌唱得很好。

② There is as much water in this cup as in that one. 这个杯子里的水和那个杯子里的水一样多。

③ The girl doesn't look like her mother. 那女孩长得不像她妈妈。

④ The robot can't work like man. 机器人不会像人一样工作。

如果需要加强语气,在这两个词之前加上 just 之类的词即可。

⑤ All the plants and animals need air just as they need water. 所有的植物和动物都需要空气,就像他们需要水一样。

⑥ Tom gets up at 6 o'clock just like his mother. 汤姆和妈妈一样 6 点起床。

二者的含义不同之处是,like 只是单纯表示比较,而且通常不是同类事物进行比较,as 可表示同类事物比较。

⑦ The ship looks like a high building. 这艘船看起来就像一座高楼。

⑧ The sky was like blue ocean. 天空像海洋一样深蓝。

⑨ This cup is as large as that one. 这个杯子和那个杯子一样大。

（2）当"正如……"的意义讲时,语法结构的不同之处是,as 作关系代词或关系副词,指全句所谈到的内容,引出非限制性定语从句,在从句中一般做主语或宾语,like 作介词。

① Metals have many good properties, as has been stated before. 正如前面所提到的,金属有很多好的属性。

② As has been mentioned above, more and more college students want to study abroad after graduation. 如上所述,越来越多的大学生想毕业后出国学习。

③ She, like thousands of others, is fascinated by this work. 她和无数其他人一样被这份工作吸引了。

（3）as 与 like 有时可以换用。在非正式的美国英语中 like 可用作连词,代替 as。

① Nobody loves you like I do, baby. 亲爱的,没有人像我这样爱你。

在非正式的文体中,like 常被用来代替 as if。

② Tom said,"You feel like you could reach out and touch it." 汤姆说:"你感觉到好像你能伸出手触摸到它一样。"

(4) as 常用于下列词组：as you know, as we agreed, as you suggested,在这些词组中,as 的实际意义不是比较,也不是相似,而是同一事物或人。

① As he knew, she wasn't much good at letter-writing. 据他所知,她写信写得不是很好。

② As all his friends agree, he was unusually warm-hearted, loving and generous. 他所有的朋友都知道,他是一个特别善良、充满爱心和慷慨的人。

巩 固 练 习

一、单项选择。

1. He is very old, _____ he still works very hard.
   A. but   B. however   C. when   D. /
2. _____ you are dismissed.
   A. Neither you go nor   B. Either you go or
   C. Whether you go or   D. Both you go and
3. They had camped once before, _____ they knew what to take.
   A. because   B. now   C. so   D. since
4. Why these things happened was _____ the driver had been careless.
   A. because of   B. owing to   C. due to   D. that
5. Although it's raining, _____ are still working in the fields.
   A. they   B. but they   C. and they   D. so they
6. _____ we have satisfied you, you have no grounds of complaint.
   A. So   B. Since that   C. Now that   D. By now
7. Write clearly _____ your teacher can understand you correctly.
   A. since   B. for   C. because   D. so that
8. You'll miss the train _____ you hurry up.
   A. unless   B. as   C. if   D. until
9. Francis did the task _____ his brother.
   A. as good as   B. as better as
   C. as well as   D. as best as
10. A: I thought he hated the TV.
    B: You are right, _____ he still watches the program.
    A. yet   B. besides   C. also   D. then
11. We must get up early tomorrow, _____ we'll miss the first bus to the Great Wall.
    A. so   B. or   C. but   D. however
12. I hurried _____ I wouldn't be late for class.
    A. since   B. so that   C. as if   D. unless
13. _____ the day went on, the weather got worse.

A. With B. Since C. While D. As

14. Young _____ she is, she knows quite a lot.

A. When B. However C. As D. Although

15. Although he is considered a great writer, _____.

A. his works are not widely read
B. but his works are not widely read
C. however his works are not widely read
D. still his works are not widely read

16. It was not _____ she took off her glasses _____ I realized she was a famous film star.

A. when; that B. until; that C. until; when D. when; then

17. _____ the 2016 Olympic Games will be held in Paris is not known yet.

A. Whenever B. If C. Whether D. That

18. You will be late _____ you leave immediately.

A. unless B. until C. if D. or

19. —I don't like chicken _____ fish.
—I don't like chicken, _____ I like fish very much.

A. and; and B. and; but C. or; and D. or; but

20. —What was the party like?
—Wonderful. It's years _____ I enjoyed myself so much.

A. after B. before C. when D. since

21. —Would you like to come to dinner tonight?
—I'd like to. _____ I'm too busy.

A. And B. So C. As D. But

22. Mother was worried because little Alice was ill, especially _____ Father was away in France.

A. as B. that C. during D. if

23. Although brought up in China, _____ he is well known for his novel about Russia.

A. however B. and C. but D. yet

24. She thought I was talking about her daughter, _____, in fact, I was talking about my daughter.

A. whom B. where C. which D. while

25. Would you like a cup of coffee _____ shall we get down to business right away?

A. and B. then C. or D. otherwise

26. If we work with a strong will, we can overcome any difficulty, _____ great it is.

A. what B. how C. however D. whatever

27. _____ we'll go camping tomorrow, I will get things ready tonight.

A. If B. Whether C. That D. Where

28. After the war, a new school building was put up _____ there had once been a theatre.

A. that B. where C. which D. when

29. Why do you want a new job _____ you've got such a good one already?

A. that	B. where	C. which	D. when

30. —I'm going to the post office.

    — _____ you're there, can you get me some stamps?

A. As	B. While	C. Because	D. If

二、改错题，注意某些连词的恰当使用。

1. We become more and more impatient of interruptions when the years go on.
2. It was not until it began to rain when I noticed his umbrella left in my car.
3. At the age of six, my father took me to the circus for the first time.
4. He acted like he had never been in a museum before.
5. You'll be permitted to bring a watch so that you may keep track of the time during you are taking the test.
6. It was not long since they made their appearance.
7. It was not so much the amount of the money but the money itself that surprised him.
8. There may not be much choice between this one or that.
9. We must eat for we may live.
10. Which do you like better, coffee and black tea?

第十六章 介 词

16.1 介词的定义和分类

16.1.1 介词的定义

介词(Preposition)又叫做前置词,一般置于名词之前。它是一种虚词,一般不重读,在句中不单独作任何句子成分,只表示其后的名词或相当于名词的词语与其他句子成分的关系。

16.1.2 介词的种类

1. 按构成分类

(1) 简单介词(Simple Preposition),即单一介词,如 at,in,of,since 等。

(2) 复合介词(Compound Preposition),由两个介词组成,如 as for,as to,into,out of 等。

(3) 二重介词(Double Preposition),由两个介词搭配而成,但没有复合介词那样固定,如 from under,from behind,until after 等。

(4) 短语介词(Phrasal Preposition),由短语构成,如 according to,because of,in spite of,on behalf of,with reference to 等。

(5) 分词介词(Participle Preposition),由现在分词构成,如 regarding,concerning,including 等。

2. 按词义分类

(1) 表地点(包括动向),如 about,above,after,along,among,at,before,behind,below,beneath,beside,between,beyond,by,down,from,in,into,off,on,over,through,throughout,to,under,up,upon,with,within,without 等。

注:有不少表地点的介词表动向,除很明显的 across,around,near,towards 外,还有 among,behind,beneath,between,on,to,under 等。

(2) 表时间,如 about,after,around,as,at,before,behind,between,by,during,for,from,in,into,of,on,over,past,since,through,throughout,till(until),to,towards,within 等。

(3) 表除去,如 besides,but,except 等。

(4) 表比较,如 as,like,above,over 等。

(5) 表反对,如 against,with 等。

(6) 表原因、目的,如 for,with,from 等。

(7) 表结果,如 to,with,without 等。

(8) 表手段、方式,如 by,in,with 等。

(9) 表所属,如 of,with 等。

(10) 表条件,如 on,without,considering 等。

(11) 表让步,如 despite,in spite of,notwithstanding 等。

(12) 表关于,如 about,concerning,regarding,with regard to,as for,as to 等。
(13) 表对于,如 to,for,over,at,with 等。
(14) 表根据,如 on,according to 等。
(15) 表其他,如 for(赞成),without(没有)等。

16.2 介词短语

16.2.1 介词短语的构成

介词后面一般由名词、代词或相当于名词的其他词类、短语或从句作它的宾语。介词和它的宾语构成介词短语。

介词短语的构成形式有下面几种:
(1) 介词+名词,如 He lives **in the city**. 他住在城里。
(2) 介词+名词性从句,如 I am curious **as to what she will say**. 我很好奇她会说什么。
(3) 介词+代词,如 I know nothing **about her**. 我对她一无所知。
(4) 介词+动名词短语或者其复合结构,如 He is interested **in playing golf**. 他对打高尔夫很感兴趣。
(5) 介词+连接词或者连接副词引导的从句或者不定式,如 Your success will largely depend **upon how you do it**. 你的成功很大程度上取决于你做这事的方式。
(6) 介词+数词,如 Five **from ten** is five. 十减五等于五。
(7) 介词+形容词,如 We know her **of old**. 我们认识她很久了。
(8) 介词+副词,如 They worked all day and had a hurried lunch **in between**. 他们工作一整天只在期间草草地吃点午饭。

16.2.2 介词短语的作用

介词短语可以在句中作多种成分。

1. 作表语

The book you want is **on the table**. 你要的那本书在桌子上。

2. 作宾语

He came out from **behind the tree**. 他从树后面出来。(behind the tree 作介词 from 的宾语)

3. 作宾补

I noticed a man **behind me**. 我发现我身后有个人。

4. 作定语(后置定语)

I don't know the little girl **in his car**. 我不认识他车里的小女孩。

5. 作状语

(1) 作地点状语。
We live **in Hangzhou**. 我们住在杭州。
(2) 作时间状语。
She got here **at four**. 她是 4 点到这儿的。

(3) 作方式状语。

They came here **by train**. 他们乘火车来这儿。

(4) 作原因状语。

The game was postponed **because of rain**. 因为下雨运动会被推迟了。

(5) 作条件状语。

There will be no living things **without water**. 没有水就没有生物。

(6) 作目的状语。

He ran **for shelter**. 他跑去避雨。

(7) 作让步状语。

They play football **in spite of the rain**. 他们冒雨踢足球。

(8) 作程度状语。

To what extent would you trust them? 你对他们信任程度如何？

16.3 介词和其他词类的搭配

在英语中，介词常常和形容词、名词、动词等构成固定搭配来表示固定的意义。

16.3.1 形容词＋介词

1. 形容词＋about

anxious about 担心，certain about 确定，concerned about 关心，enthusiastic about 热心的，excited about 对……感到兴奋的，happy about 对……感到高兴的，worried about 担心，crazy about 对……狂热的

2. 形容词＋at

shocked at 吃惊的，amazed at 惊讶的，angry at 生气的，astonished at 震惊的，clever at 擅长于，good at 擅长于做……的，slow at 对……反应慢的，quick at 做……敏捷的

3. 形容词＋for

appropriate for 适合……的，convenient for 对……来说方便的，eager for 渴望的，famous for 以……而闻名的，fit for 对……适宜的，good for 对……来说有好处的，late for 做……迟到的，necessary for 为……所必需的，responsible for 对……负责的，right for 对……来说是正确的

4. 形容词＋from

absent from 缺席的，distant from 遥远的，free from 不受……限制的，safe from 安全的，separate from 分离的

5. 形容词＋in

absorbed in 专心于，disappointed in 对……感到失望，interested in 有兴趣的，lacking in 缺乏，lost in 迷失于……，poor in 贫乏，rich in 富含

6. 形容词＋of

ashamed of 感到羞耻的，aware of 意识到，capable of 有能力的，confident of 有信心的，composed of 由……构成，conscious of 意识到，fond of 喜欢，ignorant of 对……一无所知的，independent of 独立的，proud of 骄傲的，worthy of 值得

7. 形容词＋on/upon

keen on 热衷于　rough on 严厉的,刻薄的　dependent on 依赖

8. 形容词＋to

sensitive to 敏感的,acceptable to 可以接受的,available to 可以获得的,accustomed to 习惯的,attractive to 对……有吸引力的,beneficial to 有益处的,contrary to 相反地,devoted to 献身于、致力于,equal to 等同于,opposite to 与……相反的,parallel to 与……平行的,relevant to 与……有关的,similar to 相似的,thankful to 感谢的

9. 形容词＋with

angry with 对……感到恼火的,annoyed with 对……烦恼的,associated with 与……相关的,bored with 对……感到厌倦的,busy with 忙于,crowded with 到处都是……的、拥挤的,faced with 面对着,familiar with 熟悉的,patient with 对……有耐心的,pleased with 对……满意的,popular with 受……欢迎的, strict with 对……严格的

16.3.2　介词和名词的搭配

1. 介词＋名词

by accident 偶然；on account of 因为,由于；in addition 另外；on average 平均,一般来说；at (the) best 充其量,至多；for the better 好转,改善；on board 在船(车、飞机)上；out of breath 喘不过气来；on business 因公,因事；in any case 无论如何,总之；in case 假使,以防(万一)免得；by chance 偶然,碰巧；in charge (of) 负责,主管；in common 共用,共有,共同；in conclusion 最后,总之；on the contrary 反之,正相反；out of control 失去控制；at all costs 不惜任何代价；in danger 在危险中,垂危；out of date 过期(时)的；in debt 欠债；in difficulties 处境困难；off duty 下班；on duty 值班,上班；on earth 究竟,到底；for example 例如；in fact 其实,实际上；on fire 烧着；on foot 步行；on guard 警惕,防范；in general 通常,大体上；to one's surprise 让某人惊讶的是

2. 名词＋介词

absence from 缺席,不在；access to ……的入口,通路；appeal for 魅力,吸引力；belief in 对……的信仰,相信；complaint of /about 报怨,控告；confidence in 对……的信任,相信；contradiction between 矛盾,不一致；contribution to 贡献,捐献,促成；desire for 渴望；dispute about 争论,辩论；encounter with 遭遇,遇到；entrance to ……的入口,入场；faith in 对……的信任,信仰；interference in/with 干涉,阻碍；objection to sth. ……反对；solution to ……的解决办法；wish for 欲望,愿望

16.3.3　介词和动词的搭配

1. 动词＋介词

care about 关心；care for 喜欢；take care of 照顾；dream about 梦到；dream of 梦想；hear about 听到关于……的详情；hear of 听到……的事/话；hear from 得到……的消息；look at 注视,考察；look for 找,指望；look after 照应,看守；think about 思索,考虑；think of 想起,企图；wait for 等候；worry about 担心；adhere to 坚持

2. 动词＋宾语＋介词

prefer...to... 喜欢……不喜欢……, prevent...from... 阻止……做某事

3. 动词＋副词＋介词

catch up with 赶上（超过）；work hard on(at) 努力学习；get on with 与某人相处；do well in 在……方面做得好；take out of 带走，拿出；climb up to 往上爬到……

16.4 相似介词的辨析

16.4.1 in, to, on 和 off 在方位名词前的区别

（1）in 表示 A 地在 B 地范围之内。
Taiwan is in the southeast of China. 台湾在中国东南部。
（2）to 表示 A 地在 B 地范围之外，即二者之间有距离间隔。
Japan lies to the east of China. 日本位于中国东方。
（3）on 表示 A 地与 B 地接壤、毗邻。
North Korea is on the east of China. 北朝鲜与中国东部接壤。
（4）off 表示"离……一些距离或离……不远的海上"。
① They arrived at a house off the main road. 他们到了离大路不远的一所房子。
② New Zealand lies off the eastern coast of Australia. 新西兰位于澳大利亚不远的东海岸。

16.4.2 at, in, on, by 和 through 在表示时间上的区别

1. at 指时间

at 指时间表示以下几种情况：
（1）时间的一点、时刻等。
They came home at sunrise (at noon, at midnight, at ten o'clock, at daybreak, at dawn). 他们日出时（正午时，午夜时，十点，天亮时，黄昏时）回家了。
（2）较短暂的一段时间，可指某个节日或被认为是一年中标志大事的日子。
He went home at Christmas (at New Year, at the Spring Festival, at night). 他圣诞节（新年，春节，晚上）回家

2. in 指时间

in 指时间表示以下几种情况：
（1）在某个较长的时间（如世纪、朝代、年、月、季节以及泛指的上午、下午或傍晚等）内。
in 2004, in March, in spring, in the morning, in the evening, etc.
（2）在一段时间之后。一般情况下，用于将来时，谓语动词为瞬间动词，意为"在……以后"。
The meeting will begin in fifteen minutes. 会议 15 分钟后开始。
谓语动词为延续性动词时，in 意为"在……以内"。
These products will be produced in a month. 这些产品将在一个月之内生产出来。
注：after 用于将来时间也指一段时间之后，但其后的时间是一个时间点，而不是一段时间。
My friend will come to see me after half past six. 我朋友 6 点半后来看我。

3. on 指时间

on 指时间表示以下几种情况：

(1) 具体的时日和一个特定的时间，如某日、某节日、星期几等。

On Christmas Day(On May 4th), there will be a celebration. 在圣诞节（五四）那天，将有一个庆典。

(2) 在某个特定的早晨、下午或晚上。

He arrived at 10 o'clock on the night of the 5th. 他5号晚上10点钟到的。

(3) 准时，按时。

If the train should be on time, I should reach home before dark. 如果火车准时，我在天黑前就到家了。

4. by 指时间

by 指时间表示以下几种情况：

(1) 不迟于，在（某时）前。

① Please hand in your paper by twelve o'clock. 请12点之前交卷子。

② Jack had made some friends by the time you came. 杰克在你来之前已经交了几个朋友了。

(2) 在……间，在……的时候。

He worked by day and slept by night. 他白天工作晚上睡觉。

5. through 指时间

through 指时间，意为"从……开始到结束"，此时与 throughout 相同。

They searched for the missing child all through the night. 他们找那个走失的孩子找了一夜。

16.4.3　near, by, beside, at 表示"在……附近"时的区别

(1) near 表示相对的近，实际距离可能还很远。

Suzhou is near Shanghai. 苏州离上海很近。

(2) by 和 beside 都表示靠近，实际距离不可能很远，但 beside 比 by 更具体地表示出"在……旁边"的意思。

He was sitting beside her. 他坐在她身旁。

(3) at 也有"在旁边"的意思，但多表示有目的的行为所处的位置，而 by 和 beside 仅表示位置关系。

① The students are sitting at the desks listening to the teacher. 学生们正坐在课桌旁认真听老师讲课。

② Several students are sitting by / beside the window talking about a film. 几个学生正坐在窗户旁谈论一部电影。

16.4.4　at, in 和 on 表示地点时的区别

1. at 表示地点

(1) 用于指较小的地方。

I shall wait for you at the station. 我在车站等你。

（2）用于门牌号码前。

He lives at 115 Zhongshan Road. 他住在中山路115号。

2. in 表示地点

（1）用于指较大的地方。

He lives in Shanghai. 他住在上海。

（2）虽然是很小的地方，如果说话人住在那里，也可用 in。商店、学校、机关等，若看作一个地点(point)用 at，若看作一个场所(place)用 in。

① I met him at the post-office. 我在邮局碰到了他。

② I'm now working in the post-office. 我现在在邮局上班。

3. on 表示地点

on 表示地点一般指与面或线接触，意为"在……上；在……旁"。

① The picture was hanging on the wall. 墙上挂着那幅画。

② New York is on the Hudson River. 纽约在哈得逊河畔。

16.4.5　besides, except, except for, but 表示"除……外"的区别

（1）besides 表示"除了……以外，还有……"，具有附加性质。

Besides Mr. Wang, we also went to see the film.（王先生也去了）除了王先生外，我们也去看了电影。

注：besides 用于否定句中时，与 except, but 同义，可互换。

We have no other books besides / except these. 除了这些书，我们没有别的书了。

（2）except 表示"……除外"，具有排它性。

We all went to see the film except Mr Wang.（王先生没去）除了王老生我们都去看了电影。

（3）except for 表示"除了……"，即表示除去整体中的一部分。

The composition is very good except for a few spelling mistakes. 这篇作文除了有几个拼写错误还是很好的。

（4）but 意为"除了"，与 except 同义，except 强调被排除的部分，but 则强调整句的内容，常修饰否定意义的代词。

Nobody knew it but me. 这件事除了我没人知道。

16.4.6　above, over, on, up 表示"在……上"的区别

（1）above 指"……上方"，表示相对高度，不一定在正上方，其反义词为 below。

We're flying above the clouds. 我们正在云层上面飞行。

（2）over 指"在……正上方"，表示垂直上方，其反义词为 under。

The bridge is over the river. 桥在河的正上方。

（3）on 表示"在……上面"，与物体表面接触，与 beneath 相对。

① There is a map on the wall. 墙上有一幅地图。

② The earth felt soft beneath our feet. 我们脚下的土地感到很软。

（4）up 表示动作的方向往上，反义词为 down。

Please hang the picture up. 请挂上这幅画。

16.4.7　by, through, with 表示"方式、方法、手段"的区别

1. by 表方式

（1）表示以一般的方法或方式。

No one in those days could live by writing poems. 在过去没人能靠写诗谋生。

（2）表示传达、传递的方式或媒介。

How did you send the letter, by airmail or by ordinary mail? 用什么方式寄这封信呢,用航空还是普通邮件?

（3）表示用交通工具、通信工具后接名词单数,不加冠词。

He came by train, but his wife came by bus. 他坐火车来的,但是他妻子坐公共汽车来的。

注意下面两句的区别:

① Did you come by train? 你是坐火车来的吗?

② Did you come in his car / on you bike? 你是坐他的汽车(骑车)来的吗?

"by ＋抽象名词"构成的词组有 by accident / by chance / by diligence / by effort / by force / by heart / by luck / by mistake / by hard work。

2. through 表示"以;通过;经由"

He succeeded through hard work. 经过努力的工作他成功了。

3. with 表示方式

（1）表示行为方式,意为"以;带着;用"。

We are well provided with food and clothing. 我们被提供以充足的食物和衣服。

（2）表示使用具体的工具或手段。

The girl drew the picture with a pencil. 女孩用铅笔画的画。

注:在表示手段时,by, through, with 有时也可换用,但 with 的意思更明确。

Through / By / With his efforts, he succeeded in making so many useful inventions. 经过他的努力,他成功地完成了那么多有用的发明。

16.4.8　through, with, from, for, at 表示原因的区别

（1）through 表示原因,作"因为"解,常和 neglect, carelessness, mistake, fault 等词连用,表示偶然或消极的原因,如疏忽、过错、不慎等。

① He cut himself through carelessness. 因为不小心他砍伤了自己。

② The experiment failed through one fault of ours. 这项实验由于我们的一个失误而失败。

（2）with 表示原因,指由于外界而影响到内部,意为"因为;由于"。

The shabby lady was shivering with cold. 那个寒酸的妇女冻得发抖。

（3）from 表示动机、疲劳、痛苦、死亡等原因。

She did it from a sense of duty. 她出于责任感做了这件事。

（4）for 常表示为了某一目的、事业的原因。

Forgive me for keeping you waiting. 请原谅我让你久等了。

（5）at 表示原因,指"听到;看到;想到"等。

At the news they felt very glad. 听到这个消息她们感到很高兴。

16.4.9　between, among 表示"在……之间"的区别

between 指在两个人或两个事物之间，among 表示在三个或三个以上的人或事物之间。如：

① There is a football match between Class One and Class Two on the playground. 操场上一班和二班正进行一场足球比赛。

② The speaker was standing among the audience. 演讲者站在观众中间。

16.4.10　in, after 表示"在……之后"的区别

"in ＋段时间"表示将来的一段时间以后，"after＋段时间"表示过去的一段时间以后，"after＋将来点时间"表示将来的某一时刻以后。

① My mother will come back in three or four days. 我妈妈三四天后回来。

② He arrived after five months. 五个月后他到了。

③ She will appear after five o'clock this afternoon. 今天下午五点后她会出现。

16.4.11　from, since 表示"自从……时"的区别

from 仅说明什么时候开始，不说明某动作或情况持续多久；since 表示某动作或情况持续至说话时刻，通常与完成时连用。

① He studied the piano from the age of three. 从三岁起他学了钢琴。（表示从他三岁起，没有强调现在是否还在学习钢琴。）

② I have known you since I was five. 从五岁起我就认识你。（表示我从五岁起至今一直都认识你）

16.4.12　on, about 表示"关于……"的区别

on 表示关于书，文章或演说，是严肃的，或学术性的，可供专门研究这一问题的人阅读；about表示内容较为普通，不那么正式。

① There will be a lecture on economics this afternoon. 今天下午将有一个有关经济的演讲。

② He is writing a book on cooking. 他在写一本有关烹调的书。

③ He told me a lot about his life in the summer vocation. 他告诉我许多有关他的暑假生活。

16.4.13　after, behind 表示"在……后面"的区别

这两个词在表示空间位置时都是"在……后面"的意思，但 after 用于动态，behind 用于静态；after 还可以表示时间，而 behind 不能表示时间。

① Go after me. 跟我走。

② He sat behind me. 他坐在我后面。

③ Come to my office after the meeting. 散会后到我的办公室来一下。

巩 固 练 习

1. _____ hearing the good news, they jumped with joy.
   A. For B. To C. On D. At
2. His father will be back from London _____ a few days.
   A. since B. in C. on D. after
3. He usually goes to work on time _____.
   A. except for raining days   B. besides it rains
   C. but that it rains   D. except on rainy days
4. Did you have trouble _____ the post office?
   A. to have found B. with finding C. to find D. in finding
5. If you keep on, you'll succeed _____.
   A. in time B. at one time C. at the same time D. on time
6. The train leaves _____ 6:00 pm, so I have to be at the station _____ 5:40 p.m. at the latest?
   A. at; until B. for; after C. at; by D. before; around
7. _____ the gate and you'll find the entrance _____ the park _____ the other side.
   A. Through; to; on   B. Along; of; on
   C. Down; to; at   D. Up; of; by
8. One _____ five will have the chance to join in the game.
   A. within B. among C. in D. from
9. — Do you go there _____ bus?
   — No, we go there _____ a train.
   A. in; on B. on; on C. by; in D. by; with
10. I made the coat _____ my own hands. It was made _____ hand, not with a machine.
    A. in; in B. in; with C. with; by D. with; with
11. The trees _____ front of the house are _____ the charge of Mr. Li.
    A. in; in B. at; in C. in; by D. from; in
12. The old man died _____ cold _____ a cold night.
    A. from; at B. of; in C. of; on D. for; during
13. My uncle lives _____ 116 Changhe Street. His room is _____ the sixth floor.
    A. at; on B. to; at C. on; in D. of; to
14. I don't think you can work out the maths problem _____ her help.
    A. since B. unless C. with D. without
15. He is running _____ the wind towards the station _____ Tom running _____ the right.
    A. down; and; on   B. against; with; on
    C. for; with; in   D. with; while; to
16. In Hangzhou Mr. Black was so struck _____ the beauty of nature that he stayed _____

another night.

    A. at; on   B. with; at   C. for; in   D. by; for

17. Don't read _____ the sun. It's bad _____ your eyes.

    A. in; to   B. under; for   C. with; to   D. in; on

18. The woman _____ a blue dress is my teacher.

    A. in   B. on   C. of   D. at

19. The boat is passing _____ the bridge.

    A. through   B. below   C. under   D. across

20. Two planes are flying _____ the city.

    A. through   B. over   C. on   D. below

21. Do you see the kite _____ the building.

    A. over   B. cross   C. on   D. above

22. The United States is _____ the south of Canada and _____ the east of Japan.

    A. to; in   B. on; to   C. in; beside   D. at; on

23. My hometown lies _____ the city. _____ I often go to the city by bike.

    A. 50 miles in the east; However   B. to the east 40 miles of; But

    C. in the east 45 miles from; But   D. 35 miles east of; However

24. The man stood _____ the window, watching the boys playing outside.

    A. in   B. by   C. with   D. to

25. Japan lies _____ the east of China.

    A. on   B. to   C. in   D. with

26. Is the street too narrow for the bus to go _____?

    A. through   B. across   C. on   D. in

27. A mother camel was walking _____ her son _____ the desert.

    A. without; along   B. with; through   C. next to; pass   D. beside; through

28. Uncle Wang arrived _____ No. 14 Middle School half an hour ago.

    A. at   B. in   C. to   D. /

29. Did your friend send you something _____ the end of last week?

    A. at   B. by   C. in   D. to

30. The monument _____ those heroes stands _____ the foot of the mountain.

    A. of; at   B. to; on   C. for; by   D. to; at

31. Wood is of ten made _____ paper.

    A. by   B. from   C. of   D. into

32. _____ research _____ the universe scientists have put a lot of information _____ computers.

    A. With; over; at   B. On; at; to

    C. In; about; into   D. For; with; through

33. When a piece of ice is taken _____ a warm room, it gets smaller and smaller until _____ the end it disappears completely.

    A. in; in   B. out of; at   C. into; in   D. to; by

34. A woman fell _____ the boat _____ the water.
    A. off; into   B. at; below   C. down; under   D. away; in
35. The tables in the restaurant are so close together that there's hardly any room to move _____ them.
    A. among   B. between   C. in the middle of   D. at the centre of
36. We visited him at his workplace _____ the young trees and ask him about his work.
    A. in   B. among   C. between   D. at

第十七章 感 叹 词

17.1 感叹词的定义

感叹词(Interjection)是用以表达说话人情感或感情的词语。感叹词是虚词,在意义上与句子有关联,但在结构上一般作独立成分看待,不作任何句子成分。感叹词一般放在句首,后用逗号(,),感情较强时可用感叹号(!),有时也可放在句中。

① Oh, it's you. 啊,是你呀。
② Wow! You hurt me. 哇! 你弄疼我了。
③ We had looked forward to lovely week by the sea, but alas, it rained every day. 我们希望在海边度过愉快的一周,可是唉,天天下雨。
④ That little boy of yours, oh, is such a dear! 你那个小弟弟,唉,真逗人喜欢!

17.2 常用的感叹词及其用法

常用的感叹词有:ah 啊,bravo 好样的, o(h) 啊,aha 啊哈,alas 唉(哎呀,嗨),blast 糟糕,bosh 胡说, come 喂(得啦), dear 天哪,(my)goodness 天哪, hum 哼, haha 哈哈, heigh-ho 嗨嗬,hurrah 太好了(好哇), hush(嘘), hmm 哼, hallo 嗨(喂), hello 嗨(喂), hi 嗨(喂), hey 嗨(喂),nonsense 胡说, now 那么(好了), Oh Lord 天呀, Good Lord 天呀, Good heavens 天呀,gosh 啊呀, oops 哎哟(哟), ouch 哎哟, pish 呸, tut-tut 啧(咳), well 呃(嗯,啊呀,好了),whew(phew)嘿, ugh 喔喻, wow 喔, hell 妈的, damn 他妈的, shit 妈的。

(1) ah 表示惊奇、高兴、讨厌、懊悔、藐视、威胁等,可译为"呀、啊"等。
① Ah, yes, Jeanne married a man with a lot of money. 啊,对啦,珍妮嫁给了一个很有钱的人。
② Ah, what a wonderful idea! 啊,这个主意真不错啊!
③ Ah, how pitiful! 呀,多可惜!
④ Ah, here is the thing I am after. 哎呀,我找的东西在这儿呢。

(2) oh 表示惊讶、指责、痛苦、称赞、懊恼等,可译为"哦"、"哎呀"、"噢"、"啊"、"呀"等。
① "Oh, who was that?" Mr. Black asked. "哦,是谁?"布莱克先生问。
② "Oh, who was on the phone?" my mum asked. "哦。刚才是谁打的电话?"妈妈问道。
③ "Oh, oh!" he cried. "My stomach! My head! oh! oh!" "哎呀,哎哟!"他大声道,"我的肚子! 我的头! 哎哟! 哎哟!"
④ Oh, what a smart Lady! 噢,多么聪明的女士啊!

(3) dear 表示后悔、难过、怜悯、同情、吃惊、盼望等,可译为"哎呀、天哪"等。与其相似的表达还有 dear me, my goodness, good gracious, goodness me 等,此类词多为女性使用。

① Dear me! What awful weather! 哎呀！多糟的天气！

② Oh, dear, dear! Where can Harry be? 天哪,天哪,亨利会在哪儿？

③ My goodness, how handsome he is! 天啊,他真帅！

(4) Oh Lord, Good Lord, Good heavens, Heavens 表示惊讶、兴奋等,可以译为"天啊"、"老天爷",多为男人所使用。

① Oh Lord, it's you! 天啊,是你！

② Good heavens, here you are! 天啊,你在这儿啊！

(5) well 表示快慰、让步、期望、讥讽、解释、责备、犹豫等,可译为"好吧、不过、好啦、嗯"等。

① Well, he is just a friend of mine. 好啦,他只是我的一个朋友而已。

② Are you sure? Well, perhaps you are right. 你能肯定吗？嗯,也许你说得对。

③ Well, you must come to lunch tomorrow. 不过,你明天一定要来吃午饭。

(6) now 表示警告、命令、请求、说明、安慰等,可译为"喂、喏、好了"等,有时也可不必译出。

① Now, now, you two; Don't fight again. 喂,喂,你们俩,别再打了。

② Now, now, my boy! It's all right! There's no need to cry! 好了,好了,孩子,没事了,别哭了。

③ Now, let's play basketball. 喏,咱们打篮球吧！

④ Now! Be careful. 喂,小心啊！

(7) come 表示鼓励、不耐烦、引起注意、安慰等,可译为"喂、好吧、说吧、得啦"等。

① Oh, come, tell me about the wonderful show. 嗨,说吧,跟我说说这次精彩演出吧。

② Come, we must hurry. 喂,我们得赶紧啦！

③ Come, come, get him his change. Tod, get him his change. 好吧,好吧,快把钱找给他,托德,快把钱找给他。

④ Come, come! What were you really doing behind the bicycle sheds? 喂！喂！你还在车棚里磨蹭啥？

(8) there 表示得意、鼓励、同情、悲哀、不耐烦、失望、安慰、挑衅、引起注意等,可译为"哟、瞧、好啦、得啦"等。

① There! There! Never mind, you'll soon feel better. 好啦,好啦,不要紧,你马上会好的。

② There, there, you said too much. 得啦,得啦,你说得太多了。

③ There—what's that? 哟,那是什么？

(9) man 表示兴奋、轻蔑、不耐烦、引起注意、可译为"啊、嗨"等。

① "He is just a kid, man!" said the teacher. "嗨,他只是个孩子,"老师说道。

② Hurry up, man. 嗨,快点。

③ We have won the match, man! 啊,我们胜利了。

(10) boy 表示高兴、兴奋、惊奇等,可译为"嘿、哇、哼、怎么样"等。

① Boy, oh, boy! Our team's going to win! How fantastic! 哇,怎么样！我们队要赢了！真是太好了！

② Boy! You look great in the dress. 嘿,你穿上这件礼服棒极了！

③ Oh, boy! I just had a wonderful dream! 嘿,我刚才做了个好梦。

(11) 此外常用的还有 why 表示惊讶,不耐烦;ouch 表示突然疼痛;alas 表示悲哀、忧伤;hush 表示要求肃静、安静;bravo 用来表示称赞或喝彩;aha 表示惊奇或胜利;tut-tut 表示不赞成或烦恼时的咂嘴声;wow 表示惊奇、赞叹或钦佩;blast 表示烦恼;hurrah 表示欢喜、赞成;ugh 表示厌恶或恐惧并带有相应的面部表情;damn, shit 及 hell 表示恼怒、失望或厌恶等。

① Why, it's you! 呦,原来是你啊!
② Ouch, I break my leg! 哎哟,我的腿折了。
③ Alas, I failed the exam! 唉,我没考过!
④ Hush! The baby is sleeping. 嘘,小宝宝在睡觉。
⑤ Bravo! Well done! 好啊,干得好!
⑥ Aha, so that's where she lives! 啊哈,原来她住在那里!
⑦ Tut-tut, you are late again! 啧啧,你又迟到了!
⑧ Wow, how marvelous the shanghai world Expo is! 哇,上海世博会真壮观啊!
⑨ Hurrah! Hurrah! We won the game! 哇,我们赢得比赛了!
⑩ Ugh! This medicine tastes nasty! 喔,这药好苦!
⑪ Shit! /Damn it! /Hell! Someone has stolen my car! 该死的,有人偷了我的车!

第十八章 句 子 类 型

18.1 按照句子的用途分类

英语句子按其交际用途可以分为陈述句(Declarative Sentence)、疑问句(Interrogative Sentence)、祈使句(Imperative Sentence)和感叹句(Exclamatory Sentence)。

18.1.1 陈述句

陈述句(Statement,或 Declarative Sentence)可用来说明事实、看法,描述动作、状态,阐明道理、原因等,是日常生活中用得最多的一种句子。它在表达意思上有两种形式,即肯定句形式和否定句形式。

① Chinese is one of the major languages in the world. 中文是世界主要语言之一。
② It is not an easy job to learn English well. 学好英语不是件易事。
③ She is doing her term paper. 她在写学期论文。
④ This is a beautiful garden. 这是一座漂亮的花园。
⑤ Wealth does not mean happiness. 富有并不意味着幸福。
⑥ Being over-slept, he was late for class today. 由于睡过了头,他今天上课迟到了。

18.1.2 疑问句

疑问句是用来提出问题的,按其语法结构和交际功能不同可分为四种类型。

1. 一般疑问句(General Question)

(1) 一般疑问句是就某件事或某种情况的"是与否"提问。因此,它的回答不是 yes 就是 no,或相当于 yes 或 no 的词语;回答时所用的句子可以是完整句,也可以是省略句。另一方面,凡是疑问句一般说来都应该是倒装语序。

① —Are you a student? 你是学生吗?
   —Yes, I am a student. 是的,我是。
② —Do you like dancing? 你喜欢跳舞吗?
   —Yes, I do. 是的,我喜欢。

(2) 在招待客人或向人表示愿意提供某种帮助时,通常在一般疑问句用肯定词。

① Would you like some coffee? (some 是肯定词)你愿意喝杯咖啡吗?
② May I get you some sugar? (some 是肯定词)我可以给你加些糖吗?

(3) 一般疑问句的缩略否定形式,即"操作词+n't+主语",在表示惊讶、失望的含义时通常用非肯定词。

① Haven't you finished your homework yet? 你怎么还没有做完作业?(yet 是非肯定词)

但是如果一般疑问句的缩略否定形式使用肯定词时,表示提问人对答案的肯定意向。

② Haven't you finished your homework already? 你不是已经做完作业了吗?

一般疑问句的缩略否定形式还可以表示对美好事物的赞叹。

③ Isn't she beautiful? 她真美啊!

④ Isn't he a clever boy? 他真是个聪明的孩子!

2. 特殊疑问句(Specidl Question)

(1) 特殊疑问句是对某件事或某种情况的某一方面的具体内容提问,因此,对哪一方面的具体内容提问,就需要使用相应的特殊疑问词,如时间(when)、地点(where)、原因(why)、方式(how)、人物(who)、名称(what)等。另外,回答的内容也应该是具体的。

① —Who invented the light bulb? 谁发明了电灯泡?
  —Edison(did). 爱迪生。

② —Why is Mary absent from duty today? 玛丽今天为什么没有上班?
  —She is preparing for going abroad. 她要出国,正在做准备。

(2) 特殊疑问句的强调形式可以用来表示惊讶、愤怒等感情。强调的方法是疑问词加ever 或加上如 on earth,in the world,the devil,the hell,the goodness 等表示惊讶、诅咒的词。

① Who ever beat my son? 到底是谁打了我的儿子?

② What on earth does it mean? 那到底是什么意思?

③ How in the world do you manage to do that? 你究竟是如何做到的呢?

④ What the hell are you doing? 你究竟在干什么啊?

3. 选择疑问句(Alternative Question)

选择疑问句可以对句子中的任何成分设置选择问题,选择部分由连词 or 连接,or 之前的部分读升调,其后的部分读降调。回答是时候要根据情况来进行选择,而不是简单的 yes 或 no。

选择疑问句有两种形式。

(1) 一种是以一般疑问句为基础。

① —Is your father or your mother a doctor? 你爸是医生还是你妈是医生?
  —My mother is. —我妈是医生。

② —Are you going to school or back home? 你是去学校还是回家?(选择谓语)
  —(I'm)Going home. 我回家。

(2) 一种是以特殊疑问句为基础。

① When would you like to come, today or tomorrow? 你想什么时候来,今天还是明天?

② How shall we get there, by bus or by train? 我们怎么去那儿,乘公交车还是火车?

4. 反意疑问句(Disjunctive Question)

反意疑问句又叫附加疑问句(Tag Question),是指当提问的人对前面所叙述的事实不敢肯定,而需要向对方加以证实时所提出的问句。其结构前一部分是一个陈述句,后一部分是一个简单的问句。完成后一部分简单问句时,要根据前面陈述句的动词时态和人称来选择适当的助动词进行提问,前后两部分的人称和动词时态要保持一致。如果前一部分用肯定式,后一部分一般用否定式;反之,前一部分为否定式,后一部分要用肯定式,即"前肯定后否定,前否定后肯定"。

① Mary is an English major, isn't she? 玛丽是英语专业的学生,对吗?

② He cannot speak French, can he? 他不会讲法语,对吗?

关于反意疑问句构成的几种特殊形式:

1) 陈述句主语是某些不定代词的反意疑问句

(1) 当陈述部分的主语是 everyone, everybody, someone, no one, nobody, somebody 等指人的合成代词时,反意问句的主语在正式语体中常使用 he。

① Nobody wants to go there, does he? 没人想去那里,是吗?

② Everyone knows him, doesn't he? 大家都认识他,对吗?

而在非正式文体中往往用 they。

③ Anyone can do that, can't they? 任何人都能做到那点,对吗?

④ No one is interested in that, are they? 没人对那个感兴趣,是吗?

(2) 当陈述部分以不定代词 one 做主语时,反意问句的主语在正式常合场用 one,非正式场合用 he。

One can't be always careful, can one? /can he? 一个人不可能总是很小心,是吗?

(3) 当陈述部分的主语是表示物的不定代词 everything, something、anything, nothing 等时,反意问句的主语用 it。

① Everything seems all right, doesn't it? 看来一切都好,是吗?

② Nothing is in the box, is it? 盒子里什么也没有,对吗?

2) 陈述部分含有否定词或半否定词的反意疑问句

陈述部分带有 never, hardly, scarcely, seldom, no, none, rarely, nowhere, few, little 等否定词或半否定词时,反意问句的动词要用肯定形式。

① Few people have come to the island, have they? 几乎没人来过这个岛上,是吗?

② Hardly has he heard from her these days, has he? 最近他几乎没有收到她的信,是吗?

③ We seldom eat out, do we? 我们很少外出吃饭,是吗?

如果陈述部分的否定意义只是由单词加否定前缀构成时,其后的反意疑问句一般要用否定形式。

④ He is unhappy, isn't he? 他不高兴,是吗?

3) 陈述部分的主语是指示代词的反意疑问句

陈述部分主语是指示代词 this, that 时,其后的反意疑问句用主语 it。

① This is important, isn't it? 这很重要,是吗?

陈述部分主语是指示代词 these, those 时,其后的反意疑问句用主语 they。

② Those are mine, aren't they? 那些是我们的,对吗?

4) 祈使句的反意疑问句

祈使句后加一个反意疑问句,使祈使句变得更加委婉。肯定祈使句的反意疑问句通常用 will you, won't you, would you, can you, can't you 等来表达不同的含义。在否定的祈使句后的反意疑问句通常只用 will you。

(1) 表示"请求",肯定祈使句的反意疑问句用 will you。

① Give me a hand, will you? 请帮我一把,好吗?

② Pass me a book, will you? 请把书递给我,好吗?

(2) 表示"邀请"、"劝诱"时,肯定祈使句后的反意疑问句用 won't you。

Have another cup of tea, won't you? 再来杯茶,好吗?

(3) 表示"催促"、"不耐烦"时,肯定祈使句后的反意疑问句用 can't you。

Stop talking, can't you? 不要讲了,好吗?

(4) 用"Let's..."开头的肯定祈使句表示"提议、建议、主张",其后的反意疑问句用 shall we。

① Let's forget the unhappy things, shall we? 让我们忘记不高兴的事情,好吗?

但是以 Let us... 或 Let me... 开头的祈使句后的反意疑问句,表示允许,则要用 will you。

② Let us go now, will you? 我们现在就走,好吗?

(5) 否定祈使句的反意疑问句只用 will you。

① Don't take away my dictionary, will you? 不要拿走我的词典,好吗?

以 Let's not... 开头的祈使句后的反意疑问句用 all right 或 OK。

② Let's not go fishing, all right? 我们不去钓鱼,好吗?

③ Let's not talk about it any more, OK? 我们不再谈论此事了,好吗?

5) 复合句的反意疑问句

(1) 当陈述部分是一个(带 that 引导宾语从句的)主从复合句时,反意问句部分要和主句的主语和谓语保持对应关系。

① He said he was a teacher, didn't he? 他说他是一名老师,是吗?

② You don't mind if I go now, do you? 如果我现在走你不介意,是吗?

但是,当陈述部分的主语是 I suppose, I think, I believe, I imagine, I expect 等结构时,反意疑问句的主语和谓语要和 that 从句的主语和谓语保持一致关系,而且要注意到否定的转移问题。

③ I don't think he will come, will he? 我认为他不会来,是吗?

④ I heard that he was very honest, wasn't he? 我听说他很诚实,是吗?

(2) 当陈述部分是并列句时,附加疑问句的主谓语要和离它最近的句子的主谓保持对应关系。

John isn't a hard-working student, for he has been late for three times, hasn't he? 约翰不是一名用功的学生,因为他已经迟到三次了,是吗?

6) 关于助动词和情态动词的反意疑问句

(1) 陈述部分含有 have/has/had to 时,其后的反意疑问句用 do 的相应形式。

① You have to go, don't you? 你不得不走,是吗?

② He has to stay in bed all day, doesn't he? 他不得不整天呆在床上,是吗?

③ I had to keep it well, didn't I? 我必须把它保存完好,是吗?

但是在陈述句中用 have/has/had got to 来代替 have/has/had to 时,反意疑问句用 have 的相应形式。

④ Ann has got to see a doctor, hasn't she? 安必须去看医生,对吗?

⑤ You haven't got to go to school on Sunday, have you? 你不必星期天上学,是吗?

陈述部分有 had better/would rather 时,其后的反意疑问句用 hadn't/wouldn't。

⑥ You'd better not stay here, had you? 你最好不要待在这里,好吗?

⑦ They would rather take this one, wouldn't they? 他们宁愿拿这个,是吗?

（2）陈述部分含情态动词 ought to，其后反意疑问句用 oughtn't 或 shouldn't 均可。

① I ought to come here, oughtn't I? 我应该来这里，是吗？

② You ought to go by ship, shouldn't you? 你应该乘船走，对吗？

（3）陈述部分含情态动词 used to，其后反意疑问句用 usedn't 或 didn't 均可。

① Tom used to live here, usedn't he? 汤姆以前住在这里，是吗？

② They used to work in the shop, didn't they? 他们过去常在这个商店工作，是吗？

（4）陈述部分有 needn't 时，附加疑问句部分用 need 但有时也可用 must。

You needn't do that, need you? /must you? 你不必那样做，是吗？

（5）当陈述部分含有情态动词 must，其意义表示"必须、必要"时，其后的反意疑问句用 mustn't 或 needn't。

① You must do it today, mustn't you? 你必须今天做，对吗？

② She must look after her sister, needn't she? 她必须照顾她妹妹，对吗？

如果 must 的含义表示"一定是、想必"等推测意义时，其后的反意疑问句则要依据句中的谓语动词的时态结构采用 be/have/did/do＋not 等相应形式。

③ He must be ill, isn't he? 他一定生病了，是吗？

④ You must have seen the film before, haven't you? 你以前一定看过这部电影，是吗？

如果陈述部分用了 must have＋P.P.（过去分词），但明示或暗示了过去的时间，其反意疑问句用过去时。

⑤ He must have seen her yesterday, didn't he? 他昨天一定见过她，是吗？

7）反意疑问句的其他特殊形式

（1）陈述部分是"I'm..."结构时，其后的反意疑问句用 aren't I?

I am a student, aren't I? 我是一名学生，是吗？

（2）陈述部分是 there be 或 there live, there stand, there used to be 等结构时，其后的反意疑问句主语用 there。

① There is something wrong with your bike, isn't there? 你的自行车出了些故障，是吗？

② There lived a king here many years ago, didn't there? 许多年前这里住着一位国王，是吗？

（3）陈述部分的主语是动词不定式、动名词短语以及词组或从句时，其后的反意疑问句主语用 it。

① Doing eye exercises is good for your eyes, isn't it? 做眼保健操有益于你的眼睛，是吗？

② What the teacher said is true, isn't it? 老师的话是对的，是吗？

（4）感叹句后的反意疑问句，谓动词用 be 的现在时否定形式，主语根据具体内容而定。

① What a clever girl, isn't she? 多么聪明的女孩，对吗？

② How beautiful the flowers are, aren't they? 这些很漂亮，对吗？

（5）陈述部分由 neither... nor, either... or 连接的并列主语时，疑问部分根据其实际逻辑意义而定。

Neither you nor I am a teacher, are we? 你不是老师，我也不是，对吗？

18.1.3 祈使句

祈使句往往是用来表示说话人的请求、命令、要求、建议等。祈使句分为第二人称、第一人称、第三人称祈使句。

1. 第二人称祈使句

第二人称祈使句的主语常被省略，因为这个主语很明确地是听话人"you"，它的否定形式是句首用 Don't ＋ 动词原形，或是 Not to ＋ 动词原形。

① Be quiet, please! 请安静！

② Stand up! 起立！

③ Don't smoke in the office. 不要在办公室抽烟。

④ Not to be careless when you're driving a car. 你开车时不要粗心。

2. 第一人称祈使句

如果说话人以自己为祈使对象，便可以用第一人称祈使句"Let me＋不定式"。

① Let me try again. 让我再试一次吧。

② Let me think what to do next. 让我想一下下一步做什么。

如果祈使对象包括说话人和听话人在内，便可以用"Let's＋不定式"结构。

③ Let's do it now. 我们现在就动手做吧。

④ Let's have a rest. 我们休息一会儿。

第一人称祈使句的否定形式是在句首加 Don't，但在正式场合下是在 Let me 或 Let's 后面加 not。

⑤ Don't let me interrupt you. 不要让我打断你。

⑥ Let's not do anything at present. 目前我们不要做任何事情。

3. 第三人称祈使句

第三人称祈使句的结构是 Let him/them/名词词组＋不定式。

① Let the baby sleep. 让孩子睡吧。

② Let him clear up the mess. 让他收拾吧。

它的否定形式经常是在句首加 Don't。

③ Don't let him go. 不要让他走。

18.1.4 感叹句

感叹句表示说话人的喜悦、气愤、惊讶等强烈的情绪。这类句子中，有很多是由 what 或 how 引起的。what 用来强调名词，how 则强调形容词、副词或动词。这类句子的构成只需将所强调或所感叹的对象放到句首；句子无需倒装，要用正常语序。

① What a fine day it is today! 今天天气多好啊！

② How touching the story is! 这个故事真感人啊！

③ What a lovely son you have! 你有个多可爱的儿子啊！

当然，如果不用这种句型，而句子(无论是哪种句子)本身又表示了上述的种种情绪，那么该句也就成了感叹句。

④ I wish I had a car! 我真希望有辆车啊！

⑤ Many happy returns of the day! 今天的收获不小啊！

⑥ Splendid! 太棒了!

18.2　按照句子的结构分类

如果按照句子的结构分类,英文句子可分为三个类别:简单句(Simple Sentence)、并列句(Compound Sentence)和复合句(Complex Sentence)。这里所说的结构,主要是指句子中主语和谓语之间所构成的关系。

18.2.1　简单句

简单句只有一个主谓关系。句子可能有两个或更多的主语,也可能有两个或更多的谓语,但是句子中的主谓关系只有一个。

① China and Chinese people are incredibly progressing in many aspects.
(两个主语,一个谓语)中国和中国人民在以非常的速度日益进步。

② Computers mean a lot to human beings and are paid more and more attention by people.
(两个谓语,一个主语)计算机对人类社会意味着很多东西,并越来越受到人们的重视。

英语的简单句有五种基本句型:

基本句型一:Ｓ Ｖ（主＋谓）

基本句型二:Ｓ Ｖ Ｐ（主＋谓＋表）

基本句型三:Ｓ Ｖ Ｏ（主＋谓＋宾）

基本句型四:Ｓ Ｖ Ｏ Ｏ(主＋谓＋间宾＋直宾)

基本句型五:Ｓ Ｖ Ｏ Ｃ（主＋谓＋宾＋宾补）

1. 基本句型一

此句型的句子有一个共同特点,即句子的谓语动词都能表达完整的意思。这类动词叫作不及物动词,后面可以跟副词、介词短语、状语从句等。

(1) The water is boiling. 水开了。

(2) The train will leave soon. 火车就要开了。

2. 基本句型二

此句型的句子有一个共同的特点:句子谓语动词都不能表达一个完整的意思,必须加上一个表明主语身份或状态的表语构成复合谓语,才能表达完整的意思,这类动词叫做系动词。系动词分两类:be, look, keep, seem 等属一类,表示存在的情况;get, grow, become, turn 等属另一类,表示变化。be 本身没有什么意义,只起连系主语和表语的作用。其他系动词仍保持其部分词义。

① This is an English-Chinese dictionary. 这是本英汉辞典。

② The dinner smells good. 午餐闻起来很香。

③ He felt unwell today. 他今天感觉不舒服。

④ Everything looks different. 一切看来都不同了。

⑤ He is growing tall and strong. 他长得又高又壮。

⑥ The trouble is that they are short of money. 麻烦的是他们缺少钱。

⑦ Our well has gone dry. 我们的井干枯了。

⑧ His face turned red. 他的脸红了。

3. 基本句型三

此句型句子的共同特点是,谓语动词都具有实义,都是主语产生的动作,但不能表达完整的意思,必须跟有一个宾语,即动作的承受者,才能使意思完整,这类动词叫做及物动词。常用于这句型的动词有：attempt, dare, decide, desire, expect, hope, intend, learn, need, offer, pretend, promise, propose, purpose, refuse, want, wish 等。

① Who knows the answer? 谁知道答案?

② He has refused to help them. 他拒绝帮他们的忙。

③ He admits that he was mistaken. 他承认犯了错误。

4. 基本句型四

此句型的句子有一个共同特点,谓语动词必须跟有两个宾语才能表达完整的意思。这两个宾语一个是动作的直接承受者,另一个是动作的间接承受者。

① She ordered herself a new dress. 她给自己订制了一套新衣裳。

② She cooked her husband a delicious meal. 她给丈夫煮了一桌好菜。

③ He brought you a dictionary. 他给你带来了一本字典。

5. 基本句型五

此句型的句子的共同特点是,动词虽然是及物动词,但是只跟一个宾语还不能表达完整的意思,必须加上一个补充成分来补足宾语,才能使意思完整。常用于这种句型的动词有 appoint, call, choose, elect, entitle, find, make, name, nominate(命名)。

① They appointed him manager. 他们任命他当经理。

② They painted the door green. 他们把门漆成绿色。

③ They found the house deserted. 他们发现那房子无人居住。

④ I saw them getting on the bus. 我看见他们上了那辆公共汽车。

除了这五种基本句型之外,还有一种"there＋be＋主语＋状语"的句型。这是英语中的一个特殊句型,表示"存在"或"有……"。句中的 be 可以换成 live, exist, appear 等表示"存在、出现、消失"的不及物动词。引导词 there 可以换成"here"或表示"地点、方向"的副词或介词。

① There is a clock on the table. 桌子上面有一个钟。

② Once there lived a king called Lear. 从前有一位王名叫李尔。

③ There seems to be some misunderstanding. 看起来有些误会。

④ Here comes the bus. 公共汽车向这边驶来了。

18.2.2 并列句

并列句有两个或两个以上的主谓结构。这些主谓结构之间的关系是并列的、对等的。从语法上讲,所谓"并列"、"对等"是指任何一个主谓结构都能独立地表达意思,谁也不从属于谁。尽管如此,这些主谓结构在意思或逻辑上有一定程度的内在联系。否则,它们就可能被分别写成简单句,而没有必要写在一起构成并列句了。在并列句中,要使两个或几个主谓结构(分句)连接在一起,就要用并列连词。并列连词用来连接平行对等(即互不从属)的分句。按其表示的不同意思有下面几种：

(1) 表示转折意思,如 but, yet, however, nevertheless, while(而,另外一方面), whereas 等。

① Everything in the world is outside you but health belongs to yourself. 一切都是身外之物,只有健康属于自己。

② He has learned English for only one year, yet he can communicate with people in English. 他才学一年英文,但已能用英文与人交流了。

③ John has his shortcomings; however, that doesn't mean he is not qualified for the job. 约翰有缺点,但这不等于说他不胜任这份工作。

(2) 表示因果关系,如 or, so, therefore, hence 等。

① You'd better take an umbrella with you, for it's going to rain. 要下雨了,你最好带把伞。

② I've got a meeting to attend, so I have to go now. 我要去开个会,我得走了。

③ You are in the right, therefore we should support you. 你是对的,所以我们该支持你。

④ The town was built on the side of a hill, hence it's named Hillside. 这个小镇建在山旁,所以叫"山旁"。

(3) 表示并列关系,如 and, or, either... or, neither... nor, not only... but (also), both... and, as well as 等。

① She came to my house yesterday evening, and I went to hers. 昨晚她来我家了,我却去她家了。

② Do it this way or you'll be in trouble. 你就这么办,不然你会有麻烦的。

③ Either you tell him the truth, or I do it. 不是你告诉他事实,就是我来告诉。

④ He doesn't know your address, neither / nor do I. 他不知道你的地址,我也不知道。

18.2.3 复合句

复合句明显地不同于简单句,因为它有两个或两个以上的主谓结构。从表面上看,它与并列句相似。其实不然,并列句的几个主谓结构之间的关系是并列的、对等的;而复合句中的主谓结构之间的关系不是并列的、对等的,其中只有一个主谓结构是主要的,其他的主谓结构都从属于这个主要的主谓结构,该主要的主谓结构称作句子的主句(Main Clause);其他的主谓结构称作句子的从句或子句(Subordinate Clause)。

复合句里的从句种类较多,引起不同的从句要用不同的从属连词。关于从属连词的具体使用将在"从句"的有关章节里再作介绍。另外,这里所说的"从属"关系,是指从句只有和主句在一起才能有意义;从句若从主句那里独立出来就无法表达意义了。

① Because they talk at home while the television is on, many people think they can talk at movies as well. 许多人在家里是边看电视边谈话,所以他们认为在电影院也可以如此。(状语从句)

② Whether he comes or not doesn't make any difference to me. 他来与不来对我都一样。(主语从句)

③ There is disagreement among economists about what money is and how money is measured. 什么是货币以及怎样计量货币,经济学家之间存有分歧。(宾语从句)

④ China is not what it used to be. 中国不是它过去的样子了。(表语从句)

⑤ Is there any proof that the food of plant differs from that of animals? 有没有什么证据说明植物性食品不同于动物性的呢?(同位语从句)

⑥ Taxes consist of money that people pay to support their government. 税款是人们支持政府而交的钱。(定语从句)

巩 固 练 习

为下列句子加上正确的反意疑问句。

1. The little boy hurt his foot, _____ _____?
2. You were late yesterday, _____ _____?
3. The little girl could hardly speak at the age of 3, _____ _____?
4. There is little water left, _____ _____?
5. There are few people in the cinema, _____ _____?
6. He never comes to school late, _____ _____?
7. Nobody knows him here, _____ _____?
8. Few people knew this word, _____ _____?
9. The king was unhappy, _____ _____?
10. That book is useless to us, _____ _____?
11. He dislikes dancing, _____ _____?
12. Everyone is having a good time on the farm, _____ _____?
13. Nothing has happened here, _____ _____?
14. Nobody likes that brown dog, _____ _____?
15. Don't make any noise, _____ _____?
16. Let's go to the cinema together, _____ _____?
17. Let us pay a visit to Shenzhen, _____ _____?
18. David says you will come in time, _____ _____?
19. I think they knew little about it, _____ _____?
20. We think he is wrong, _____ _____?
21. We don't believe he will come, _____ _____?
22. There were only six people now, _____ _____?
23. There will be a football match tomorrow, _____ _____?
24. You'd better not stand in the row, _____ _____?
25. You'd like to go there, _____ _____?

第十九章 直接引语和间接引语

19.1 直接引语和间接引语的定义

直接引述别人的原话,叫直接引语。用自己的话转述别人的话,叫间接引语。间接引语在多数情况下构成宾语从句。直接引语一般前后要加引号,间接引语不用引号。

Mr Black said, "I'm busy." 布莱克先生说:"我很忙。"(直接引语)

Mr Black said that he was busy. 布莱克先生说他很忙。(间接引语)

19.2 直接引语如何变为间接引语

一般来说,直接引语转换为间接引语时,人称、时态、时间状语和地点状语、句子的结构等都要有变化。

19.2.1 人称的变化

人称的变化可以根据"一主、二宾、三不变"的原则来进行变换。

(1)"一主"指在直接引语中的第一人称变为间接引语时,要和主句中的主语在人称上保持一致。

He said, "I am forty."(直接引语)他说:"我四十岁了"。

He said that he was forty.(间接引语)他说他四十岁了。

(2)"二宾"指直接引语中的第二人称变为间接引语时,要和主句中的间接宾语保持人称一致。

He said to Lily, "Are you coming tomorrow?"(直接引语)他对莉莉说:"明天你来吗?"

He asked Lily if she was coming the next day.(间接引语)他问莉莉第二天是否来。

(3)"三不变"指直接引语中的第三人称变为间接引语时,人称不变。

She said to me, "Is he an English teacher?"(直接引语)她对我说:"他是英语老师吗?"

She asked me if he was an English teacher.(间接引语)她问我他是不是英语老师。

19.2.2 时态的变化

如果主句的谓语动词是现在时,直接引语变成间接引语时,从句的时态无需变化。如果主句的谓语动词是过去时,直接引语变成间接引语时,从句的时态要做出相应的改变,如下表所列。

直接引语	间接引语
一般现在时	一般过去时
现在进行时	过去进行时
现在完成时	过去完成时
一般将来时	过去将来时
一般过去时	过去完成时
过去完成时	过去完成时
将来进行时	过去将来进行时
将来完成时	过去将来完成时
can, may, must, ought to, needn't	could, might, must(had to), ought to, needn't/didn't need to/ didn't have to
shall, will	should, would

注：直接引语变成间接引语时，从句时态无需改变的情况有如下几种：

（1）当主句的谓语动词是一般现在时的时候。

He always says, "I am tired out."（直接引语）他总说："我累坏了"。

He always says that he is tired out.（间接引语）他总说他累坏了。

（2）当主句的谓语动词是将来时的时候。

He will say, "I'll try my best to help you."（直接引语）他会说："我会尽力帮助你。"

He will say that he will try his best to help me.（间接引语）他会说他会尽力帮助我。

（3）当直接引语部分带有具体的过去时间状语时。

He said, "I went to college in 1994."（直接引语）他说："我一九九四年上大学"。

He told us that he went to college in 1994.（间接引语）他告诉我们他一九九四年上了大学。

（4）当直接引语中有以 when, while 引导的从句，表示过去的时间时。

He said, "When I was a child, I usually played football after school."（直接引语）他说："我小时候总是放学后踢足球。"

He said that when he was a child, he usually played football after school.（间接引语）他说他小时候总是放学后踢足球。

（5）当直接引语是客观真理或自然现象时。

Our teacher said to us, "Light travels faster than sound."（直接引语）我们老师对我们说："光的传播速度比声音的快。"

Our teacher told us that light travels faster than sound.（间接引语）我们老师告诉我们光的传播速度比声音的快。

（6）当引语是谚语、格言时。

He said, "Practice makes perfect."（直接引语）他说："熟能生巧。"

He said that practice makes perfect.（间接引语）他说熟能生巧。

（7）当直接引语中有情态动词 should, would, could, had better, would rather, might, must, ought to, used to, need 时。

① The doctor said, "You'd better drink plenty of water."（直接引语）医生说："你最好多喝水。"
The doctor said I'd better drink plenty of water.（间接引语）医生说我最好多喝水。
② He said, "She must be a teacher."（直接引语）他说："她一定是一名老师。"
He said that she must be a teacher.（间接引语）他说她一定是一名老师。
③ He said, "She ought to have arrived her office by now."（直接引语）他说："她本应该现在就到了她的办公室。"
He said that she ought to have arrived her office by then.（间接引语）他说她本应该那时就到了她的办公室。
④ The teacher said, "You needn't hand in your compositions today."（直接引语）老师说："今天你们不必交作文。"
The teacher said we needn't/didn't need to/didn't have to hand in our compositions that day.（间接引语）老师说那天我们不必交作文。

19.2.3 指示代词、时间状语、地点状语及方向性动词的变化

指示代词、时间状语、地点状语及方向性动词的变化如下表所列。

词类	直接引语	间接引语
指示代词	this	that
	these	those
时间状语	now	then
	today	that day
	tomorrow	the next/following day
	yesterday	the day before
	the day after tomorrow	two days after, in two days' time
	the day before yesterday	two days before
	three days ago	three days before
	this week/month	that week/month
	last week/month	the week/month before
	next week/month	the next/following week/month
地点状语	here	there
动词	bring	take
	come	go

注：如果就在当地转述，here 不必变为 there，come 不必改为 go，如果就在当天转述，则 today, yesterday, tomorrow 等状语也不必变化。

She said to us, "I'll come here tomorrow."（直接引语）她对我们说："我明天来这里。"
She told us she would come here tomorrow.（间接引语）她告诉我们她明天来这里。

19.2.4 句子结构的变化

1. 陈述句的直接引语变间接引语时

此时用连词 that 引导(that 在口语中常可省略),主句的谓语动词可用直接引语中的 said,也可用 told sb. 来代替。

He said,"I'll give you an examination next Monday."(直接引语)他说:"下周一我要测试你们。"

He said to us that he would give us an examination the next Monday.(间接引语)他给我们说下周一他要测试我们。

He told us that he would give us an examination the next Monday.(间接引语)他告诉我们下周一他要测试我们。

2. 直接引语是疑问句时

此时还应该把直接引语中的疑问句改为陈述句语序,句尾加上句号。

(1) 直接引语为一般疑问句,变为间接引语的时,要用连词 whether 或 if 将其引出,使其成为间接引语的宾语从句。如果主句的谓语动词是 said,则将其改为 asked,如果谓语动词的后面没有间接宾语,可以加上一个间接宾语 me,him,her,us 等。

① "Is there anything wrong, Madam?"said the policeman.(直接引语)"有什么麻烦事吗,女士?"警察说。

The policeman asked the woman if(whether) there was anything wrong.(间接引语)警察问这位妇女是否遇到了麻烦。

② My friend asked," Do you like English?"(直接引语)我朋友问:"你喜欢英语吗?"

My friend asked me whether (if) I liked English.(间接引语)我朋友问我是否喜欢英语。

(2) 当直接引语是特殊疑问句时,间接引语常是由该特殊疑问词所引导的宾语从句。

① The boy was wondering,"How does the computer work?"(直接引语)男孩自忖道:"电脑是怎么运行的呢?"

The boy was wondering how the computer worked.(间接引语)男孩想知道电脑是如何运行的。

② Mary said,"What are you dong, Mike?"(直接引语)玛丽说:"你在干什么,麦克?"

Mary asked Mike what he was doing.(间接引语)玛丽问麦克他在干什么。

(3) 直接引语是选择疑问句时,间接引语通常只能改为由"whether"引导的宾语从句。同时要注意语序的变化。

He asked me,"Do you study English or French?"(直接引语)他问我:"你学的是英语还是法语?"

He asked me whether I studied English or French.(间接引语)他问我学的是英语还是法语。

(4) 直接引语是反义疑问句时,间接引语用连词 whether 或 if 来引导。

"It's Mary, isn't it?"asked Jane.(直接引语)"是玛丽,是吗?"詹妮问。

Jane asked whether (if) it was Mary.(间接引语)詹妮问是不是玛丽。

3. 直接引语为祈使句时

(1) 一般情况的祈使句在由直接引语变为间接引语时要将动词原形变为动词不定式,主句根据语气来选用 ask，tell，order，demand，warn，command 等及物动词,其否定句是在动词不定式之前加 not。

① "Don't take off your coat," she said to her sister. （直接引语）"不要脱外套",她对她姐姐说。

She told her sister not to take off her coat. （间接引语）她告诉她姐姐不要脱外套。

② "Do some shopping for me, please. ", he said to her. （直接引语）"请给我买些东西"。他对她说。

He asked her to do some shopping for him. （间接引语）他请她替他买些东西。

③ "You must do everything as I do", the professor said. （直接引语）"你必须按我做的去做"教授说。

The professor ordered his students to do everything as he did. （间接引语）教授命令他的学生们按他所做的那样去做。

（2）转述"let's..."开头的表示建议、劝告等含义的祈使句时,可以用"suggest/say that"从句,也可以用"suggest＋doing"结构。

He said, "Let's have a rest. "（直接引语）他说："我们休息一下吧。"

He suggested that we should have a rest/suggested our having a rest. （间接引语）他建议我们应该休息一下。

（3）在 suggest，insist，demand，shout，cry 等动词后常用 that 引导的宾语从句来转述原来的祈使句。但要注意使用虚拟语气。

He insisted, "Have a cup of tea and you will feel better. "（直接引语）他坚持说："喝杯茶你就会觉得好多了。"

He insisted that I (should) have a cup of tea and then I would feel better. （间接引语）他坚持让我喝杯茶然后我就会感觉好多了。

4. 直接引语是感叹句时

感叹句一般很少变为间接引语。如果必须转述,通常用其他词语来表达原句的意义和情感。

①"What a brave boy!"the man said. （直接引语）"多么勇敢的男孩啊！"这个男人说。

The man remarked with admiration what a brave boy he was. （间接引语）这个男人赞美说他是很勇敢的男孩。

②"Goodness me!" he said, "What a great deal of work you have done!"（直接引语）"天啊！"他说："你做了那么多的工作啊！"

He expressed considerable surprise that I had done such a great deal of work. （间接引语）他很吃惊地说我做了那么多的工作。

③ He said,"Alas! How foolish I have been!"（直接引语）他说："哎呀！我多么蠢啊！"

He confessed with regret that he had been very fool. （间接引语）他后悔地说他很蠢。

④ He said to me,"How do you do?"（直接引语）他对我说"你好！"

He greeted me. （间接引语）他同我打了招呼。

⑤ He said to them, "Good night!"（直接引语）他给他们说"晚安！"

He wished them good night. （间接引语）他祝他们晚安。

⑥ He said, "Happy new year!"（直接引语）他说："新年好！"

He wished me a happy new year. （间接引语）他祝我新年快乐。

巩 固 练 习

把下面的直接引语句变为间接引语。

1. "You should be more careful next time," his father said to him.
2. Mr. Wang said, "I will leave for Shanghai on business next month, children."
3. "I haven't heard from my parents these days," said Mary.
4. The geography teacher said to us, "The moon moves around the earth and the earth goes round the sun."
5. She said to him, "It's time that you left here."
6. Zhang Hong said to me, "Doctor Wang passed away in 1948."
7. John said to his parents, "I had learned 500 Chinese words by the end of last term."
8. The history teacher said to them, "The Chinese Communist Party was founded on July 1st, 1921."
9. He said, "Are you a student?"
10. "Have you anything interesting I can read, George?" she said.
11. "She's here to ask for help, isn't she?" he asked.
12. "Where are you going?" the father asked his son.
13. "Are you sorry for what you have done?" the mother asked the naughty boy.
14. She said, "Did you meet this man at the station two hours ago, Mr. Li?"
15. "Write your names on your papers first," the teacher said to us.
16. "Please come here again tomorrow," her friend said to her.
17. "Let me pack the parcel for you," he said.
18. "Don't make so much noise in class, boys and girls," said the teacher.
19. "What a lovely day it is!"
20. "Happy New Year to you!" he said.

第二十章 名词性从句

20.1 概　述

在句子中起名词作用的各种从句统称为名词性从句(the Noun clause)。名词可作句子的主语、表语、宾语(包括介词宾语)或同位语,名词性从句的语法作用与名词相同。因此,根据它们在句中所起的语法作用,这类从句又可分为主语从句、表语从句、宾语从句和同位语从句。

20.2 名词性从句的引导词

根据引导名词性从句的连词在从句中的作用,名词性从句的引导词共分为三类。
(1) 连接词:that,whether/if,as if/though,whether...or。
(2) 连接代词:who/whoever,whom/whomever,whose,what/whatever,which/whichever。
(3) 连接副词:when,where,how,why。

20.2.1 连接词(Conjunction)

只起连接主句和从句的作用,在从句中不作句子成分。常用的引导名词性从句的连接词有四个 that,whether/if,as if,whether...or,其中 that 无意义(在引导宾语从句时还可省略,但是若引导的宾语从句作介词的宾语则不能省略),whether/if 表示"是否"(其中 if 只引导宾语从句,在主语从句、表语从句和同位语从句中只用 whether,whether...or 的意思是"是……还是"或者"是否",as if/though 的意思是"好像"。

① <u>That we go swimming everyday</u> does us a lot of good. 每天游泳对我们很有益处。(主语从句)

② Your great fault is **that** <u>you are careless</u>. 你最大的失误是你太粗心了。(表语从句)

③ They came to the conclusion <u>that not all things can be done by a computer.</u> 他们得出结论:并非所有的事情都可通过计算机完成。(同位语从句)

④ She always complains (**that**) <u>he is down on her.</u> 她总是抱怨他瞧不起她。(宾语从句)

20.2.2 连接代词(Conjunctive Pronoun)

连接代词既具有连词的作用,用来连接主句与从句,同时也具有代词的作用,在从句中作主语、宾语、表语、定语。常用的引导名词性从句的连接代词有 who/whoever,whom/whomever,whose,what/whatever,which/whichever,其中 who 表示"谁",主格,作从句的主语;whom 表示"谁",宾格,作从句的宾语;whose 表示"谁的",所有格,作从句的定语;what 表示"什么,……的东西",指物,作从句的主语、宾语、表语或定语;which 表示"哪个/些",指人或物,作从句的主语、宾语、表语或定语;whoever/ whomever(=anyone who/whom)表示"无论谁",作用分别与 who/ whom 相同;whatever 表示"无论什么",指物,作用与 what 相同;whichever 表示"无论哪个/些,作用与 which 相同。

① **Who** did the work is unknown. 这件工作是谁干的,大家都不知道。(主语从句,who 作从句的主语)

② Do you know **who he expects will give as a talk**? 你知道他希望谁为我们做报告吗? (宾语从句,who 作从句的主语)

③ **Whoever makes mistakes** must correct them. 无论谁犯了错误都必须改正。(主语从句,whoever 作从句的主语)

④ **Whom** we should help is an important question. 我们应当帮助谁是个重要问题。(主语从句,whom 作从句的宾语)

⑤ **What/Whatever** clothes I should wear depends on myself. 穿什么衣服我说了算。(主语从句,what/whatever 作从句主语的定语)

再如:

① Here are the chairs. Tell me **which /whichever** (ones) are worth buying. 椅子都在这里,告诉我哪些值得买。(宾语从句,which /whichever 作从句的主语或者定语)

② I asked him **whose** bag was stolen. 我问他谁的包丢了。(宾语从句,whose 作从句中主语 bag 的定语)

20.2.3 连接副词 (Conjunctive Adverb)

连接副词既具有连词的作用,用来连接主句与从句,同时也具有副词的作用,在从句中作状语。常用的引导名词性从句的连接副词有 when,where,how,why,其中 when 表示"什么时候";where 表示"什么地方";why 表示"为什么"; how 表示"怎样,如何"。

① He knows **where** you live. 他知道你住哪儿。(宾语从句,where 作从句的地点状语)

② I'd like to know **when** they will let him out. 我想知道他们什么时候放他出来。(宾语从句,when 作从句的时间状语)

③ This is **how** we parted. 我们就是这样分手的。(表语从句,how 作从句的方式状语)

④ **Why** he did it remains a puzzle for ever. 他为什么这么做永远是个谜。(主语从句,why 作从句的原因状语)

20.3 名词性从句的种类

根据名词性从句在句中所起的语法作用可分为主语从句、表语从句、宾语从句和同位语从句。

20.3.1 主语从句(Subject Clause)

在主句中作主语的从句叫做主语从句,它的位置与陈述句基本结构中的主语相同,在句子的最前面。

① **That** the boy didn't take medicine made his mother angry. 小孩子不吃药,这使他妈妈很生气。

② **Whether** he will accept the invitation **or not** is not clear. 他是否会接受邀请还不清楚。
③ **Who** can operate the new machine is not known. 不知道谁会开这台新机器。
④ **Whoever** comes will be welcome. 无论谁来都受欢迎。
⑤ **What/Whatever** clothes I should wear depends on myself. 穿什么衣服我说了算。
⑥ **Why** he did it remains a puzzle for ever. 他为什么这么做永远是个谜。
⑦ **How** they are going to solve the problem is still a puzzle. 他们如何解决这个问题仍然是个谜。

注：(1) 主语从句放在句首，句子常常显得比较笨重，因此常把它移至句子末尾，而用 it 来做形式上的主语。其中 that, whether 引导的主语从句用 it 作形式主语尤为多见。因此，上面的例②可改写为下面的形式。

It is not clear **whether** he will accept the invitation **or not**. 他是否会接受邀请还不清楚。

再如：
① It is strange **that** she came alone yesterday. 很奇怪，她昨天一个人来了。
② It is a pity **that** Mary can't attend our English meeting. 真可惜，玛丽不能出席我们的英语晚会。
③ It is natural **that** they should have different views. 他们有不同的意见和观点是很自然的。
④ It was uncertain **whether** he could come or not. 他是否能来还不确定。

(2) 有些用 it 作形式主语的主语从句结构已形成常用的固定句型。常见的有下面四种结构：

A. It is ＋动词的过去分词＋that－clause

It is said that...	据说……
It is believed that...	有人相信……
It is thought that...	有人认为……
It is suggested that...	有人建议……
It is announced that...	有人通知……
It is reported that...	据报道……
It is proved that...	已证明……
It is hoped that...	希望……
It is supposed that...	据推测……
It is well known that...	众所周知……
It was told that...	有人曾经说……
It is estimated that...	据估计……
It may be said without fear of exaggeration that...	可以毫不夸张地说……
It must be admitted that...	必须承认……
It must be pointed out that...	必须指出……
It will be seen from this that...	由此可见……
It is asserted that...	有人主张……
It is generally considered that...	大家认为……

B. It is ＋形容词＋that-clause

It is important that...	重要的是……
It is possible that...	可能……
It is probable that...	很可能……
It is (un)likely that...	很可能/很不可能……
It is clear that...	很清楚……
It is necessary that...	有必要……
It is queer that...	奇怪的是……
It is strange that...	奇怪的是……

C. It is ＋名词＋that-clause

It is a great pleasure that...	令人高兴的是……
It is a fact that...	事实是……
It is good news that...	……是好消息
It is a question that...	……是个问题
It is common knowledge that...	……是常识
It is a shame that...	……遗憾的是……
It is a waste of time that...	……是浪费时间

D. It ＋动词＋that-clause

It seems that...	好像是……
It struck me that...	令我震惊的是……
It happened that...	碰巧……
It has turned out that...	结果是……

① **It** is such a pleasure **that** you are here. 令人高兴的是你在这里。

② **It** is believed **that** he is a criminal. 人们认为他是罪犯。

③ **It** happened **that** he was in Beijing then. 他当时碰巧在北京。

④ **It** is a waste of time **that** you try to persuade him to change his mind. 你想说服他改变主意纯属浪费时间。

⑤ It seems that we all agree. 我们大家似乎都同意。

20.3.2 宾语从句

放在及物动词或者介词之后作宾语的从句叫做宾语从句（Object Clause），宾语从句可作及物动词的宾语，也可以作介词的宾语。

1. 作动词的宾语

① I know (**that**) she is kind and hospitable. 我知道她很善良，而且好客。

② Here are the chairs. Tell me **which**/**whichever** (ones) are worth buying. 椅子都在这里，告诉我哪些值得买。

③ Do you know **when** we shall have a meeting? 你知道我们什么时候开会吗？

④ The teacher asked me **whether or not** I finished my work. 老师问我是否完成了作业。

⑤ His mother ever explained **why** he had been dismissed. 他妈妈曾经解释过他为什么被解雇。

注:(1) 在 demand, order, suggest, decide, insist, desire, request, command 等表示要求、命令、建议、决定等意义的动词后,宾语从句常用"(should)＋动词原形"作谓语,should 还可以省略。

① I insist **that she (should) do** her work alone. 我坚持要她自己工作。

② The commander ordered **that troops (should) set off** at once. 司令员命令部队马上出发。

(2) think, believe, imagine, suppose 等动词引起的否定性宾语从句中,将从句中的否定形式前移到主句中即可。

① We **don't think** you are here. 我们认为你不在这。

② I **don't believe** he will do so. 我相信他不会这样做。

(3) 在 hope, believe, imagine, suppose, guess, think, I'm afraid 等词或结构的后面,可以用 so 代替一个宾语从句,此宾语从句通常是上文提到过的一件事,其否定形式用本动词的否定式,如 I hope so, I believe so, I suppose so, I guess so, I think so, I'm afraid so,其否定形式:I don't believe so, I don't suppose so, I don't guess so, I don't think so,但要注意 hope 和 I'm afraid 的否定式与上面不同:I hope not, I'm afraid not。

—Do you think it is going to rain? 你觉得会下雨吗?

—I'm afraid so. 恐怕要下雨。

2. 作介词宾语

① He was interested in **whatever** he heard and saw there. 他对在那里听到和看到的一切都感兴趣。

② I was greatly surprised at **what** my little son said. 我儿子讲的话使我大吃一惊。

③ I know nothing about him except **that** he is an orphan. 除了他是一个孤儿的情况以外,对他我一无所知。

注:(1) that 在引导宾语从句时可以省略,但是若引导的宾语从句作介词的宾语则不能省略。

① She always complains **(that)** he is down on her. 她总是抱怨他瞧不起她。(that 可以省略)

② I know nothing about him except **that** he is an orphan. 除了他是一个孤儿的情况以外,对他我一无所知。(that 不可以省略)

(2) 若主句含有复合宾语,即主句是"主语＋谓语＋宾语＋补语"结构,宾语若是从句,则习惯在宾语的位置放上形式宾语 it,而把真正的宾语从句置于句子最后,这就是"主语＋谓语＋形式宾语 it＋补语＋宾语从句"结构。

① I think **it** best **that** you should stay here. 我认为你最好留在这儿。

② I took **it** for granted **that** you would stay with us. 我认为你和我们在一起是理所应当的。

(3) that 引导的宾语从句作介词的宾语时,可在从句前加一个形式宾语 it,这就是"介词＋it＋that"结构,it 可被看作是 that 从句的先行词。

① You may depend on **it that** they are valuable. 你放心,这些东西有价值。

② I'll see to **it that** everything is ready ahead of time. 我将负责提前做好一切准备。

3. 作形容词的宾语

在一些特定的系表结构中(如形容词 happy, glad, delighted, excited, pleased, satisfied, surprised, disappointed, worried, sure, certain, afraid 等作表语时),后面常跟宾语从句。

① I am not certain **whether** he will come and join us. 我没有把握他能否来参加我们的活动。

② I am delighted **that** my 60-year-old father has passed the difficult test. 非常高兴,我60岁的父亲通过了这次很难的测试。

注:(1)宾语从句的句子语序要用陈述语序。

① I want to know **what** he has told you. 我想知道他告诉了你什么。

② She always thinks of **how** she can work well. 她总是在想怎样能把工作做好。

③ She will give **whoever** needs help a warm support. 凡需要帮助的人,她都会给予热情的支持。

(2)注意宾语从句中的时态呼应。当主句动词是现在时,从句根据自身的句子情况,而使用不同时态。当主句动词是过去时态,从句则要用相应的过去时态,如一般过去时、过去进行时、过去将来时等。当从句表示的是客观真理、科学原理、自然现象,则从句仍用现在时态。

① I know (that) he **studies** English every day. 我知道他每天学英语。

(从句用一般现在时)

② I know (that) he **studied** English last term. 我知道他上学期学了英语。

(从句用一般过去时)

③ I know (that) he **will study** English next year. 我知道他明年要学英语。

(从句用一般将来时)

④ I know (that) he **has studied** English since 1998. 我知道他从一九九八年就学习英语了。

(从句用现在完成时)

⑤ The teacher **told** us that Tom **had left** us for America. 老师告诉我们汤姆已经离开我们去美国了。

(从句用过去完成时)

20.3.3 表语从句

在主句中作表语的从句叫表语从句(Predicative Clause)。引导表语从句的连词与引导主语从句的连词大致一样。表语从句位于连系动词后,有时用 as if 引导。其基本结构为主语 + 系动词 + 表语从句。常用的系动词有 be,seem,remain,look 等。

① The reason why I didn't go to America was **that** I got a new job in Beijing. 我没去美国的原因是我在北京找到了一份新工作。

② My suggestion is **that** you should make good use of your time. 我的建议是你该好好利用你的时间。

③ The question is **whether** he can finish the work on time. 问题在于他能不能按时完成这项工作。

④ That is **why** I lost my temper yesterday. 这就是我昨天发脾气的原因。

注:表语从句还可由 as if/as though(宛如,好像),because(因为)引导。

① It looks **as if** it is going to rain. 看起来天要下雨。

② It is **because** he is too young. 这是因为他太年轻。

20.3.4 同位语从句

同位语从句(Appositive Clause)说明其前面的名词的具体内容,可跟同位语从句的名词有 advice,demand,doubt,fact,hope,idea,information,message,news,order,problem,promise,question,request,suggestion,truth,wish,word 等抽象名词。

① We were very happy at the news **that** our team won. 我们听到我们队赢的消息非常激动。

② I don't believe the rumor **that** he murdered his wife. 我不相信他谋杀了他妻子的谣言。

注:(1) 同位语从句通常由 that 引导,也可由 whether,when,which,who,how,what,why 等引导。

① I have no idea **whether** he likes it or not. 我不知道他是否喜欢它。

② Next comes my question **why** you want it. 其次就是我提出的问题:你为什么要它?

(2) 同位语从句有时不是紧跟在有关的名词后面,而是被其他的词隔开了。

① The question came up at the meeting **whether** we had enough money to build a new library. 会上提出了我们建图书馆的经费是否够的问题。

② The rumor spread **that** he murdered his wife. 谣传他谋杀了他妻子。

③ Three days later,word came that our country had sent up another man-made satellite. 三天后消息传来,我国又发射了一颗人造卫星。

(3) 同位语从句与定语从句的区别。定语从句与同位语从句相似的位置,使许多学生往往混淆,阻碍了对文章的理解。那么,如何正确地区分定语从句与同位语从句呢?

定语从句是形容词从句,其作用相当于一个形容词,是用来修饰前面的名词或代词的;同位语从句是名词性从句,其作用相当于一个名词,是对前面的名词作进一步解释的。

① We heard the news (**that**) he had told her. 我们听到他对她说的消息。

② We heard the news **that** he had won the game. 我们听到消息说他赢得了比赛。

例①中的 that 从句的作用相当于一个形容词,其作用是修饰 the news,是定语从句;例②中的 that 从句的作用相当于一个名词,是对 the news 内容的进一步说明,是同位语从句。

定语从句的引导词在从句中充当一定的成分,可作主语、宾语、状语等。而同位语从句中的引导词 that,whether 在从句中只起连接作用,不作任何句子成分,但其他引导同位语从句的引导词,在从句中充当成分。

① A plane is a machine **that** can fly. 飞机是一种能飞的机器。

② The fact **that** they didn't finish the work has to be faced. 必须面对事实,他们没有完成工作。

例①中的引导词 that 在从句中充当句子成分,作从句的主语,故为定语从句;例②中的 that 只起连接作用,引导从句解释 fact 的内容,不作任何句子成分,故为同位语从句。

引导定语从句的关系代词在从句中作宾语,可以省略;而同位语从句的引导词一般不能省略。

① The news (**that**) she heard is true. 她听到的消息是真的。

② The news **that** she will go abroad is true. 她将出国这消息是真的。

例①是定语从句,that 作从句的宾语,可省略;例②是同位语从句,that 不能省略。

巩 固 练 习

一、单项选择。
1. Along with the letter was his promise _____ he would visit me this coming Christmas.
   A. which　　　　B. that　　　　C. what　　　　D. whether
2. They always give the vacant seats to _____ comes first.
   A. whoever　　　B. whomever　　C. who　　　　D. whom
3. We agreed to accept _____ they thought was the best tourist guide.
   A. whichever　　B. whoever　　　C. whatever　　D. whomever
4. _____ men have learned much from the behavior of animals is barely new.
   A. That　　　　B. Those　　　　C. What　　　　D. Whether
5. _____ we can't get seems better than _____ we have.
   A. What; what　B. What; that　　C. That; that　D. That; what
6. It is generally considered unwise to give a child _____ he or she wants.
   A. however　　　B. whatever　　　C. whichever　　D. whenever
7. The possibility _____ the majority of the labor force will work at home is often discussed.
   A. which　　　　B. that　　　　C. what　　　　D. whether
8. We are not looking into the question _____ he is worth trusting.
   A. which　　　　B. that　　　　C. what　　　　D. whether
9. _____ will win the match is still unknown.
   A. What　　　　B. Which　　　　C. Who　　　　D. Whom
10. _____ the English evening will be held has not yet been announced.
    A. Where　　　B. What　　　　C. Why　　　　D. That
11. I have no idea _____ has happened to him.
    A. what　　　　B. which　　　　C. who　　　　D. whom
12. _____ there is life on the moon is an interesting question.
    A. Whether　　B. What　　　　C. Why　　　　D. That
13. This is _____ our problem lies.
    A. what　　　　B. which　　　　C. where　　　D. how
14. It looks _____ it is going to rain.
    A. that　　　　B. which　　　　C. as if　　　　D. whether
15. The thought came to him _____ Mary had probably fallen ill.
    A. which　　　　B. that　　　　C. what　　　　D. whether
16. _____ is a fact that English is being accepted as an international language.
    A. There　　　　B. This　　　　C. That　　　　D. It
17. A computer can only do _____ you have instructed it to do.
    A. how　　　　B. after　　　　C. what　　　　D. when
18. He asked _____ for a violin.

A. did I pay how much B. I paid how much
C. how much did I pay D. how much I paid

19. What the doctors really doubt is _____ my mother will recover from the serious disease soon.
    A. when B. how C. whether D. why

20. Sarah hopes to become a friend of _____ shares her interests.
    A. anyone B. whomever C. whoever D. no matter who

21. —I drove to Zhuhai for the air show last week.
    —Is that _____ you had a few days off?
    A. why B. what C. when D. where

22. I read about it in some book or other, does it matter _____ it was?
    A. where B. what C. how D. which

23. —I think it is going to be a big problem.
    —Yes, it could be.
    —I wonder _____ we can do about it.
    A. if B. how C. what D. that

24. Information has been put forward _____ more middle school graduates will be admitted into universities.
    A. while B. that C. when D. as

25. I still remember _____ this used to be a quiet village.
    A. when B. how C. where D. what

二、用本章所学句型翻译句子。

1. 遗憾的是我没见着那个女演员。
2. 他碰巧出去了。
3. 奇怪的是你竟然不知道这件事。
4. 你有必要把真相告诉他。
5. 事实是我不喜欢运动。
6. 他好像已经知道这件事了。
7. 我认为他不是故意这么做的。
8. 有人主张把会议推迟到下周。
9. 据报道,70多人在那次事故中死亡。
10. 众所周知,他爷爷50年前去了台湾。

三、在下列名词性从句中填入正确的连接词。

1. The reason is _____ he is unable to operate the machine.
2. Mary wrote an article on _____ the team had failed.
3. Elephants have their own way to tell the shape of an object and _____ it is rough or smooth.
4. People have heard _____ the President has said, and they are waiting to see _____ he will do.
5. A computer can only do _____ you have instructed it to do.

6. A story goes _____ Elizabeth I of England liked nothing more than being surrounded by clever and qualified noblemen at court.
7. A modern city has been set up in _____ was a wasteland ten years ago.
8. You are saying that everyone should be equal, and this is _____ I disagree.
9. The other day, my brother drove his car down the street at _____ I thought was a dangerous speed.
10. Do you have any idea _____ is actually going on in the classroom?

四、改错。

1. If we'll go camping tomorrow depends on the weather.
2. It is estimate that a round trip to Mars would take more than a year and a half.
3. A man cannot be really happy if that he enjoys doing is ignored by society as of no value or importance.
4. Although Anne is happy with her success, she wonders that will happen to her private life.
5. What you didn't know the rules won't be a sufficient excuse for your failure to report.

第二十一章 定语从句

21.1 概 述

修饰某一名词或代词,或修饰整个主句的从句,叫做定语从句。被定语从句所修饰的词叫做先行词,定语从句通常由"关系词"引出。引导定语从句的关系词,起着纽带的作用,把从句和它修饰的词,即主句中的某一名词或者代词连接起来,同时代替先行词在从句中担任一个语法成分,如主语、宾语、表语、定语或状语等。

21.2 关系词的分类

按照在定语从句中的语法作用,关系词可分为关系代词和关系副词。
(1) 关系代词,如 who, whom, whose, that, which, as。
(2) 关系副词,如 when, where, why。

① Is he the man who/that wants to see you?
   先行词   定语从句
他就是想见你的那个人吗?(who/that 是关系代词,既引导定语从句,又代替先行词,the man 作从句的主语)

② This is the room **where** his father once lived.
    先行词   定语从句
这是他爸曾经住过的房间。(where 是关系副词,既引导定语从句,又代替先行词 the room 在从句中作地点状语)

③ They rushed over to help the man whose car had broken down.
        先行词   定语从句
那人车坏了,他们都跑过去帮忙。(whose 是关系代词,即引导定语从句,又代替先行词 the man, 作从句的定语)。

④ Please tell me the reason why you missed the plane.
      先行词   定语从句
告诉我你为什么误了飞机。(why 是关系副词,既引导定语从句,又代替先行词 the reason,在从句中作原因状语)。

21.3 关系代词及其引导的定语从句

关系代词可以指代表示人或物的先行词,并在从句中作主语、宾语、表语、定语等。关系代词的功能比较如下表所列。

关系代词	指代功能	语法功能	例 句
who	指代人	主语	① **The man who** stole your car has been arrested. 偷你车的那个人已被逮捕。
		表语	② He is no longer **the man who** he used to be. 他不再是以前那样的人了。
		宾语 （口语中代替 whom）	③ **The man（who）**I met told me to come here. 我碰见的那个人让我到这儿来。
whom （见注1）	指代人	宾语	④ **The man（whom）**I met told me to come here. 我碰见的那个人让我到这儿来。 ⑤ **The man（whom）** I traveled with couldn't speak English. 和我一起旅行的那个人不会说英语。
whose （见注2）	指代人	定语	⑥ She is looking for **the boy whose** mother has just died. 她正在寻找刚失去妈妈的那个孩子。
	指代物	定语	⑦ He lives in **the house whose** window faces south. 他住在窗户朝南的那个房子里。
that （见注1）	指代人	主语	⑧ **The man that** stole your car has been arrested. 偷你车的那个人已被逮捕。
		宾语	⑨ **The man（that）**I met told me to come here. 我碰见的那个人让我到这来。
		表语	⑩ He is no longer **the man（that）** he used to be. 他不再是以前那样的人了。
	指代物	主语	⑪ **The bus that** has just left is for Beijing. 刚刚离开的汽车是去北京的。
		宾语	⑫ Is this **the photo（that）**you took in Shanghai? 这是你在上海照的照片吗？ ⑬ This is **the pan（that）** I boiled the milk in. 这是我煮牛奶的锅。（作介词 in 的宾语）
		表语	⑭ My hometown is not **the dirty village（that）** it used to be. 我的家乡不再是过去那个脏乱的村庄了。
which （见注1）	指代物	主语	⑮ **The bus which** has just left is for Beijing. 刚刚离开的汽车是去北京的。
		宾语	⑯ Is this **the photo（which）** you took in Shanghai? 这是你在上海照的照片吗？ ⑰ This is **the pan（which）** I boiled the milk in. 这是我煮牛奶的锅。（作介词 in 的宾语）

(续)

关系代词	指代功能	语法功能	例 句
as	指代人	主语	⑱ **Such women as** knew Tom thought he was charming. 认识汤姆的女人认为他很有魅力。
		宾语	⑲ **Such women as** I know are very hard-working. 我认识的这些女人很勤劳。
as	指代物	主语	⑳ I bought **the same** kind of **clothes as** are sold in the store. 我买了和这个店里卖的一样的衣服。
		宾语	㉑ She wears **the same** kind of **clothes as** her sister usually does. 她和她姐姐穿同样的衣服。

注:(1) 关系代词 whom, which, that 可作动词的宾语,也可作介词的宾语。当 whom, which 作介词的宾语时,可把介词前提到 whom, which 前。但是,that 作介词的宾语时,介词不可前提。上表中的例句⑤、例句⑬可改写为下面的形式。

① The man **with whom** I traveled couldn't speak English. 和我一起旅行的那个人不会说英语。

② This is the pan **in which** I boiled the milk. 这是我煮牛奶的锅。

但是,含有介词的动词短语一般不拆开使用,如 look for, look after, take care of 等。

This is the watch which/that I am looking for. (正确)这就是我在找的手表。

This is the watch for which I am looking. (错误)

(2) 用 that 不用 which 引导定语从句的几种情况。

① 先行词为 all, everything, nothing, something, anything, little, much 等不定代词。

There is **little** (**that**) I can use. 几乎没有我可以用的东西。

② 先行词被 all, every, no, some, any, little, much 修饰。

I have read **all** the books (**that**) you gave me. 我读完了你给我的所有的书。

③ 先行词被序数词或者形容词最高级或者 the very, the only, the last 修饰。

This is **the best** novel (**that**) I have read. 这是我读过的最好的小说。

④ 有两个以上分别表示人和物的先行词。

He talked about **the teachers and schools that** had been praised. 他谈到了受表扬的学校和老师。

⑤ 主句是以 who 或 which 开头的特殊疑问句。

Who's the person **that** is standing there? 站在那边的人是谁?

(3) 关系代词 whose 引导定语从句,作从句中某一名词的定语(即 whose＋名词),既可指代人,也可指代物。指代人时,"whose＋名词"可以用"the ＋名词＋of whom"或者"of whom ＋ the ＋名词"替换。指代物时,"whose＋名词"可以用"the ＋名词＋of which"或者"of which ＋ the ＋名词"替换。上表中的例句⑥、例句⑦可改写为下面的形式。

She is looking for the poor boy **the mother of whom** has just died. 或者

She is looking for the poor boy **of whom the mother** has just died.

她正在寻找刚失去妈妈的那个可怜的孩子。

He lives in the house **the window of which** faces south. 或者

He lives in the house **of which the window** faces south.

他住在窗户朝南的那个房子里。

(4) 当关系代词 who, whom, which, that 引导定语从句，作动词或者介词的宾语时可以省略。但是，当关系代词 whom, which 引导定语从句，作介词的宾语且介词前置时，whom, which 不可省略。上表中例句③、例句④、例句⑨、例句⑤、例句⑫、例句⑯、例句⑬、例句⑰可改写为下面的形式。

The man I met told me to come here. 我碰见的那个人让我到这儿来。

The man I traveled with couldn't speak English. 和我一起旅行的那个人不会说英语。

The man with whom I traveled couldn't speak English. 和我一起旅行的那个人不会说英语。

Is this the photo you took in Shanghai? 这是你在上海照的照片吗？

This is the pan I boiled the milk in. 这是我煮牛奶的锅。

This is the pan in which I boiled the milk. 这是我煮牛奶的锅。

(5) as 引导限制性定语从句，常用于一些固定搭配中，如 such...as，the same...as，so...as 等，例句见上表 as 栏。

21.4　关系副词及其引导的定语从句

关系副词可以指代表示时间、地点和原因的先行词，并在从句中作状语。关系副词的功能比较如下表所列。

关系代词	指代功能	语法功能	例　句
when	时间	状语	I shall never forget **the day when** I arrived in Beijing. 我将永远不会忘记我到北京的那一天。
where	地点	状语	This is **the village where** he was born. 这就是他出生的村庄。
why	原因	状语	She didn't tell me **the reason why** she refused the offer. 她没有告诉我她为什么拒绝帮助。

注：(1) 关系副词 when, where, why 引导定语从句，作从句中的状语，在语法意义上关系副词相当于"介词＋关系代词"，when 相当于 at/on/in/during which；where 相当于 at/in which；why 相当于 for which。上表中的例句可以改写为下面形式：

I shall never forget **the day on which** I arrived in Beijing. 我将永远不会忘记我到北京的那一天。

This is **the village in which** he was born. 这就是他出生的村庄。

She didn't tell me **the reason for which** she refused the offer. 她没有告诉我她为什么拒绝帮助。

(2) 当先行词是 the way 时，引导定语从句的关系词是 by which，也可以用关系代词 that

引导,关系代词 that 也可以省去。

① I don't like **the way** <u>in which</u> you speak to your parents. 我不喜欢你对父母说话的方式。

② I don't like **the way** <u>that</u> you speak to your parents. 我不喜欢你对父母说话的方式。

③ I don't like **the way** you speak to your parents. 我不喜欢你对父母说话的方式。

(3) 当先行词是表示时间、地点、原因和方式的名词时(如 the day, the village, the reason, the way),引导定语从句的关系词不一定就是关系副词或者"介词+关系代词"。若先行词作了定语从句的状语,用关系副词或者"介词+关系代词"引导定语从句;若先行词作了定语从句的主语、宾语或者表语,则用关系代词引导定语从句。

① I still remember **the day** <u>when/on which</u> I first came to the school. 我仍然记得第一次上学的日子。(先行词 the day 作从句的时间状语)

② I still remember **the days** <u>which/that</u> we spent together. 我仍然记得我们一起度过的岁月。(先行词 the days 作从句的宾语)

③ **The house** <u>where/in which</u> I lived ten years ago has been pulled down. 我十年前住的房子已经被拆掉。(先行词 the house 作从句的地点状语)

④ This is **the village** <u>which/that</u> we visited last year. 这是我们去年参观过的村庄。(先行词 the village 作从句的宾语)

⑤ Please tell me **the reason** <u>why/for which</u> you missed the plane. 请告诉我你为啥没赶上飞机。(先行词 the reason 作从句的原因状语)

⑥ **The reason** <u>which/that</u> you give me is unacceptable. 你提出的理由是不可接受的。(先行词 the reason 作从句的宾语)

21.5 限制性定语从句和非限制性定语从句

根据定语从句与先行词的关系,定语从句可分为限制性定语从句和非限制性定语从句。限制性定语从句对主句进行修饰限制,它是主句不可或缺的一部分,少了它,主句意义就不完整,甚至没有意义,它紧跟先行词,且不用逗号与主句隔开,常译为先行词的前置定语。非限制性定语从句对主句进行附加情况的说明,它起补充说明的作用。非限制性定语从句的先行部分既可以是主句中的一个词,也可以是整个主句,少了它,主句意义仍然完整,且常用逗号与主句隔开,常译为主句的并列句。

① All the books **that** were damaged are to be thrown away. 毁掉的这些书要被扔掉了。(限制性定语从句)

② All the books, <u>which</u> were damaged, are to be thrown away. 这些书要被扔掉了,这些书毁掉了。(非限制性定语从句)

③ Rats ran about the attic all night, <u>which</u> kept me awake. 一晚上耗子在阁楼上跑来跑去,这弄得我睡不着。(非限制性定语从句)

注:同一个定语从句,是限制性的还是非限制性的,在意义上是有区别的。

① Grandma Liang has **a son** <u>who/that</u> serves in the army. 梁奶奶有一个当兵的儿子。(梁奶奶也许还有其他儿子,但不是军人)(限制性定语从句)

② Grandma Liang has **a son**, <u>who</u> serves in the army. 梁奶奶有一个儿子,他是军人。

(梁奶奶只有这一个儿子)(非限制性定语从句)

21.5.1 限制性定语从句和非限制性定语从句的引导词

限制性定语从句和非限制性定语从句的引导词是有区别的。21.1 节概述中所列关系代词和关系副词都可引导限制性定语从句。引导非限制性定语从句的关系词有:关系代词 who, whom, which, as, whose 和关系副词 when, where, 如下表所列。

种类	关系代词	关系副词
限制性定语从句	who, whom, whose, that, which, as	when, where, why
非限制性定语从句	who, whom, whose, which, as	when, where

也就是说,关系代词 that 和关系副词 why 不能引导非限制性定语从句。
21.2 节和 21.3 节中表格中所用例句均为限制性定语从句。

21.5.2 非限制性定语从句

who, whom, whose, when, where 引导非限制性定语从句和引导限制性定语从句一样, who/whom 指人,分别作从句的主语、宾语。whose 表示人或者物,作定语从句中某一名词的定语。when, where 分别表示时间和地点,作从句的状语。

① I've invited **Diana**, <u>who lives in the next flat</u>. 我邀请了戴安娜,她住在隔壁公寓。

② **Tom**, <u>whom everyone suspected</u>, turned out to be innocent. 大家都怀疑汤姆,结果他却是无辜的。

③ **Mrs. Green**, <u>for whom I was working</u>, was very generous. 我为格林太太工作,她很大方。

④ **The boy**, <u>whose father is an engineer</u>, studies very hard, 那位小男孩学习很努力,他的父亲是位工程师。

⑤ We will put off the picnic till **next week**, <u>when the weather may be better</u>. 我们要把野餐的时间推到下周,那时天气会好点。

⑥ They reached **Beijing** yesterday, <u>where a negotiation of sale will be held</u>. 他们昨天抵达北京,有一个关于销售的谈判在那儿举行。

但是,which 和 as 引导限制性定语从句和非限制性定语从句时,情况却不同。which 引导限制性定语从句时,其先行词是一个名词或者代词;而在引导非限制性定语从句时,其先行词可以是一个名词或者代词,也可以是主句的一部分,还可以是整个主句。as 引导限制性定语从句时,常用于一些固定搭配中,如 such...as, the same...as 等;而在引导非限制性定语从句时,情况和 which 相似,其先行词是整个主句。as 在非限定性定语从句中作主语、表语或宾语,且引出的从句位置比较灵活,可位于句首或句末,也可插入主句中间,通常均由逗号将其与主句隔开,有"正如……","就像……"之意。

① She gave me **this sweater**, <u>which she had knitted herself</u>. 她把这件毛衣给了我,这是她自己织的。

② Peter **drove too fast**, <u>which was dangerous</u>. 皮特开车太快,这很危险。

③ **Rats ran about the attic all night**, <u>which kept me awake</u>. 一晚上耗子在阁楼上跑来跑

去，这弄得我睡不着。

④ He hung around for **hours, during which** time I washed a lot of clothes. 他在外面晃悠了几个小时，这段时间里我却洗了好多衣服。

⑤ **He is absent, as** is often the case. 他没来，他老是这样。

⑥ **John, as** we had expected, **was admitted into the university.** 正如我们所料，约翰被那所大学录取了。

⑦ **As** is known to the United States, **Mark Twain is a great American writer.** 美国人都知道，马克·吐温是一位伟大的美国作家。

注：(1) which 和 as 引导非限制性定语从句时的区别有以下几方面。①which 引导非限制性定语从句时，其先行词可以是一个名词或者代词（见①句和④句），也可以是主句的一部分（见②句），还可以是整个主句（见③句）；as 引导非限制性定语从句时，其先行词是整个主句。②as 引出的定语从句位置比较灵活，可位于句首（见⑦句）或句末（见⑤句），也可插入主句中间（见⑥句），通常均由逗号将其与主句隔开，as 有"正如……"，"就像……"之意。which 引出的定语从句一般不放于主句前（见上①句、②句、③句、④句）。

(2) 介词在非限制性定语从句中不能后置，关系代词也不能省略。

Mr Smith, from whom I have learned a lot, is a famous scientist. 史密斯先生是一位著名的科学家，我从他那儿学到了许多东西。

(3) "介词＋关系代词"前可有 some, any, none, both, all, neither, most, each, few 等代词或者数词，即"some/any/none/both/all/neither/most/each/few ＋ of ＋ which/whom"结构。

① He loved his parents deeply, both of whom are very kind to him. 他爱他的父母，他们对他很好。

② In the basket there are quite many apples, some of which have gone bad. 篮子里有好多苹果，有些已经坏掉。

③ There are forty students in our class in all, most of whom are from big cities. 我们班共有 40 个学生，他们大多来自于大城市。

巩 固 练 习

一、单项选择。

1. Don't talk about such things of _____ you are not sure.
   A. which   B. what   C. as   D. those
2. Is this the factory _____ you visited the other day?
   A. that   B. where   C. in which   D. the one
3. Is this the factory _____ he worked ten years ago?
   A. that   B. where   C. which   D. the one
4. The wolves hid themselves in the places _____ could not be found.
   A. that   B. where   C. in which   D. in that
5. This book will show you _____ can be used in other contexts.
   A. how you have observed   B. all that you have observed

C. that you have observed   D. how that you have observed
6. That tree, _____ branches are almost bare, is very old.
   A. whose   B. of which   C. in which   D. on which
7. I have bought the same dress _____ she is wearing.
   A. as   B. that   C. which   D. what
8. He failed in the examination, _____ made his father very angry.
   A. which   B. it   C. that   D. what
9. We're talking about the piano and the pianist _____ were in the concert we attended last night.
   A. which   B. whom   C. who   D. that
10. The girl _____ an English song in the next room is Tom's sister.
    A. who is singing   B. is singing   C. sang   D. was singing
11. Those _____ not only from books but also through practice will succeed.
    A. learn   B. who   C. that learns   D. who learn
12. Didn't you see the man _____?
    A. I nodded just now   B. whom I nodded just now
    C. I nodded to him just now   D. I nodded to just now
13. Is there anything _____ to you?
    A. that is belonged   B. that belongs   C. that belong   D. which belongs
14. He has lost the key to the drawer _____ the papers are kept.
    A. where   B. in which   C. under which   D. which
15. Antarctic, _____ we know very little, is covered with thick ice all the year round.
    A. which   B. where   C. that   D. about which
16. It's the third time _____ late this month.
    A. that you arrived   B. when you arrived
    C. that you've arrived   D. when you've arrived
17. May the fourth is the day _____ we Chinese people will never forget.
    A. which   B. when   C. on which   D. about which
18. We are going to spend the Spring Festival in Guangzhou, _____ live my grandparents and some relatives.
    A. which   B. that   C. who   D. where
19. He is not _____ a fool _____.
    A. such, as he is looked   B. such, as he looks
    C. as, as he is looked   D. so, as he looks
20. Is that the reason _____ you are in favor of the proposal?
    A. which   B. what   C. why   D. for that
21. He must be from Africa, _____ can be seen from his skin.
    A. that   B. as   C. who   D. what
22. He has two sons, _____ work as chemists.
    A. two of whom   B. both of whom

C. both of which   D. all of whom

23. I, _____ your good friend, will try my best to help you out.
    A. who is   B. who am   C. that is   D. what is
24. He is a man of great experience, _____ much can be learned.
    A. who   B. that   C. from which   D. from whom
25. I don't like _____ you speak to her.
    A. the way   B. the way in that
    C. the way which   D. the way of which
26. _____ is known to the world, Mark Twain is a great American writer.
    A. That   B. Which   C. As   D. It
27. The residents, _____ had been damaged by the flood, were given help by the Red Cross.
    A. all their homes   B. all whose homes
    C. all of whose homes   D. all of their homes
28. Language is a city, to the building of _____ every human being brought a stone.
    A. which   B. that   C. it   D. this
29. _____ might be expected, the response to the question was very mixed.
    A. As   B. That   C. It   D. What
30. We need a chairman _____.
    A. for whom everyone has confidence   B. in whom everyone has confidence
    C. who everyone has confidence of   D. whom everyone has confidence on

二、改错。

1. The book that I borrowed it from the library is well written.
2. The house stood at the place which the roads meet.
3. Did you see the young man whom was chosen the League secretary?
4. We shall visit the university where my father teaches there.
5. The person whom you want to see comes.
6. Can you think of anyone who's house is on a pile of rocks?
7. The day which I was to start arrived at last.
8. I have known the reason which she is so worried.
9. This is the girl who practice playing the piano every day.
10. The watch which her mother gave it to her works very well.
11. This is the shop which keep open till eleven at night.
12. Is she the girl who her grandfather was a Red Army man?
13. The worker who repaired our house live next door to Li Hua's.
14. The girl studies music plays the violin very well.
15. The house in where we live is very large.
16. The street which lead us to the Beijing Station is wide and long.
17. Do you know the driver who caused the traffic accident where a man was killed?
18. Has she returned you the novel that you lent it to her last Friday?

19. This is the one hundredth letter which she has received from that boy.
20. This is the woman to who my mother talked just now.

三、翻译下列句子。

1. 这是本月上映的最好的一部影片。
   This is the best film _____.
2. 你可以拿你感兴趣的任何一本书。
   You can take any book _____.
3. 人们喜欢住在空气新鲜、噪声很少的地方。
   People like to live in a place _____.
4. 你在会上看到的那个女孩是个出名的游泳运动员。
   The girl _____ is a well-known swimmer.
5. 他就是我们昨天在报纸上见到照片的那个工人。
   He is the very worker _____.
6. 他进大学的那一天非常高兴。
   He was very happy on the day _____.
7. 我总不太明白他犯这样一个错误的原因。
   I never really understand the reason _____.
8. 不要读那些你看不懂的书。
   Don't read such books _____.
9. 很快,他们来到一座小房子旁,房子前面坐着一个男孩。
   Soon they arrived at a small house _____.
10. 这就是我昨天丢的那本书。
    This is the same book _____.

第二十二章 状语从句

22.1 概述

在复合句中起副词作用、作状语的分句称为状语从句。状语从句可以修饰谓语、非谓语动词、定语、状语或整个句子。状语从句一般由连词(从属连词)引导,也可以由词组引导。从句位于句首或句中时通常用逗号与主句隔开,位于句尾时可以不用逗号隔开。

① **Where** there is smoke, there is fire. 无风不起浪。
② Let's set out **when** the sun has risen. 太阳出来时我们动身出发。

22.2 状语从句的种类

状语从句按其意义和在主句中的作用可分为以下几类。
(1) 时间状语从句(Adverbial Clause of Time)。
(2) 地点状语从句(Adverbial Clause of Place)。
(3) 原因状语从句(Adverbial Clause of Cause)。
(4) 条件状语从句(Adverbial Clause of Condition)。
(5) 目的状语从句(Adverbial Clause of Purpose)。
(6) 结果状语从句(Adverbial Clause of Result)。
(7) 让步状语从句(Adverbial Clause of Concession)。
(8) 比较状语从句(Adverbial Clause of Comparison)。
(9) 方式状语从句(Adverbial Clause of Manner)。

22.3 时间状语从句

在复合句中用作时间状语的分句叫做时间状语从句,引导时间状语从句的从属连词和词语有:
(1) 表示"当……时候",如 when,whenever,while,as。
(2) 表示"一……就……",如 as soon as,immediately,directly,instantly,the moment,the minute,the instant,no sooner... than,hardly/scarcely/ rarely... when。
(3) 表示"直到……才……",如 till,until。
(4) 表示"在……之前"或者"在……之后",如 before,after。
(5) 表示"每次"、"下次"或者"第一次",如 each time,every time,next time,the first time。
(6) 表示"到……为止",如 by the time。

(7) 表示"自从……",如(ever)since。

(8) 表示"一旦……",如 once。

22.3.1 表示"当……时候"的从属连词引导的时间状语从句

表示"当……时候"的从属连词有 when 当……时候,whenever 无论……时候,while 当……时候,as 在……的同时,一边……一边……。

① Mozart started writing music **when** he was four years old. (当)莫扎特四岁的时候开始写音乐作品。

② **When** you think you know nothing, then you begin to know something. 当你以为自己一无所知的时候,你就是在开始知道一些事了。

③ **Whenever** it rains, the roof leaks. 无论什么时候下雨,房顶都漏雨。

④ Strike **while** the iron is hot. 趁热打铁。

⑤ He visited a lot of places **while** he was traveling. 他在旅途中参观了许多地方。

⑥ You can feel the air moving as your hand pushes through it. 当你的手在空气中挥动时,你能感觉到空气在流动。

注:when, while 和 as 的区别。when 引导的从句的谓语动词可以是延续性的动词,又可以是瞬时动词;并且 when 有时表示"就在那时",这时常被看作并列连词。while 引导的从句的谓语动作必须是延续性的,强调主句和从句的动作同时发生(或者相对应),并且 while 有时还可以表示对比。as 表示"一边……一边……",as 引导的动作是延续性的动作,一般用于主句和从句动作同时发生。

① When she came in, I was eating. 她进来时,我在吃饭。(瞬时动词)

② When I lived in the countryside, I used to carry some water for him. 当我住在农村时,我常常为他挑水。(延续性的动词)

③ We were about to leave when he came in. 我们就要离开,就在那时他进来了。(并列连词表示"就在那时")

④ While my wife was reading the newspaper, I was watching TV.
(was reading 是延续性的动词,was reading 和 was watching 同时发生)

⑤ I like playing football while you like playing basketball. 我喜欢踢足球,而你喜欢打篮球。(表示对比)

⑥ We always sing as we walk. 我们总是边走边唱。(as 表示"一边……一边……")

22.3.2 表示"一……就……"的从属连词引导的时间状语从句

表示"一……就……"的从属连词有 as soon as,immediately,directly,instantly,the moment,the minute,the instant,no sooner...than,hardly/scarcely/rarely...when 等。

① As soon as I reach Canada, I will ring you up. 我一到加拿大就给你来电话。

② I will write to you **the moment** I get home. 我一到家就给你写信。

③ I told him the news **the minute** he came back. 他一回来我就把消息告诉他了。

④ He went out **immediately** he had eaten. 他一吃完饭就出去了。

⑤ **No sooner** had I left my house than it began to rain. 我一离开家天就开始下雨。

⑥ **Hardly** had he begun to speak when the audience interrupted him. 他一开始说话观众

就打断了他。

注：hardly(scarcely, rarely)…when, no sooner…than 相当于 as soon as 之意，但是主句用过去完成时，从句用一般过去时。当 hardly, scarcely, rarely 和 no sooner 位于句首时，主句用倒装语序。

① He had hardly fallen asleep when he felt a soft touch on his shoulder. 他刚要入睡就感到肩膀上被轻轻碰了一下。

② He had no sooner arrived home than he was asked to start on another journey. 他刚到家，就被要求开始另一旅程。

③ No sooner had the sun shown itself above the horizon than he got out of bed to work. 太阳刚从地平线上升起，他就起床劳动去了。

④ Hardly had I sat down when he stepped in. 我刚坐下，他就进来了。

22.3.3 表示"直到……才……"的从属连词引导的时间状语从句

till, until 都可以作连词，连接时间状语从句，也可以作介词，与其他词构成介词短语，在句中作时间状语。

① **Don't** open the door **till / until** the rain stops. 雨停了才开门。(till 和 until 是连词，后跟句子)

② I worked until he came back. 我一直工作到他回来。(till 和 until 是连词，后跟句子)

③ Xiao Ming **didn't** leave home **till / until** his father came back. 小明直到他爸爸回来才离开家。(till 和 until 是连词，后跟句子)

④ Xiao Ming didn't leave home till / until eleven o'clock. 小明直到 11 点种才离开家。(till 和 until 是介词，后跟名词)

注：till 和 until 一般情况下可以互换，但是在强调句型中多用 until。并且要注意的是，如果主句中的谓语动词是瞬时动词时，必须用否定形式；如果主句中的谓语动词是延续性动词时，用肯定或否定形式都可以，但表达的意思不同，如：

① I didn't go to bed until(till) my father came back. 直到我父亲回来我才上床睡觉。

② It was not until the meeting was over that he began to teach me English. 直到散会之后他才开始教我英语。(强调句)

③ I worked until he came back. 我工作到他回来为止。

④ I didn't work until he came back. 直到他回来我才开始工作。

22.3.4 表示"在……之前"或者"在……之后"的从属连词引导的时间状语从句

before 在……之前，after 在……之后。before 引导的从句一般表示主句的动作发生在从句动作之前，如从句是过去时，主句一般要用过去完成时。after 引导的从句，表示主句的动作发生在从句的动作之后，如主句是过去时，从句一般要用过去完成时。

① Mr. Brown had worked in a bank for a year **before** he came here. 布朗先生来这之前已经在一家银行里工作一年了。

② He went home **after** he had finished his homework the other day. 前几天他做完作业之后回的家。

③ We had sailed 4 days and 4 nights <u>before we saw land</u>. 我们航行了四天四夜才看到陆地。(……多久才)

④ I hadn't touched her <u>**before** she cried</u>. 我没碰着她,她就哭喊起来。(没有……就)

⑤ Please write it down <u>**before** you forget</u>. 趁着你没忘,请把它记下来。(趁还没有……)

⑥ It will be four days <u>before they come back</u>. 他们四天后才能回来。(多久后才能)

⑦ It won't be long <u>**before** we meet again</u>. 不久我们就会再见面的。(不久就会)

⑧ It was a long time <u>**before** I got to sleep again</u>. 好长时间后我才睡着。

⑨ It wasn't long <u>**before** I got to sleep again</u>. 不久我就睡着了。

22.3.5 表示"每次"、"下次"或者"第一次"的从属连词引导的时间状语从句

引导此类状语从句的从属连词有 each time 每次, every time 每次, next time 下次, the first time 第一次。

① **Each time** he came to Harbin, he would call on me. 每次来哈尔滨,他都来看我。

② **The first time** I saw her, I was struck by her beauty. 我第一次见她,就被她的美貌打动了。

22.3.6 表示"到……为止"的从属连词引导的时间状语从句

by the time 引导时间状语从句,所在句子的主句用完成时。

① **By the time** he gets home, his father has already gone. 他到家的时候,他爸爸已经走了。

② **By the time** I got to school, the class had already began. 我到校时,已经开始上课了。

22.3.7 表示"自从……"的从属连词引导的时间状语从句

since 表示自过去的一个起点时间到目前(说话时间)为止的一段持续时间。since 引导的从句的谓语动词可以是延续性的动词,又可以是瞬时动词。主句一般用现在完成时,从句用一般过去时。since 还可以用作介词,后跟名词。since 自从,从……以来; ever since 从那时起一直到现在,此后一直。

① Mr. Green has taught in that school <u>**since** he came to China three years ago</u>. 自格林先生三年前到中国以来,他就在这所学校教书。

② Where have you been <u>**since** the party</u>? 自上次聚会,你一直在哪里?(since 用作介词,后跟名词)

注:在"It is/was……since"句型中,主句中的谓语动词也可用一般时态。

① It is /has been a long time <u>since I met you last</u>. 自从我上次见你,已经好久了。

② It was / had been years <u>since I had seen her</u>. 自从我上次见到他,已经有好多年了。

③ It is five months <u>since our boss was in Beijing</u>. 我们老板离开北京有五个月了。

22.3.8 表示"一旦……"的从属连词引导的时间状语从句

① **Once** you object to a man, everything he does is wrong. 一旦你反对一个人,那么他做的一切都是错的。

② **Once** you understand this rule, you'll have no further difficulty. 一旦明白了这条规

则,就再也没有困难了。

注:时间状语从句中常用一般时态表示将来,即用一般现在时表示一般将来;用一般过去时表示过去将来。

① It will be 5 years before we meet again. 我们五年后才能再见面。
② I will write to you <u>the moment I get home</u>. 我一到家就给你写信。
③ He said that he would write to me <u>the moment he got home</u>. 他说他一到家就给我写信。

22.4　地点状语从句

地点状语从句一般由 where, wherever, anywhere, everywhere 等引导。where 在……地方, wherever 无论什么地方, anywhere 任何地方, everywhere 每个地方。

① We must camp <u>where we can get water.</u> 我们必须在能找到水的地方露营。
② **Wherever** <u>the sea is</u>, you will find seamen. 有海就有海员。
③ **Wherever** <u>you go</u>, you must obey the traffic rules. 无论你到哪儿,都应该遵守那里的交通规则。
④ You can go **anywhere** you want (to go). 你可以去你想去的任何地方。
⑤ You will see it **everywhere** you go. 所到之处你都可以见到这种东西。

22.5　原因状语从句

原因状语从句可以由连词 because, since, as 引导,也可由 for, now that, considering (that), seeing(that), in that 等词引导。because 语势最强,用来说明人所不知的原因,回答 why 提出的问题。当原因是显而易见的或已为人们所知,就用 as 或 since。但如果不是说明直接原因,而是多种情况加以推断,就只能用 for。now(that)既然, seeing(that)由于, considering(that)考虑到, in that 鉴于、由于。now(that)和 since 同义,其中 that 可省去,用来表示一种新的情况,再加以推论。in that 表示"因为,基于……的理由",在句中不重读,它所引导的从句只能位于主句之后。now that 引导的从句只用现在时态。

① I didn't go to school yesterday **because** I was ill. 我昨天没去上学,因为我生病了。
② <u>**Since** everybody is here</u>, let's begin our meeting. 既然大家都来了,让我们开始开会吧。
③ <u>**As** you are in poor health</u>, you should not stay up late. 由于你身体不好,你就不该熬夜。
④ I asked her to stay to tea, <u>**for** I had something to tell her.</u> 我请她留下来喝茶,因为我有事要告诉她。
⑤ It must be daybreak, <u>**for** the birds are singing.</u> 天一定亮了,因为小鸟在叫。
⑥ <u>**Now that** you are here</u>, you'd better stay. 你既然来了,还是留下吧。(既来之,则安之)
⑦ <u>**Seeing** (**that**) the weather is bad</u>, we'll stay at home. 由于天气不好,我们要待在家里了。

⑧ **Considering**（**that**）he has only been learning English a year, he speaks it very well. 考虑到他学英语才一年,他的英文已讲得相当不错了。

⑨ I'm in a slightly awkward position **in that** he's not arriving until the 10th. 我的处境有点难堪,因为他要十号才来。

22.6　条件状语从句

条件状语从句一般由以下连词引导:if 如果,unless 如果不,除非;in case 万一;so/as long as 只要;on condition that 条件是;provided/providing that 假如;suppose/supposing 假如;only if 只要,只有,但是;if only 表示"但愿,要是……该多好"。

① I'll buy a computer **if I am able to save up enough money**. 如果我能存下足够多的钱,我就买台计算机。

② We shall go **unless it rains**. 如果天不下雨,我们就去。

③ **Suppose** it rains, what shall we do? 假如天下雨,我们怎么办?

④ In case I forget, please remind me of it. 万一我忘了,请提醒我。

⑤ **In case of** fire, ring the alarm. 万一有火灾,请按响报警器。(in case of 是介词,后跟名词)

⑥ **So long as** I can, I must do it well. 只要我能够,我一定要做好。

⑦ I can tell you the truth on condition that you promise to keep it a secret. 我可以告诉你真相了,条件是你答应保守秘密。

⑧ **Only if** a teacher has given permission **is a student allowed** to enter this room. 只有老师允许,学生才可以进这个房间。(句子倒装)

⑨ **If only** I knew her name. 我要是知道她的名字就好了。(if only 后的句子中使用虚拟式谓语)

注:条件状语从句中常用一般时态表示将来,即用一般现在时表示一般将来;用一般过去时表示过去将来,如:

① We shall go unless it rains. 如果天不下雨,我们就去。

② Suppose it rains, what shall we do? 假如天下雨,我们怎么办?

③ He said he would buy a computer if he was able to save up enough money. 他说如果他能存下足够多的钱,他就买台计算机。

22.7　目的状语从句

引导目的状语从句的连词或词语一般有:so that 为了,以便;in order that 为了,以便;in case 以防;for fear(that) 唯恐,以免;lest 唯恐,以免,为不使。

① I opened the window **so that/ in order that** fresh air might come in. 我把窗户打开以便新鲜空气进来。

② I lent him 500 Yuan **so that/ in order that** he might go for a holiday. 为了他能去度假,我借给他 500 元。

③ Take your umbrella **in case** it rains. 带上你的雨伞,以防天下雨。

④ He is working hard **for fear that** he should fail. 他正努力学习,唯恐考不及格。

⑤ **Lest** anyone should think it strange, let me assure you that it is quite true. 我向你们保证那是真事,以免有人觉得奇怪。

22.8　结果状语从句

结果状语从句一般由(so)that, so...that, such...that, so much/many...that 引导,它们都表示"如此……以至于……"。such 是形容词,修饰名词或名词词组,so 是副词,只能修饰形容词或副词。so 还可与表示数量的形容词 many, few, much, little 连用,形成固定搭配。

so foolish	such a fool
so nice a flower	such a nice flower
so many / few flowers	such nice flowers
so much / little money	such rapid progress
so many people	such a lot of people

so many 已成固定搭配,a lot of 虽相当于 many,但 a lot of 为名词性的,只能与 such 搭配。

① He speaks **so** fast <u>that no one can catch him</u>. 他说话太快,无人能听明白。

② She spoke **so** fast <u>**that** nobody could catch what she was saying</u>. 她说话如此之快,竟没有人听出来她在讲什么。

③ She is **so** good a girl <u>**that** we all like her</u>. 她是这么好的一个女孩,我们都喜欢她。

④ She is **such** a good girl <u>**that** we all like her</u>. 她是这么好的一个女孩,我们都喜欢她。

⑤ They are **such** good students <u>**that** the teacher has praised them many times</u>. 他们是如此好的学生,老师多次表扬他们。

⑥ He told us **such** a story <u>**that** we all laughed</u>.
= He told us **so** funny a story <u>**that** we all laughed</u>.
他讲了个很有趣的故事,(以至于)我们都笑了起来。

⑦ She got **so** little education <u>**that** she could hardly read</u>. 她几乎没受什么教育,她几乎不认识什么字。

⑧ She got up late **so that** <u>she failed to catch the early bus</u>. 她起床这么晚,以至于没有赶上早班车。

注:结果状语从句中有 so...that, such...that 结构,限制性定语从句中有 such...as, so...as 结构,他们之间有什么区别?

引导限制性定语从句的 such...as, so...as 结构中的 as 是关系代词,它既代替先行词(即前面的名词或者代词),同时又作从句中的主语或者宾语;结果状语从句中 so...that, such...that 结构中的 that 只起连接句子的作用,没有指代功能。因此,当主句中用 such 或者 so 时,要判断后面从句的成分是否完整,若从句中缺少成分,则为定语从句,用 such...as, so...as 结构;若从句成分完整,则为结果状语从句,用 so...that, such...that 结构。

① Such women _____ knew Tom thought he was charming. 认识 Tom 的女人认为他很有魅力。

(本句中从句缺少主语,填入的词要作从句的主语,同时代替前面的名词 women,即 Such women knew Tom,因此是定语从句,填 as。)

② She is such a good girl _____ we all like her. 她是这么好的一个女孩,我们都喜欢她。

(本句中从句成分完整,填入的词在从句中没有位置,同时也没有指代作用,因此是状语从句,填 that。)

22.9　让步状语从句

引导让步状语从句的连词有:although 虽然;though 虽然;even if /though 即使,纵然,尽管;as 尽管;while 尽管;whoever(no matter who)不管谁;whatever(no matter what)无论什么;whenever(no matter when)无论什么时候;wherever(no matter where)无论哪里;however (no matter how)无论怎样;whether...or 不论……还是。

though, although 表示"虽然",都不能和 but 连用。但是它们都可以同 yet (still) 连用。as 引导让步状语从句时,常放在作表语、状语或谓语的一部分的形容词、名词、副词或动词原形之后。如果是单数名词或形容词的最高级作表语,不再用冠词。

① Although he is rich, but he is not happy.（错误）
Although he is rich, yet he is not happy.（正确）
虽然他很富有,然而他并不快乐。

② Although we have grown up, our parents treat us as children.（正确）
Although we have grown up, our parents still treat us as children.（正确）
尽管我们已经长大了,可是我们的父母仍把我们看作小孩。

③ **Though/Although** he is old, he is quite strong. 尽管他年事已高,身体依然很强健。

④ Old **though/as** he is, he is healthy. 尽管他年事已高,身体依然很健康。

⑤ Try **though/as** you will, you won't manage it. 尽管你想试一试,你是不会成功的。

⑥ Much **though/as** I admire him as a writer, I don't like him as a man. 尽管作为作家我很欣赏他,但是作为一个人,我是不喜欢他的。

⑦ Doctor **though/as** he is (=Though he is a doctor), he knows medicine no better than I. 虽然他是医生,但他和我一样都不懂医学。

⑧ Hard **though/as** he tried, he was unable to make much progress. 他虽然竭尽全力,但是没能取得多大进步。(though 引导的让步状语从句也可和 as 一样引起句子的倒装,但 although 却不行。)

⑨ **Even if/though** I were starving, I wouldn't ask a favor of him. 即使我被饿死,我也不会求他帮忙。

⑩ **Whenever/No matter when** I see him, he is at his books. 我无论什么时候见他,他总是在看书。

⑪ While I am willing to help, I do not have much time available. 虽然我愿意帮忙,但是没有多少时间。(while 用于句首=although)

又如:

① **Whoever(No matter who)** wants to speak to me on the phone, tell them I'm busy.

不管谁要我接电话,就说我现在正忙着呢。

② **Whether it rains or not**, we're playing football on Sunday. 无论下不下雨,我们星期天一定踢足球。

③ **Whether** she is sick **or** well, she is always cheerful. 无论她身体好坏,她总是高高兴兴的。

22.10 方式状语从句

方式状语从句通常由 as, as if/though, as...so 引导。as 像……一样,按照;as if/though 好像。as if/though 引出的状语从句谓语多用虚拟语气,表示与事实相反,有时也用陈述语气,表示所说情况是事实或实现的可能性较大。

① You must do everything **as** I do. 你必须按照我说的做。

② She stood up **as if** she wanted to go. 她站起来,好像要走。(可能性较大,用陈述语气)

③ Mum treats me **as if** I were a guest. 妈妈对我像对客人一般。(与事实相反,用虚拟语气)

④ As water is to fish, so air is to man. 我们离不开空气,犹如鱼儿离不开水。

注:as if / as though 也可以引导一个分词短语、不定式短语或无动词短语。

① He stared at me **as if** seeing me for the first time. 他目不转睛地看着我,就像第一次看见我似的。

② He cleared his throat **as if** to say something. 他清了清嗓子,像要说什么似的。

③ The waves dashed on the rocks **as if** in anger. 波涛冲击着岩石,好像很愤怒。

22.11 比较状语从句

比较状语从句一般由 than(比), as...as...(和……一样), not as/so...as(和……不一样),"the+形容词比较级/副词比较级,the+形容词比较级/副词比较级(越……越……)"等引导。

22.11.1 than 引导的比较状语从句

than 引导的比较状语从句在口语中或正式的文体中多以省略的形式出现,或省略主语和动词,或省略谓语动词。此外,比较级前面可加 much, far, still, even, a lot, a little, a great deal, four years, three times, one-third, 30%等程度状语对其修饰,说明双方相差的程度。

① The youth of today are better off than we used to be. 今天的年轻人比我们过去的境况要好。

② She likes reading **better than** (she likes) going to parties. 她爱读书而不爱去参加聚会。(省略主语和动词)

③ He has lived here **longer than** I (have lived here). 他在这儿住的时间比我长。(省略谓语动词)

④ Air in the country is much **fresher than** that in the city. 乡下的空气比城里的新鲜得多。

⑤ His house is three times **bigger than** ours (is). 他的房子是我们的四倍大。

22.11.2 as...as...(和……一样), not as/so...as(不如……那样)引导的比较状语从句

as...as..., not as/so...as 用来引导同级比较状语从句。

① Jack is **as tall as** Bob. 杰克和汤姆一样高。

② We were **as fortunate as** they were. 我们和他们一样幸运。

③ I hope she will make **as much progress as** you (have done). 我希望她将取得和你同样的进步。

④ She runs **as fast as** a boy (does). 她跑得像男孩一样快。

⑤ She is **not so(as)outgoing as** her sister(is). 她不如她姐姐外向。

22.11.3 "the＋形容词比较级/副词比较级,＋the＋形容词比较级/副词比较级"结构

"the＋形容词比较级/副词比较级,＋the＋形容词比较级/副词比较级"这种结构用来表示"越……,越……"。

① **The more** you listen to English, **the easier** it will become. 英语听得越多就越容易。

② **The harder** you work, **the greater** progress you will make. 你工作越努力,取得的进步就越大。

③ **The more** pictures I take, **the more** skilled I will become. 我拍的照片越多,我的技术就越熟练。

注：(1) no more than 表示"只不过"＝only（嫌少的意思）；not more than 表示"不如……"(前者不如后者)。

① I have no more than two pens. 我只有两支笔。

② It's no more than a mile to the shops. 去商店不过一英里。

③ Jack is not more diligent than John. 杰克不如约翰勤奋。

(2) no＋比较级＋than 表示"……和……都不……"；not＋比较级＋than 表示"……不如……"。

① He is no taller than I. 他和我都不高。（暗含 He is as short as I.）

② He is not taller than I. 他没有我高。

巩 固 练 习

一、单项选择。

1. Although it's raining, _____ are still working in the fields.
   A. they   B. but they   C. and they   D. so they

2. Write clearly _____ your teacher can understand you correctly.
   A. since   B. for   C. because   D. so that

3. You'll miss the train _____ you hurry up.
   A. unless   B. as   C. if   D. until
4. Francis did the task _____ his brother.
   A. as good as   B. as better as C. as well as   D. as best as
5. He talked about it _____ he had been there.
   A. that   B. as   C. as if   D. like that
6. _____ to New York, her father has not heard from her.
   A. Because she went   B. After she went
   C. When she went   D. Since she went
7. _____ he daydreamed, Peter saw figures in the sky.
   A. Until   B. Since   C. While   D. During
8. We arrived at the station _____ the train had left.
   A. after   B. before   C. since   D. when
9. _____ he was in poor health, he worked just as hard as everyone else.
   A. But   B. Although   C. Even if   D. If
10. Do not make the same mistake _____ I did.
    A. so   B. as   C. like   D. that
11. He ran off _____ I could stop him.
    A. before   B. after   C. since   D. when
12. _____ you told me, I had heard nothing of what happened.
    A. Till   B. Until   C. After   D. Since
13. Where have you been _____ you left home?
    A. before   B. as   C. since   D. when
14. _____ the problem of method is solved, talking about the task is useless.
    A. Until   B. Since   C. After   D. Unless
15. We have produced 15% more cotton this year _____ we did last year.
    A. as   B. than   C. like   D. white
16. He will come _____ you ask him.
    A. whether   B. unless   C. if   D. while
17. _____ he will come or not is still unknown.
    A. If   B. Where   C. That   D. Whether
18. I don't know _____ to stay at home or go out.
    A. whether   B. if   C. how   D. where
19. He spoke loudly _____ the audience could hear him clearly.
    A. so   B. that   C. so that   D. in order to
20. It rained heavily, _____ the basketball match had to be put off.
    A. so that   B. when   C. otherwise   D. therefore
21. You are certainly right, _____ others may say.
    A. what   B. whatever   C. that   D. as
22. I'll discuss it with you _____ you like to come.

| A. when | B. where | C. whoever | D. whenever |

23. _____ you work, you must always serve the people heart and soul.

| A. Wherever | B. Whenever | C. Where | D. When |

24. _____ you understand this rule, you will have no further difficulty.

| A. Once | B. At once | C. Only | D. Only then |

25. _____ difficult the task may be, we must fulfill it this month.

| A. No matter how | | B. No matter what |
| C. No matter when | | D. No matter where |

26. We can surely overcome these difficulties _____ we are closely united.

| A. so far as | B. so long as | C. as soon as | D. as well as |

27. Please write me _____ you arrive in New York.

| A. as well as | B. so long as | C. as far as | D. as soon as |

28. Scientists say it may be five or ten years _____ it is possible to test this medicine on human patients.

| A. since | B. before | C. after | D. when |

29. Liquids are like solids _____ they have a definite volume.

| A. in that | B. for that | C. with that | D. at that |

30. You see the lightning _____ it happens, but you hear the thunder later.

| A. the instant | B. for an instant | C. on the instant | D. in an instant |

二、状语从句填空。

1. Give me your telephone number _____ I need your help.
2. _____ we have all the materials ready, we should begin the new task at once.
3. _____ they will not come to join us, we have to change our plan.
4. We'll visit Europe next year _____ we have enough money.
5. _____ you are leaving tomorrow, we can eat dinner together tonight.
6. _____ he works hard, I don't mind when he finishes the experiment.
7. _____ difficulties we may come across, we'll help one another to overcome them.
8. He was punished _____ he should make the same mistake again.
9. There was such a long line at the exhibition _____ we had to wait for about half an hour.
10. We hadn't met for 20 years, but l recognized her _____ I saw her.

第二十三章　it 的用法

it 除作单数第三人称代词，还可以在句子中充当主语，用来表示气候、时间、距离、温度、日期等，即虚义 it；也可以作形式主语，即先行 it；还可以在分裂句中作引导词，即"分句引导词"it。

23.1　代词 it 的用法

用于指人或者人以外的一切生物、无生命的东西和事情。一般指说话者心目中已经了解或所指的生物、无生命的东西或事情，没有性别的区分；可以是可数名词，也可以是不可数名词，在句子中既可作主语，也可以作宾语。

23.1.1　指示代词 it(常用以指人)

(1) 指代说话者心目中不太清楚的那个人，常在打电话或敲门时用。
① —Who was it? 是谁(打来的电话)？
　—Was it Susan？(打电话的)是苏珊吗？
　—Yes, it was. 是的，我是。（根据上下句，"it was"也可不译出来。）
② —Who is knocking at the door? 谁在敲门？
　—It's me. 是我。
(2) 指说话者心目中的那个人。
—Is it your sister, Kate？（那旧照片上的 baby）是你姐姐凯特吧？
—No! 不是。
—Is it your brother? 是你哥哥吧？
—No! 不是。
—I know—it's you! 我知道了，(那)是你。
(3) 指代性别不详的婴幼儿或在不计较性别时，也可用 it 来指人。
① The child smiled when it saw its mother. 这小孩一见到母亲就笑了。
② I don't know who it is. 我不知道他是谁。
③ What a beautiful baby—is it a boy? 多漂亮的宝宝，是个男孩吗？
(4) 在回答用指示代词表示人的特殊问句时，常用 it 指人。
—Who's that? 那人是谁？
—Is it Kate? 是凯特吗？
—Yes, I think you're right. It's Kate. 是的，我想你说对了，是凯特。

23.1.2　代替上文提到过的整个事情

① I love jogging, It keeps me fit. 我喜欢慢跑，它能使我保持健康。
② That pot is valuable, it's more than 2000 years old. 那个陶壶很珍贵，它有 2000 多年

历史了。

③ Well, you mustn't play on the road. It's dangerous. 哦,你不能在公路上玩。这太危险了!

④ It was hard work, but they really enjoyed it. 它是艰苦活,可他们都乐意去干(它)。

23.1.3 代表抽象事物

① The committee has met and it has approved the proposal. 委员会已经开过会,同意了这项建议。

② It is all my fault. 都怪我。

23.1.4 指动物和植物、一些无生命的东西

① —Oh, that's Lucy's hat. 噢,那是露茜的帽子。
   —It looks like a cat! 它看上去像只猫!

② —Where's tea grown? 什么地方种植茶?
   —It's grown in the southeast of China. 中国东南部种植茶。

③ Is it your watch? 这是你的手表吗?

④ Look at the rain! It's heavy, isn't it? 看这雨!雨很大,对吗?

23.2 虚义 it 的用法

虚义 it 是"非指代性"it,不同于做人称和指示代词 it 的用法,虚义 it 可以在句子里担任具体意义的主语、宾语和表语。

23.2.1 虚义 it 作主语

(1) 虚义 it 作主语,指天气、时间、距离和环境等。

① It's summer in Australia now. 现在澳大利亚是夏天。

② It is sunny today. 今天阳光灿烂。

③ It is raining cats and dogs. 正下着倾盆大雨。

④ It is our wedding adversary. 今天是我们的结婚周年纪念日。

⑤ It is five miles to the college from here. 这里离学院有五英里。

⑥ It gets very noisy here in the rush hour. 这儿在上下班高峰期很嘈杂。

(2) 虚义 it 也可以在某些以 appear, happen, turn out, see, look 等动词作谓语的句子里作主语,后面接 that 从句。

① It looks as if you were young. 你看上去非常年轻。

② It appears that he is an skilled worker. 他看起来是一位非常熟练的工人。

(3) 虚义 it 也可在一些习惯用语中作主语。

① It is hard to say. 这不好说。

② It can't be helped. 这没用。

23.2.2 虚义 it 作宾语和表语

(1) 虚义 it 也常在某些习惯用语中作宾语,但 it 并无此具体意义。

① You should catch it for your rashness. 你应该为你的莽撞付出代价。

② You must fight it out. 你必须奋斗到底。

此外还有:cab it 乘车,come it strong 做得过分,make it 办成,take it out of sb. 拿某人出气。

(2) 当虚义 it 作表语时,有时整个句子的意思不易理解,所以要特别留心,注意正确理解其含义。

① Stop acting as though you were it. 别自以为了不起。

② In a sport clothing, he was it. 他穿着一身运动装,帅极了。

23.3 先行 it 的用法

先行 it 是指在句中使用 it 作形式主语或形式宾语,以代表后面的真正主语或真正宾语,使其显得平衡有序。先行 it 的使用能避免句子结构不平衡。真正主语或真正宾语通常是不定式结构、ing 分词结构或名词性从句。

23.3.1 it 作形式主语

1. 不定式作真正主语

(1) be + 名词 + 不定式。

① It would be a pity to miss this golden opportunity. 错过这个黄金机会非常可惜。

② It's a good habit to get up early and go to bed early. 早睡早起是好习惯。

③ It must be great fun to fly to the moon in a spaceship. 乘宇宙飞船飞往月球一定很有趣。

(2) be + 形容词 + 不定式。

① It is interesting to play with snow in winter. 冬季里玩雪是很有趣的。

② It is illegal to drive a car without a license. 无证驾驶是违法的。

③ It is difficult to translate this article. 翻译这篇文章很难。

④ It's important to keep the water clean. 保持水质清洁是很重要的。

(3) be + 介词短语 + 不定式。

① It is beyond me to do that. 我做不到。

② It was against my principle to help them. 帮助那些人违背了我的原则。

(4) 及物动词 + 宾语 + 不定式。

① It costs 2 hours to repair the TV. 修电视用了 2 个小时。

② It takes two to make a quarrel. 一个巴掌拍不响。

③ It took me a week to finish reading the book. 我花了一周时间看完这本书。

④ It cost me 260 yuan to buy the new watch. 我买这块新手表花了 260 元。

2. 动名词作真正主语

(1) be + 名词 + 动名词。

① It has been a great honor your coming to visit me. 您的来访让我倍感荣幸。

② It is no use studying for an exam at the last minute. 临时抱佛脚来应考是没用的。

(2) be + 形容词 + 动名词。

① It is useless regretting now. 现在后悔也没用。

② Is it worthwhile fighting for it? 为它打架值得吗?

③ It's bad playing in the street. 在街上玩是没好处的。

3. 以 that 引导的从句或以连接代词或连接副词引导的从句作主语

(1) It＋be＋形容词＋that 从句。

① It is necessary that the meeting be postponed. 会议务必推迟。

② It is certain that he has stolen the diamond. 肯定是他偷了钻石。

(2) It＋动词＋连接代词或副词引导的从句。

① It does not matter much whether he comes or not. 他来不来无所谓。

② It is known when and where the meeting will be held. 都知道会议的时间和地点。

23.3.2　it 作形式宾语

1. 不定式作真正宾语

① I found it difficult to explain to him what happened. 我发现向他解释发生了什么很困难。

② He mades it a rule to get up before dawn. 他习惯于天亮前起床。

2. 动名词作真正宾语

① I consider it impossible getting everything ready in a while. 我认为这么短的时间内什么都准备好是不可能的。

② He thought it no use going over the subject again. 他认为再讨论这个问题没有用了。

③ We think it no good reading in bed. 我们认为躺在床上看书无益处。

3. that 引导的名词性分句作真正宾语

① I took it for granted that she would be coming. 我想当然地认为她会来。

② We must make it clear to the public that something should be done to stop pollution. 我们必须让公众意识到是采取措施来防止污染的时候了。

③ I think it necessary that we have the meeting. 我认为开这个会是必要的。

23.4　分裂句引导词 it

(1) 分裂句是以 it 为引导词的强调句型,它的结构形式是：It ＋ be 的一定形式 ＋ 中心成分 ＋that/who 从句。

① It was Jane that/who called this morning. 是珍妮今天上午打来电话。

② It was a parcel that she brought him. 她带给他的是一个包裹。

(2) 分裂句是由普通陈述句转换而来的,通过这种结构可以强调除谓语动词以外的大多数句子成分。如以下句子：

John gave Mary a handbag at Christmas. 约翰在圣诞节给了玛丽一个提包。

根据上下文和语义意图,说话人可以通过分裂句分别强调主语、间接宾语、直接宾语、状语,使之成为信息中心。

① It was John that/who gave Mary a handbag at Christmas. 是约翰在圣诞节给了玛丽

一个提包。

② It was Mary that John gave a handbag (to) at Christmas. 约翰在圣诞节的提包是给玛丽的。

③ It was a handbag that John gave Mary at Christmas. 约翰在圣诞节给玛丽的是一个提包。

④ It was at Christmas that John gave Mary a handbag. 是在圣诞节约翰给了玛丽一个提包。

(3) 分裂句的时态一般应一致,即主句与从句的时态应皆用现在时,或皆用过去时,或皆用将来时。

① It is not I who am angry. 发怒的不是我。

② It was my two sisters who knew her best. 是我的两个姐妹最了解她。

③ It will not be you who will have to take the blame for this. 对此须受责难的将不是你。

(4) 有时分裂句的谓语动词还可以采取复杂形式。

① It may have been at Christmas that John gave Mary a handbag. 可能是在圣诞节约翰给玛丽一个提包。

② It might have been John who gave Mary a handbag. 很可能是约翰给了玛丽一个提包。

(5) 分裂句可以强调多种多样的状语成分。

① It was when she was about to go to bed that the telephone rang. 是在她即将上床睡觉时电话铃响了。

② It was because I wanted to buy a dictionary that I went to town yesterday. 我昨天是由于想买一本词典而进城的。

③ It was not until his father came back that Tom went to bed yesterday. 昨天汤姆是直到他父亲回来才上床睡觉的。

(6) 表语通常不可以作分裂句的中心成分,如在规范英语中通常不说:

① It is beautiful that she is. 她很漂亮。

② It is chairman of the Committee that he is. 他是委员会的主席。

但是宾语补语是可以这样用的,如:

① It is the chairman of the committee that they elected him. 他们选他作为委员会主席。

② It is green that they have painted the wall. 他们把墙壁漆的是绿色。

注:(1)当强调的中心成分为主语,指人时可用连词 that 或 who,强调其余的成分时,连词一律用 that。

(2) 分裂句中的 that 与 who 在非正式文体中可以省略。

① It was the President himself spoke to me. 是总统亲自和我谈了话。(省去从句主语 who)

② It was the dog I gave the water to. 我是给那条狗水的。(省去从句的宾语 that)

③ It was yesterday I first noticed it. 我是昨天开始注意到的。(省去从句连词 that)

有时还可省去句首的 it is,如:

A good, honest trade you are learning, Sir Peter! 彼得爵士,你学的是很好而诚实的一

行啊!

(3) 分裂句中的被强调部分有时可放在句首。

① Now was it that his life was done, and the fate which he could not escape was upon him. 就在这时,他的生命完结了,他所逃不脱的命运降临了。

② When was it that he arrived at the village? 是何时他到达了这个村子?

③ Why was it that he was late for school? 他是因为什么上学迟到的?

巩 固 练 习

一、单项选择。

1. — I'm sorry I broke your mirror.
   —Oh, really _____.
   A. It's OK with me B. It doesn't matter
   C. Don't be sorry   D. I don't care

2. I appreciate _____ if you would turn the radio off.
   A. it B. that C. these D. them

3. The Parkers bought a new house but _____ will need a lot of work before they can move in.
   A. they B. it C. one D. which

4. The volleyball match will be put off if it _____.
   A. will rain B. rains C. rained D. is raining

5. _____ from Beijing to London!
   A. How long way it is   B. What long way is it
   C. How long way is it   D. What a long way it is

6 _____ is a fact that English is being accepted as an international language.
   A. There B. This C. That D. It

7. —Do you know our town at all?
   —No, it is the first time I _____ here.
   A. was B. am going C. came D. have been

8. Was it in 1969 _____ the American astronaut succeeded _____ landing on the moon?
   A. when; on B. that; on C. when; in D. that; in

9. Was _____ that I saw last night at the concert?
   A. it you B. not you C. you D. that yourself

10. It is the ability to do the job _____ matters.
    A. one B. what C. that D. it

11. —What was the party like?
    —Wonderful. It's years _____ I enjoyed myself so much.
    A. after B. before C. when D. since

12. —He was nearly drowned once.
    —When was _____ ?

— _____ was in 1998 when he was in middle school.

A. that; It B. this; That C. this; It D. that; This

13. Tom's mother kept telling him that he mustn't smoke, but _____ didn't help.

A. he B. which C. it D. they

14. When you go outing with your sisters, you must see to _____ that they are safe.

A. everything B. it C. that D. yourself

15. —How do you like _____ here so far, Mr. David?

—Well, I've really enjoyed meeting many nice people here and everything here is quite different.

A. it B. them C. that D. this

16. —There is something wrong with my left shoulder. I hurt it while I was doing gym. I've got a pain here too.

— Let me take a look at your shoulder. Where _____ hurt?

A. do you B. does it C. do they D. does that

17. —Who is making so much noise in the garden?

— _____ the children.

A. It is B. They are C. That is D. There are

18. Who was _____ that called him "comrade"?

A. one B. that C. it D. her

19. Joan had often heard _____ said that Marley had no money.

A. one B. once C. it D. her

20. _____ doesn't seem to have been any difficulty solving the problem.

A. It B. He C. There D. That

21. _____ is it _____ has made Peter _____ he is today?

A. What, that, that B. That, that, what
C. What, what, that D. What, that, what

22. I don't think _____ possible to master a foreign language without much memory work.

A. this B. that C. its D. it

23. It was not _____ she took off her dark glasses _____ I realized she was a famous film star.

A. when; that B. until; that C. until; when D. when; then

24. It was how the young man had learned five foreign languages _____ attracted the audience's interest.

A. so that B. that C. what D. in which

25. It was _____ he said _____ disappointed me.

A. what; that B. that; that C. what; what D. that; what

26. In fact, _____ is a hard job for the police to keep order in an important football match.

A. this B. that C. there D. it

27. The news that they failed their driving test discouraged him, _____?

A. did they B. didn't they C. did it D. didn't it

28. It is these poisonous products _____ can cause the symptoms of the flu, such as headache and aching muscles.

   A. who   B. that   C. how   D. what

29. _____ fun it is to jump into a pool or go swimming in summer!

   A. What a   B. How   C. How a   D. What

30. Was _____ at the air battle on June 8, 1944, _____ was led by Captain Johnson _____ Peter lost his life?

   A. it; when; that   B. that; that; who
   C. it; which; that   D. it; which; when

二、结合 it 的用法翻译下列句子。

1. 冬天,天色晚得早。
2. 问她没有用,她什么都不知道。
3. 从这儿到车站有两英里(路程)。
4. 你见过下冰雹吗?
5. 由你来决定该怎么办?
6. 据说他已去过美国两次了。
7. 可惜你错过了那次音乐会。
8. 看来,他很害怕。
9. 牛奶已经泼翻,哭也无用(即做无益的后悔无济于事)。
10. 几个月之后我们才又见面。

第二十四章 一 致

一致指句子成分之间或词语之间在语法形式上的协调关系。主谓一致是指主语和谓语动词在人称、数等方面保持一致,其主要方面是数的一致,与数的一致相联系的有主谓人称一致。

在现代英语中,动词 be 有不同的人称形式 am, is, are, was, were。主语人称不同,动词 be 的形式也就不同;动词 have 有第三人称单数形式 has,其余动词只有现在时第三人称单数,才有特殊的-s 形式,其余人称的单复数,都无特殊形式。

24.1 主谓一致的三个基本原则

处理主谓一致关系可根据以下三个原则:语法一致原则、概念(或意义)一致原则和邻近一致原则。

24.1.1 语法一致原则

语法一致指谓语动词必须在人称和数上与主语保持形式上的一致,即主语是单数形式,谓语动词也是单数形式;主语是复数形式,谓语动词也是复数形式。

① She watches TV for 2 hours every day. 她每天看两小时的电视。
② Every student comes in time. 每位同学都准时到了。
③ Few families are really perfect. 家家都有本难念的经。

24.1.2 概念一致原则

概念一致,指主谓语的一致不受语法形式的限制,而是随着主语所表达的内在含义而定。如果主语形式是复数,但表示单数概念,谓语动词用单数;反之,主语形式是单数,但表示复数概念,谓语动词用复数。

① Ten minutes is enough. 十分钟足够了。
② The class are taking notes. 全体学生正在记笔记。

24.1.3 邻近一致原则

邻近一致原则是指谓语动词的单复数形式不以主语的语法形式或实际意义为依据,而以靠近它的单复数形式为依据。

① Either she or I am going to the exhibition. 我和她有一个去看展览。
② Neither she nor you are going to blame. 你和她都没责任。

上述三个原则表面看来有时有矛盾现象,但在具体运用中,它们互相协调,并不矛盾。在运用中如果出现难以确定哪一原则的情况下,一般来说要遵循语法一致的原则。

24.2 以集体名词作主语的主谓一致

集体名词,如 committee,family,team,cattle,group,government 等,在意义上是复数,而在语法形式上是单数。以此类名词作主语的主谓一致问题,往往在于对"语法一致"和"意义一致"两种原则的选择。这种选择要遵循以下几个方面的要求。

24.2.1 通常用作复数的集体名词

有些集体名词,如 cattle, militia, poultry, people, police, vermin 等,通常用作复数,之后的谓语动词也要用复数形式。

① The police have caught the murderer. 警察抓住了凶手。
② Our militia were quartered in that country. 我们的民兵驻扎在县城里。

24.2.2 通常用作不可数名词的集体名词

有一些集体名词,如 merchandise, equipment, machinery, foliage, furniture 等,通常用作不可数名词,后面的谓语动词用单数。

① The foliage in autumn is hard to clean up. 秋天的落叶很难清扫干净。
② All the machinery in the factory is made in local. 工厂里的机器都是本地生产的。
③ All the furniture is made in England. 所有的家具都是英国制造。

24.2.3 既可作单数也可作复数的集体名词

有一些集体名词,如 audience, class, committee, council, crew, enemy, family, jury, government, public 等,既可以用作单数,也可以用作复数。如果将这些名词所代表的集体视为一个整体,谓语动词就用单数。

① My family has a reunion every year. 我家每年有一次大团圆。
② The public is focusing on that political scandal. 公众正在关注政府丑闻。

如果将侧重点放在组成集体的成员上,谓语动词用复数,请比较:

① There was a large audience at the concert. 音乐会的听众甚多。
② The audience are dressed in a variety of way. 观众有着各式各样的打扮。
③ The committee is to deal with the problem. 委员会正在处理那个问题。
④ The committee here approved that proposal unanimously. 委员会各委员一致通过那项提议。

24.3 表示确切数量的名词词组作主语时的主谓一致

(1) 在数学运算中,通常把数词词组看成一个整体,谓语动词用单数。

① Two plus three is five. 二加三等于五。
② Eight minus two leaves six. 八减二等于六。

但两数相加或相乘,谓语动词可用单数或复数。

① Four and four is/are eight. 四加四等于八。
② Twice three is/are six. 三乘三等于六。
如果最后一个数是 one 时,谓语动词用单数。
① Two times one is two. 二乘一等于二。
如果最后一个数用作复数名词时,谓语动词通常用复数形式。
② Two threes are six. 三乘二等于六。

(2) 如果作主语的名词词组是由"分数(或百分数)＋of-词组"构成,其动词形式依 of 词组中名词类别而定。

① Two-thirds of the area has been reclaimed for tree planting. 这个地区的三分之二面积要求种上树。
② Over forty percent of the country was ruined in the earthquake. 在地震中,这个县超过百分之四十的地方被夷为平地。

(3) 如果主语由"**one in/one out of** ＋复数名词"构成,在正式语体中,动词用单数;在非正式语体中,动词可按"就近原则"来确定单、复数形式。
One in five soldiers has/have been badly injured in the battlefield. 五分之一的战士在战场上受了重伤。

24.4　表示非确切数量的名词词组作主语时的主谓一致

当主语为表示非确定数量的名词词组时,可依据以下原则解决主谓一致问题。

(1) "**a number of** ＋复数可数名词"作主语,谓语动词用复数;"**the number of** ＋复数可数名词"作主语,谓语动词用单数;"**numbers of** ＋复数可数名词"作主语,谓语动词用复数。

① A number of people were injured in the riot. 许多人在暴乱中受伤。
② A large number of alldience cheered up at the performance of Chinese men's gym-nastics team in the 2008 Olympic Games. 许多观众看了 2008 年奥运会上中国男子体操队的表现后,倍受鼓舞。
③ The number of coin-collectors is increasing rapidly. 集币者的数量正在飞速地增加。
④ Numbers of students were questioned in the class. 很多学生在课堂上被提问到了。

(2) 由"**a lot of/ lots of /plenty of/ heaps of/ loads of/ scads of**"等后接可数名词作主语时,谓语动词用复数;后接不可数名词作主语时,谓语动词用单数。

① There are lots of /heaps of people who don't approve it. 有很多人不同意。
② There is plenty of space around the house. 房子四围还有很大空间。
③ Loads of apples have been picked. 很多苹果被摘掉了。
④ A lot of money was spent for travel. 旅游花了很多钱。

(3) 词组"**a (great/ good) deal of；a/an (large/ small) amount of；a (large/small) quantity of**"后面一般接不可数名词,这种结构形式作主语时,谓语动词用单数。

① A (great) deal of money was spent for the party. 聚会的花销巨大。
② A large amount of damage was done in a very short time. 短时间内造成了巨大的损失。

amount 和 quantity 的复数形式作主语时,后面可以是不可数名词或者复数可数名词,谓语动词都要用复数。

① Large amounts of money were spent on this bridge. 建造那座桥花了很多钱。

② Great quantities of fish have recently been caught in this river. 最近在这条河里捕捞了很多鱼。

(4) 在"a kind/ sort/ type of；this kind/ sort/ type of"之后通常跟单数可数名词或不可数名词,动词用单数。

① This kind of guy offends me. 这个家伙惹恼我了。

② This sort of apple is sour. 这种苹果是酸的。

③ That type of TV is out of date. 这种电视已经过时了。

出现在 these/those kinds of, many/ several kinds of 之后的名词,既可以是单数可数名词或不可数名词,也可以是复数可数名词,后面的谓语动词都用复数。

① There are many different kinds of snake in the mountain. 山上有许多不同种类的蛇。

② There are several sorts of cheese in this supermarket. 在超市里有很多种奶酪。

③ Those kinds of insects are useful. 这些种类的昆虫是有益的。

(5) "**more than one** ＋单数可数名词,**many a** ＋单数可数名词"作主语时,谓语动词用单数；"**a great/ good many** ＋复数可数名词"作主语时,谓语动词用复数。

① More than one problem was solved. 解决的问题不止一个。

② There's many a slip twist the cup and the lip. 事情往往功亏一篑。

③ There are a good many workers in the factory. 工厂里有许多工人。

"more ＋复数可数名词＋than one"结构一般要求谓语动词用复数形式。

④ More houses than one have been destroyed in that hurricane. 在飓风中被毁掉的房子不止一座。

(6) 当"**most, half, part, portion, proportion, enough, the majority, the remainder, the rest**"等作主语时,谓语动词根据主语的意义用单数或复数。

① Half of the students were failed in the exam. 有一半的学生没通过考试。

② Half of the land is cultivated. 有一半的土地得到了开发。

③ A large proportion of the teachers are post-graduates. 老师中很多人都是研究生。

④ Part of the lake is devoted to tourism. 湖的一部分被开发成旅游景区。

⑤ The rest of the story needs no telling. 剩下的故事不必再说了。

(7) 定冠词＋ 形容词/分词作主语时,如果泛指一类人时,谓语动词用复数；如果表示个别人时,谓语动词用单数；如果表示抽象概念,谓语动词用单数。

① The sick are well attended in hospital. 患者在医院里得到了很好的照顾。

② There lives a rich man and a poor man. The rich helps the poor a lot. 那里住着一个富人和一个穷人。富人给了穷人很多帮助。

24.5　以-s 结尾的名词作主语时的主谓一致

英语可数名词的复数形式是在词尾＋s 或＋es,也有一些以-s 结尾的名词并不是可数名词,这类词有的作单数用,有的作复数用,有的既可以作单数也可以作复数。因此,在谓语动词的使用上,要注意以下几点。

1. 下列以-s结尾的词通常用作单数

(1) 疾病名,如arthritis(关节炎),bronchitis(支气管炎),rickets(软骨病),mumps(腮腺炎),phlebitis(静脉炎)等,这类名词通常用作单数。

① German measles is a dangerous disease for pregnant women. 风疹对于孕妇是一种危险的疾病。

② Arthritis is a disease causing pain and swelling in the joints of the body. 关节炎是一种造成身体某些关节极为疼痛并发肿胀的疾病。

但有些表示疾病的名词既可用作单数,也可用作复数,例如:

① Mumps is/are fairly rare in adults. 腮腺炎在成年人中相当罕见。

② Rickets is/are caused by malnutrition. 软骨病是由营养不良造成的。

(2) 游戏名,如craps(掷骰子),darts(掷镖),dominoes(多米诺),draughts(国际跳棋),fires(放烟火),marbles(弹球)等,通常用作单数。

① Dominoes is one of the most popular games in the world and was not confined to children. 多米诺是世界上最流行的游戏,不仅仅限于儿童。

② Darts is essentially a free and easy game. 掷镖游戏是一种自由而且容易玩的游戏。

但有个别表示游戏名称的名词用作复数,当有的名词指游戏工具时用作复数,例如:

③ We can play cards in the leisure time. 闲暇时,我们可以玩纸牌。

④ Three darts are thrown at each turn. 每轮投三种镖。

⑤ Marbles are various in kind and quality. 各种弹子在品种和质量上都有差别。

(3) 学科名称,如economics(经济学),physics(物理学),statistics(统计学),politics(政治学),tactics(兵法),optics(光学),acoustics(声学),mathematics(数学),linguistics(语言学)等,通常用作单数。

① Politics is the key subject in our school. 政治学是我校的重点学科。

② Mathematics is an exact science. 数学是一门精确的学科。

③ Tactics is an important study for the soldier. 对于战士来说,兵法是一门非常重要的学问。

④ Linguistics is a complex subject for the beginners of language. 对于语言初学者来说,语言学是非常难懂的。

但当这些名词表示学科以外的其他意义时,也可用作复数,例如:

⑤ His mathematics are weak. 他的运算能力差。

⑥ What are his politics? 他的政治观点是什么?

⑦ The acoustics in the New hall are above reproach. 新大厅的音响设备无可挑剔。

⑧ Athletics have been greatly promoted in this university. 这所大学大力提倡体育运动。

⑨ Statistics prove nothing in this instance. 统计学在这一事例上不说明问题。

(4) 以-s结尾的国家名称,如the United Nations, the United States, the Netherlands等作为单一政治实体,故用作单数。

The United States is a country of people with various origins. 美国是一个由多种族构成的国家。

2. 以-s结尾的名词在句中作主语时谓语动词通常用作复数

(1) 由两部分组成的物品,如glasses, scissors, spectacles, pincers, shorts, pajamas,

trousers 等。

① The trousers are dirty.

但如果此类名词有单位词修饰时,那么动词的单复数形式由单位词的单复数形式决定。

② One pair of scissors is enough. 一把剪子就够了。

③ Two pairs of pincers are on the desk. 桌子上有两把钳子。

(2) 地理名称中表示山脉、群岛、海峡、瀑布等名词用作复数。

① The Himalayas are youngest mountains in the world. 喜马拉雅山脉是世界上最年轻的山脉。

② The Niagara Falls are perhaps the most famous waterfall in the world. 尼亚加拉大瀑布可能是世界上最著名的瀑布。

(3) 由-ing 结尾的名词,如 belongings,sharings,fillings,lodgings(租住房),clippings(剪下来的东西),diggings(挖出来的东西),earnings(收入),surroundings(环境)等,通常用作复数。

① The lodgings in this district have been kept on record in police station. 这个地区的租住房被详细地记录在派出所里。

② The sweepings of the class have been disposed of. 教室里的垃圾被清理掉了。

但也有一些以-ing 结尾的名词既可以用作单数,也可以用作复数,如 tidings(消息)。

Good tidings has/have cheered them up.

好消息让他们高兴起来。

(4) 一些常以-s 结尾的名词,如 arms(武器),clothes,contents(目录、内容),fireworks,goods,remains(遗体),stairs,suburbs(郊区),morals(道德、品行),archives(档案),eaves(屋檐)等,通常用作复数。

① High wages make him happy. 高薪使他非常满意。

② The goods are transported by air. 货物是空运的。

③ The arms are scattering on the battlefield. 战场上到处都是散落的武器。

④ The contents at this reference book are easy to understand. 这本参考书的内容非常容易理解。

3. 单复数同形的名词

以-s 结尾的单数、复数同形的名词,如 headquarters(总部),series(系列),species(种类),barracks(营房),works(工厂)等,在其后面的谓语动词的单复数形式取决于此类名词的意义。

① A headquarters was set up to direct the operation. 一个用于指挥行动的总部成立起来了。

② Their headquarters are in basement. 他们的总部设在地下室里。

24.6 并列结构作主语时的主谓一致

并列结构作主语的主谓一致常见于以下几种情况:

(1) 由 **and** 连接的并列主语,根据语法一致的原则,谓语动词一般用复数形式。如果并列主语指的是一个整体,或在意义上指的是同一个人或物,同一事件或同一概念时,根据概念一致的原则,谓语动词用单数形式。

① Jim and Tom are good friends. 吉姆和汤姆是好朋友。

② The hunting and the fishing in that village were good that year. 今年那个村的渔猎收成都不错。

③ The poet and writer has come. 那个诗人兼作家来了。

④ Care and patience is needed in study. 学习需要细心和耐心。

（2）当 and 连接的并列名词词组中带有 each/every and each/every，或 many a 等限定词时，后面的谓语动词通常用单数。

① Every boy and every girl in the room is glad to hear that story. 这个房间里的男孩、女孩都喜欢听那个故事。

② Many a man and woman is asked to help. 许多人需要帮助。

（3）由 both...and 连接的词语如果是指两个人或物，谓语动词用复数。

① Both rice and wheat are grown in our village. 我们村子种植大米和小麦。

② Both bread and butter were sold in this grocery. 杂货店出售面包和黄油。

（4）用 or，either...or，neither...nor，not only...but also 等连接的词语作主语时，通常根据邻近一致的原则，谓语动词的形式和相邻的词语保持一致。

① He or his brothers were to blame. 应该怪他和他的兄弟们。

② Either the shirt or the sweater is a good buy. 这些衬衣，要不就是这件毛衣，买上去是很合算的。

③ Neither you nor he is responsible. 你和他都没有责任。

④ Not only the students but also their teacher has been there. 老师和学生都在那里。

（5）由 as well as，rather than，more than，no less than，as much as，in addition to，with，along with，except，together with 等连接的词语作主语时，通常把这些词语当作介词看待，谓语动词形式与这些词组前面的词语一致。

① The girl, as well as the boys, has learned to ride. 女孩和男孩一样都学会了骑车。

② A man with two children has come. 一个男人带着两个孩子来了。

③ I as well as they am ready to help you. 不仅他们愿意帮助你，我也愿意帮助你。

④ The car, in addition to the house, was destroyed by the fire. 车，连同房子一块被火烧掉了。

24.7 不定代词作主语时的主谓一致

不定代词都是第三人称，用作主语时单数和复数有以下几类情况：

（1）**all、some** 替代可数名词，谓语动词用复数，替代不可数名词时用单数。

① Some approve and some disapprove. 一些人同意，一些人反对。

② Some enjoy the performane of women's rhythmic gymnastics, for it connects sports and arts together closely. 有些人喜欢女子艺术体操表演，因为它把体育和艺术紧密结合起来。

③ All is correct. 都对了。

④ All are happy to come here. 所有的人很高兴来这儿。

（2）**any** 可以替代不可数名词和可数名词，替代不可数名词时用单数，替代可数名词一般用作复数,有时也可以用单数。

① I don't think any is left. 我想没有剩下的了。

② I guess any of them have come. 我想他们中间有人来过。

(3)**both** 和 **several** 一般用作复数。

① Both his cousins are called Tom. 他的两个堂兄弟都叫汤姆。

② Several of buildings are destroyed in the earthquake. 好几栋建筑物在地震中倒塌了。

(4) **each** 常用作单数。

① Each of the workers has their own advantage. 每个工人都有特长。

但后面如果有较长的定语时,谓语动词也可根据邻近原则用复数。

② Each of the visitors into the Olympic Sports Stadium must be checked strictly for safety. 每位进入鸟巢的人都必须进行严格的安全检查。

(5) **none** 可代表单数可数名词、复数可数名词和不可数名词,谓语形式根据所替代意义用常数或复数。

① None of us are perfect. 人无完人。

② None of this money is mine. 没有一分钱是我的。

③ None are so deaf as those that will not hear. 聋子莫过于不愿听人言之人。

(6) **many** 和 **few** 做主语,谓语动词常用复数;**much** 和 **little** 常用作单数;**more and most** 根据替代的是可数或不可数名词,决定谓语动词用复数或单数。

① Many of us are students. 我们中间有一部分是学生。

② Few of the girls like sporting. 喜欢体育的女孩不多。

③ Much of what he says is true. 他说的许多话是事实。

④ There is little we can help. 我们帮不上忙。

⑤ Most of the people were saved from the fire. 许多人被从火场救出。

⑥ Most of the lawn is seriously demaged. 草地的大部分被毁掉了。

但在 many is (was) the time (thing, etc.) (that) 这一固定结构中则要求用单数名词。

⑦ Many was the time I went to that cinema. 我去过那个电影院很多次。

(7) **either** 用作主语时,谓语动词一般用单数,但在非正式英语中"either ＋of＋复数名词(代词)"结构之后则用复数。**neither** 作主语,谓语动词可根据要求采用单数或复数。

① I do not think either of them have gone. 我想他们两个都还没走。

② Either of them is gone. 他们两个人走了一个。

③ Neither of the books is satisfactory. 两本书都不令人满意。

④ Neither of them are welcome. 他们两个都不受欢迎。

(8) 由 **some**, **any**, **no**, **every** 和 **body**, **one**, **thing** 构成的复合不定代词作主语时,谓语动词用单数。

① Somebody is speaking there. 那里有人说话。

② Nobody was listening. 没人听。

③ Everyone has his own idea. 每个人都有自己的想法。

但有时当 everybody, anybody, nobody 后边有复数名词时,谓语动词也可用复数形式,符合邻近原则。

④ Nobody, not even the children, were interested. 没有人,甚至于孩子,都不感兴趣。

24.8 其他方面的主谓一致

24.8.1 以名词性分句作主语的主谓一致

(1) 由 what, who, why, how, whether 等引导的名词性分句作主语,后面的谓语动词通常用单数。

① What I think is no business of yours. 我怎么想和你没关系。
② Whatever he says is of no importance. 无论他说什么都不重要。
③ Whoever says that is wrong. 无论谁说这话都不对。

(2) 由 and 连接的并列名词性分句作主语,如果主语表示两件不同的事情,动词用复数。

Where the accident happened and who badly hurt in it were recorded. 事故的地点和伤者都被记录下来。

(3) 在主系表结构中,如果主语补语是复数名词,那么谓语动词也可用复数。

① What I want are details. 我需要的是细节。
② What the disaster area need are foods and medicines. 灾区急需的是食物和药品。

24.8.2 以非限定分句做主语的主谓一致

非限定分句,一般是指不定式分句和动名词作主语,其后的谓语动词用单数。

① To study a foreign language requires patience and tenacity. 学习外语需要耐心和毅力。
② To finish such work needs ten years. 要完成这项工作需要十年时间。
③ Reading books is a good way to broaden our view. 读书有助于拓宽视野。

若有 and 连接的并列非限定分句作主语,是指的两件事,谓语动词可用复数。

④ To preview the lesson and to review it will help you remember the points. 课前预习和课后复习可以帮助你记住要点。

24.8.3 关系分句中主谓一致

关系分句中谓语动词单、复数形式通常依关系代词的形式而定。

(1) 关系代词在句中作主语的时候,谓语动词应与先行词的人称和数一致。

① I, who am your friends, advise you to stop it. 我,作为你的朋友,建议你停下来。
② I, who am your classmate, will share the work with you. 我是你的同学,要和你分担这项工作。
③ You, who are my partner, should help me. 你作为我的搭档,应该帮助我。
④ The recorder that has been given to me is home-made. 给我的那台录音机是国产的。

(2) 在"one of+复数名词+关系分句"结构中,谓语动词的单复数一般依先行词的数而定。

① He is one of the students who have failed in exam. 他是众多落榜生中的一员。
② I am one of those people who are ready to help victims in the earthquake. 许多人时刻准备援助地震灾区的受害者,我是他们中的一份子。

如果这类结构之前有定冠词 the 或者有 the only/ the very 等限定词和强调词时,关系分句动词形式依 one 而定用单数。

③ He is the only one of the survivors who escapes from the flood. 他是唯一一个从洪水中幸免于难的人。

24.8.4　分裂句中的主谓一致

在分裂句中,that/who-分句的动词形式通常依先行项而定。典型的有:It is I/me＋who/that-分句。在此类分句中,who 分句动词现在时在人称和数的形式上与 I 等先行词表示一致。

① It is you who are right. 你是对的。

② It is not she who has been wrong. 错的不是她。

但如果分裂句中心成分是宾格代词,随后的分句动词通常用第三人称单数。

③ It is me that is to blame. 受责备的应该是我。

④ It is me that has committed a mistake. 是我犯了一个大错。

24.8.5　倒装句中的主谓一致

(1) 在倒装结构中,主语即使是复数名词,谓语动词往往也用单数,尤其是在非正式英语中。

① In our family comes workers also one teacher. 我的家族出了许多工人,也出了一位教师。

② In the midnight was heard the horns of two pistol cars. 半夜,两辆巡逻车的警笛响起来了。

(2) 在 there be 开头的存在句中,谓语动词的单、复数形式一般取决于随后的主语的单、复数形式。

① There are three ways which lead to village. 有三条路可以通往村子里。

② There is a note left on the floor. 地面上有张纸条。

24.9　数词与名词的一致

数词有时与名词在形式上不一致,但在逻辑上是一致的。

① **Cinemas** were one of the few places where they could relax. 电影院是他们能够放松一下的少数地方之一。

② Mrs. Jane is worth ten of her daughter. 简太太比得上她的 10 个女儿。

③ I would not sit thirteen to dinner. 我在宴会上绝不坐第 13 个座位。

数词用作定语时,与名词的一致比较简单。

④ two photos 两张照片

⑤ ten kilos 10 公斤

有些单位词,如 pair,couple 等,与以上的基数词连用时,用单形或复形皆可。

⑥ two pair(s) of gloves 两双手套

⑦ four couple(s) of rabbits 四对兔子

在 one and a half(quarter,etc.)后一般应用复形名词,但亦可用单形名词。

⑧ one and a half hours 一个半小时（为避免用单形名词或复形名词的疑虑,最好说 one hour and a half）

现就一些常见情况具体分类讨论如下：

(1)"一以上的基数词＋连字符＋表时间的名词"结构用作定语时,其名词一般应用单形。

① a ten-second pause 一次 10 秒钟的停顿

② a five-minute break 一次 5 分钟的休息

③ a two-hour test 一次 2 小时的测试

如不用连字符,其名词则常用复形。

④ a ten minutes rest 一段 10 分钟的休息

⑤ a two months training 为期 2 个月的训练

⑥ five years service 5 年的工龄

也可用名词所有格。

⑦ four hours'delay 4 小时的延误

⑧ a ten days'wonder 10 天的奇迹

当"一以上的基数词＋连字符＋表时间的名词＋连字符＋old"结构用作定语时,其名词一般用单形。

⑨ a two-year-old baby 一个 2 岁的宝宝

但 old 如代之以其他形容词,则一般须用复形。

⑩ a four-years-long waiting 一个长达 4 年的等待

(2)"一以上的基数词＋连字符＋表长度、距离等的名词"结构用作定语时,其名词一般用单形。

① a ten-inch ruler 一把 10 英寸的尺子

② a sixty-acre market 一个占地 60 英亩的市场

③ a three-foot-long stick 一根 3 英尺长的棍棒

④ a two-hundred-foot wide river 一条宽 200 英尺的河

在非正式英语中,面积常用单形 foot。

⑤ My classroom is about eight foot by twelve. 我的教室大约有 12 英尺长 8 英尺宽。

(3) 在表示房子的高度时,常用单形名词 **storey**(或 story)表楼房的层次。

① a five-story building 一座 5 层高的楼(亦可说 a fivestoried building)

但一般应说：four stories high.

说人的高度时,一般应用复形 feet。

② He is six feet four(inches tall). 他身高六英尺七英寸。

但在非正式文体中,人们亦常用单形 foot。

③ He is only five foot four. 他身高只有五英尺四英寸。

表深度的说法与表高度的说法一样。

(4) 表重量的 **ton** 与数词连用时可用单形或复形。

① a five-ton weight 重 5 吨之物(用单形)

② a 200,000 tons ship 一艘 20 万吨的船(用复形)

名词 stone 多用单形。如：

③ A full-grown man in Asia averages about eleven stone. 亚洲的成年人平均体重约为 11 英石。(亦可用 stones)

(5) 表价值的定语修饰 **note** 和 **bill** 等名词时,定语中名词用单形。

① a 100-pound note 一张 100 英镑的钞票

② a ten-dollar bill 一张 10 美元的钞票

单形 penny 和复形 pence 皆可用。

③ five three-penny(或 three-pence)stamps 5 张 3 便士的邮票

pound 多用复形。

④ four pounds sixty-five 4 英镑 65 便士

⑤ the six thousand pounds prize 6 千英镑的奖金

巩 固 练 习

一、单项选择。

1. Neither he nor I _____ for the plan.
   A. were   B. is   C. are   D. am
2. My family as well as I _____ glad to see you.
   A. was   B. is   C. are   D. am
3. My father, together with some of his old friends, _____ there already.
   A. will be   B. had been   C. has been   D. have been
4. There are two roads and either _____ to the station.
   A. is leading   B. are leading C. lead   D. leads
5. Nine plus three _____ twelve.
   A. are making   B. is making   C. make   D. makes
6. Twenty miles _____ a long way to cover.
   A. seem to be   B. is   C. are   D. were
7. Very few _____ his address in the town.
   A. has known   B. are knowing C. know   D. knows
8. When and where this took place _____ still unknown.
   A. has   B. is   C. were   D. ar
9. I know that all _____ getting on well with her.
   A. were   B. are   C. is   D. was
10. The rest of the novel _____ very interesting.
    A. seem   B. is   C. are   D. were
11. Our family _____ a happy one.
    A. are   B. was   C. are   D. is
12. The boy sitting by the window is the only one of the students who _____ from the countryside in our school.
    A. was   B. were   C. is   D. are
13. More than one answer _____ to the question.

A. had given B. were given
C. has been given D. have been given

14. The students in our school each _____ an English dictionary.
    A. are having B. had C. has D. have
15. The pair of shoes _____ worn out.
    A. had been B. have been C. were D. was
16. A professor and a writer _____ present at the meeting.
    A. had been B. were C. is D. was
17. Those who _____ singing may join us.
    A. is fond of B. enjoy C. likes D. are liking
18. There _____ a knife and fork on the table.
    A. are B. is seeming to be C. seem to be D. seems to be
19. Over 80 percent of the population _____ workers.
    A. will be B. are C. is D. was
20. The whole class _____ greatly moved at his words.
    A. is B. had C. were D. was
21. The wounded _____ good care of here now.
    A. is taking B. are taking C. are being taken D. is taken
22. Deer _____ faster than dogs.
    A. will run B. are running C. runs D. run
23. The police _____ a prisoner.
    A. are searched for B. is searching
    C. are searching for D. is searching for
24. It was reported that six _____ including a boy.
    A. had killed B. was killing C. were killed D. was killed
25. The United Nations _____ in 1945.
    A. was found B. was founded C. were founded D. were found
26. I, who _____ your good friend, will share your joys and sorrows.
    A. was B. are C. is D. am
27. Between the two buildings _____ a monument.
    A. is standing B. standing C. stands D. stand
28. Laying eggs _____ the ant queen's full-time job.
    A. have B. has C. are D. is
29. Peter, perhaps John, _____ playing with the little dog.
    A. seems B. were C. are D. is
30. Many a student _____ that mistake before.
    A. had made B. has been made C. have made D. has made

二、改错。

1. Bill was standing at the side of the car, talking to two men who was helping him to repair it.

2. Playing football not only makes us grow up tall and strong but also give us a sense of fair play and team spirit.
3. Now my picture and the prize is hanging in the library.
4. But then there is always more mysteries to look into.
5. But not all information are good to society.
6. So now, a concert cost so much. I may just listen to music.
7. If I listen to my own records, there are no need to spend money.
8. You will probably want to join the Stamp Collectors' Club which exist to add more stamps to your collection.
9. One evening she told me that something happened when their parents was out.
10. A man of abilities is needed.
11. More than one person are involved in this.
12. This is one of the best books that has appeared.
13. The number of stamp-collectors are growing apace.
14. Three-fourths of the people is illiterate.
15. None of them in the house was in their beds.

第二十五章 强 调

在英语语法中,强调就是通过句序的特殊调整以及运用一些强调型词语,把需要强调的部分表述出来。强调涉及两个方面,在书面语中,一般采用分裂句的形式来表示强调,也可以采用将强调的部分后置或前置的方法;还有一种同汉语表达方式较接近的方法,即运用强调性词语。第二,在口语中,强调一半是靠语音、语调的不同将被强调的部分表现出来。如被强调的词语的语调往往要比正常情况下读音高、声音洪亮,词中的元音拉得较长。有时还可以有意识地在被强调部分前停顿一下,如 It is me who want to go outside. 这句话我们要强调"me",那么读的时候"me"这个词的元音[iː],就要比正常的情况下念得更长些。

25.1 分 裂 句

分裂句是英语中特有的一种强调句型,也是最常用的一种强调句型。它由 it 做引导词,基本句型为 It is/was ＋被强调部分＋适当的引导词＋从句。如果被强调的部分是物,大都是 that 来引导,有时也用 which,指人通常用 who(whom)引导从句;如果强调的部分是状语,指时间、地点等也用 that 来引导从句,不用 when,where。

分裂句可强调主语、宾语、时间状语、地点状语、方式状语及 because 引导的原因状语。如果引导的部分是主语时,从句中的谓语动词要与被强调的主语保持一致。

(1) 强调句型中的时态一般会用两种,即一般现在时和一般过去时,若原句的动词为一般过去时、过去完成时及过去进行时,就用 It ＋ was＋被强调部分＋适当的引导词＋从句;若原句中的动词为其他时态,则使用 It ＋ is ＋被强调部分＋适当的引导词＋从句。

① It was John who /that bought an old bike yesterday in a marketplace. 是约翰昨天在市场上买了辆旧自行车。(强调主语)

② It was an old bike that John bought yesterday in a marketplace. 昨天约翰在市场买的是辆旧自行车。(强调宾语)

③ It was yesterday that John bought an old bike in a marketplace. 约翰是昨天在市场上买了辆旧自行车。(强调时间状语)

④ It was in a marketplace that John bought an old bike yesterday. 约翰昨天是在市场上买了辆旧自行车。(强调地点状语)

⑤ It was because he didn't pass the exam that his father gave him a good beating. 是因为考试不及格他爸爸把他痛打一顿。

(2) 除了用 It is / was 以外,用 what,who 等也可以引导这样的分裂句。

① When is it that you will set off? 你到底什么时候出发?

② Who was it that told you this? 是谁告诉你这件事的?

(3) 此外还有一些常用的固定强调句型,如 not...until 的强调形式是 It is / was not un-

til...that...,表示"是直到……才……"的意思。

① He and the other doctors did not leave until the operation was over. 他和其他医生等手术做完后才离开。

= It was not until the operation was over that he and the other doctors left.

注：在强调句型中只用 until,不用 till,由于 that 前已有否定词 not,故 that 后的句子要用肯定式。

② I won't believe you until I've seen you in the jar with my own eyes. 直到我亲眼看你在坛子里,我才相信你的话。

= It is not until I've seen you in the jar with my own eyes that I will believe you.

也可以用下面的倒装句型来强调以 not until 引导的时间状语：not until＋时间状语（或从句）＋助动词 did＋主谓。

③ Jack's father didn't buy him a computer until he went to college. 直到杰克上大学爸爸才给他买了台计算机。

= It was not until he went to college that Jack's father bought him a computer.

= Not until he went to college did Jack's father buy him a computer.

(4) 如前所述,一般分裂句是不可以用简单陈述句的谓语动词作为中心成分的。如果要强调谓语动词,就得采用另外一种强调句型,这种句型又叫做"拟似"分裂句。

① I gave her a book. What I did was (to) give her a book. 我所做的是给她一本书。

② He took a plane to Beijing. What he did was (to) take a plane to Beijing. 他所做的是乘飞机去北京。

③ The student is going to write an article. What the student is going to do is(to) write an article. 这个学生要做的是写一篇文章。

"拟似"分裂句的主语通常是由 what 引导的名词性从句,从句的主动词通常是 do 的一定形式。这种分裂句的主语补语通常是不定式结构,可带 to,也可不带 to,它构成"拟似"分裂句的信息中心。

"拟似"分裂句还可采取另外一种形式,即"what-从句＋be＋名词词组"的形式。

④ What he gave her was a handbag. 他给她的是个提包。

也可采取"名词词组＋be＋what-从句"的形式。

⑤ A handbag was what he gave her. 提包就是他给她的。

25.2 后　　置

英语句子中较显要的部分是句首和句尾,而其中以句尾更为显要。原因在于句尾部分给人印象长久,而且把重要的部分后置,还会给读者留下深刻印象,因此把需要强调的部分后置到句尾是强调的重要方法之一。试比较以下每组句子：

① The boy tried to catch the ball, but he failed in the end.

The boy tried to catch the ball, but in the end he failed.

（后移之后便强调了"他失败"的结果。）

② We all know that he made up the story. 我们都知道他编造了那一套。

We all know that he made the story up. 我们都知道他说的那一套是编造的。

（从这组比较句中可以看出，短语动词的部分后移同样能产生强调的效果。在后一句中强调"他说的那一套是编造的"，而前一句突出表现的，则不是编造这种手段，而是编造的内容，即 story。）

③ This is the most beautiful dress, I think. 我想这是最漂亮的衣服了。

This dress, I think, is the most beautiful dress. 这件衣服，我想，是最漂亮的。

（通过对"is the most beautiful"的后移，强调了这是最漂亮的一件衣服。）

④ She told me the secret. 她告诉我那个秘密了。

She told the secret to me. 她把那个秘密告诉我了。

（第二句强调了"她把那个秘密告诉了我，而不是别的什么人"这样的意思。）

还有一种句型也可把它称作后置，例如：

⑤ That he will pass the exam is impossible. 他通过考试是不可能的。

It is impossible that he will pass the exam. 他不可能通过考试。

第二个句子中突出了从句部分，从而强调了"He won't pass the exam."用于这种句式的此类形容词有 necessary, important, hard, surprising, clever, amazing 等。

25.3　前　　置

还可以通过将需强调的部分前置的方式来表示强调。

(1) 把句中强调的部分前置，达到强调的效果。

① What do you think of that book? 你认为那本书如何？

That book, what do you think of it? 那本书，你认为如何？（将句中的宾语前置，强调"那本书"）

② She ran slowly to the classroom. 她慢慢地向教室跑去。

Slowly she ran to the classroom. 慢慢地，她向教室跑去。（状语前置）

③ My name is Jane, so you can call me Jane.

Jane my name is, so Jane you can call me.（补足语前置）

有时倒装句亦可用来表示强调。如上组句子"Jane my name is"，这样的句子也可以用这样的方法表达：Jane is my name。因此可以说，有时倒装与强调之间的关系是密不可分的。

④ Many a time have I climbed that hill. 我不止一次登上那座山。

⑤ Only in this way can we solve the problem. 只有通过这种方式，问题才能够解决。

(2) 被动语态的使用，是把宾语动作的对象前置，从而达到强调的目的。

① The solders expelled the invaders from the border. 战士们将侵略者赶出了边境。

The invaders were expelled from the border by the solders. 侵略者被战士们赶出了边境。

② We often regard the victory of that war as something of a miracle. 我们经常把这场战争的胜利看成一个奇迹。

The victory of that war is often regarded as something of a miracle. 这场战争的胜利经常被我们看成一个奇迹。

(3) so 这个单词前置后可用来强调肯定的部分。

① You have finished your homework? 你做完作业了吗？

So I have. 是的，我做完了。

② It is sunny outside. 今天阳光明媚啊。
So it is. 是啊。

25.4　用 if 来表示强调

if 从句＋I don't know who/what，etc. does/is/has，etc. 主语部分也可以用 nobody does/is/has，etc. 或 everybody does/is/has，etc. 来代替(这里的 if 从句往往是正话反说，反话正说)。

① If he can't do it，I don't know who can. 要是他做不了这件事，我不知道还有谁能做。（强调只有他能做）

② If Jim is a coward，everybody is. 要是吉姆是个胆小鬼，那么人人都是胆小鬼。（强调吉姆不是胆小鬼）

25.5　强制性词语

除了用一些特殊的语法和语序外，还有一些方法也常常用来表示强调。

（1）用助动词"do(does/did)＋动词原形"来表示强调，有时 do 还可加在 be 的前面表示强调。

① Do be careful! 千万小心！
② I do like swimming. 我的确喜欢游泳。
③ He did go there last night. 他昨晚的确去过那儿。

（2）用形容词 very，only，single，such 等修饰名词或形容词来加强语气。

① That's the very textbook we used last term. 这正是我们上学期用过的教材。
② You are the only person here who can speak Chinese. 你是这里唯一会讲汉语的人。
③ Not a single person has been in the shop this morning. 今天上午这个商店里连一个人都没有。
④ How dare you buy such expensive jewels? 你怎么敢买这么贵的宝石呢?

（3）用 ever，never，very，just 等副词和 badly，highly，really 等带有-ly 的副词来进行强调。

① Why ever did you do so? 你究竟为什么要这么做？
② He never said a word the whole day. 一整天，他一句话也没说。
③ You've got to be very，very careful. 你一定得非常非常小心。
④ This is just what I wanted. 这正是我所要的。
⑤ I really don't know what to do next. 我的确不知道下一步该怎么做。

（4）用 in the world，on earth，at all 等介词短语可以表达更强的语气(常用于疑问句)。

① Where in the world could he be? 他到底会在哪儿?
② I don't know it at all. 我一点也不知道。
③ What on earth are you doing there? 你到底在那儿干什么?

（5）用重复来表示强调。

① He thought and thought, and suddenly he got a good idea. 他想啊想啊,突然想到了一个好主意。

② He ran and ran, and at last he caught up with others. 他跑啊跑,终于赶上了其他人。

25.6 用破折号或黑体字表示强调

① It's because of hard work—ten years of hard work. 那是因为艰苦的工作——十年艰苦的工作!

② He began the work in **late May**. 他在五月底开始的这项工作。(强调时间)

巩 固 练 习

1. It was last year _____ you taught me how to drive.
   A. when   B. that   C. where   D. which
2. It was _____ he said _____ disappointed me.
   A. that; what   B. what; that
   C. what; what   D. that; that
3. It was in the factory _____ produced TV sets _____ our friend was murdered.
   A. which; which B. that; which   C. that; that   D. where; that
4. _____ find my wallet, Tom?
   A. Where did you that   B. Where was it you
   C. Where have you   D. Where was it that you
5. It was not until 1920 _____ regular radio broadcast began.
   A. while   B. which   C. that   D. since
6. It is the ability to do the job _____ matters, not where you came from or what you are.
   A. one   B. it   C. what   D. that
7. It is these poisonous products _____ can cause the symptoms of the flu, such as headache and aching muscles.
   A. who   B. that   C. how   D. what
8. I feel it is your husband who _____ for the spoiled child.
   A. is to blame   B. is going to blame
   C. is to be blamed   D. should blame
9. It was for this reason _____ her uncle moved out of New York and settled down in a small village.
   A. which   B. why   C. that   D. how
10. —Where was it _____ the road accident happened yesterday?
    —In front of the market.
    A. when   B. that   C. which   D. how
11. It is _____ who _____ reasonable.

A. me; am B. me; is C. I; am D. I; is

12. It was the dean _____ walked by.
    A. where B. who C. what D. which

13. It was not until she had arrived home _____ her appointment with the doctor.
    A. did she remember
    B. that she remembered
    C. when she remembered
    D. had she remembered

14. It was in Beihai Park _____ they made a date for the first time _____ the old couple told us their love story.
    A. where; that B. that; that C. where; when D. that; when

15. —Why was _____ you lost all your keys?
    —It was because of my carelessness.
    A. that B. wha C. it that D. one

16. It was _____ I met Mr. Smith in London.
    A. many years that
    B. for many years since
    C. since many years ago when
    D. many years ago that

17. Was _____ Bill, _____ played basketball very well, _____ helped the blind man across the street?
    A. that; that; who
    B. it; that; that
    C. it; who; that
    D. this; who; who

18. Was it in 1969 _____ the American astronaut succeeded _____ landing on the moon.
    A. when; on B. that; on C. when; in D. that; in

19. Was it in this palace _____ the last emperor died?
    A. that B. in which C. what D. he

20. Was it during the Second World War _____ he died?
    A. that B. while C. in which D. then

21. It _____ Mike and Mary who helped the old man several days ago.
    A. was B. are C. were D. had been

22. It was not until 1920 _____ regular radio broadcasts began.
    A. which B. when C. that D. since

23. She said she would go and she _____ go.
    A. didn't B. did C. really D. would

24. It was the training _____ he had as a young man _____ made him such a good engineer.
    A. what; that
    B. that; what
    C. that; which
    D. which; that

25. — Were all three people in the car injured in the accident?
    — No, _____ only the two passengers who got hurt.
    A. there were B. it were C. there was D. it was

第二十六章　省略与倒装

26.1　省　略

省略是一种避免重复，突出关键词语，并使上下文紧密连接的语法手段。它可分为一般性省略和定型化省略。定型化省略实际上是一个独立的句子，它已形成了相对固定的习惯用法，而省略的部分却不能填充进去。

① Good morning.
② So far so good.
③ Thanks.

这都属于固定化省略之列。本章所要阐述的是第一种省略，即一般性省略，它通常是指省略掉对构成完整的语法结构所必需的，而通过上下文又能弄懂的某个词或几个词。

① (I) Hope to see you again.
② (Is there) Anything wrong?
③ He is good at swimming and (good at) boxing.

从上述例句中可以看出，有的句子省略了主语和谓语，有的省略了并列句中的相同成分，从而使语言更加简练，结构更加严谨。一般性省略是有规律可循的，大致分为以下几类：名词性省略、动词性省略、从句性省略、并列句中的省略和复合句中的省略。

26.1.1　名词性省略

名词性省略主要表现在句子的主语或宾语部分的省略。但名词在并列句中作中心词时以及在比较句中最高级形容词后也有类似的省略。

(1) 作主语时名词的省略。

① The tall boy could touch the roof easily, but the short (boy) found it difficult. 个子高的男孩能够轻松够到房顶，小个子的男孩子却够不到。
② She did not care whether the guests would stay or (whether the guests would) go. 她不在乎客人的去留。
③ The girl was longing for, (the girl) was longing for her favorite doll. 小女孩在期盼着，期盼着心爱的玩具。

(2) 作宾语时名词的省略，这种省略现象在并列句中出现得比较多。

① Let's do the dishes. I will wash and you dry. 让我们洗碗吧。我来洗，你来擦干。(wash 与 dry 之后皆省去了宾语 dishes)
② Do you want to borrow (book) or buy this book? 这本书，你是想借还是想买？

(3) 有时名词在并列句中作中心词亦可以省略，这主要是因为前后所用名词相同。

① The boys prefer blue color and the girls prefer red (color). 男孩喜欢蓝色，女孩喜欢

红色。

② My brother likes boiled food but I like fried (food). 我哥哥爱吃煮的食物,而我喜欢油炸的。

以下情况在从句中也常常出现。

③ I prefer the first (solution). Why do you choose the second solution? 我倾向于第一种方案,你为什么选择第二种?

④ The teacher gave two (books), while most of the students like only one book. 老师给了两本书,但大多数学生只喜欢其中的一本。

(4) 在表达含有比较意义的句子中最高级形容词后的名词通常可以省略。

① Of those shoes, she chose the most expensive (shoes). 她在那些鞋中挑了一双最贵的。

② This is the worst (news) I heard today. 这是我一天中听到的最坏的消息。

如果上下文很明确,在 last, next 等形容词后的名词亦可以省略。

③ I needn't mention it in the phone, since I told you in my last (phone). 没必要在电话里再提这个事了,上次我已经告诉你了。

④ What is the last (thing) we shall do? 我们最后做什么?

(5) 在形容词后的名词省略。

① In the 1960's the black (people) are looked down upon by the white (people) in the United States. 在20世纪60年代的美国,黑人遭到了白人的歧视。

② She prefers white dress to red (dress) in such occasion. 在这样的场合,她更喜欢穿白色的礼服而不是红色的。

在前两个例句中,所保留下来的定冠词,"the+形容词"这种结构通常是指一类人或事物。

③ She is going to get her dress at the tailor's (shop). 她准备去裁缝店取衣服。

④ I stayed too long at my uncle's (house). 我在叔叔家待的时间不短了。

26.1.2 动词性省略

动词性省略指句子中谓语部分的省略,表现在助动词、主动词及全部动词的省略。不定式中存在的动词省略现象,亦可被视为动词性省略。

(1) 系动词 be 的省略。这种省略现象不仅存在于简单句中,在复合句,特别是在并列句中也常常出现这样的省略,常用于口语中。

① (Is) every gone? 人都走了吗?

② (Is there) anything you want to tell me? 有什么事要告诉我吗?

③ Johnson (is) ready for sports meet. 约翰逊准备参加运动会。

④ She (is) in tears. 她泪流满面。

简单句中的这种现象多在疑问句中出现,前例句①、例句②便属于这种情况。此外,还有主语+be 同时省略的现象。

⑤ (I am) sorry to bother you. 不好意思打扰你了。

⑥ She is clever, but (she is) too careless. 她很聪明,就是太马虎了。

(2) 助动词的省略。重复的助动词,通过上下文,借助谈话当时的情景可将不言自明的助动词省略,后一种情况一般表现在口语和疑问句中。在这种情况下,有两个主动词时,一般只重复前一个。

① (Have)The workers finished their work? 工人们已经完工了?

② Sister will be cleaning the rooms and I (will be) cooking the meal. 姐姐打扫房间,我去做饭。

在上下文很明了的情况下也可将主语和助动词同时省略。

③ (You have)Finished all the excercises? 你完成所有的练习了?

④ (We have)Got to go now. 我们得走了。

(3) 主动词的省略。在含有助动词的谓语动词中,常常只用助动词即可,而将主动词省略。这种情况下,一般是主动词在前面的句子中已经出现过。

① He said he had help that poor family, but he hasn't (helped them). 他说他已经资助过那个贫困家庭了,而实际上他没有。

② —Has the TV set been turned off? 电视关了吗? —Yes, it has (been turned off). 已经关了。

③ Some agree with me, but others didn't (agree with me). 有的人同意我的看法,有的人不同意。

省略主动词时,常常连同动词后面的词(如上面的最后一个例句中的 with me)一起省略。同样,主动词前边的词(主语)也常常与主动词一同省略。

④ —How do you go to school? 你怎么去学校?
—(I go there) By bus. (我)乘车(去)。

⑤ —Do you work in the steel plant? 你在钢厂工作吗?
—No,(I work)in a power plant. 不,(我在)发电厂(工作)。

(4) 全部谓语的省略。这里主要指的是助动词与主动词同时省略。在没有助动词时所省去的谓语动词,与我们上面所论述过的主动词的省略基本相同。

① I will wash up today and my sister (will wash up) tomorrow. 今天我洗碗,姐姐明天(洗碗)。

② We will do the best (we can do). 我们将尽(我们的)力而为。

③ Jim has done a good job, but Bob(has done)a bad one. 吉姆做得很好,但是鲍勃(做得)不好。

④ Only one of us was injured, and he (was injured) just slightly. 我们当中只有一个人受了伤,而且(受到的)只是轻伤。

在不影响理解的情况下有时可将谓语前的主语或将其后面的宾语一同省略。

⑤ —When will you come again? 你什么时候再来?
—(I will come)In a few days. (我)过一段时间(再来)。

⑥ —Who will help us? 谁来帮助我们?
—Peter(will help us). 彼得(将来帮我们)。

(5) 不定式中动词的省略。动词在不定式中的省略一般有下列几种情况:在名词后作定语、在及物动词后作宾语、在代词后作宾语补足语以及在部分情态动词或助动词后都有这种省略现象存在。

① I would like to go aboard,if I have a chance to (go aboard). 如果有机会(出国),我将很乐意出国。

② He got up very late, only because he didn't want (got up). 他很晚才起床,因为他不想起床。

有时动词不定式的符号 to 也可以省略,这种现象一般出现在特定的动词(如 go,help 等)后面,以及在不定式做表语时。

③ His sister often helps him(to)do his homework. 他的姐姐经常帮助他(去)做作业。

④ At that time what he could do was(to)run away. 那时候,他所能做的只是(去)逃跑。

⑤ Go (to) tell mother something has gone wrong. 去告诉妈妈,事情有点不对劲。

(6) 在 no,but 后,谓语动词省略其后的宾语时往往与动词一同省略。

① —I think you can do it well. 我认为你能做好。
　　—No, I can't(do it well). 不,我做不了(很好)。

② —Why didn't the old man ask others for help? 为什么那位老人不向其他人求助?
　　—But he did (ask others for help). 但是他已经求了(别人帮助他了)。

26.1.3　从句性省略

这一节里所论述的从句省略,指的是在主从复合结构中往往可以省略其整个从句部分。这主要是对宾语从句的省略,以及对一些特定的词如 so,not 后面所跟的从句的省略。

(1) 宾语从句的省略。在用 I don't know,I'm afraid not,Yes,I know 等类似的惯用语来回答某些特殊疑问句和一般疑问句时,在对别人的陈述句表示肯定时,可以认为在其后面省略了宾语从句。在比较状语从句中也常常将从句中及物动词后的宾语从句省略。

① —How did he come here? 他是怎么来这儿的?
　　—I don't know(how he came). 我也不知道(他是怎么来的)。

② —The film is very interesting. 电影非常有意思。
　　—Yes. I know(it is very interesting). 是的,我知道(电影很有趣)。

③ It took us longer time than we expected (it would take us).
　　我们实际花费的时间要比我们预计(花费)的长。

(2) 在 so,not 后从句的省略。当 so,not 这两个词分别跟在 think,expect,hope,fear,believe,suppose 等词的后面时,so 便代替了整个从句。因此有些语法学家也把这种情况称作代替。在这里着重强调的是被省略的这个从句部分。

① —Has father come back? 爸爸回来了吗?
　　—I think so(=I think that father has come back). 我想是的(我想爸爸已经回来了)。

② —Can you finish it today? 今天你能完成吗?
　　—I fear not(=I fear that I can't finish it today). 恐怕不行(我想今天完不成)。

③ —Is the class over? 下课了吗?
　　—It seems not (It seems that the class is not over). 看起来还没有(看起来还没下课)。

26.1.4　并列句中的省略

并列句中所出现的省略现象比较明显,这主要是因为前后两句出现的重复现象较多,在不影响理解的情况下通常把其相同的部分省略,因此在并列句中便出现了主语、谓语、表语、宾语、状语、定语及其他成分的省略。

其中的主语、宾语和谓语的省略,在前面的名词性省略和动词性省略中已分别论述过,这里不再赘述。

(1) 并列句中表语的省略。这种省略一般在第二分句中,但当两个分句的系动词不同时,表语的省略也可能出现在第一分句中。

① These oranges, some are ripe but others are not (ripe). 这些橘子有的熟了,有的还没有(熟)。

② He looked (tired), and (he) indeed was tired. 他看起来很累了,实际上(他)确实累了。

(2) 并列句中状语的省略。在前后两个分句中相同的状语常常可以省略。

① Some danced (in the hall) and some sang in the hall. 在大厅里一些人在唱歌,也有一些人(在大厅里)跳舞。

② You idled (the whole afternoon) but the others worked very hard the whole afternoon. 其他人整个下午都在忙碌,只有你(整个下午)游手好闲。

(3) 并列句中定语的省略。在并列句中如果名词有相同的定语,那么第二、第三个名词的定语通常可以省略。这里的定语包括指示词、物主代词、名词所有格、形容词、分词、介词、短语、不定式以及做前置或后置定语的从句。

① His brother and (his) sister are both studying at Oxford. 他的哥哥和(他的)姐姐都就读于牛津大学。

② Have you lost a green pen or (a green) pencil? 你丢的是绿色的钢笔还是(绿色的)铅笔?

③ Both the teacher (of the class) and the students of the class are very active. 课堂上的学生和(课堂上的)老师都非常活跃。

④ We should give them some short stories (to read) and poems to read. 我们应该给他们读一些诗歌、(读)一些小故事。

⑤ It's not me (who is responsible for it) but you who should be responsible for it. 不是我(应该负责任),而应该是你负责任。

(4) 并列句中其他相同部分的省略。除了前面所论述的现象外,为了避免重复,相同的冠词、介词、限定词等都可以省略。

① Please pass me those books and (those) papers. 请递给我那些书和(那些)文件。

② The girl saw a man and (a) woman coming towards her. 那个女孩看到一个男人和(一个)女人正朝她走来。

③ He has business both in China and (in) Japan. 他在中国和(在)日本都有生意。

④ Paul failed in the exam because he was lazy and (because he was) dull. 保罗考试没有及格,因为他懒惰并且(因为)愚笨。

26.1.5 复合句中的省略

不仅简单句中存在省略现象,在各种从属连词及关系词所引导的从句中,也存在着省略现象。无论是在主句前或在主句后,只要与主句有相同的部分,通常都可以省略。此外,有一些连词和关系词在一些特定的结构中也可省略。

(1) 状语从句的省略。在各种状语从句中,比较从句所出现的省略现象最为频繁,其次便是条件、时间、让步等从句。

① He speaks Chinese better than (he speaks) Japanese. 他说汉语要比(他说)日语好。

② He glances about as if (he is) in search of something. 他四下张望,仿佛在寻找什么东西似的。

③ Often she would weep when (she was) alone. (她)一个人时常常哭泣。

在以 if,though,when,while 等连词引导的时间、条件、方式、让步等状语从句中,一般在从句与主句的主语相同的情况下,如果有形容词、副词、名词、数词、介词短语等作表语,其中的主语＋be 常常可以省略。

④ She told her pupils not to talk while (they were) reading. 她告诉她的学生在(他们)读书的时候不要说话。

⑤ He would never do this unless (he was) compelled. 他绝不会这样做,除非(他)是被迫的。

⑥ If (you were) in doubt, ask your local library. 若(你)有疑问,可向当地图书馆咨询。

(2) 定语从句中的省略。在定语从句中虽然存在着其他部分的省略现象,但较为突出的却是关系词的省略,它除了在作从句的宾语时可省之外,在一些特定的结构中,作从句中的主语、状语和表语时都可省略。

① The man (who was) over there is our school master. 那边的人是我们的校长。

② I have lost the book (that) I bought the day before yesterday. 我把前天买的书给丢了。

③ She is not the cheerful girl (that) she used to be. 她不如以前活泼了。

在由 there be 或 here be 引导的倒装句中,当关系代词作主语时通常可以省略。

④ There is something (that) makes him feel sad. 一定有让他难过的事。

⑤ Here is the news (that) will make all of you excited. 这儿有一个肯定让你们高兴的消息。

⑥ There was a fisherman (who) lived in a small hut. 在一间茅屋里住着一位渔夫。

(3) 主语从句中的省略。主语从句的引导词 that 常省略。这种省略多存在于口语中,有时在强调句中也可能出现这种现象。

① It is true (that) there is something wrong. 肯定有不对的地方。

② It was necessary (that) there should be someone to take care of the old man. 必须有人来照顾这位老人。

(4) 宾语从句中的省略。在宾语从句中除了重复部分省略外,所出现的更多的省略现象则是在如 think,believe,know,hear,hope,say 等后面的连词 that 的省略。

① I'm sure(that) it is suitable to you, but (it is) not (suitable) to me. 我肯定它适合你,但是它不适合我。

② I'm afraid (that) we have to stay here. 恐怕我们走不了了。

③ Browns hope (that) their son will become a doctor. 布朗夫妇希望他们的儿子将来能成为一名医生。

26.2 倒 装

英语句子按语序,可分为正常语序(Normal Order)和倒装语序(Inverted Order)两类。倒装语序的格式很多,常见的有谓语或部分谓语提到主语前,宾语或表语提到主语前。为了强调把其重要的部分移到句首,含有 if 的条件句省略从属连词要倒装,有一些感叹句要倒装,在表示祝愿、否定、祈使的句子里也常出现倒装的现象。倒装的形式根据 H. Fowler(福勒)的归纳有以下八种原因:①疑问;②命令;③假设;④平衡;⑤衔接;⑥点题;⑦否定;⑧韵律。这些倒装可概括为两点:一是一定的语法结构和习惯用法要求倒装,二是修辞上的特殊安排要求倒装。

修辞性倒装在 19 世纪曾风靡一时。随着英语的发展,有些形式倒装由于长期使用已形成习惯用法,还有一些随着语法学家对其语言现象的归期和总结已形成固定用法。本章主要对语法和惯用法的倒装,以及修辞倒装分别加以论述。

26.2.1 语法和惯用法的倒装

倒装在英语句子中屡见不鲜,但有一些倒装有规律可循,这是由于一定语法结构所要求的。例如:Do you speak English? 这个表示疑问的英语句子,在语法结构上要求它必须倒装。还有一些是由于使用得既普遍又长久,已成为习惯,这些都是这一节要论述的内容。

(1) 疑问句倒装。这里主要指一般疑问句和特殊疑问句的倒装。

① Are you from here? 你是本地人吗?

② Is that man your schoolmaster? 那个人是你校长吗?

反意疑问句的倒装在句子的后部。

④ You like this book, don't you? 你喜欢这本书,不是吗?

⑤ He is a hard student, isn't he? 他是一个刻苦的学生,不是吗?

在间接疑问中通常不用倒装。

⑥ He asked me whether I could spare him a few minutes. 他问我有没有时间。

(2) 感叹句有时也要求倒装。在这种情况下,它们的形式与否定疑问句相同,但表达的是一种强烈的情感,在美国英语中尤其是这样。

① Isn't it a beautiful scenery! 多美的景色啊!

② Here comes the bus! 公交车来了!

③ How gracefully they danced! 他们跳得多优美啊!

(3) 在某些虚拟语气的句子中倒装可用来代替 if。

① Had I come earlier, I would have caught the bus. 如果我早来一点,就可以赶上车了。

② Were I Tom, I would refuse. 如果我是汤姆,我会拒绝。

(4) 除了省略后的假设条件句有倒装的现象外,有时在比较和让步状语从句中也会出现倒装。

① Change your mind as you will, you will gain no additional support. 你即使改变主意,也不会得到援助。

② Look as I would up and down, I could see no human being. 尽管我上下张望,还是看不到一个人。

(5) 在 there be 存在句中也常常需要倒装。

① There must be something out of order. 一定是出了什么乱子。

② There is a man at the door wants to see you. 门口有一个人要见你。

在这种句式中,其中的 be 可由 lie, exist, live, appear, occur, stand 等词代替。

③ Once upon a time, there lived a fisherman. 很久以前,那里住着一个渔夫。

④ There seems to be some misunderstanding about the matter. 在这个问题上似乎有些误会。

(6) 与存在句相类似的,还有以 here,there,now,then 等表示地点和时间的副词为首的句子,一般也要倒装。

① Now comes your turn. 轮到你了。

② Here is the post man. 邮递员来了。

③ Then comes the most exciting hour. 最激动人心的时刻到了。

用于这种句型的动词一般为 come,go,fall 等不及物的单个动词。如果句子中的主语是代词,则不必倒装。

④ There he comes. 他来了。

⑤ Here it goes like this. 事情是这样的。

在这类句子中除了用 here,there 这样的副词做地点状语外,用介词短语的时候也很多。

⑥ At the top of the hill stands a pagoda. 在山顶上有座亭子。

⑦ Round the corner comes a bus. 拐弯处来了一辆公交车。

(7) 在书面语的直接引语中,常有 replied Tom,shouted the man,answered the boy,grunted Peter 等类似的词语。这些词语告诉读者谁说了些什么,怎样说的。可以看到在这些词语中动词通常在主语前,当主语较长时则更是如此。

① "I will lend you a hand,"said the little boy. 小男孩说道:"我会帮助你的。"

② "Let us go this way."suggested the shy guide. 那个害羞的向导说:"请这边走。"

当主语是代词时,通常不需要倒装。

③ "I know it quite well" he answered. 他回答说:"我知道,这很好。"

(8) 在祝愿句中也常出现倒装的现象。

① Long live the peace! 和平万岁!

② May you be successful! 祝你成功!

③ Would we were young forever! 但愿我们青春常在!

(9) 除以上句式外,一些特定的词在句中也常常引起倒装,so 就是其中之一。

① My husband likes music and so do I. 我和我的丈夫都喜欢音乐。

② His father is an engineer and so is he. 他们父子都是工程师。

除此之外,so...that 句型常引起部分倒装,so+形容词和 so+副词的结构分别作主语补足语前置和状语前置。

③ So dangerous was the job that nobody dare to take it. 那项工作太危险了,以致于没人敢做。

④ So slowly did the old man walk that he missed the bus. 那位老人走得太慢了,以致于没赶上公交车。

(10) only 位于句首并后跟状语或者是由 only 引导的从句位于句首也常引起倒装。

① Only then could the work be really begun. 只有那时这工作才真正开始。

② Only after a hard study can you master this language. 只有努力学习,你才能掌握这门语言。

③ Only when she came home did he learn the news. 直到她回家时他才知道这消息。

在 not only...but also 句型中也会出现部分倒装。

④ Not only did we have nothing to eat, but also we lost our way. 我们不但没有吃的了,而且还迷路了。

⑤ Not only did he finish his own work, but also he helped the others. 他不但完成了自己的工作,还帮助了别人。

含否定意义的状语放在句首时往往引起局部倒装。

⑥ Not a word did he say. 他一言不发。

⑦ Never in my life have I seen such a thing. 我一生中从未见过这样的事。

除了完全否定词外,一些半否定词置于句首也会产生类似的倒装。

⑧ Scarcely had he arrived when they asked him to leave again. 他刚一来,他们又请他离去。

⑨ Seldom have we felt as comfortable as here. 我们很少像在这里住得那么舒适。

能用于这种句型的词还有 never, little, no sooner, seldom, rarely, nowhere, in vain 等。

(11) 当方式、频率状语被移到句首时常常会引起部分倒装。

① Seldom have I seen such brutality. 我很少见这样残忍的行为。

② Gladly would I pay more if I could get better serive. 如果我能得到更好的服务,我将非常乐意多付钱。

26.2.2 修辞倒装

英语句子还有另一类倒装,它会使整个句子读起来更清楚、更平稳,使句子衔接得更紧密,使对比更鲜明,使重点更突出,这就是本节所要叙述的修辞倒装。这种倒装与语法和习惯用法相比较,无规律可循,只能依照上下文而定,因此随意性较强。

(1) 为了避免头重脚轻,有些句子往往要采取一定形式的倒装。

① Thus began the fierce argument between the two groups. 两派之间展开了唇枪舌战。

② Higher and higher flew the white balloon till it vanished in the clouds. 白色气球越升越高,最后消失在云层中。

③ In the far distance was seen the glittering surface of a metal. 好远就看见一块金属在闪闪发光。

(2) 为了使上下文衔接得更紧密,有时也要采取一定形式的倒装。

① What you did was important, but more important was the way you did things. 你做什么事固然重要,但你做事的方式更重要。

② Jim prepared two pens. One of these he would give to his brother, the other he would keep himself. 吉姆准备了两只钢笔。一支给哥哥,另外一支自己用。

(3) 利用倒装的形式有时会使句子中所产生的对比更醒目、更强烈。

① Gifts he had but money he had none. 他虽有才却又无财。

② My paintings the visitors admired. My sculptures they disliked. 游客喜欢我的油画却不喜欢我的雕塑。

③ In New York it is hot and humid during the summer. In Los Angeles it is hot and dry. 夏天的纽约又热又潮,而洛杉矶是又热又干。

(4) 为了使句子描述得更生动,表达得更清楚,常常采用倒装的手段。

① Up went the arrow into the air. 嗖的一声箭射向天空。

301

② Following the roar, out rushed a tiger from among the bushes. 随着一声低吼,灌木丛中突然窜出来一只猛虎。

26.2.3 强调性倒装

这是为了强调某一句子成分而进行的倒装。强调与倒装的关系极为密切,强调性倒装句是英语语法中比较重要的知识点,也是本节阐述的重点,这种倒装大致有下列几种。

1. 谓语置于句首

(1)谓语动词置于句首。

① I'm going back to motherland to fight for it, believe you me. 我要回到祖国为此而斗争,你相信我吧。

② At last he finds himself in a garden, full of beautiful flowers of strange forms, and watered by streams of crystal in which are swimming marvellous fish with scales of rubies and gold. 最终他发现自己来到一个花园,这里到处是奇异的花卉,还有清澈的溪水,里面游着珍贵的具有红玉般和金黄色鱼鳞的鱼。

有时倒装结构为"主要动词+主语+助动词"。

③ Stay I can't. 我不能留下。

④ Yield he would not. 屈服,他是不干的。

有时倒装结构为"主要动词+宾语+主语+助动词",其主要动词往往是重复前文中的动词。

① They have promised to finish the work and finish it they will. 他们保证完成这项工作,而且他们一定会完成的。

② Save him she could not; but she avenged him in the most terrible fashion afterwards. 她不能救他,但后来她以最可怕的方式为他报了仇。

有时倒装结构为"助动词+主语+(主要动词)"。

③ Johnson was taken completely by surprise by the news, as was Susan. 这消息完全出乎约翰逊的意料,也完全出乎苏珊的意料。

④ They looked upon him as a trusted friend, as did many others he had deceived. 他们和他所欺骗的许多人一样,也把他看作可以信赖的朋友。

(2)过去分词置于句首。

① Also discussed was a revenue-raising proposal to hike the sales tax... 也讨论了增加销售税的提高税收建议……

② Also said to be under consideration is a performance in Beijing. 据说也考虑在北京上演。

(3)现在分词+be+主语。

① Covering much of the earth's surface is a blanket of water. 地球表面上许多地方都布满了水。

② Facing the lake was a little inn. 湖的对面是一个小旅店。

这种倒装结构多半已变成词序固定的句型。在新闻文体中,现在进行时的现在分词亦可进行倒装。

③ Throwing the hammer is champion William Anderson, who is a hard-working shepherd in the Highlands of Scotland. 正在掷链球的是冠军威廉·安德森,他是苏格兰高地上的一位勤劳的牧民。

(4) 引述动词＋主语＋直接引语,这种结构常用于新闻体。

① Declared prosecutor Roy Amlot,"It was one of the most callous acts of all time." 检察官罗伊·阿默朗特宣称:"这是最最淡漠无情的行为之一。"

② Said he,"We confront great evils and we need great solutions." 他说道:"我们面对着重大的邪恶,我们需要重大的决策。"

2. 表语置于句首

(1) 形容词＋连系动词＋主语。

① Present at the meeting were Professor Gorge, Professor Brown, Sir Hugh and many other celebrities. 到会的有乔治教授、布朗教授、休爵士以及许多其他知名人士。

② Far be it from me to condemn him in any way. 我决不会以任何方式谴责他。

(2) 过去分词＋连系动词＋主语。

① Gone are the days when they could do what they liked to the Chinese people. 他们能够对中国人民为所欲为的日子一去不复返了。

(3) 介词短语＋be＋主语。

① Among the goods are Christmas trees, flowers, candles, turkeys and toys. 货品中有圣诞树、花卉、蜡烛、火鸡和玩具。

② Amid the gaseous pollutants they inhale are carbon monoxide, sulphur dioxide, nitrogen oxides, hydrochloric acid, ammonia and hydrocarbons. 在他们所呼吸的污染气体中有一氧化碳、二氧化硫、氮氧化物、盐酸、氨和碳氢化合物。

(4) 不定式＋be＋主语。

First to mention is the dilemma we are in, and next we need now. 首先要提到的是我们目前的困境,然后再提我们急需的物资。

3. 宾语置于句首

① "Yes", said the youth shortly. "是的",那个小伙子简短地说道。

② Someone once said Australia is a country born to alcoholism. A man would pay $5 to get drunk and $8 to get home, goes the jest. 有人说过,澳大利亚是一生性嗜酒的国家。有一个笑话说,那里的人会花5美元喝醉后,再花8美元回家。

4. 状语置于句首

(1) 某些副词＋倒装结构。

① Just then along came Tom. 就在这时,汤姆来了。

② Just then in walked the lady with a radiant face. 正值此时刻,一位女士容光焕发地走了进来。

注:短语动词的小品词一般不可前置,如不可说 Up cracked the soldier. 又如,上述例句中如用人称代词则不可倒装,必须说 In she walked.

③ Then did I throw myself into a chair, exhausted. 这时我累得一下就坐在椅子上了。

④ Only in this way can you learn Chinese. 只有这样你才能学会汉语。

注:副词 only 后接非状语时则不可倒装。

⑤ So bright was the moon that the flowers bright as by day. 皓月当空,花朵就像白天时

303

那样鲜艳。

⑥ Crack goes the whip. 啪的一声鞭子响了。

(2) 介词短语＋倒装结构。

① By his side stood his lovely daughter. 在他的旁边站着他可爱的女儿。（介词短语表示地点）

② Many a time as a boy have I climbed that hill. 我在童年时期曾多次爬过那座山。（介词短语表示时间）

③ With it was mingled far-away cheering. 远处的欢呼声与此融在一起。（介词短语表伴随）

(3) 表示否定的词语＋倒装结构。

① Never did he speak about his own merits. 他从不讲他自己的功绩。

② Seldom has a devoted teacher been so splendidly rewarded. 一位忠诚的教师很少受到如此好的报答。

③ Hardly had he arrived when she started complaining. 他一到家，她就抱怨起来。

④ Little did I think that we were talking together for the last time. 我没有想到我们这次谈话竟成诀别。

⑤ No sooner had he arrived than he went away again. 他刚到家就又走了。

⑥ Not only did they present a musical performance, but they also gave a brief introduction to the history of Western brass instruments. 他们不但进行了音乐表演，而且简短地介绍了西方铜管乐器的历史。

巩 固 练 习

一、省略句练习，单项选择。

1. Tom wanted to play football with his friends in the street, but his father told him _____.
   A. not to   B. not to do   C. not do it   D. do not to
2. —Do you think Jack is going to watch a football match this weekend?
   —_____.
   A. I believe not   B. I believe not so
   C. I don't believe it   D. I don't believe
3. —What do you think made the girl so glad?
   —_____ a beautiful necklace.
   A. As she received   B. Receiving
   C. Received   D. Because of receiving
4. Father advised me not to say anything until _____ at the meeting.
   A. asking   B. to ask   C. asked   D. ask
5. —Have you watered the flowers?
   —No, but _____.
   A. I am   B. I'mm going   C. I'm just going to   D. I will go
6. —He hasn't gone to the office up to now.

—Well, he _____.
A. should　　　B. ought to　　　C. ought to go　　　D. ought to have

7. —The war is very likely to break out in the near future.
   —I _____. if the situation goes as it is.
   A. hope so　　　B. hope not　　　C. am afraid not　　　D. am afraid so

8. —You ought to have given them some advice.
   —_____, but who cared what I said?
   A. So ought you　　　B. So I ought　　　C. So I did　　　D. So did you

9. The man we followed suddenly stopped and looked as if _____. whether he was going in the right direction.
   A. seeing　　　B. having seen　　　C. to see　　　D. to have sen

10. _____ he come, the problem would be settled.
    A. Would　　　B. Should　　　C. Shall　　　D. If

11. —Can I see you at 3:00 pm next Monday?
    —I _____. I will have flown to New York long before thsn.
    A. am afraid not
    B. am afraid so
    C. am afraid to
    D. am afraid not to

12. —Is that a book on farming? If so, I want to borrow _____.
    —Yes, it is.
    A. this　　　B. it　　　C. one　　　D. the one

13. _____, I will help you with your work.
    A. If am possible
    B. If it possible
    C. If possible
    D. Possible

14. —How are you getting on with your work?
    —Oh, I'm sorry. Things aren't going so well as _____.
    A. plans　　　B. planning　　　C. planned　　　D. to plan

15. —Are you a volunteer now?
    —No, but I _____. I worked for the City Sports Meeting last year.
    A. used to　　　B. used to be　　　C. used to do　　　D. was used to

16. —Are there any English story-books for us students in the library?
    —There are only a few, _____.
    A. if any　　　B. if there　　　C. if some　　　D. if has

17. —Why didn't you come to Mike's birthday party yesterday?
    —Well, I _____, but I forgot it.
    A. should　　　B. must　　　C. should have　　　D. must have

18. —Have you ever been to Shanghai?
    —_____.
    A. Not yet　　　B. Haven't　　　C. Yet not　　　D. Still not

19. —Be sure to get up earlier tomorrow morning.
    —_____. I'll be as early as a bird.

A. OK, I will   B. I'm afraid I can
C. Of course not   D. No, I will

20. —What's the matter with you?
    —I didn't pass the test, but I still _____.
    A. hope so   B. hope to   C. hope it   D. hope that

21. —Is she really ill?
    — _____. She's in hopital.
    A. I hope so   B. I'm sure   C. I don't think so   D. I'm afraid s

22. —You look happy today, Mary.
    —I like my new dress and Mother _____, too.
    A. likes   B. does   C. is   D. do

23. —Who's got all the money?
    —He _____.
    A. does   B. is   C. was   D. has

24. They got to Beijing earlier _____.
    A. as we did   B. as we do   C. than we did   D. than we were

25. —Would you like to have a try once again?
    — _____.
    A. Yes, I like   B. No, I don't like it
    C. Yes, I want very much   D. Yes, I'd like to

26. —Are you angry?
    —Yes. He should at least answer when _____.
    A. speaking   B. spoken to   C. spoken   D. speaking to

27. —How about the price of these refrigerators?
    —They're equal in price to, if not cheaper than, _____ at the other stores.
    A. others   B. it   C. that   D. the ones

28. —Why didn't you come to join her party?
    —Sorry, I _____, but I had an unexpected visitor.
    A. would do   B. should
    C. would have   D. was going to have

29. —I hear Mr Zhang was badly injured in the accident.
    — _____, let's go to see him.
    A. If such   B. If so   C. If not   D. If any

30. _____, the experiment will be successful.
    A. If carefully doing   B. If did carefully
    C. If carefully done   D. If doing carefully

二、倒装句练习。
(一)单项选择。
1. Only after liberation _____ to be treated as human beings.
    A. did they begin   B. they had begun

  C. they did begin   D. had they begun
2. Not only _____ to stay at home, but he was also forbidden to see his friends.
  A. he was forcing   B. he was forced
  C. was he forcing   D. was he forced
3. Not until his father was out of prison _____ to school.
  A. can John go   B. John can go
  C. could John go   D. John could go
4. Never before _____ seen such a stupid man.
  A. am I   B. was I   C. have I   D. shall I
5. Rarely _____ such a silly thing.
  A. have I heard of   B. I have heard of
  C. I have been hearing of   D. have I heard from
6. Little _____ about his own health though he was very ill.
  A. he cared   B. did he care   C. does he care   D. he cares
7. Seldom _____ him recently.
  A. I met   B. I have met   C. have I met   D. didn't I meet
8. Hardly _____ down _____ he stepped in.
  A. had I sat; than   B. I had sat; when
  C. had I sat; then   D. had I sat; when
9. No sooner _____ asleep than she heard a knock at the door.
  A. she had fallen   B. had she fallen
  C. she had fell   D. had she fell
10. He did not see Smith. _____.
  A. Neither did I   B. Nor didn't I
  C. Neither I did   D. So didn't I
11. I don't know how to swim, _____.
  A. and my sister doesn't neither   B. nor my sister can
  C. nor does my sister   D. and my sister does either
12. —You ought to have given them some advice.
  — _____, but who cared what I said?
  A. So ought you   B. So I ought
  C. So did you   D. So I did
13. —It was hot yesterday.
  —_____.
  A. It was so   B. So was it   C. So it was   D. So it did
14. She's passed the test. _____.
  A. So am I   B. So have I   C. So I have   D. Also I have
15. A: You like football very much. B: _____.
  A. So do I   B. It is the same with me
  C. I do too   D. So I do

16. _____, he is honest.
    A. As he is poor					B. Poor is he
    C. Poor as he is					D. Poor as is he
17. _____, he knows a lot of things.
    A. A child as he is					B. Child as he is
    C. A child as is he					D. Child as is he
18. _____, you can't lift yourself up.
    A. Even you're strong				B. Strong as you are
    C. How strong you are				D. In spite you're strong
19. So carelessly _____ that he almost killed himself.
    A. he drives					B. he drove
    C. does he drive					D. did he drive
20. Early in the day _____ the news _____ the enemy were gone.
    A. come; that   B. came; that   C. comes; that   D. came; what
21. Only when you realize the importance of foreign languages _____ them well.
    A. you can learn					B. can you learn
    C. you learned					D. did you learn
22. Look, _____.
    A. here the bus comes				B. here is the bus coming
    C. here comes the bus				D. here the bus is coming
23. "Where is Kate?" "Look, _____. She is at the school gate."
    A. there she is					B. there is she
    C. here you are					D. here it is
24. Which of the following sentences is correct?
    A. In the teacher came				B. In did come the teacher
    C. In did the teacher come			D. in came the teacher
25. Out _____, with a stick in his hand.
    A. did he rush					B. rushed he
    C. he rushed					D. he did rush

(二) 句型转换。改写下列各句,把黑体的副词放在句首,并使主、谓语倒装。

1. I have **never** heard a speech as exciting as this.
2. The mark was **so** small that I could hardly see it.
3. I **hardly** turned off the light when my brother came in.
4. It has **at no time** been more difficult for us to pass the examination.
5. We can succeed **only** in this way.
6. He did **not** speak a word at the meeting.
7. Mary **not only** complained about the food, but also refused to pay for it.
8. She had **no** sooner begun to speak than I sensed that something was wrong.
9. Mike has helped me with my English **many a time**.
10. There was a sudden gust of wind and his hat went **away**.

巩固练习参考答案

第一章

1. 主语—动词
2. 主语—动词—宾语—补语
3. 主语—动词—宾语—宾语
4. 主语—动词—补语（表语）
5. 主语—动词—宾语—宾语
6. 主语—动词—宾语—补语
7. 主语—动词—宾语—宾语
8. 主语—动词—宾语—补语
9. 主语—动词—宾语—补语
10. 主语—动词—宾语—补语
11. 主语—动词—补语（表语）
12. 主语—动词—宾语—补语
13. 主语—动词—宾语
14. 主语—动词
15. 主语—动词—补语（表语）
16. 主语—动词—宾语—补语
17. 主语—动词—宾语—补语
18. 主语—动词—补语（表语）
19. 主语—动词—宾语—宾语
20. 主语—动词—宾语—补语

第二章

一、
policemen	geese	shelves
teeth	wives	buses
leaves	babies	mosquitoes
knives	cities	brushes
thieves	flies	boxes
foxes	days	kilos
halves	wolves	glasses
aircraft	lorries	calves
pianos	gases	women
parties	oxen	potatoes
children	feet	roofs

monkeys　　　　　　dishes　　　　　　　ladies
watches　　　　　　 mice　　　　　　　 inches
tomatoes　　　　　　heroes　　　　　　 photos
toys　　　　　　　　lives　　　　　　　classes
busses　　　　　　　branches　　　　　 wishes

二、1. sheep　　 2. geese　　 3. oxen　　 4. knives　　 5. wolves　　 6. fishermen
　　7. mice　　 8. teeth　　 9. policewomen　 10. Women　 11. phenomena 12. strata
　　13. aircraft　 14. feet　　 15. fish　　 16. leaves

三、1. This shop sells both men's and women's clothes.
　　2. Do they sell babies' clothes?
　　3. He's looking at the dog' teeth.
　　4. This is a woman's bicycle.
　　5. June 1st is Children's Day.
　　6. You can buy aspirin at the chemist's(a drug store).
　　7. He has a doctor's degree.
　　8. We have a week's holiday during the Spring Festival.
　　9. I bought ten dollars' worth of stamps.
　　10. I've been to the butcher's(the baker's, the barbar's).
　　11. I'm going to have dinner at my aunt's.
　　12. I went to John's, but he was at his sister's.

第三章

一、1—5　CBDAA　6—10　DBCBC　11—15　CACDC　16—20　DCACA
　　21—25　ABCBD 26—30　BDDBA

二、1. 0/0　　　　2. 0/the/the　　　3. 0/the/0/0/the　　4. The/0/the/the/the
　　5. the/0/0　　6. the/0/0/0　　　7. The/0/the　　　　8. the/the

第四章

一、1—5　BCBDC　6—10　ABCAB　11—15　CAACA　16—20　CACAA
　　21—25　DCBDC 26—30　CBDAB

二、1. who　　2. whom　 3. whose　 4. which　 5. whom　 6. whose　 7. (that)
　　8. whom　 9. whose　10. (that)　11. who　 12. whom　13. which　14. which

三、(略)

第五章

一、1—5　CDDDB　6—10　ACACB　11—15　CBDDA　16—20　ACAAB

二、(一) 1. March 8th　　2. August 1st　　3. December 25th　　4. October 1st
　　　　 5. April 12th　 6. September 31st　7. June 21st　　　 8. July 30th
　　(二) 1. 1949(nineteen forty-nine)　　　2. 2008(two thousand and eight)
　　　　 3. 1804(eighteen oh four)　　　　 4. 1600(sixteen hundred)
　　　　 5. 658 B.C(six fifty-eight B.C.)　6. 2000 B.C. (two thousand B.C)
　　　　 7. 720 A.D. (seven twenty A.D)　 8. 2010(two thousand and ten)
　　(三) 1. Part 3　　　　　2. Section 67　　　　3. Chapter twelve

  4. Book Four   5. Flight 108(one oh eight)   6. Carriage No. 5

  7. Bus No. 103(one oh three)   8. Channel 23

(四) 1. 8:00 a.m.

  2. 9:15(a quarter past nine 或 nine fifteen)

  3. 2:30(half past two 或 two thirty)

  4. 5:45(a quarter to six 或 five forty-five)

  5. 12:55(five to one 或 twelve fifty-five)

  6. 7:00 a.m.   7. 2:15 p.m.   8. 11:05 p.m.

(五) 1. Two one nine four oh seven three oh

  2. Three seven two oh two two (double two) seven seven (double seven)

  3. Extension 009(oh oh mine)

  4. Extension 137(one three seven)

第六章

1—5 ADCBB   6—10 BBDDA   11—15 DCBAD   16—20 BCCBC

第七章

一、1—5 BDBAA   6—10 DDDBD   11—15 BBCBA   16—20 DCAAA

  21—25 CDAAB 26—30 CADCC   31—35 DDBCB   36—40 BBDAB

第八章

一、1. not to read   2. keep   3. waiting   4. are   5. has been   6. missed   7. had been on   8. interested   9. seeing   10. going   11. find   12. put on   13. to eat   14. watching   15. broken   16. not to come home   17. have taken place   18. have heard from   19. took   20. would have met   21. giving   22. telling   23. doing   24. were playing   25. has been away   26. didn't go   27. was put   28. laughing   29. bring   30. had visited

二、1—5 BDADD   6—10 AABDC   11—15 ADDCC   16—20 ADBDC

  21—25 DBCDC 26—30 ADBCD   31—35 CCDBB   36—40 DCCBA

第九章

一、1. can be finished   2. was paid to   3. will be sung   4. needn't be done   5. will be looked after   6. is used   7. was made to do   8. has been given   9. Was, built   10. will be put   11. is said to be hiding   12. is often mended   13. was done away with   14. won't be hurt   15. were made to work   16. Was, broken by him   17. have been sold   18. are being turned out   19. must not be planted   20. can be dug

二、1. are, told   2. will be put   3. must be sent   4. are sold   5. is, made, is made   6. was given   7. Can, be taken   8. is cleaned   9. can be seen   10. have been watered   11. were made   12. are growing   13. is learnt   14. are used   15. was built   16. must not be put   17. will be drawn   18. can be made   19. has opened   20. was founded

第十章

一、1—5 ADCDC   6—10 DBCCC   11—15 BDBBD   16—20 BBBDB

  21—25 BDABA 26—30 BBBDC   31—35 BCDCD   36—40 ABCBC

第十一章

1. to sing 2. work 3. die, surrender 4. to love 5. change 6. play 7. escape 8. to go 9. not ask 10. make 11. (to) give 12. drop 13. take, drink 14. marry 15. to explain 16. become 17. have made 18. have visited 19. be correcting 20. have won 21. have been working 22. have recovered 23. have been given/be given 24. be discussing/have been discussing 25. to have worked 26. be sent 27. be sent 28. be fooled 29. be invited 30. be loved, needed 31. be told 32. read 33. let 34. seek 35. read 36. be constantly reminded 37. write 38. be used 39. understand 40. wash

二、1—5 ABCAA   6—10 ACCAA   11—15 DBCBA   16—20 BACDB

第十二章

一、1—5 BBCCB   6—10 DDBDD   11—15 BDBBB   16—20 CDBCD
    21—25 BACBA 26—30 DCCCB

第十三章

1—5 CCCBC   6—10 BBBDC   11—15 DBBBC   16—20 CDCCD
21—25 ACCBD

非谓语动词专练

1—5 CBDBD   6—10 CBAAA   11—15 CBCCB   16—20 CADCA
21—25 ADBCA 26—30 CCBCC   31—35 CABBB   36—40 BBADC
41—45 ACAAA 46—50 CDABD

第十四章

三、(略)

1. B other than 与否定词(如 not, hardly 等)连用,意为"只(能)是"。

2. D much less 更不用说。

3. A no better than before 和以前情况一样差。

4. B far, a lot, much 等都可修饰比较级,意为"……得多"。anyone else 的所有格形式为 anyone else's。

5. C …is he any better? 他好些了吗?

6. C freely 自由地,无拘无束地。free 也可用作副词,意为"无偿地,免费地"。

7. A much 可用于 to one's disappointment/surprise/joy…结构前,以加强语气。

8. C lately 近来;late 迟,晚。

9. C 修饰人的嗓音、眼神、眼泪、叫声和表情等,常用过去分词。under way 已经开始并进行着。

10. C cannot…too… 无论……都不过分。题意为"我们非常钦佩他的勇敢"。

11. B be particular about 对……挑剔的、讲究的。

12. B anyhow 无论如何,不管怎样。

13. D immediately 除了作副词外,还可用作连词,意为"一……就……"。

14. C not a bit 一点也不;not a little 非常;plenty of 充足的,大量的,用于修饰名词。

15. C something worth doing 相当于 something that is worth doing。

16. C actually 相当于 in fact。

17. A practical 实际的,符合情况的;actual 真实的,实际的;content 满足的,满意的;familiar 熟悉的。

18. D 题意为"孩子们未经允许就在花园里摘花,史密斯先生很生气。"句中 cross 相当于 angry。

19. C serious 认真的,严肃的。注意:true 侧重指事情的真实。

20. B keep still 保持一动不动。calm 强调心情的平静;silent 沉默,不讲话;quiet 表示安静。

21. B 句中 second to none 意为"第一的,无人能比的",然后,根据转折连词 but 可知应填 hardly。

22. A 此处指的是"病后,身体不太强壮",故选 A。

23. B though 作副词时,常位于句末,意为"不过,然而"。

24. D 此处 alone 为副词,应放在名词或代词后面,意为"仅仅,只"。

25. B very, too, quite, fairly 和 so 一般不用来修饰比较级。

26. D pleasant 意为"令人愉快的,讨人喜欢的";pleased 指(人)满意的,高兴的。

27. B a popular way 一种流行的、受欢迎的方式。

28. D 多个形容词修饰同一名词时,其排列顺序为:限定词(如 a, the, my, all 等),描绘性形容词(如 strong, beautiful, fine 等),表示大小、长短、高低的形容词,表示年龄、新旧、颜色的形容词,表示国家、地区、出处的形容词,表示构成事物材料的形容词(如 wooden, glass 等)+名词。

29. C 题意为"虽然那个年轻人对众多事情都很精通,但他并不是完美无缺的"。perfect 完美的。

30. A 数目(the number of...)应用大小来衡量(如:big, small 和 large)。

第十五章

一、1. A but 和 however 都表转折,但要注意 however 后要加逗号。

2. B 否定概念的并列。

3. C 状语从句必须用从属连词引导。

4. D 表语从句若不缺失成分,必须由 that 引导而且不能省略。

5. A Although 为从句标志,主句不能再加连词。

6. C Now that 既然。

7. D so that 引导目的状语从句。

8. A 9. C 10. A 11. B 12. B 13. D

14. C Young as she is 为倒装句,等于 Although she is Young,...

15. A

16. B It was not until...that 是强调句型的一种固定结构。

17. C 引导主语从句、前有介词、后跟不等式、表选择等只用 Whether 不用 if(是否)。

18. A 19. D 20. D

21. D 拒绝邀请常用 but 引出借口表示委婉。

22. A 不难判断这是一个含有时间状语从句的主从复合句,during 是介词,因而选 A。

23. D 24. D 25. C

26. C however great it is 是一个方式状语从句 however=no matter how。

27. A 28. B 29. D 30. B

二、1. when → as,随着。

2. when → that, It is(was) not until...that 是 not...until 的强调句型。

3. At the age of six → When I was six years old, At the age of six 用于句中是指 my father。

4. like → as if, as if 可以引导虚拟语气的结构。

5. during → while, during 是介词,不可引导从句。

6. since → before, not long before(不久……就……)。

7. but → as, not so much...as(与其说……不如说)。

8. or → and, between...and...(在……与……之间)。

9. for—that, that(so that, in order that)+may(might)(为了……)表示目的的连接词,而 for 为表示原因的连接词。

10. and—or,表示选择。

第十六章

1. C on (one's) doing 意为"当……时",相当于 when 引导的时间状语从句。如:On (my) asking for information, I heard a loud noise outside.

2. B 表示"从现在起多长时间之后"用 in。

3. D except 后接动词不定式可与 but 连用,但 except 后还可接 that, when, where 等从句或介词短语,在表示对细节加以纠正之意时用 except for。

4. D have trouble/difficulty in doing sth./with sth. 是一个习惯用法,表示"做某事吃力、费劲"。

5. A in time 除平时熟悉的"及时"之意外,还有"迟早"的意思,相当于 sooner or later。

6. C 具体时间即点时间前常用介词 at,表示"到……为止"用 by。

7. A through 指"从某事物的内部空间穿过";entrance 后习惯接 to;表示"在……边"用 on。

8. C "one in five"指"五人中有一个",即"one out of five"。

9. C "乘坐交通工具"时,用 by+抽象名词(无冠词的名词)或用 in/on 加冠词再加交通工具。

10. C "由手工制作"用固定词组 with one's hands 或 by hand。

11. A in front of 表示"在……前面";in the charge of 表示"在……掌管/控制下"。

12. C die of 用于疾病、情感、饥饿、寒冷等原因造成的死亡,die from 指除了疾病、情感、饥饿、寒冷以外的原因造成的死亡,on a cold night 为特定时间。

13. A 在相对小的地点或门牌前用 at;房间"在第几层"用"on...floor"。

14. D "在……帮助下"用 with,"没有……帮助"用 without。

15. B "逆/顶风而跑"用 against;"with +宾+宾补"表示伴随;表示"在左/右边"用 on。

16. D "be struck by"意为"被……迷住/打动",stay for the night 表示"留下来过夜"。

17—21 AACBD 22—26 BBBBA 27—31 BBADD 32—36 CCABB

第十八章

1. didn't he 2. weren't you 3. could she 4. is there 5. are there 6. does he 7. do they 8. did they 9. wasn't he 10. isn't it 11. doesn't he 12. aren't they 13. has it 14. does he/ do they 15. will you 16. shall we 17. will you 18. doesn't he 19. did they 20. isn't he 21. will he 22. weren't there 23. won't there 24. had you 25. wouldn't you

第十九章

1. His father told him that he should be more careful the next time.
2. Mr. Wang told the children that he would leave for Shanghai on business the next month.
3. Mary said that she hadn't heard from her parents those days.
4. The geography teacher told us that the moon moves around the earth and the earth goes round the sun.
5. She told him that it was time that he left there.
6. Zhang Hong told me that Doctor Wang passed away in 1948.
7. John told his parents that he had learned 500 Chinese words by the end of last term.
8. The history teacher told them that the Chinese Communist Party was founded on July 1st, 1921.
9. He asked whether I was a student.
10. She asked George if he had anything interesting she could read.
11. He asked whether she was there to ask for help or not.
12. The father asked his son where he was going.
13. The mother asked the naughty boy if he was sorry for what he had done.
14. She asked Mr. Li whether he had met that man at the station two hours before.
15. The teacher told us to write our names on our papers first.
16. Her friend asked her to go there again the next/ following day.
17. He offered to pack the parcel for me.
18. The teacher told the boys and girls not to make so much noise in class.
19. He/ She exclaimed that it was really a lovely day.
20. He wished me a Happy New Year.

第二十章

一、1—5 BABAA　　6—10 BBDCA　　11—15 AACCB　　16—20 DCDCC
　　21—25 ADCBA

二、1. It's a pity that I didn't meet the actress.
　　2. It happened that he was out.
　　3. It is strange that you know nothing about it.
　　4. It is necessary that you tell him the truth.
　　5. It is the fact that I don't like sports.
　　6. It seems that he has known it.
　　7. I don't think he did it on purpose.
　　8. It is asserted that the meeting be put off till next week.
　　9. It is reported that more than 70 persons died in the accident.
　　10. It is well-known that his grandfather went to Taiwan 50 years ago.

三、1. that　2. why　3. whether　4. what, what　5. that　6. that　7. what　8. where
　　9. what　10. what

四、1. If 应改为 Whether
　　2. estimate 应改为 estimated

3. that 应改为 what

4. that 应改为 what

5. What 应改为 That

第二十一章

一、1—5 AABAB 6—10 AAADA 11—15 DDBBD 16—20 CADBC
21—25 BBBDA 26—30 CCAAB

二、1. 去掉 it 2. which→where 3. whom→who 4. 去 there 5. come→came/has come
6. who's → whose 7. which → when 8. which → why 9. practice → practices
10. 去掉 it 11. keep→keeps 12. who her→whose 13. live→lives 14. studies→who studies 15. where→which 16. lead→leads 17. where→in which 18. 去掉 it
19. which→that 20. who→whom

三、1. that has been shown this month 2. that interests you best

3. where there's fresh air and little noise

4. (who, whom, that) you saw at the meeting

5. whose picture we saw in the newspaper yesterday

6. when (on which) he entered the university

7. why he made such a serious mistake

8. as you cannot understand

9. in front of which sat a small boy

10. I lost yesterday

第二十二章

一、1—5 ADACC 6—10 DCABB 11—15 ABCBB 16—20 CDACA
21—25 BDAAA 26—30 BDBAA

二、1. In case 2. Now that/Since 3. Seeing that 4. If/provided/providing that/supposing/suppose 5. Since 6. As/So long as 7. Whatever/No matter what 8. Lest
9. That 10. as soon as/ the moment/ the minute/ directly/ immediately/ instantly

第二十三章

一、1—10 BABBD DDDAC 11—20 DACBA BBCCC 21—30 DDBBA DDBDC

二、1. It is getting dark earlier in winter.

2. It is no use asking her because she didn't know anything about it.

3. It's two miles from here to the bus station.

4. Have you seen it hailing?

5. It is up to you decide what to do.

6. It is said that he has been to the U.S.A. twice.

7. It's a pity that you've missed the concert.

8. It seems that he is much afraid.

9. It's no use crying over spilt milk.

10. It was several months before we met again.

第二十四章

一、1—10 DCCDD BCBBB 11—20 DCCDD BBDBC 21—30 CDCCB DCDDD

二、1. was 改为 were 2. give 改为 gives 3. is 改为 are 4. is 改为 are 5. are 改为 is 6. cost 改为 costs，7. are 改为 is 8. exist 改为 exists 9. was 改为 were 10. abilities 改为 ability 11. are 改为 is 12. has 改为 have 13. are 改为 is 14. is 改为 are 15. was 改为 were

第二十五章

1—5 BBCDC   6—10 DBACB   11—15 CBBAC   16—20 DCDAA
21—25 ACBDD

第二十六章

一、1—5 AABCC   6—10 DDCCB   11—15 ABCCB   16—20 ACAAB
21—25 DBDCD   26—30 BDCBC

二、

(一) 1—5 ADCCA   6—10 BCDBA   11—15 CDCBD   16—20 CBBDB
21—25 BCADC

(二) 1. Never have I heard a speech as exciting as this.
2. So small was the mark that I could hardly see it.
3. Hardly did I turn off the light when my mother came in.
4. At no time has it been more difficult for us to pass the examination.
5. Only in this way can we succeed.
6. Not a word did he speak at the meeting.
7. Not only did Mary complain about the food, but also refused to pay for it.
8. No sooner had she begun to speak than I sensed that something was wrong.
9. Many a time has Mike helped me with my English.
10. There was a sudden gust of wind and away went his hat.

参 考 文 献

[1] 张道真. 实用英语语法. 北京:商务印书馆,1998.
[2] 张道真. 现代英语用法词典. 北京:外语教学与研究出版社,2001.
[3] 章振邦. 新编英语语法教程. 上海:上海外语教育出版社,2004.
[4] 董亚芬. 大学英语精读. 上海:上海外语教育出版社,1992.
[5] 潘欢怀. 现代英语实用句法. 北京:北京师范大学出版社,1988.
[6] 朗文当代英汉双解词典. 香港:朗文出版(远东)有限公司词典编译出版部,1998.
[7] 薄冰. 薄冰英语语法. 北京:开明出版社,1998.